HISTORICAL ARCHAEOLOGY

AND THE
IMPORTANCE OF MATERIAL THINGS II

Edited by

Julie M. Schablitsky & Mark P. Leone

The Society for Historical Archaeology
SPECIAL PUBLICATION NUMBER 9

2012

J.W. Joseph, SHA Journal Editor

Cover illustration by Tracey Fedor, with permission

J.W. Joseph, Julie Schablitsky, and Mark Leone, Copy Editors
Tracey L. Fedor, Compositor and Designer
New South Associates, Stone Mountain, GA

Table of Contents

J. W. Joseph Preface

In 1975, the Society for Historical Archaeology (SHA) convened its 8th annual conference in Charleston, South Carolina. Program Chair Stanley South saw the Charleston Conference as an opportunity for a thematic discussion on theory in historical archaeology and he called on Leland Ferguson to organize such as session. As Ferguson purveyed the field at that time, however, he recognized the conflict between practitioners of various theoretical viewpoints and he instead sought to create a forum in which archaeologists would build from a common ground rather than argue differences. He succinctly termed this common foundation of the field "the Importance of Material Things." Ferguson sought contributions from archaeologists Jim Deetz, Lewis Binford, William Rathje, Mark Leone, and Jim Fitting and folklorist Henry Glassie. Their papers were subsequently compiled and published as the Society for Historical Archaeology's second Special Publication.

Historical Archaeology and the Importance of Material Things (Ferguson 1977) would go on to become the SHA's best selling publication, running through multiple printings until finally going out of print. At the SHA Annual Meeting in Amelia Island in 2010, I spoke with Leland Ferguson about the volume and raised the possibility that it be re-published using the SHA's Print on Demand (POD) press. Ferguson, as well as others I spoke with, was enthusiastic about the prospect. Ferguson wondered whether a current consideration of historical archaeology and its analysis of the material world might not benefit the field. Taking history as my guide, I contacted Julie Schablitsky, Program Chair for the 2012 SHA Annual Meeting in Baltimore, to ask if she would be interested in chairing a session on this topic with the ambitious objective to publish the papers prior to the conference. Julie enthusiastically accepted the challenge, and called on Mark Leone as a collaborator.

The selection of participants for this volume was a greater challenge than it was for Ferguson, as historical archaeology has more voices now than it did then. Schablitsky and Leone sought participants who could speak to the material past from different places, both physically and theoretically. Their selection was thorough and deliberate, and the final slate fits the benchmark that Ferguson originally employed, as the participants are all archaeologists whose voices we want to hear.

In this volume, various archaeologists offer their analyses and ideas on the importance of material things and the ways in which historical archaeology allows us to see the past differently, and sometimes see a different past. While the field has changed dramatically over the past 35 years, two of the most prominent areas of change are evident herein. First, our scale of analysis has expanded from sites to landscapes, from structures to systems, and from artifact typology to material culture's role in expressing beliefs and identity. The historical archaeologists in this volume examine the complex interplay of people, places, and things and base their analysis on the sum of the parts. As a result, all of the papers employ comparison to understand and interpret the meanings of different social spaces in the same setting, as well as to compare and contrast different places and societies.

The second evident change is that our discipline is now global in scope. Historical archaeology, post-medieval archaeology, the archaeology of the modern world, by all of its various names represents a collective scholarship focused on the spread of cultures, economies, technologies, and materials throughout the world. This new platform, when coupled with Internet-

2

based technologies, allows data to be easily shared across broad spaces and offers the potential for a far greater level of comparative analysis in the coming years. And it places a greater emphasis on historical archaeology to use the importance of material things to analyze and explain human behavior. This volume provides a summation of where we are now as well as where future paths may lead as we encounter the past from a global perspective.

I thank Julie Schablitsky, Mark Leone, and the authors for bringing this volume to completion, and look forward to seeing where historical archaeology takes us in the near century.

J. W. Joseph
New South Associates
6150 East Ponce de Leon Avenue
Stone Mountain, GA 30083

Mark P. Leone

A Program for a Comparative Historical Archaeology

Where has the last 35 years brought historical archaeology? Very far. But we still have not reached our potential—it is hoped the essays contained here will move our field closer to our potential as a scientific discipline. Indeed, the writings in this collection have two qualities that mark an advance in historical archaeology. They are comparative, which resolves a serious dilemma. And, second, they utilize objects far more comfortably in their analyses than has often been the case in the field. "Things" are important but not trivialized by being removed from their broader historical context. Rather, "things" are used to explore and describe context.

Much has been resolved since the publication of *The Importance of Material Things* (Ferguson 1977). Structural analysis and cognitive analysis are dead, as far as I can see. Lewis Binford's ideas (South 1978a and 1978b) did not translate easily into historical archaeology. Instead, James Deetz became the hero of our field. *In Small Things Forgotten* (1977) is perhaps *the* founding text, but small things do not make the field. Big patterns of many things make historical archaeology a worthwhile endeavor, as these essays demonstrate effectively.

Science lost. Advocacy won. Politics for others, not for archaeologists, took the lead. The history of others won. The tie to history as a discipline, lost. When science lost and advocacy won, comparative work in our field languished. We will see if it flourishes again now. Parallel to the preference against comparison, which was not successfully counterbalanced by scholars like Charles Orser (1996), began public advocacy, originally a public opening of archaeology. There are two unrelated but often confused components to public archaeology. The earliest to emerge was the opening of sites in many different ways to people beyond the profession. Parallel to this, but separate

too, is the idea that archaeology not only was a way to see people who did not write a history for themselves, but who also deserved allies in presenting and using their history. Public archaeology as advocacy was natural to historical archaeology if historical archaeology's purpose was to study the invisible peoples of European expansion from 1460 on. These are conquered and subordinated people and their descendants. This is a popular and worthy idea, but has not become a comparative idea within the field. Such practice retrieves people's historical integrity and in some cases does so remarkably well. Public advocacy takes the integrity of cultural presentation we found coming from Deetz's students and which is exemplified in *In Small Things Forgotten*, and moves its object to descendant groups, where it is effective and can be politically powerful. This does not mean such studies cannot be comparative, but they usually are not.

During the founding years of historical archaeology, Stanley South (1978a and 1978b), long a friend and colleague of Lewis Binford, argued for and showed how comparative methods could be used to distinguish between types of sites and between functions within them. Binford (1968), and to a lesser degree Kent Flannery (1964), introduced a strong presentation into prehistoric archaeology that made, permanently from my perspective, the field a comparative endeavor. Population dynamics, plant genetics, Pleistocene retreats, and transected ecological zones on a worldwide basis became the frame of reference behind the understandings of how the earth was populated, farming founded, cities born, and civilized, and literate life begun. Prehistoric archaeology was a recognized scientific success. Along with this large transformation of the parent field was paleoanthropology, then called "fossil man," better called the fossil evidence for human emergence and evolution, which was a huge scientific endeavor in itself.

In the midst of these profound, and it turns out, illuminating changes, historical archaeology could not compete in knowledge production, and its leaders all understood this issue. Inter- and intra-site comparison produced comprehensive archaeology from plantations, forts, villages, and townhouse lots. But, it stopped before understanding plantation economics, the economic purpose of missions, territorial expansion for harnessing raw resources for transatlantic and transpacific trade, baroque urban planning for imperialism, and land speculation for profit. No one wrote about these within historical archaeology. Eventually, many individual scholars did not even believe they needed to, or should.

Historical archaeology had no framework for being comparative. In fact, as some of its leaders sought a divorce from prehistoric archaeology, a divide was created with the whole of the prehistoric past, not just with prehistoric archaeology. An affinity was developed with the long term mood of cultural anthropology for not comparing. Here Deetz, deeply influenced by Henry Glassie (1975) and early cognitive anthropology, took the position that still dominates our field--understanding internal integrity is most important. *In Small Things Forgotten* actually meant: No comparison of one culture to another. Initially, this was Deetz's implication and the work that the majority of his students stressed, which is the integrity of the meaning of artifacts within a society. This approach in Deetz's hands lead to the comparison of ceramics, gravestones, and house forms in eastern New England that leaves me still amazed at its insight and daunted by its scope. Even with the runaway success of this book in our field it produced no viable offspring. In his rewriting of the book, Deetz suggested comparison of the North Atlantic coast with Cape Town and 17th century culture there, and other places. But, there was neither a method nor a reason for comparison. There was no theory to achieve comparison and from within Deetz's combination of structural method and a Geertz-like focus on meaning, there could not be. In this volume, Matthew H. Johnson with a more historical approach and a consideration of trade and politics, but not a materialist approach, sets a more successful stage for recovering the comparative initiative that

Deetz tried. Martin Gibbs tries the same thing for the Spanish in the 16th century across the Mid-Atlantic and Mid- and South Pacific.

Now, and in a fruitful and progressive way, Alan Mayne (2008: 93-118) accurately characterizes the epistemology of, and thus the basis for comparative knowledge within, historical archaeology. *The Importance of Ambiguity* is one of the best and most comprehensive reviews of historical archaeology available. Mayne argues that historical archaeologists use their data and see that there is ambivalent material everywhere in history that can create new, different, and alternative ways for seeing the narrative histories written for a people, nation, group, institution, and class. He does not use ambiguity in quite the same sense that Lewis Binford (1987) did, but it is quite close, and is powerful.

The result of this work, and the big achievement of recent historical archaeology, is to say that something else happened, too. Someone else was working, too. It says: Think about it this way, too. Mayne calls this stance ambiguity and he means that material from the ground or from the built environment frequently does not fit a given history. Therefore, the material from historical archaeology makes a commentary on the history of the people, processes, or nation whose ruins it comes from. Because the excavated material is always going to be different, it is always going to be available to say something a historian did not think of, or could not know. For Alan Mayne, ambiguity means more than one side. For Lewis Binford (1987), who introduced middle range theory into prehistoric archaeology, ambiguity was the attempt to match— really see the mismatch—between ethnographic observations and something similar from the ground that was to be illuminated by the analogy with something ethnographic. The difference between the ethnography and the archaeology was called ambiguity and was to be highlighted so that an archaeologist could build a better explanation of a past society. Better meant more thorough as well as different from the accepted explanation.

In historical archaeology in the last 35 years, the ambiguity, or differences, between the traditional historical explanations, including local, folkloristic, and popular histories, have lead to some of our field's main advances. Virtually everyone agrees that the archaeology of black Americans, which is usually called African American historical archaeology, constitutes an advance and thus a contribution to the knowledge behind our country's progress as a whole.

The knowledge of slavery and free African Americans before and after Emancipation is knowledge because it was created, or was actually constituted as important discoveries, against popular and professional positions that said such knowledge was gone, or never even existed. The ambiguity that Alan Mayne (2008: 93-118) talks about is achieved because the foils about an African American past were found to be so strong. These include the ideas that cultural knowledge was lost during the Middle Passage (Frazier 1939: 7-8), absence of literacy lead to no recording of black history (Frazier 1939: 21-22), folklore was so epistemologically weak that it was an unreliable source of African origins (Mintz and Price 1992:10), and the material culture used by black Americans was made by others and could offer few, if any, clues to specific African origins of African American culture (Mintz and Price 1992:53).[1] Indeed, there was no African American culture. Black Americans had a version of American or European culture and that was debased by poverty and illiteracy. These have become the foils against which ambiguity was announced by historical archaeology. Historical archaeology could show that all these popular, received, and literary traditions were actually tropes or poses, not the truth. However, in order to make scientific progress — prove a position of generality to be incorrect — the ambiguity had to be created. Mayne missed this point, although Lewis Binford (1987) did not and never ceased to build the pointed difference between a received position and the data he — or any scientist — found.

To be sure, sometimes the contrasts have to be sharpened to make a point clear. A truer reading of the African American case shows scholarly understandings of many different African cultures with many different forms, as well as survivals, in the Americas in Creole cultures. The use of ambiguity puts this point second to the initial announcement of a stark contrast. There are many such powerful contrasts in this volume.

Adam Heinrich and Carmel Schrire in their essay, and Johnson in his, take the lives on the margins that are discovered and re-centered by historical archaeologists in South Africa and New England respectively and frame them into an effort to examine worldwide colonialism and capitalism. All three authors see the whole world, not just the margins that needed redeeming. The breadth, scope, reading of primary documents, and willingness to talk to a needy world about the origins of the system that grasps us more and more each year is what allows historical archaeology not just a rich future, but an indispensable one. Anyone reading Heinrich and Schrire or Johnson will be exhilarated. Similar exhilaration comes with the writings of Stacey Lynn Camp, Paul R. Mullins, Julie M. Schablitsky, Christopher N. Matthews, and Matthew M. Palus. The larger problem is seen from time to time in them, as each writes. It is not completely clear to me, but I think that if each were to see his and her study the way Mayne advises, the more general point in each would be gripping.

Take a minute and ask with me why no other subject matter in historical archaeology has been probed and prodded like African American archaeology? Consider that the archaeology of women, gender, or children has not evolved beyond academic recognition. The archaeology of religion is stagnant. All the technical progress in nautical, maritime, or underwater archaeology has not brought intellectual attention for it. The archaeology of labor is just beginning to take off. The archaeology of poverty hardly exists. Modern material culture studies finds it has to find its point. Even the archaeology of advocacy and politics has come close to destroying its base while strengthening the people it wants to serve. These statements are not an insult, but a challenge. All of these avenues of inquiry will come alive, or be rejuvenated and more effective, in the near futrue. But how?

Find a good foil. Find a problem. Announce it. Use ambiguity the way that Alan Mayne and Lewis Binford proposed. Say we inherit a certain understanding. Then say, with archaeological discoveries we find that something different was the case. For example, Gibbs sees that the Pacific in the 16th century is virtually vacant in our current understanding of Spanish colonization. He builds a contrasting case by showing Spanish settlement of some of the Solomon Islands. The resulting illumination is the Spanish imperial design of a trading network from Peru to the Philippines with supporting colonies at both ends of the Pacific, and along the way. He is writing for historical archaeologists who did not know this sweep. It was not that no one at all knew this. It was that his American and British audience did not know it this way. Nor had we the opportunity to envision it against the same but later sweep of the British across the North Atlantic that Johnson describes. The ambiguity comes from understanding how the Spanish colonial empire looks from one perspective and then challenging the received view by telling a different and more robust story.

The same contrast has been used by Mullins. It is not at all that he is studying bric-a-brac. Those are his data. The ambiguity Mullins uses comes because he asserts that knick knacks are not normal artifacts. They aren't bottles, coins, or dishes. They are anomalous. Then he attaches them to everyday life which, using both de Certeau (1988) and Vaneigen (1971), he calls revolutionary—or, at least, potentially revolutionary. Mullins does not explicitly set himself up against the group of archaeologists and other scholars who argue that consuming things is a way to declare freedom and independence through agency and thus find resistance to capitalist class categories. He opposes this line of argument, but you have to be a well-read historical archaeologist to know that. Instead, he has this amazing quote from Raoul Vaneigem (1971) about everyday life. "People who talk about revolution and class struggle without referring explicitly to everyday life, without understanding what is subversive about love and what is positive in the refusal of constraints, such people have corpses in the mouths" (Vaneigem 1979:74). Mullins is making two important moves. He is acknowledging de Certeau's critique of Foucault and making a place for material culture, simultaneously. De Certeau's *The Practice of Everyday Life* (1988) makes an effort to show how the practices of daily life can be seen as sites of resistance to the practices which reinforce the power of the state, particularly as described by Foucault. Mullins offers material culture like bric-a-brac as a vehicle for such a move. I believe he is trying to say that moments and parts of people's lives are outside of the oppressive control of most of the large structures of capitalism. There is no existence outside those structures for many people. But there can be moments of liberation from them, Mullins argues.

The structures of capitalism like colonialism, slavery, factory and asylum life, schools, mission churches, and the police have within and around them places and behaviors like frontiers, woods, and yards; strikes, ideas, and the Gospels; and the barricades that also need to be seen and recovered by archaeologists for a better description of modern life. The ambiguity provided by historical archaeology as identified by Alan Mayne and also known to us through its methodological use by Lewis Binford helps identify what we are going to find.

Our data for this are the urban street performances and sidewalk politics described by Matthews as the places where African American New Yorkers attempted to claim their rights and eventually succeeded in doing so. And also by Schablitsky who found and understood a whole house built from the ground to the roof as a safe place by African Americans in Maryland, not 10 miles from downtown Washington, D.C. With her discovery, we have ambiguity we didn't have before, and a lead as well. Every other site where African American religious practices from Africa have been discovered was one that was altered from a European original and made later into a safe place. The house was European, or European American; the use of hoodoo/conjure/West African spirit practices was added. Now, we have a whole building thought through from the foundation on up, and probably a landscape thought in the same way, too. We could call this variation, and usually do. But it is more productive to see the variation as ambiguity because it offers us the opportunity to say that it causes a different understanding of a different culture.

Ambiguity means that contrast between what we call an inherited history, now often called a master narrative and its tropes, and the object, that includes lost peoples and processes. The point in Mayne's hands is to write a better, fuller, and different history. A more truthful and liberating one, too. Ambiguity in Binford's hands has more potential. Binford compares similar but distant situations from different cultures in order to illuminate a misunderstood situation in the past. He urges us not to see similarities, but to identify differences, or places where our data do not fit, and to say why, and to form a hypothesis about the difference. If we were to treat class and ethnic or racial difference this way, we might see workers, African Americans, Pacific Islanders, the South African natives, and others as quite different, but with the intent—clearly identified by Habermas (1970, 1979, 1984, 1989)—to see the integrity of their lives and their opinions of Western capitalist structures as a needed and privileged commentary.

Ambiguity builds two foils for Palus. His is an essay about public utilities like water, sewer, electric, and gas lines. The ambiguity does not come from the services these provide for all of us now. The ambiguity comes from asking why are these called utilities and not agents of taxation, like the poll tax. Why not call them agents of the state used to extend state control? Or, inspired by Shanon Dawdy (2010), why not call them stratified ruins since we excavate all kinds of dead service lines and broken pipes and come to understand that the overhead lines we see on our streets often contain old lines that are also dead but not removed?

Palus points out that under the guise of public health and public safety, communities within a city are subordinated to uniform codes and uniform taxes by being forced, home by home, and business by business, to have running water, sewerage, gas, and electric service for their own good. We knew this didn't we? He tells us. Well, what we didn't know was that wells, cisterns, wood stoves, kerosene lights, and outhouses, used by people for millennia, worked quite well but provided independence for many and were closed down in order to provide uniform operation of government control and the imposition of uniform fees, where before there were none. Thus, ambiguity comes from piercing the ideologies and the chants about needing public health and public safety and seeing them instead as excuses for extending state control.

The second source of ambiguity for Palus is his refusal to see buried service lines and pieces of broken sewer pipe and broken electric features as ruining a more valuable archaeological resource. He salvages the normal archaeological frustration with utility trenches and big sewer pipe pieces and makes these important discoveries that show how an area or neighborhood was colonized, or, using Foucault (1991:87-104), was subject to governmentality. Ambiguity comes from

seeing that public health and safety is not that alone. He sees that a gas pipe trench through an 18th century deposit isn't a ruin of a ruin, but a record of a mistake: a discovery.

Ambiguity powers Camps' analysis in two ways. Despite our interest in labor, Camp connected labor to immigration and citizenship. Despite our interest in the downtrodden, she connected the archaeology of internment camps to immigrants and cheap labor, showing we never intended to grant full citizenship and other rights and full respectability to cheap labor. The state does not want the American dream to be fulfilled by hard work, education, and speaking proper English. Ambiguity works in Camp's analysis because historical archaeologists do not compare, even though we think we might be better off intellectually if we did. What happened when she saw Mexican immigrant workers near Los Angeles from the early 20th century and Japanese interns from the era of World War II? Instead of coming up with artifacts that did not say much, she compared arid, wasted landscapes surrounded by no privacy, constant intrusive surveillance, and a management who saw the subjects as alien beings, not humans.

Ambiguity in Camp's hands leads to the roots of a pattern in American history called by Matthews two kinds of citizenship with one class always having less freedom. This is not the kind of statement historical archaeologists usually make and sometimes it is not even what some think they should say. But they did, and we should.

Recently, Dawdy (2010:761-793) pointed out that anthropology gave up comparisons because we were using an offensive notion of the primitive. I don't think prehistorians ever fully gave up comparisons, but certainly they are not concerned with the old idea of the primitive. Dawdy's (2010: 764) writing points out that comparisons within archaeology are largely absent today and that within historical archeology there is a fixed division between the modern world and everything that went before that prevents comparison. Hers is an insightful point. The point of the essays in this volume is to restart the process of comparison using a set of methods that will facilitate the process, rather than letting the members of the field guess at how it might be done.

Here is how comparison might work. First, find that larger issue by asking what is there that you disagree with. There must be an issue, a problem, something, as Lewis Binford used to say, that strikes you as ridiculous, some mistake that is embedded in scholarly work or an assumption that you just know is incorrect. Heinrich and Schrire knew that South African historical archaeology had to deal with the origins of racism embedded within Apartheid histories. Johnson knew that the focus of historical archaeology on New England and the Chesapeake and the failure to understand English history had created a parochial myopia among some. Palus knew that utility trenches could not be dismissed as a nuisance. Light at night and water that runs when you want it to are as central to modern life as you can get. Further, when electricity is called power, there is something in the metaphor that requires attention.

Mullins understood that there was more to desire than window shopping and cheap trinkets. Chris Matthews saw the need in New York City to look behind the North's ability to blame slavery on the South thereby exempting itself not just from a role in slavery, but also from a role in slave holding in its own past. Camp saw two patterns and called them one. She saw the marginal conditions of camps for Mexican workers in Los Angeles and American internment camps for Japanese U.S. citizens and called both groups immigrants. She began to tell U.S. history using a more generalized pattern. She began to compare by identifying a single issue: how the United States takes immigrants and creates two classes of people in its own society and does so as a part of its basic structure.

Gibbs realized that the tiny dots we think of as the Pacific Islands were seen as a whole by Spanish colonial ambitions in the 16th century and from Madrid, to Lima, to Manila. And he has said so. Our myopia on both Spanish colonization and the life of Pacific native societies is the problem he identified. Schablitsky has operated on a smaller scale but to the same effect. How do we establish the integrity of African American culture? When she found and described, not an African house pattern built as a slave quarter, but an American house for American purposes embodying African traditions built by African Americans from the ground up, she found something new. If the shotgun house is an African tradition in the Deep South, then a house built with hoodoo materials in its walls from below ground to four feet above is the same. It is not someone else's culture. It is new and it starts a search.

There is a second move needed to establish a comparative historical archaeology and that move is clearer from Binford than from Mayne. Do we compare using analogies, or do we acknowledge when things do not fit and ask why and find out why they do not? To do the second, comparisons have to be precise by describing what is being compared with careful attention to what does not match. This often requires a theory of description such as a surveillance system (Agamben 1998) or a known set of parameters like faunal remains and how age and sex are manifested in skeletons of sheep and cattle. Historical understanding of a single cultural entity like England for Johnson or Spain for Gibbs is a concern for and description of a long cultural cycle that is a chronological comparison rather than one between different places and societies. These long cycles allow us to see planning, trajectories of ideas, and the emergence of conflicts. These are influenced by Marx (Althusser 1970) and Braudel (1979 a, b) but at the heart they are the powerful histories of states, empires, and regions that frequently provide us hypotheses of large processes that give sense and order, even if tentatively. This is a kind of comparison and includes productive overviews like Breasted's idea of a Fertile Crescent and of a Northwest Quadrant (Quigley 1961), Vavilov's (1992) and Binford's (1968) on the origins of domestication, Childe's (1950) and Adams' (1966) on the origins of cities, and on the ebb and return of the Pleistocene's ice ages as reconstructed through palynology.

The authors here, including myself, and other archaeologists like Dawdy are attempting to rebuild a productive and sound comparative analysis. A comparative stand should lead our field to comment on Foucault on power and Agamben on surveillance, Deetz and Hume on the common elements of British settlement, on Edmund Wilson (1975) on "American Slavery, American Freedom," and whether there must always be an American under class. We should comment on authors like Raboteau (1980), Smith (1994), and Chireau (2003) on whether Afro-Christianity is a new kind of Christianity and is like Voudon, Santeria, and Candomblé, and other diasporic religions. How is hoodoo, or conjure, or North American practices that use spirits like other new religions of oppressed groups? This is where comparative anthropology made sense. Can it again?

Dawdy's tentative invitation has at its central archaeological initiative the study of modern ruins in the midst of American cities. What can seeing factory remnants and landfills tell us? This is a good, useful question. To pose it, she shows that much of historical archaeology since the 1980s like Chuck Orser's (1996; Orser and Fagan 1995) and my work (2005) focuses on the harm and evil produced by capitalism. She is, of course, correct. A well-done comparative analysis could focus on the origins of British liberty, a revision of Christianity by Africans, and the maintenance of native integrity in the context of colonialism. This might work. There does need to be a link between survival and flourishing integrity in colonialism and the attention Habermas urges us to pay to the native critiques made by those within, but alienated from, profit making societies. Camp, Gibbs, and Matthews propel the voices of people made into second class members of society and with these authors we can see what such people sound like. Many historical archaeologists have accepted this as a form of analysis, and it is sometimes comparative. Its intent is to promote democratic participation, democratic processes, and even survival of democratic government (Friedman 1992, 2003). Is there a reason we cannot write simultaneously to illuminate structures, which is freeing, but to also listen to those captured within those structures who describe them to us?

References

ADAMS, ROBERT
1966   *The Evolution of Urban Society.* Aldine Publishing
        Company, Chicago, IL.

AGAMBEN, GIORGIO
1998   *Homo Sacer: Sovereign Power and Bare Life.* Translated
        by D. Heller-Roazen. Stanford University Press, CA.

ALTHUSSER, LOUIS
1970   *For Marx.* Translated by Ben Brewster. Vintage Books,
        New York, NY.

BINFORD, LEWIS R.
1968   Post Pleistocene Adaptations. In *New Perspectives in
        Archaeology.* Sally R. Binford and Lewis R. Binford,
        editors, pp. 313-341. Aldine Publishing Company,
        Chicago, IL.
1987   Researching Ambiguity: Frames of Reference and
        Site Structure. In *Method and Theory for Activity Area
        Research: An Ethnoarchaeological Approach.* Susan Kent,
        editor, pp. 449-512. Columbia University Press, New York,
        NY.

BRAUDEL, FERNAND
1979a   *The Wheel of Commerce.* Translated by Sian Reynolds.
        Harper and Row, New York, NY.
1979b   *The Perspective of the World.* Translated by Sian
        Reynolds. Harper and Row Publishers, New York, NY.

CHILDE, GORDON V.
1950   "The Urban Revolution." *The Town Planning Review*
        21(1): 3-17.

CHIREAU, YVONNE P.
2003   *Black Magic: Religion and the African American Conjuring
        Tradition.* University of California Press, Berkeley.

DAWDY, SHANNON L.
2010   Clockpunk Anthropology and the Ruins of Modernity.
        Current Anthropology 51(6):761-791.

DE CERTEAU, MICHEL
1988   *The Practice of Everyday Life.* Translated by Steven
        Randall. University of California Press, Berkeley.

DEETZ, JAMES
1977   *In Small Things Forgotten: An Archaeology of Early American Life*. Anchor Press/Doubleday, Garden City, NJ.

FERGUSON, LELAND (EDITOR)
1977   *Historical Archaeology and the Importance of Material Things*. Special Publication Series, Number 2. Society for Historical Archaeology.

FLANNERY, KENT
1964   Microenvironments and Mesoamerican Prehistory. *Science*. 143(3607):650-654.

FOUCAULT, MICHEL
1991   Governmentality. In *The Foucault Effect: Studies in Governmentality*. Graham Burchell, Colin Gordon and Peter Miller, editors, pp. 87-104. University of Chicago Press, IL.

FRAZIER, FRANKLIN E.
1939   *The Negro Family in the United States*. University of Chicago Press, IL.

FRIEDMAN, JONATHAN
1992   The Past in the Future: History and the Politics of Identity. *American Anthropologist* 94(4):837-859.
2003   Globalizing Languages: Ideologies and Realities of the Contemporary Global System. *American Anthropologist* 105(4):744-752.

GLASSIE, HENRY
1975   *Folk Housing in Middle Virginia*. University of Tennessee Press, Knoxville.

HABERMAS, JURGEN
1970   Toward a Theory of Communicative Competence. *Inquiry* 13: 360-376.
1979   *Communication and the Evolution of Society*. Beacon Press, Boston, MA.
1984   The Theory of Communicative Action. *Vol. 1, Reason and the Rationalization of Society*. Beacon Press, Boston, MA.
1989   *The Theory of Communicative Action. Vol. 2, System and Lifeworld*. Beacon Press, Boston, MA.

HERSKOVITS, MELVILLE JEAN
1941   *The Myth of the Negro Past*. Beacon Press, Boston, MA.

LEONE, MARK P.
2005   *The Archaeology of Liberty in an American Capital: Excavations in Annapolis*. University of California Press, Berkeley.

MAYNE, ALAN
2008   On the Edges of History: Reflections on Historical Archaeology. Review Essay. *American Historical Review*, February 2008: 93-118.

MINTZ, SIDNEY W. AND RICHARD PRICE
1976   *The Birth of African-American Culture: An Anthropological Approach*. Beacon Press, Boston, MA.

ORSER, CHARLES E.
1996   *A Historical Archaeology of the Modern World*. Plenum, New York, NY.

ORSER, CHARLES E., JR. AND BRIAN M. FAGAN
1995   *Historical Archaeology*. Harper Collins Publishers, New York, NY.

QUIGLEY, CARROLL
1961   *The Evolution of Civilizations*. The Macmillan Company, New York, NY.

RABOTEAU, ALBERT J.
1980   *Slave Religion: The "Invisible Institution" in the Antebellum South*. Oxford University Press, New York, NY.

SMITH, THEOPHUS
1994   *Conjuring Culture: Biblical Formations in Black America*. Oxford University Press, New York, NY.

SOUTH, STANLEY A.
1978a   Research Strategies for Archaeological Pattern Recognition in Historical Archaeology. *World Archaeology* 10(1):36-50.
1978b   Pattern Recognition in Historical Archaeology. *American Antiquity* 43(2):223-230.

VANEIGEN, RAOUL
1971   *The Revolution of Everyday Life*. Translated by John Fullerton and Paul Sieveking. Rising Free Collective, London, England.

VAVILOV, NIKOLAY

1992   *Origin and Geography of Cultivated Plants.* Translated
        by Doris Love. Cambridge University Press, Cambridge,
        England.

WILSON, EDMUND S.

1975   *American Slavery, American Freedom.* W.W. Norton
        Company, New York, NY.

Endnote

1   For contra arguments see Melville Jean Herskovits' *The
        Myth of the Negro Past* (1941).

Mark P. Leone
Department of Anthropology
University of Maryland College Park
1111 Woods Hall
College Park, MD 20742

Stacey Lynn Camp

The Utility of Comparative Research in Historical Archaeology

What is important is that there is direction to our research that goes beyond an individual site and that ties into research questions of broader importance: questions that require a comparative approach to resolve... Historical archaeology is, and must remain, a comparative endeavor built on well-excavated, catalogued, conserved, and reported data.

-Lees (1999:63)

ABSTRACT

Performing comparative work is especially important when it comes to the issue of race relations in the United States, a topic that has been of great interest to historical archaeologists since the discipline's founding. This is because the basic tenets of racist ideology stemmed from the same source: Western capitalism. In performing comparative work, I argue that our scholarship can work against racist thought that dehistoricizes its social origins by making it seem natural and innate to humankind. This chapter illustrates the utility in such an approach by comparing and contrasting the experiences of two racialized groups living in the early 20th century Western United States: Mexican Americans and Japanese Americans.

Introduction

Tape deck broken, no radio signal, air condition staggering in 100-degree heat. With two undergraduates in tow, I made my way across the Western United States on a 21-hour road trip from Idaho to Colorado in an old university Chevy Suburban in the summer of 2010. What compelled me to spend an entire week driving from Moscow, Idaho to Granada, Colorado with two undergraduates I barely knew outside of the classroom? Initially, the answer to this question seemed straightforward: to better inform my own archaeological project and public outreach efforts at a contemporaneous Japanese American internment camp located outside of Kooskia, Idaho by studying the field and laboratory procedures used at Amache, a World War II Japanese American internment camp (Clark 2008, 2010; Clark et al. 2008; Skiles and Clark 2010). The Kooskia Internment Camp (Wegars 2001, 2010) is unique in that it was occupied by a small all-male Japanese American population that was predominantly comprised of first generation migrants (also known as *Issei*), whereas previously studied internment camps, such as Amache, imprisoned a large multi-generational and -gendered population. By standardizing data collection and analysis between sites like Amache and Kooskia, archaeologists may be able to shed light on how generational and gender differences were expressed through Japanese internees' use of material culture. Towards this end, we observed public outreach efforts, met former internees, toured Amache Preservation Society's museum, obtained digital copies of field and laboratory forms, learned how to excavate gardens associated with internment camps, and even hired two of Amache's former crew chiefs to work on the Kooskia Internment Camp Archaeological Project (http://www.uidaho.edu/class/kicap).

Comparative research across camps can thus potentially address important historical questions regarding how Japanese internees' responses to internment fractured along gender and generational lines. But as Dr. Bonnie Clark led my students and me on a tour of Amache, I realized that there was something

Figure 1. Migrant worker housing at Amache Internment Camp, July 2010. (Photograph by author, 2010).

more to this trip than merely systematizing archaeological data collection and analysis across internment camps. While looking at the archaeological remnants of a garden built near one of the mess halls at Amache, I noticed a small group of trailers in a fenced area about 100 ft. away (Figure 1). I inquired about the settlement and learned that it was migrant housing for seasonal Mexican agricultural workers. These workers are likely part of H-2 guest worker program that the Southern Poverty Law Center has likened to a "modern-day system of indentured servitude" (Southern Poverty Law Center 2007:2) where workers are "bound to the employers who *import* them [emphasis added]" (Southern Poverty Law Center 2007:1). Under the H-2 program, workers live in substandard housing, have no chance of gaining citizenship in the United States, have no access to medical benefits or compensation if injured on the job, and can face "blacklisting, deportation, or other retaliation" if an employee files a formal complaint against his or her employer (Southern Poverty Law Center 2007:1).

Although the contemporary conditions of Mexican immigrants are not necessarily synonymous with the experiences of Japanese American internees, the source of the isolation and invisibility of both modern and historic labor forces remains the same: the assumption that these two groups are racially and biologically inferior to the prototypical Anglo American citizen, an ideology that arose out of European imperialism and capitalism (Omi and Winant 1994; Sanjek 1994; McClintock 1995; Stoler 2006). This is the only rational explanation for why we continue to allow people to live in a setting that mimics the barracks of Amache's historic internment camp. Clearly "race still matters in the world today because the contradictory realities of racism are being reproduced in the

disjunctures of the late twentieth-century world" (Harrison 1995:65).

The racialization of both Japanese and Mexican immigrants has its roots in the formation of the United States' capitalist economy. As Brodkin elaborates, "Africans, Europeans, Mexicans, and Asians each came to be treated as members of less civilized, less moral, less self-restrained races only when they were recruited to be the core of the US capitalist labor force" (2000:245). In other words, "race making is class making, just as much as class making is race making" (Brodkin 2000:245). If we, as historical archaeologists, wish to take seriously scholars' calls (Leone et al. 1987; 1999; Orser 1998, 2001, 2004; Leone and Parker 1999; Funari et al. 1999) for an historical archaeology of global capitalism, then we must not only look at its various forms in specific temporal and geographical locations but also identify the similarities between racialization processes. In performing comparative work, our scholarship can work against racist thought that dehistoricizes its social origins by making it seem innate to humankind or that reduces racism to "psychological disposition, an emotive affect (action), a dis-order - and so as ab-normal and unusual" (Goldberg 1997:19). In doing the latter, "racist...acts are thus transformed silently into emotive expressions, into crimes of passion" (Goldberg 1997:19) rather than perceived as structural issues. McGuire (1982), one of the first historical archaeologists to broach the topics of ethnicity and race, similarly emphasized the importance of examining ethnicity from a "cross-cultural perspective" (1982:161).

Comparing racializations - the process through which groups are categorized as socially separate from a dominant group - and responses to racialization is important because in a capitalist economy, the segmentation of lower-classes into socially constructed "races" acts to naturalize the lower-class status of blue-collar laborers; the same system masks the processes (including unequal wages, unsanitary labor conditions, etc.) involved in the production of goods so that the consumer remains unaware of how the goods they are consuming were produced within a web of labor inequality. Race, then, has to a large extent determined who can work, when they can work, and what kinds of work (e.g. service vs. professional) they can do. Hence, as one of the principal mechanisms structuring and determining how labor is organized in the United States, race "has always been a central strand of state administration; a silent (and sometimes not so silent) barrier to kinship and adoptability; a condition of advancement and advantage, of power and privilege; and a mark of preference and improvement, of intellectual prowess and jury participation, of law's empire and social injustice, of ethnic excludability and historical denial, of social invisibility and sociospatial segregation" (Goldberg 1997:10).

In acknowledgement, historical archaeologists have long explored and exposed the roots and social consequences of capitalism (c.f. McGuire and Paynter 1991; Shackel 1993; Johnson 1996; Leone and Potter 1999; McGuire and Reckner 2005; Mrzowoski 2006) and, to a great extent, the construction of ethnic or racial boundaries required to maintain a highly stratified, class-based economy (c.f. Mullins 1999; Delle et al. 2000; Orser 2001). This robust body of scholarship provides a sound theoretical and methodological foundation from which we can compare and contrast the experiences of racialized groups. What remains underexplored within this literature is how gender and age came into play in the racialization process and, in turn, how racialized groups' responses to Western imperialism differed along such vectors of identity. Racial identity not only came to define an individual's place in society during the emergence of a capitalist economy; one's age and gender likewise predetermined the types of jobs one could occupy and their position in society. Together, this tripartite of age, race, and gender determined the range of economic and social possibilities available to individuals inhabiting early 20th century America (Enloe 1990; diZerega Wall 1994; Bederman 1995).

Honing in on how different generations and genders within racialized groups responded to their

marginalization can help counter assumptions central to racist thought that groups such as the "Japanese" or "Mexicans" are homogenous races who act in a similar manner due to their shared ethnic background. Comparing the plights of two racialized groups also continues in the tradition of critical race scholarship that historicizes the concept of race, helping researchers to better "understand how and why a ranked hierarchy of races has been put to such destructive uses, been affirmed 'scientifically,' been challenged repeatedly, and yet still dies so hard" (Sanjek 1994:1-2). Historical archaeological studies of immigrants in the Western United States have inadvertently reified these racial categories by studying them as bounded entities. For instance, in the case of Overseas Chinese archaeology, "most archaeological studies have conceptualized Overseas Chinese communities as insular, segregated enclaves in which residents have minimal interactions with non-Chinese people and cultures" (Voss 2005:426). If historical archaeologists continue to focus on specific racialized groups, we risk making invisible the economic hierarchy of "races, colors, religions, and cultures" (Sanjek 1994:10) within the global capitalist system and, in essence, we naturalize their imagined biological differences. In an effort to avoid this essentializing tendency, the experiences of two immigrant groups - Mexican and Japanese immigrants - inhabiting the early 20th century Western United States are juxtaposed in this chapter. As we will see, while both groups faced similar forms of social and spatial discrimination, their responses to it were dependent on their age, citizenship status, and gender. These differences become apparent through extra-site comparison, an approach championed (yet still relatively underutilized) by a number of historical archaeologists since the discipline's origins.

Comparative Research in Historical Archaeology: An Abbreviated History

In its earliest days, historical archaeology was envisioned as a discipline that would supplement rather than augment history. As such, many of the first articles published in our discipline's flagship journal, *Historical Archaeology*, described and detailed factual information about artifact manufacturing and production processes without relating this information to human behavior and historical trends. Bernard L. Fontana, President of the Society for Historical Archaeology, critiqued this myopia, commenting: "...if we persist in cataloguing artifacts rather than thoughts; if we continue to map sites rather than outlines of human behavior; and if we go on digging unique mounds of debris in place of unearthing middens of cultural tradition, we will have consigned our endeavors to the golf course: a gentlemen's game to be played at leisure, affording exercise and conversation and, above all, one which requires little thinking" (1970:2). Yet these early attempts at standardizing artifact classification and cataloging procedures established a common vocabulary through which historical archaeologists could discuss similarities and differences across assemblages. Their descriptive efforts laid the foundations necessary for contemporary scholars to move beyond typologies and explore new applications of theory to historical data.

Despite the discipline's initial concentration on artifact histories, the founding members of the Society for Historical Archaeology envisioned the discipline as being interdisciplinary and comparative. At one of the society's first business meetings, the scope and purpose of the discipline were discussed. Those present nearly unanimously agreed that historical archaeology's statement of purpose needed to be defined broadly in order to encourage comparisons between the material culture found in the New World and other parts of the globe. For instance, Carlyle Smith remarked that "we must go to the Old World, even for digging at times, to illuminate New World problems" (Society for Historical Archaeology 1967:8), while Ivor Noel Hume argued that "there was comparability of artifacts between East Africa and Virginia" (Society for Historical Archaeology 1967:8). Wilcomb Washburn and Mayer-Oakes similarly pushed for a definition of the society that reflected its transnational foci and temporal diversity, with Washburn moving to delete references to "national boundaries" and specific "cultural periods" from the society's statement of purpose (Society for Historical Archaeology 1967:8).

One of the discipline's most noted scholars, James Deetz, furthered this agenda in his book, *In Small Things Forgotten,* a work historical archaeologists consider canonical. In it, Deetz shows how multiple ethnic groups imprinted their own worldviews upon North America's colonial landscape. For instance, colonists imposed an explicitly European "Georgian Order" on the North American landscape that can be seen in colonial architecture. Deetz also shows that African Americans similarly replicated shotgun-style houses found in their homeland of West Africa despite European American attempts to eradicate African cultural practices. Reflecting this perspective, Deetz, in the 1996 edition, makes a case for historical archaeology to "adopt a global perspective on its data, for when the first European sailing ships set out for distant parts of the world, a chain of events never before seen in human history was set into motion" (Deetz 1996:5). Leone (1996) similarly found that an Annapolis, Maryland socialite, William Paca, applied the principles of the Georgian Order - a style marked by segmentation of space and "bilateral symmetry" (1996:373) - to his garden and estate layout. According to Leone, this design made Paca's elite status appear natural, masking the socio-historical conditions (in particular, slavery) that allowed him to accumulate wealth and status. As these early examples illustrate, the best historical archaeological research requires thinking across cultures and national borders.

The rise of processualist thought within archaeology, which emphasized employing replicable scientific methodologies to make generalizations about human behavior (c.f Binford 1962, 1978), inspired a turn towards a new type of comparative research in historical archaeology: one that aimed to identify specific, predictable patterns of consumer behavior that could be directly correlated with ethnicities, genders, and classes (e.g. South 1977, 1978). Miller (1980, 1991), for example, compiled sets of ceramic price indices that would allow archaeologists to calculate the relative cost of an assemblage. Historical archaeologists then used Miller's indices to measure and compare the wealth and/or class standing of different households (c.f. Spencer-Wood 1987), though as some later pointed out, wealth and class are not one in the same (Wurst 1999); an individual can possess items that communicate an air of sophistication and wealth without having regular access to capital.

Though not explicitly championing Miller's indices, Praetzellis et al. (1988) similarly asserted that the middle-class' consumption patterns served "as a source of inspiration and emulation for the fashions and pretenses of their social inferiors" (1988:195) in mid- to late-19th century America. They proposed excavating middle-class homesteads to identify consumer patterns typical of the group. The archaeological assemblages of lower-class or ethnic minorities could then be compared against this middle-class model of consumer behavior to determine their relative assimilation to dominant consumer practices (as defined by the middle-class according to Praetzellis et al.). Other scholars argued that Miller's price indices did not acknowledge individual choice and the symbolic meaning behind artifacts. Cook et al., for example, took issue with the deterministic nature of price indices, arguing that they reduced consumer choice to being "seen as either determined by economics or as a small, at best passive, voice, inaudible, submerged in the noisy black box of mass culture" (1996:50).

Some of the first attempts at exploring race and ethnicity in historical archaeology also centered on pattern recognition, with scholars looking for "distinct cultural patterns in language, social structure, economic organization and belief," patterns that were often assumed to have "clearly defined correlates in material culture" (Schulyer 1980:viii). Such research involved seeking out objects that could be associated with ethnic groups - such as opium pipes for the Chinese; these efforts mirrored some of the earliest culture-history studies in archaeology, where scholars like A. L. Kroeber assumed that "a unique material culture" reflected a "wholly distinct past culture" (Orser 2007:11). As historical archaeology evolved and came to be defined as a subfield committed to "those of little note" (Scott 1994), more refined ways of interpreting expressions of ethnicity, race, and group affiliation developed.

These studies complicated earlier work that made one to one correlations between objects and an ethnic group by demonstrating that materiality was not merely a reflection of one's racial designation, but instead used as a tool by marginalized groups to transform their socially imposed identity. For instance, Praetzellis and Praetzellis' (2001) research on Chinese merchants in historic Sacramento showed that different racialized groups used material culture in ways that price indices cannot accommodate. These merchants displayed expensive European-American ceramics and goods to attract Anglo American customers, but used Asian American products inside their homes (Praetzellis and Praetzellis 2001). Mullins' work (1999, 2001; this volume) likewise raised questions about the applicability of price indices and pattern analysis in historical archaeology. He asserts that Victorian-era bric-a-brac, figurines designed to "evoke pleasant yet inchoate sentiments about a romanticized past, household class identity, Western cultural and racial roots, patriarchy, personal style, aristocratic behavior, or any number of things" (2001:160), found in mid- to late-19th century African American homesteads in Oakland, California should not be interpreted as passive reflection of a racialized minority's desire to assimilate to Euro-American culture. Rather, Mullins sees these objects as expressing a "radical critique of whiteness by paradoxically embracing its genteel rules and commodity forms, thereby countering the white exclusivity associated with those rules and goods" (2001:161).

Because of studies like these and the shift away from processualist thought in the discipline, historical archaeologists now generally shy away from seeking out patterns across sites associated with racialized groups. Nonetheless, a few historical archaeologists have made advances in comparing racializations across the globe, though this type of comparative work currently remains the exception. Charles E. Orser, Jr.'s (2007) recent publication, *The Archaeology of Race and Racialization in Historic America*, examines how two seemingly disparate cultural groups (Chinese Americans and Irish Americans) occupying two entirely different social and historical milieus (California and New York) were racialized in a remarkably similar fashion. In making this claim, Orser attempts to demonstrate the incongruencies and contradictions inherent in racial categories that continue to be perceived as "natural" or "biological" in contemporary American society. By looking at the transatlantic and global linkages between Irish citizens subjected to

British governance, Irish settlements in the United States, and Africans colonized by Western imperialism, Orser discovers an international trafficking of racial categories and stereotypes across borders and cultural groups, that resulted in a surprisingly uniform and static vocabulary of racial classifications and stereotypes. In making this claim, Orser shows that racism has its genesis in the emergence of Western capitalism.

Martin Hall has similarly unpacked some of the international structures and "networks" that inform discourses of racializations. Though continents and oceans apart, the histories of the Cape region of Africa and colonial Chesapeake in the United States, the former occupied by the Dutch and the latter by the British, were shaped by a similar, Western European ethic grounded in "merchant capitalism that drove exploitation and colonial settlement" (Hall 2000:18). What resulted between the two regions was a "set of economic imperatives that in turn generated similarities of form" (Hall 2000:18). In both settings, the Dutch and the British confronted indigenous populations with preconceived and globally distributed images displaying the colonized's supposed inferiority, and, as a result, "the transcripts of colonial settlement were repeated many times over in widely different parts of the world" (Hall 2000:18). Despite a concomitant to the global dissemination of European economic systems, the way empires and colonization played (or faded) out was determined by the colonized and not the colonizers. This, Hall explains, is why we find unique material signatures, such as differences in Dutch and Euro-American architecture, in Africa and America.

Orser and Hall's transnational genealogies of racializations provide a compass to guide and direct future historical archaeologies of race, power, and inequality. They illustrate the utility of the comparative approach by exploring the global histories of racialized discourses. In the next section, then, I draw upon my own research at two separate early 20th century sites in the Western United States associated with Japanese American and Mexican American immigrants. By comparing the remarkably similar experiences of two racialized groups, it becomes apparent that the racism they faced was not limited to each individual ethnic group but rather reflective of larger structural issues and goals of the American empire. Archaeological data

suggests that their reactions to racialization, however, differed within and across the Japanese American and Mexican American communities.

Comparative Research in Practice

Early 20th century America witnessed an unparalleled influx of immigrants hailing from all parts of the world (Daniels 2004). American expansion into and urbanization of the Western frontier required an immigrant labor force who could build railroads, extract precious resources, and construct and take menial jobs in cityscapes at little cost to the United States government and corporations. These employees had to be willing to engage in dangerous and highly mobile work, moving "between the agricultural harvests of California, the lumber camps of the Pacific Northwest, and the copper mines of Alaska. Many others moved over a seasonal or longer-term pattern between the agricultural, mining, construction, and lumber camps of California, or coupled crop work in California with stints in munitions factories in Iowa, grain harvests in the Dakotas, and mining in the Rockies" (Walker 2008:3).

Already made economically vulnerable due to the transient and risky nature of their work, this "floating army" (Walker 2008) of laborers faced additional hardships that came in the form of racial discrimination and structural marginalization. Despite their contributions to the construction of the West, immigrants repeatedly found their acceptance in American society subject to the economic imperatives of the American nation. In times of war, intense immigration to the United States, or economic turmoil, naturalized immigrants found that their citizenship privileges were questioned. Despite building successful businesses, developing thriving communities, and even securing political positions within their neighborhoods, cities, counties, states, or nation, immigrants often found that their rights to act and live as American citizens could be subject to revocation. For example, in response to the shifting demographic composition of the United States, federal and Western state acts and laws excluded both Mexican and Japanese immigrants from accessing the economic and social benefits extended to Anglo American citizens.

Even when citizenship was extended to some members of these racialized groups, it was always subject to revocation. In the case of the internment of Japanese Americans and Japanese migrants during World War II, the "U.S. government never formally stripped Japanese Americans of their citizenship" (Ngai 2004:175); however, their citizenship was "nullified...exclusively on the grounds of racial difference" (Ngai 2004:175). Interestingly, the citizenship privileges of certain individuals of Japanese heritage were maintained, primarily due to the economic necessities of the American nation. In Hawaii, where "one-third of the Hawaiian population was of Japanese ancestry," Japanese Americans were not forced into internment camps because "their labor was crucial to the civilian and military economy of the islands" (Burton et al. 1999:29). The citizenship rights of nearly 250,000 (Ngai 2004:8) individuals of Mexican heritage were similarly swept under the rug in the 1930s when over half a million Mexican Americans and Mexican migrants were repatriated back to Mexico by the United States government (Guerin-Gonzales 1994:1). For many Japanese American and Mexican American migrants, conferral and attainment of American citizenship held little promise in a country where one's race or ability to serve the United States' capitalist economy rather than legal citizenship determined how fellow European American citizens treated them.

This complicates historical archaeology models that link consumption to an expression of ones citizenship aspirations (this point is discussed further in Camp 2012). In a time when an individual's consumption habits were used as a barometer to measure his or her loyalty to the nation and his or her citizenship aspirations, some members of early 20th century marginalized ethnic groups recognized that their consumption patterns or any other form of behavior for that matter would not necessarily lead to their acceptance within Anglo American society. This was made apparent with the passing of legislative acts such as California's Alien Land Law of 1913, which prevented individuals of Asian ethnicity from owning "agricultural land" (Daniels 1993:14). Early 20th century scholars of Mexican immigrant communities also noted

the incongruency between an immigrant's naturalization and acceptance into American society. As one researcher wrote in reference to Mexican Americans, "citizenship is disappointing to him for he is still likely to be treated as a Mexican and a foreigner. Citizens of the United States as a rule do not distinguish between naturalized and unnaturalized Mexicans" (Bogardus 1934:78).

The above and below ground archaeological data historical archaeologists study can speak to the structural inequalities that persist in our modern world. Perhaps equally important is historical archaeologists' ability to reveal how these structures can never fully squelch a group's or individual's culture. Archaeological data can help us understand how such groups envisioned their own national aspirations and yearnings for belonging in a culture that persistently pushed immigrant groups aside in favor of imperial goals.

Site Histories: Kooskia and Mount Lowe

On 19 February 1942, over 120,000 individuals of Japanese heritage were forced to leave the comfort and solace of their communities and relocate to internment camps spread throughout some of the harshest locales in the Western United States (Helphand 2006:156). Seen as enemies of the state during World War II, Japanese Americans were given an ultimatum: abandon their homes within six to twenty-one days or be imprisoned.

As the United States' first and only attempt in using Japanese male internees as a labor force, Idaho's Kooskia Internment Camp provides privileged insight into how Japanese American men, in particular, coped with internment and isolation from their families. The Kooskia Internment Camp was occupied by a diverse group of 265 Japanese American and Japanese men who were charged with the daunting and dangerous task of completing the construction of Highway U.S. 12 (located between Idaho and Montana) (Wegars 2010). Some male internees voluntary opted to leave the comfort of their families and move from internment camps in Minidoka, Idaho; Santa Fe, New Mexico; and Fort Missoula, Montana to work at the Kooskia Internment Camp. Other internees living at Kooskia were forcibly removed (Wegars 2010:16) by the United States government from Mexico, Panama, and Peru in an attempt to exchange the internees for American prisoners of war held in Japan.

Preliminary archaeological testing at the Kooskia Internment Camp took place over a four-week period of time in the summer of 2010. The goal of the project was to locate archaeological data associated with the Kooskia Internment Camp and to distinguish between the site's multilayered occupational periods by exploring the horizontal and vertical distribution of artifacts. Before the site was transformed into an internment camp, it was used by the Nez Perce and later, as a Civilian Conservation Corps (CCC) camp and federal prison. Once the internment camp closed in May 1945, buildings were removed from the landscape. Today, the site lacks signage, extant buildings, or any other material markers indicating that it was anything more than a modern hiking trail and popular camping spot. The Kooskia Internment Camp Archaeological Project (http://www.uidaho.edu/class/kicap) seeks to install signage, nominate the site for the National Register of Historic Places, and work with stakeholder groups and the local community to encourage site stewardship and protection.

The second site, Los Angeles' Mount Lowe Resort and Railway (1893-1936), is demographically similar to Kooskia. The site was primarily occupied by first generation Mexican migrants who were hired by the world-renowned tourist attraction to repair its incline railway, the steepest one of its kind at the time. Unlike Kooskia, however, employees were not forced against their will to labor or live at the site. Interestingly, not one of the 14 Mexican immigrant railway laborers worked at the site for more than 10 years, as census schedules for the resort demonstrate. Instead, new first generation Mexican immigrant laborers appear in the United States Federal Census for 1910, 1920, and 1930 (Camp 2009). With the help of Brian Marcroft, a local historian, the remains of the Mexican railway workers' housing were located in 2004 and then we excavated the archaeological component in 2005 and 2006. Archaeological work took place inside the homestead's kitchen, bedroom, and dining room as well as the exterior landscape, which featured an associated cesspool and garden.

Comparative Work across Sites

Despite sharing different migration histories and ethnic backgrounds, Japanese and Mexican immigrants encountered like forms of hostility and racism upon their arrival on America's shores. In particular, the landscapes and the built environment they occupied communicated remarkably uniform messages to first generation immigrants: cooperate with corporate- or government-imposed sanctions and rules or you will be punished. As the architecture reveals, the living conditions within internment and work camps dehumanized and stripped its occupants' of sense of individuality or personhood. The material environment can be read as a reflection of the tension between America's need of immigrants to support its capitalist economy and its simultaneous disinterest in extending citizenship to such workers.

Though the occupants of work camps were not involuntarily confined, severely unequal power relations characterized the situation in which they were placed and the method in which they arrived at work sites. Resource extraction and the construction of railways brought Anglo American nationals to live across the U.S.-Mexico border in the late 1800s. American-owned railway and mining camps established clear "color lines" between Anglo American and Mexican employees; pay scales, worker housing, and job affiliation were all determined by one's national affiliation and physiological characteristics. For example, "Mexican miners and railroad workers generally earned one-half the amount paid to Americans for the same work" in Mexico (González 2004:123). American labor camps on Mexico's soil physically segregated Mexican and Anglo American workers by placing them in separate living quarters. Believing that individuals of Mexican heritage were biologically different from Anglo Americans, American businesses expressed no qualms about actively recruiting and employing Mexican children; Mexican men, women, and children mined ore, picked cotton, and harvested sugar beets, with each family unit receiving "only one wage" for their labor (González 2004:120).

American corporations also crossed the border to acquire labor for work in the United States. Ignoring the Alien Contract Labor Law of 1885, American railway companies like Pacific Electric Railway actively recruited Mexican nationals by traveling along railway lines and advertising higher wages and better living standards across the border (Sánchez 1993:39). These "specific recruitment patterns of American railroad companies," Sánchez explains, "set the mass migration of the early twentieth century in motion" (1993:39). Once immigrants were brought into the United States and placed in work camps, they were expected to uphold Victorian standards of cleanliness that the provided landscapes and homes simply could not accommodate. Female reformers were hired by companies like the Pacific Electric Railway Corporation to ensure worker compliance with these standards. Unfortunately, reformers overlooked the conditions surrounding the workers and instead pointed the blame at the "racial inferiority" of their charges. Reflecting the eugenic thoughts of the time, reformers believed adherence to Victorian ideologies would help further the "evolution" Mexican immigrants. In this vein, one reformer working for the Pacific Electric Railway Corporation wrote, "It is interesting to note the varying types of Mexican, as one travels from door to door, from camp to camp. The stupid, sullen Mexican of the lower type, is our problem and a very discouraging problem it is. From this type on up we have many different grades, all more or less pliable, some naturally clean and some naturally dirty" (Carr 1921).

The homesteads and the physical layouts of work camps made emulating a middle-class Anglo American ideal of domesticity nearly impossible. While outsiders critiqued the squalid conditions of railway work camps, mid-20th century scholars like Carey McWilliams directed criticism not at the workers but rather at the companies who employed them. McWilliams' research on one Los Angeles settlement of Mexican Americans, Rancho La Tajauta, uncovered that it first developed due to a railway company's "importation of a carload" of Mexican immigrants in 1906 (McWilliams [1948] 1968:169). This community, which was originally comprised of boxcars and tents, transitioned into "company built rowhouses" available for rent by several railroad companies and was still primarily occupied by

Mexican Americans in 1948 (McWilliams [1948] 1968:169). In another study, McWilliams' critically described a 35 year-old Pacific Electric camp at the intersection of San Vicente and Santa Monica "where forty Mexican families live as they might live in a village in Jalisco" (McWilliams [1948] 1968:225). Venturing inside the camp, McWilliams continued to discover additional disturbing findings: "the company has generously provided four 'outside' showers for 120 residents. It has even provided them with 'hot water' – on Mondays, Wednesdays, and Saturdays! The only facilities for washing clothes or dishes consist of outside sinks, detached from the shacks in the court, and used by all the families" (McWilliams [1948] 1968:225).

Mount Lowe's Mexican immigrant railway workers inhabited a landscape much like the ones described by McWilliams. They dealt with cramped, unsanitary living quarters that company officials portrayed as clean and orderly in official photographs of their work camps (Camp 2009). Worker housing for Mexican immigrants featured a pigpen, two incinerators that burnt the resort's waste, and a massive, cement-lined cesspool that sat less than 10 ft. away from the workers' home. The everyday activities of these elements looked something like this: human waste would pile up in the cesspool (covered by a thin board made out of plywood); pigs would urinate and defecate in their pen; and billowing gray clouds of smoke and dust from the burning incinerators turned the "natural" mountain air into smog. In 1910 alone, three married couples and two single men of Mexican ancestry lived in this company housing. Their homestead was in the only area of the resort's copious worker housing complex that featured the deadly combination of sewage (human and animal) and hotel and construction-related trash. Furthermore, in October 1914, a railway car inspection pit was built approximately 200 ft. away from the section house. The railway workers' "work" was now a few steps away from the doorstep of their house: this naturalized Mexican immigrants' association with railway labor, especially for the middle- to upper-class tourists who voyeuristically witnessed the daily lives of the railway workers as a their trolly car passed directly above the workers' home (Camp 2009).

Internees similarly found themselves in "homes" that were a far cry away from what they were accustomed to. Almost immediately after President Franklin D. Roosevelt signed Executive Order 9066 permitting the removal of Japanese Americans "from their homes" and their imprisonment (Dusselier 2008:10), Japanese Americans found themselves in temporary holding camps that ranged from racetracks to fairgrounds; these "assembly centers" were ill prepared for the volume of individuals they were to house. Some internees, for instance, found themselves living in racehorse stalls while awaiting transport to larger, more permanent camps like Manzanar and Minidoka. When transferred to larger permanent camps, internees encountered equally hostile environments. Like Mount Lowe's Mexican immigrant housing, multiple families were forced to share the same barrack. "Incomplete walls often separate barracks units, so that all conversations could be overheard" (Branton 2004:130) and intimate acts were no longer intimate. Even the most personal space, the bathroom, "did not have interior walls or doors" (Branton 2004:131). Barbed wire fences and armed guard towers formed the perimeter of most internment camps. Internees were forced to dine communally and endure lines that extended outside the halls' doors, which "sometimes caused frost bite and extreme summer temperatures... resulted in heat stroke" (Dusselier 2008:11).

The conditions at the Kooskia Internment Camp were, at times, likewise deplorable. Internees were so frustrated with their living situation that they petitioned camp officials and administrators at neighboring camps for proper medical treatment and appropriate work clothing (Wegars 2001:155). Though data processing and analysis is preliminary, artifacts such as a medicinal bottle manufactured in Japan appear to speak to internees' attempts to temporarily remedy their lack of medical facilities. To help time pass by, internees crafted traditional Japanese gaming pieces and ornate artwork from the crude elements of their environment: soil, sediment, and mortar. Kooskia lacked the barbed wire fences of other camps, however, its panoptic landscape ensured that guards could surveil internees' movement at all times. Monumental rock outcrops served as faux guard towers, while the internees' marginal racial and citizenship status was further reinforced by keeping their living space approximately one half mile separate from the camp employees' housing. Mount Lowe's Mexican railway worker housing similarly sat directly below the tourist railway they were employed to repair. Railway cars would pass over their

Figure 2. Gaming pieces recovered from the 2010 field season at the Kooskia Internment Camp. (Photograph by Mary Petrich-Guy, 2010).

homestead hourly, permitting intense surveillance as tourists glimpsed into the Mexican employees' daily lives.

Artifacts from Mount Lowe's railway workers' housing complex paint a picture of employee responses to their marginalization. At Mount Lowe, a high frequency of matching molded one- and two-line white wares and improved white wares (c.f. diZerega Wall 1994:144-47) along with both molded and painted flower and vine designed white wares presented an image of submission - a necessity in a highly supervised landscape. Failure to conform to these standards was perceived as an act of disobedience or even seen as evidence of the occupants' moral disarray (Kaplan 1998:582). As Fitts explains, "Like other forms of genteel behavior, the presence or absence of the appropriate tableware was viewed as a sign of morality or immortality" (1999:50). Visibly expressing one's compliance with the material symbols of Victorian domesticity was especially important in this particular historical case study. If employees failed to pass regular house inspections and neglected to attend demeaning demonstrations on proper eating, bathing, and bed-making, they lost access to the few pleasure activities made available to them by the Pacific Electric Railway Corporation. If "women and children in each camp" met a "certain standard of cleanliness each week," they were "awarded with free passes to Los Angeles for shopping and pleasure trips" (Elliott 1918:152). If, however, they were "careless about observing the rules," wrote Pacific Electric Engineer Clifford Elliott, they were "disqualified from receiving any such free transportation" (1918:152): perhaps the only transportation that was financially and physically available to the railway workers. These matching table wares must therefore be read in light of the consequences that would result if they failed to comply with reformer and company expectations.

Scant, but nonetheless compelling archaeological data does capture some of the practices that may have been outside the purview of reformers and company inspectors. Diagnostic ammunition, which included a metal cartridge case from a 38.40 Winchester and a 32.40 U.M.C., found at the site implies that workers may have neglected reformers' dietary recommendations in favor of traditional or locally acquired food or, at the very least, supplemented their meals beyond what they may have been given by their employers. While working for Pacific Electric Railway Corporation, it appears that the railway workers were given food (perhaps as leftovers) from the resort's hotel. Of the identifiable bones, a total of 697 mammals, 142 birds, and 8 fish were found on the section house's landscape; 614 bones were unidentifiable (Stoyka 2009:395). Some individual species were identified within these categories and included: 17 cows, 18 sheep, 12 pig, 2 cottontail rabbits, 1 turkey, 18 chicken, 5 large ducks, and 1 trout. All of these species were served at the resort with the exception of cottontail rabbits. Like the munitions, unidentified small mammals and rodents from the site's faunal assemblage may also be reflective of the workers' desire to supplement or substitute certain foods in their diet.

The latter practices have been archaeologically documented at other railway workers' camps in the region. For instance, the remains of a ground squirrel, jackrabbits, and cottontail rabbits displaying evidence of human processing and cooking were recovered from a Santa Barbara, California railway workers' house during the same occupational period (1898-1933) (Nettles and Hamilton 2005). The archaeobotanical remains, though likewise limited, also suggest that the railway workers found ways to accommodate their own food preferences beyond their employer's rigid dietary expectations. Cultivated plants found at the site include chile pepper, fig, common bean, blackberry, grape, and wild elderberry, which were also found at the same workers' camp. Chile peppers, especially symbolic of a Mexican American diet, may have been incorporated into popular dishes such as *chile rellanos* and *chile verde* (Haverluk 2002:46).

Concluding Thoughts on Comparative Research

Given the significant parallels between Mexican American and Japanese American historiographies and responses to racism, why is extra-site comparison rarely undertaken in historical archaeology? Voss (2008) offers one explanation for the relative lack of comparative research in historical archaeology and collaborative work across sites. She asserts that this negligence is due to current methodological constraints of historical archaeology research where the household or site is privileged as the primary unit of comparison and analysis (Voss 2008:37). As a result, community sites, which feature communal rather than individual middens, are neglected. Focusing on the household therefore leaves a large gap in the archaeological historiography of marginalized immigrant groups who were placed in group housing by their employers or by the United States government. Mullins (2009) has similarly expressed concern over historical archaeology's obsession with individual households and individuality, particularly the notion that individual consumption can operate outside of societal influences and structural constraints. Our interpretations of objects and consumer decisions, he argues, must be carefully "positioned within and against racial subjectivity and the persistent structural continuities of racism that are invested in particular classes and social collectivities" (Mullins 2009:210).

Despite these substantial obstacles, historical archaeologists must both reconceptualize what they consider a "site" as well as forge relationships with our colleagues to perform extra-site analyses. As successful projects at Ludlow (c.f. Wood 2002) and Annapolis (c.f. Leone et al. 1987) have shown, exposing the injustices of capitalism requires a collective, not individual, effort. The task at hand is to also push the discipline of historical archaeology in exciting and new political and interdisciplinary directions that conceptualize America as an empire. Honing in on moments in American history where imperial desires are especially visible in the archaeological signatures and historic landscapes will help us move in this direction. We must work to continue to expand this field of study beyond what its earliest practitioners described as a "handmaiden to history" and, instead, stress its role as having a hand in rewriting history.

References

ARAI, IVY D.

1999   The Silent Significant Minority: Japanese American Women, Evacuation, and Internment During World War II. In *Women and War in the Twentieth Century: Enlisted with or without Consent*, Nicole Ann Dombrowski, editor, pp. 157-176. Garland Publishing, Inc., New York, NY.

BEDERMAN, GAIL

1995   *Manliness & Civilization: A Cultural History of Gender and Race in the United States, 1880-1917.* The University of Chicago Press, Chicago, IL.

BINFORD, LEWIS

1962   Archaeology as Anthropology. *American Antiquity* 28(2):217-225.

1978   Dimensional Analysis of Behavior and Site Structure: Learning from an Eskimo Hunting Stand. *American Antiquity* 43(3):330-361.

BOGARDUS, EMORY S.

1934   *The Mexican in the United States.* University of Southern California School of Research Studies, Number Five, Social Science Series Number Eight. University of Southern California, Los Angeles, CA.

BRANTON, NICOLE

2004   *Drawing the Line: Places of Power in the Japanese-American Internment Eventscape.* Doctoral dissertation, Department of Anthropology, University of Arizona. University Microfilms International, Ann Arbor, MI.

BRODKIN, KAREN

2000   Global Capitalism: What's Race got to do with it? *American Ethnologist* 27(2):237-256.

BURTON, JEFFREY F.

2005   The Fate of Things: Archaeological Investigations at the Minidoka Relocation Center Dump, Jerome County, Idaho, Volume III. Publications in Anthropology No. 90. Western Archaeological and Conservation Center, National Park Service, U.S. Department of the Interior, Tucson, AZ.

BURTON, JEFFREY F., MARY M. FARRELL, FLORENCE B. LORD, AND RICHARD W. LORD

1999   *Confinement and Ethnicity: An Overview of World War II Japanese American Relocation Sites*. Western Archaeological and Conversation Center, National Park Service, U.S. Department of the Interior, Tucson, AZ.

CAMP, STACEY L.

2011   Consuming Citizenship? The Archaeology of Mexican Immigrant Ambivalence in Early 20th Century Los Angeles. *International Journal of Historical Archaeology* 16(2): 305-328.

2009   *Materializing Inequality: The Archaeology of Citizenship and Race in Early 20th Century Los Angeles*. Doctoral dissertation, Department of Anthropology, Stanford University. University Microfilms International, Ann Arbor, MI.

CARR, VIVA M.

1921   Camp Welfare. *Pacific Electric Magazine*, January 10, 5(8).

CLARK, BONNIE J.

2008   Artifact Versus Relic: Ethics and the Archaeology of the Recent Past. *Anthropology News* 49(7):23.

2010   The Tangible History of Amache, Phase II: Archaeology Research Design and Methodology for Field Investigations, Summer 2010. Department of Anthropology, University of Denver, Denver, CO.

CLARK, BONNIE J., APRIL KAMP-WHITTAKER, AND DANA OGO SHEW

2008   The Tangible History of Amache: Archaeology Research Design and Methodology for Field Investigations, Summer 2008. Department of Anthropology, University of Denver, Denver, CO.

COOK, LAUREN, REBECCA YAMIN, AND JOHN M. McCARTHY

1996   Shopping as a Meaningful Action: Toward a Redefinition of Consumption in Historical Archaeology. *Historical Archaeology* 30(4):50-65.

DANIELS, ROGER

1993   *Prisoners without Trial: Japanese Americans in World War II*. Hill and Wang, New York, NY.

2004   *Guarding the Golden Door: American Immigration Policy and Immigrants since 1882*. Hill and Wang, New York, NY.

DEETZ, JAMES

1996   *In Small Things Forgotten: The Archaeology of Early American Life*, expanded and revised from 1977 edition. Doubleday, New York, NY.

DELLE, JAMES A., STEPHEN MRZOWOSKI, AND ROBERT PAYNTER (EDITORS)

2000   *Lines that Divide: Historical Archaeologies of Race, Class, and Gender*. The University of Tennessee Press, Knoxville, TN.

diZEREGA WALL, DIANA

1994   *The Archaeology of Gender: Separating the Spheres in Urban America*. Plenum Press, New York, NY.

DUSSELIER, JANE E.

2005   Gendering Resistance and Remaking Place: Art in Japanese American Concentration Camps. *Peace & Change* 30(2):171-204.

2008   *Artifacts of Loss: Crafting Survival in Japanese American Concentration Camps*. Rutgers University Press, New Brunswick, NJ.

ELLIOTT, CLIFFORD A.

1918   Home Attractions Keep Track Laborers Satisfied - Solving the Labor Problem by Providing Free Section Houses With All Conveniences, Land for Gardens and Chicken Raising as Well as Free Transportation to Amusement Places for Their Employees and Families. *Pacific Electric Magazine*, July 27:150-152.

ENLOE, CYNTHIA

1990   *Bananas, Beaches, and Bases: Making Feminist Sense of International Politics*. University of California Press, Berkeley, CA.

FITTS, ROBERT K.

1999   The Archaeology of Middle-Class Domesticity and Gentility in Victorian Brooklyn. *Historical Archaeology* 33(1):39-62.

FONTANA, BERNARD L.

1970   In Search of Us. *Historical Archaeology* 4:1-2.

FUNARI, PEDRO PAULO A., MARTIN HALL, AND SIÂN JONES (EDITORS)

1999   *Historical Archaeology: Back from the Edge*. Routledge, UK.

26

GOLDBERG, DAVID THEO
1997   *Racial Subjects: Writing on Race in America.* Routledge, London, UK.

GONZÁLEZ, GILBERT G.
2004   *Culture of Empire: American Writers, Mexico, and Mexican Immigrants, 1880-1930.* University of Texas Press, Austin, TX.

GUERIN-GONZALEZ, CAMILLE
1994   *Mexican Workers and American Dreams: Immigration, Repatriation, and California Farm Labor, 1900-1939.* Rutgers University Press, New Brunswick, NJ.

HALL, MARTIN
2000   *Archaeology and the Modern World: Colonial Transcripts in South Africa and the Chesapeake.* Routledge, London, UK.

HARRISON, FAYE V.
1995   The Persistent Power of 'Race' in the Cultural and Political Economy of Racism. *Annual Review of Anthropology* 24:47-74.

HAVERLUK, TERRANCE W.
2002   Chile Peppers and Identity Construction in Pueblo, Colorado. *Journal for the Study of Food and Society* 6(1):45-59.

HELPHAND, KENNETH I.
2006   *Defiant Gardens: Making Gardens in Wartime.* Trinity University Press, San Antonio, TX.

JOHNSON, MATTHEW
1996   *An Archaeology of Capitalism.* Blackwell, Oxford, UK.

KAMP-WHITTAKER, APRIL
2010   Through the Eyes of a Child: Japanese Internment at Amache. Master's thesis, Department of Anthropology, University of Denver, Denver, CO.

KAPLAN, AMY
1998   Manifest Domesticity. *American Literature* 24:547-565.

LEES, WILLIAM
1999   Comments on 'Historical Archaeology in the Next Millennium: A Forum,' *Historical Archaeology* 33(2):63-65.

LEONE, MARK P.
1996   Interpreting Ideology in Historical Archaeology: Using the Rules of Perspective in the William Paca Garden in Annapolis, Maryland. In *Images of the Recent Past: Readings in Historical Archaeology*, Charles E. Orser, Jr., editor, pp. 371-391. AltaMira Press, Walnut Creek, CA.

LEONE, MARK P. AND PARKER B. POTTER, JR. (EDITORS)
1999   *Historical Archaeologies of Capitalism.* Kluwer Academic/Plenum, New York, NY.

LEONE, MARK P., PARKER B. POTTER, AND PAUL A. SHACKEL
1987   Toward a Critical Archaeology. *Current Anthropology* 28(3):282-302.

McCLINTOCK, ANNE
1995   *Imperial Leather: Race, Gender, and Sexuality in the Colonial Conquest.* Routledge, New York, NY.

McGUIRE, RANDALL H.
1982   The Study of Ethnicity in Historical Archaeology. *Journal of Anthropological Archaeology* 1:159-178.

McGUIRE, RANDALL H. AND ROBERT PAYNTER
1991   *The Archaeology of Inequality.* Blackwell, Oxford and Cambridge, UK.

McGUIRE, RANDALL H. AND PAUL RECKNER
2005   Building a Working Class Archaeology: The Colorado Coal Field War Project. In *Industrial Archaeology: Future Directions*, Eleanor Conlin Casella and James Symonds, editors, pp. 217-241. Springer, New York, NY.

McWILLIAMS, CAREY
1968   *North from Mexico: The Spanish-Speaking People of the United States.* Reprinted 1948 by Greenwood Press, New York, NY.

MATSUMOTO, VALERIE J.
1999   Japanese American Women and the Creation of Urban Nisei Culture in the 1930s. In *Over the Edge: Remapping the American West*, Valerie J. Matsumoto and Blake Allmendinger, editors, pp. 291-306. University of California Press, Berkeley, CA.

MILLER, GEORGE L.

1980 Classification and Economic Scaling of 19th-Century Ceramics. *Historical Archaeology* 14:1-40.

1991 A Revised Set of CC Index Values for Classification and Economic Scaling of 19th-Century Ceramics. *Historical Archaeology* 25(1):1-25.

MRZOWOSKI, STEPHEN A.

2006 *The Archaeology of Class in Urban America*. Cambridge University Press, Cambridge, UK.

MULLINS, PAUL R.

1999 *Race and Affluence: An Archaeology of African America and Consumer Culture*. Kluwer Academic/Plenum Publishers, New York, NY.

2001 Racializing the Parlor: Race and Victorian Bric-a-Brac Consumption. In *Race and the Archaeology of Identity*, Charles E. Orser, Jr., editor, pp. 158-178. The University of Utah Press, Salt Lake City, UT.

2009 Consuming Individuality: Collective Identity Along the Color Line. In *The Materiality of Individuality*, Carolyn White, editor, pp. 207-219. Springer, New York, NY.

NETTLES, WENDY M. AND COLLEEN HAMILTON

2005 Life at a Remote Railroad Section House revealed through Material Culture. Paper presented at the Society for California Archaeology Annual Meeting, Sacramento, CA.

NGAI, MAE M.

2004 *Impossible Subjects: Illegal Aliens and the Making of Modern America*. Princeton University Press, Princeton, NJ.

NISHIMOTO, RICHARD S.

1995 *Inside an American Concentration Camp: Japanese American Resistance at Poston, Arizona*, Lane Ryo Hirabayashi, editor. The University of Arizona Press, Tucson, AZ.

OMI, MICHAEL AND HOWARD WINANT

1994 *Racial Formation in the United States: From the 1960s to the 1990s*. Routledge, New York, NY.

ORSER, CHARLES E., JR.

1998 The Challenge of Race to American Historical Archaeology. *American Anthropologist* 100(3):661-668.

2001 Race and the Archaeology of Identity in the Modern World. In *Race and the Archaeology of Identity*, Charles E. Orser, Jr., editor, pp. 1-13. The University of Utah Press, Salt Lake City, UT.

2004 *Race and Practice in Archaeological Interpretation*. University of Pennsylvania Press, Philadelphia, PA.

2007 *The Archaeology of Race and Racialization in Historic America*. University Press of Florida, Gainesville, FL.

PRAETZELLIS, MARY, ADRIAN PRAETZELLIS AND MARLEY BROWN III

1988 What Happened to the Silent Majority? Research Strategies for Studying Dominant Group Material Culture in Late Nineteenth-Century California. In *Documentary Archaeology in the New World*, Mary C. Beaudry, editor, pp. 192-202. Cambridge University Press, Cambridge, UK.

PRAETZELLIS, ADRIAN AND MARY PRAETZELLIS

2001 Mangling Symbols of Gentility in the Wild West: A Case Study in Interpretive Archaeology. *American Anthropologist* 140(3):645-654.

RUIZ, VICKI

1992 Star Struck: Acculturation, Adolescence, and Mexican American Women, 1920-1950. In *Unequal Sisters: A Multicultural Reader in U.S. Women's History*, Vicki L. Ruiz and Ellen Carol DuBois, editors, pp. 346-361. Routledge, New York, NY.

SÁNCHEZ, GEORGE J.

1993 *Becoming Mexican American: Ethnicity, Culture, and Identity in Chicano Los Angeles, 1900-1945*. Oxford University Press, New York, NY.

SANJEK, ROGER

1994 The Enduring Inequalities of Race. In *Race*, Steven Gregory and Roger Sanjek, editors, pp. 1-17. Rutgers University Press, New Brunswick, NJ.

SCHUYLER, ROBERT L.

1980 Preface. In *Archaeological Perspectives on Ethnicity in America: Afro-American and Asian American Culture History*, Robert L. Schuyler, editor, pp. vii-viii. Baywood Publishing Company, Farmingdale, IL.

28

SCOTT, ELIZABETH M.
1994   Through the Lens of Gender: Archaeology, Inequality, and Those of Little Note. In *Those of Little Note: Gender, Race, and Class in Historical Archaeology*, Elizabeth M. Scott, Editor, pp. 3-24. University of Arizona Press, Tucson, AZ.

SHACKEL, PAUL A.
1993   *Personal Discipline and Material Culture: An Archaeology of Annapolis, Maryland, 1695-1870*. The University of Tennessee Press, Knoxville, TN.

SHEW, DANA OGO
2010   Feminine Identity Confined: The Archaeology of Japanese Women at Amache, a WWII Internment Camp. Master's thesis, Department of Anthropology, University of Denver, Denver, CO.

SKILES, STEPHANIE A. AND BONNIE J. CLARK
2010   When the Foreign is not Exotic: Ceramics at Colorado's WWII Japanese Internment Camp. In *Trade and Exchange: Archaeological Studies from History and Prehistory*, Carolyn D. Dillian and Carolyn L. White, editors, pp. 179-192. Springer, New York, NY.

SOCIETY FOR HISTORICAL ARCHAEOLOGY
1967   Beginnings. *Historical Archaeology* 1:1-12.

SPENCER-WOOD, SUZANNE M. (EDITOR)
1987   *Consumer Choice in Historical Archaeology*. Plenum Press, New York.

SOUTH, STANLEY
1977   *Method and Theory in Historical Archaeology*. Academic Press, New York, NY.
1978   Pattern Recognition in Historical Archaeology. *American Antiquity* 43(2):223-230.

SOUTHERN POVERTY LAW CENTER
2007   *Close to Slavery: Guestworker Programs in the United States*. Southern Poverty Law Center, Montgomery, AL.

STOLER, ANN LAURA
2006   Intimidations of Empire: Predicament of the Tactile and Unseen. In *Haunted by Empire: Geographies of Intimacy in North American History*, Ann Laura Stoler, editor, pp. 1-22. Duke University Press, Durham, NC.

STOYKA, MICHAEL
2009   Mount Lowe Archaeological Project Faunal Analysis. South Central Coastal Information Center, Fullerton, CA.

VOSS, BARBARA L.
2005   The Archaeology of Overseas Chinese Communities. *World Archaeology* 37(3):424-439.
2008   Between the Household and the World System: Social Collectivity and Community Agency in Overseas Chinese Archaeology. *Historical Archaeology* 42(3):37-52.

WALKER, MARK
2008   'The Floating Army': Transient Labor in Early 20th Century California. Paper presented at the Society for Historical Archaeology Annual Conference, Albuquerque, NM.

WEGARS, PRISCILLA
2001   Japanese and Japanese Latin Americans at Idaho's Kooskia Internment Camp. In *Guilt by Association: Essays on Japanese Settlement, Internment, and Relocation in the Rocky Mountain West*, Mike Mackey, editor, pp. 143-183. Western History Publications, Powell, WY.
2010   *Imprisoned in Paradise: Japanese Internee Road Workers at the World War II Kooskia Internment Camp*. Asian American Comparative Collection, University of Idaho, Moscow, ID.

WOOD, MARGARET
2002   Moving Towards Transformative Democratic Action through Archaeology. *International Journal of Historical Archaeology* 26(3):187-198.

WURST, LOUANN
1999   Internalizing Class in Historical Archaeology. *Historical Archaeology* 33(1):7-21.

WURST, LOUANN AND RANDALL H. MCGUIRE
1999   Immaculate Consumption: A Critique of the 'Shop till you drop' School of Human Behavior. *International Journal of Historical Archaeology* 3(3):191-199.

YAMIN, REBECCA

2002   Children's Strikes, Parents' Rights: Paterson and Five
        Points. *International Journal of Historical Archaeology*
        6(2):113-126.

Stacey Lynn Camp
Department of Sociology & Anthropology
University of Idaho
PO Box 441110
Moscow, Idaho 83844-1110

Paul R. Mullins

The Importance of Innocuous Things: Prosaic Materiality, Everyday Life, and Historical Archaeology

The everyday is platitude (what lags and falls behind, the residual life with which we fill our trash cans and cemeteries: scrap and refuse); but this banality is also what is most important if it brings us back to existence in its very spontaneity and as it is lived—at the moment when, lived, it escapes every speculative formation, perhaps all coherence and all regularity.

-Blanchot (1993:239)

ABSTRACT

Perhaps the boldest challenge of *Historical Archaeology and the Importance of Material Things* was its ambitious definition of material culture that could confront a vast range of social questions, but historical archaeologists continue to circumspectly define archaeological data, focus on the prosaic details of everyday life, and avoid anomalous goods. This paper examines the implications of a historical archaeology that answers many of the Ferguson collection's challenges, taking aim on materiality in broad terms addressing the profound social significance of apparently mundane archaeological material culture and crafting a reflective picture of everyday life and materiality.

Innocuous Things

In his introduction to *Historical Archaeology and the Importance of Material Things*, Leland Ferguson (1977:5) suggested that his goal for the 1975 symposium was to "concentrate on the importance of archaeological data—material things—and the undeveloped potential of those data." Ferguson lamented that historical archaeology was overly descriptive and needed to focus on the social dimensions of material culture, a complaint that today seems simultaneously quaint and uncomfortably relevant. On the one hand, the critique of an empirical archaeology seems dated since the vast breadth of contemporary scholarship recognizes the cultural and social dimensions of things. Yet, on the other hand, the discipline remains firmly wedded to a fine-grained and highly focused picture of everyday material patterns that often is poorly or unconvincingly connected to ambitious social and cultural questions. Over 30 years later, nagging tensions between broad social questions and highly focused material analysis continue to trouble historical archaeologists who aim to craft a socially and intellectually relevant scholarship while preserving the discipline's distinctive material insight into prosaic everyday life.

This paper examines the vast breadth of materiality tackled by *The Importance of Material Things* and confronts how such a broadly defined materiality might change African American archaeology in particular and historical archaeology in general. My interest is in complicating the ways everyday material repetition, patterns, and routine are defined in historical archaeological theory. In particular, this paper explores the dual nature of everyday life as a realm of unconscious repetitive oppression as well as a potential space for creativity if not liberation. This mission depends on outlining a broad notion of materiality, and *The Importance of Material Things* provides a useful starting point. The volume outlined a more expansive and self-reflective notion of material culture—and, by extension, historical archaeology itself—than the discipline has subsequently embraced. Ferguson recognized the breadth of material things that might reasonably become the focus of historical archaeology, acknowledging that the last half millennium was stocked with "an ever increasing proliferation of material items. Farm tools, ceramics, houses, furniture, toys, buttons, roads, cities, villages—the list continues almost *ad infinitum*" (Ferguson 1977:7). Indeed, the 1977 collection hosted a relatively unique and idiosyncratic range of things: banjos, old houses, plate scrapings, landscapes, cereal toys, a massive church, and ceramics are just a few of the myriad objects that found their way into the contributions. The papers did not seem especially concerned about narrow definitions of archaeological material culture as something distinct from broader materiality. For instance, Deetz (1977:10) ambitiously defined material culture as the dimension of the physical world that is shaped "according to culturally dictated plans," sweeping up a vast range of goods and arguing that material culture studies needed to become a central dimension of all anthropological scholarship and perhaps any social science. Henry Glassie (1977:32) similarly concluded that "artifacts can be transformed into a multitude of structures expressive of mind," and the limits on material interpretation "are drawn only by will and desire."

Despite such sentiments, North American historical archaeology's subsequent vision of materiality has been somewhat particularistic and persistently focused on, for lack of a better term, "everyday" material things. In archaeological usage the ambiguity of "everyday" materiality tends to invoke objects that are involved in broadly shared, patterned behaviors registered in quantitatively common material goods and repetitive practices, such as foodways. The discipline's focus on prosaic materiality paints everyday life as utterly quotidian, a smoothly functioning and rational daily existence registered in a backdrop of commonplace materiality and material practices. This everyday realm is composed of repeated but mostly implicit, unexpressed, and loosely codified practices.

Prosaic material things are certainly ripe for thick description, and celebrations of the everyday offer historical archaeology a powerful theoretical and political intervention against scholarship that focuses on elite material culture, reduces everyday materiality simply to ideological absorption, or ignores material culture entirely. Nevertheless, this requires a systematic theory of everyday life and materiality that situates prosaic objects within relations of power; ponders what distinguishes the everyday (or to what it is opposed); defines everyday life in the last half millennium as something distinct from a universal sociality common to every historical moment; and encompasses a much broader range of material goods than the discipline has focused on yet. Historical archaeology risks overemphasizing the uniformity in everyday life, reducing everyday consumption to its barest empirical patterns and granting significance to quantifiably common goods. The everyday is truly repetitive, but in historical archaeology its banality risks being painted as apolitical or even reactionary by focusing on its apparent uniformity.

Everyday material consumption provides a focus that, on the one hand, demonstrates modernity's successful regimentation of citizens, the ways in which behavior is profoundly shaped by normative institutions and practices that Michel de Certeau (1984:48) referred to as "organizing discourses." Henri Lefebvre (1987; 1991) saw the everyday as a dimension of life people do not consciously apprehend and recognize, and Lefebvre argued that the everyday is lived through ideological lenses that make everyday life a space of absorption into dominance. On the other hand, material culture simultaneously reveals the ways consumers negotiate the breakdowns in structural codes and defy those organizing discourses (Upton 2002:714). The everyday constitutes mundane practices that inevitably are the scene of ideological domination, but those practices foster new desires and political aspirations that hold the seeds of intervention. Michel de Certeau approached the everyday as a constellation of obstinate practices that are never fully assimilated to dominant economic and ideological forces (Highmore 2006:106). By its very nature, everyday life is an "inchoate and heterodox mix of fluid, multiple and symbolically dense practices and thoughts" that is at least partially outside the gaze of power (Gardiner 2000:16). Certeau celebrated concrete instances of creativity and subversion within existing dominance, underscoring the limits of rationality and focusing on how they are constantly revealed in the most apparently mundane everyday practices (Gardiner 2000:164). This does not conceive of everyday life simply as "resistance," instead approaching the everyday as that which cannot be utterly reduced by dominant disciplines.

Raoul Vaneigem (1979) even more radically celebrated everyday life's potential spontaneity and pleasure, championing it as a complete rejection of the sacrifices required by and the contrived desires constructed in modern consumer society. Vaneigem (1979:4) argued that all consequential radical politics must come from subjective everyday experience, proclaiming that "People who talk about revolution and class struggle without referring explicitly to everyday life, without understanding what is subversive about love and what is positive in the refusal of constraints, such people have corpses in their mouths." Vaneigem (1979:74) sought to position radical politics in the subjectivity of desire and experience, asking "[w]ho can gauge the striking-power of an impassioned daydream, of pleasure taken in love, of a nascent desire, of a rush of sympathy? Everyone seeks spontaneously to extend such brief moments of real life; everyone wants basically to make something whole out of their everyday life." Vaneigem (1979:162) suggested that consumption inevitably revealed existing and potential desires that countered domination, indicating that consumers' capacity to embrace such desires revolves "around our ability to turn against capitalism the weapons that commercial necessity has forced it to distribute." This politics channeled everyday desire and experience against moral authority, artificial consumer needs, and class separations (Plant 1992:62-63). Vaneigem argued that a genuine revolutionary politics sought to capture what people have in brief moments of everyday life, but those desires were constantly commodified, ideologically restrained by dominant roles, or hollowly fulfilled in the world of consumption.

The everyday has often been perceived as a polar opposite to institutional and ideological frameworks for life, a realm of lived experience that cannot be contained by and is outside if not openly critical of those dominant structural frameworks (Poster 2002:743-744). Scholars that focus on everyday experiences typically consider it to be something informal, tactical, spontaneous, and without centralized organization, as opposed to organized institutional spheres with concrete strategically planned goals that unfold over time. In any complex society there is perhaps some basic dimension of life that remains distanced from, if not outside, state and institutional controls, so there is perhaps something that might loosely be termed everyday life in any complex society. However, everyday life has little explanatory power for historical archaeology without recognizing the historical specificity of everyday life and materiality in the last half millennium, when the distinctions between everyday life and dominant spheres such as the state and workplace fundamentally reflect capitalism's routinized roles and commodification of human creativity and agency (Michael 2006:18). While there is some heuristic value to the basic polarization of everyday life and dominant institutional and ideological frameworks, everyday life is a complex and internally contradictory union of lived experience and reified structural frameworks (Kaplan and Ross 1987:3). Everyday life in Lefebvre's (1991:97) formulation, for instance, was perhaps less a polarized opposite than a totality of practices that was in part appropriated by structural ideologies even as it elided those structural influences in significant forms. Lefebvre still saw everyday life as fundamentally passive and characterized by banality, but it held the potential for political interventions that Mark Poster (2002:747) argues have moved politics from the workplace and state structures to broader public and popular realms.

Archaeological pictures of the everyday typically use dense material description to evoke a patterned and commonplace bedrock of things and practices. As the Program Chair for the conference that yielded *The Importance of Material Things*, Stanley South (1977) hoped that Ferguson's session would vigorously embrace theory that pushed historical archaeology beyond descriptive analysis, but by 1988 he was disappointed to conclude that the discipline "normally does not extend beyond particularistic, inductivistic exercises in identification and labeling" (South 1988:25). South lamented that historical archaeology 11 years after Ferguson's volume still persistently identified artifact patterns without linking them to cultural processes. Subsequent archaeological approaches to the everyday have often focused on pattern description and evaded anomalous things that do not seem to conform to functional artifact typologies, have not been defined as being especially significant, or are simply not considered appropriately "archaeological." Historical archaeologists generally have circumspectly viewed contemporary objects, infrequently recovered goods, or idiosyncratic things as completely "archaeological." In 2001, for instance, Charles Cleland (2001:5) groused that "much of what passes for historical archaeology is not archaeology. It seems perfectly acceptable to write or present papers that do not involve excavation or even artifacts." The result is that much of the 1977 Ferguson volume's call for a broadly defined materiality taking aim on any thing is accepted in theory but remains uncommon in practice.

The Banal Politics of Bric-a-Brac

Bric-a-brac is a class of artifacts that rarely plays a significant role in assemblage interpretations despite being constantly discussed in period literature and routinely fascinating to contemporary audiences and archaeologists alike. Ethnographic objects, items from nature, and craft goods were displayed in curiosity cabinets since the 18th century, and mass-produced curiosities joined those cabinets in the 19th century. Most of the archaeological artifacts classed as bric-a-brac are figurines, and while various sorts of miniature figures have been manufactured since prehistory they were most widely mass-produced in the 19th century. Figurines capture familiar dimensions of recognizable reality—people, animals, places, objects—but they reproduce that reality in aesthetically and ideologically distorted forms that distill the complicated symbolism of lived experience in a simultaneously spectacular aesthetics and utterly prosaic scale. In his study of miniatures, Ralph Mills (2010:11) argues that bric-a-brac's very scale and apparently familiar symbolism provide a circumspect security and a sense of order that invites consumers to imagine apparently alternative realities, which makes miniatures defensive mechanisms against experienced hardships. Bric-a-brac was innocuous in the sense that it was a commonplace, typically inexpensive, and very small object that rendered familiar subjects in apprehensible aesthetic forms, but that prosaic appearance encouraged consumers to project meaningful imagination and desire into those things.

Like almost all prosaic things, mass-produced knick knacks are material dimensions of life that are intrinsically elusive, largely inchoate, and obliquely brought into words and consciousness. The symbolic appeal of bric-a-brac was broadly defined, with some objects implying the class refinement of high art and others more firmly evoking cultural exoticism, relationships with nature, nationalism, and heritage. In 1867, for example, *The Albion* (1867:218) cast an exceptionally broad definition of bric-a-brac that revolved around its "artistic" dimensions, including "all that is precious and beautiful as well as mediocre in art, whether pictures, porcelain, ivory or wood carving, terra cotta, miniatures, jewelry, or plate." H. Byng Hall (1875:7) referred to such mass-produced goods as "industrial art," and much of the appeal of bric-a-brac was its deliberately liminal position between industrial commodities and high art. Hall argued that such objects, "if good specimens, [are] works of the most refined art," a position that confounded the notion of art as a product of unique creativity and admitted mass-produced objects into the realm of aesthetic authenticity and meaningful social symbolism. In 1853 one observer even hinted that mass-produced Parian improved on the natural materials artists used, indicating that the "colour of the Parian clay is beautifully adapted to statuary, and its softness of tone surpasses that of the finest marble" (Richards 1853:131). Parian porcelain statuary displayed at the 1851 Great Exhibition borrowed motifs from the Elgin Marbles and objects recovered at Pompeii, but other bric-a-brac examples did not so assertively fashion themselves as "high art" pieces, such as the many animal figurines on the market (The Royal Commission 1851; Barber 1893). When Henry Ward Beecher's massive bric-a-brac assemblage was auctioned in 1887, it included motifs as varied as a Ulysses S. Grant bust, a figurine of Shakespeare, hundreds of Chinese and Japanese porcelain vessels, and numerous figurines of cats, dogs, monkeys, turtles, and other animals (Kirby 1887). For decorative ideologues, bric-a-brac admitted select commodities to the realm of art, but in that sense it was ideologically incorporative because it did not threaten the status of art itself.

Despite rich period discourses on bric-a-brac, it is often archaeologically ignored. This is perhaps because it is recovered in modest quantities, since most decorative material culture was not broken at the same rate as commonly handled goods like tableware; nevertheless, many other things that are recovered in very small quantities justifiably occupy archaeological attention. Archaeologists have routinely valued quantitatively prevalent materiality over the things and practices that are less common in the archaeological record. This has yielded a rich picture of everyday patterns but paradoxically provided little sense of the numerous idiosyncrasies in everyday life. The modest quantities of bric-a-brac and its symbolic idiosyncracies defy easy analysis, so it often is buried in the depths of an artifact catalog or appears as a curious object whose picture adorns an otherwise dry technical report.

Bric-a-brac is typical of the everyday goods that largely fell outside materialist ideologies revolving around luxury items, high fashion goods, and novel styles, and it is those material ideologies that have driven Western historical narratives of consumer life, if not archaeological analysis as well (Owens et al 2010:213). Bric-a-brac is actually relatively similar to the flood of prosaic commodities that populate archaeological assemblages, but its rich symbolism and awkward fit in most archaeological typologies risks rendering it anomalous. Archaeologists often ignore uncommon material patterns and anomalous practices that provide idiosyncratic punctuation to everyday life, but such materiality that does not "make sense" on first glance harbors some of the discipline's most important insights. Amy Gazin-Schwartz (2001:266) argues that archaeologists' definitions of anomalies simply reveal our methodological, social, and disciplinary assumptions about the patterns we believe material culture should reveal. In the most rudimentary functional terms bric-a-brac is easy to define, but casting such goods simply as "decorative" objects ignores all their charged symbolism and fails to comprehend that a wide range of goods from tableware to seashells were aesthetic and ideological mechanisms in Victorian homes.

Archaeologists routinely ponder precisely what an object was meant to symbolize in the eyes of producers or consumers or reduce the objects to functional terms, but bric-a-brac's meanings and literal functions were intentionally ambiguous and idiosyncratic. Consumers were perhaps invoking the cultural meanings of high art when they decorated their homes with Parian vases, and exotic mass- or foreign-manufactured goods evoked global locales and distant cultures, but precisely what those concepts meant to any household was quite fluid. The representational logic of bric-a-brac was akin to the simulacra, which masquerade as a faithful copy of something authentic but mask and pervert reality or represent nothing especially real at all (Baudrillard 1988:170). Bric-a-brac was most widely marketed at a moment when commodity aesthetics began to mass-reproduce images, clouding the distinction between reality and representation as well as the authentic and the commodity. That representational ambiguity was a central appeal of these things (and many other commodities), and that departs from the notion that consumers acquired goods to instrumentally "communicate" particular sorts of meanings. Bric-a-brac was routinely consumed for no especially concrete reason besides its capacity to evoke generalized symbolism its consumers considered empowering in their own imaginations, if not the imaginations of others. In this sense, like all material things, bric-a-brac's meanings could never be utterly contained by dominant symbolism and ideological frameworks. The meaning of things constantly was shaped by highly contextualized, spontaneous experiences and desires even as consumer culture's ideological frameworks and the boundaries of dominant identities pulled in the opposite direction aspiring to constrain everyday desires that might well upset material and social discipline.

Bric-a-Brac and the Color Line

In the hands of African Americans bric-a-brac appropriated genteel symbolism that was routinely considered to be exclusively white, so it secured a circumspect foothold in consumer culture. In 1897, for instance, African American Bishop W.J. Gaines (1897:178-179) suggested that such goods had a "civilizing" effect, arguing that "The more intelligent of the negroes are beginning to recognize the influence of art as a factor in the improvement of their homes. They are beginning to understand its educative effect, its refining and elevating tendency. ... I have been astonished and gratified by the exhibition of pictures, bric-a-brac and ornamentations of various kinds which adorn these homes. This shows that the

minds of the better informed of my race have passed out of the stage of the semi-barbarism in which emancipation found them, and are opening to the susceptibilities of civilized life." For Gaines and many genteel observers, "art" evoked education, cultural breeding, style, and class in ways that explicitly invoked dominant ideological standards, and artistic materiality implicitly distanced African American consumers from racist caricatures that lay at the heart of those standards.

Figure 1. This well-behaved dog was recovered with the accompanying glass hat. The dog was essentially a behavioral model for a turn-of-the-century Indianapolis household, with its dress, style, demeanor, and implied dignity posing as a model for its human consumers. (Photograph by author, 2010).

Such modest goods drew African American consumers into a broad range of ideologies that were often considered color and class exclusive. For instance, the early 20th century Indianapolis, Indiana home of Ruben and Sallie Jones included a relatively typical cat figurine that used animals' domestication and discipline as a model for genteel households' own behaviors. The Jones' neighbors on California Street had a ceramic animal figurine in a late 1890s assemblage, and the dog was a similar disciplinary model, with impeccably combed hair, a stylish gilded bow, and an attentive pose that aspired to demonstrate the power of genteel discipline (Figure 1). Human figurines also routinely modeled the same genteel disciplines. For example, the ca. 1880-1920 South African farm site Vaal Krans included a figurine of a stylishly dressed sailor who breaks significantly from the stereotypical picture of sailors (Figure 2). The figurine's orderly blonde hair, beret, and kerchief underscored the civilizing effects of materiality and the disciplinary power of refined practices that could bring animals and sailors alike into Victorian culture. Such modeling invoked an ambiguous albeit largely undefined disciplinary ideal against which consumers

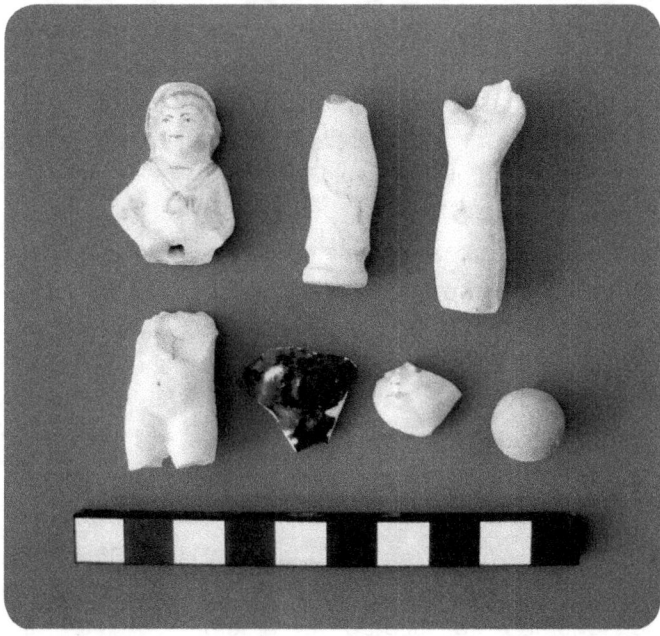

Figure 2. The sailor figurine shown in the upper left was among a modest assemblage of trinkets including dolls and toys found at the circa 1880-1920 South African farm site Vaal Krans. (Photograph by Gerda Coetzee, 2010).

measured themselves. In that sense, bric-a-brac obliquely posed a behavioral ideal that was "real" to consumers who recognized their distance from an idealized mainstream, but no especially clear ideal or mainstream actually existed in lived reality.

Some bric-a-brac was less a disciplinary model than an oblique critique of un-named social complexities. For instance, a ca. 1920-1940 figurine from the Wilson Farm Tenancy Site in New Castle County, Delaware combined the motifs of both a child sitting on a fence and a small playful kitten, doubly invoking an overly sentimental innocence that surfaced in figurines from the late-19th century onward (Affleck et al. 2010:7.28). In some hands this notion of childlike innocence was an indirect social critique of a public world many consumers saw as defamiliarizing, antagonistic, and not innocent at all. Pastoral images often performed a similar critique to such innocent figurines, attacking industrial society's material and social complexity with romanticized agrarian motifs in the somewhat incongruous form of a mass-produced commodity (Figure 3). If a consumer did not articulate that critique, the consumption of that object might be interpreted as ideological absorption rather than reflective critique. In most cases, though, such social symbolism skated along the boundaries between absorption and resistance as things assumed ever-emergent and relatively inarticulate meanings. This is typical of the tension within everyday material consumption, which is a symbiotic relationship between, on the one hand, an instrumentally rational ideology rooted in broad social and class structure and, on the other hand, an emotive, creative, and idiosyncratic symbolism that is vested in specific contexts, if not individual agents (Campbell 1987). Bric-a-brac's aesthetic novelty and ambiguous symbolism fueled creative longing that allowed consumers to imagine very different lives, yet it was simultaneously a mechanism of incorporation into unifying dominant ideological standards. Bric-a-brac was typical of the everyday practices that were firmly situated within dominant structural frameworks even as they held the seeds of interventions against those very frameworks.

By embracing dominant symbolism African Americans' bric-a-brac posed an oblique threat to racist ideologies. In 1906, for instance, Harry Stillwell Edwards (1906:212) expressed pleasant surprise at

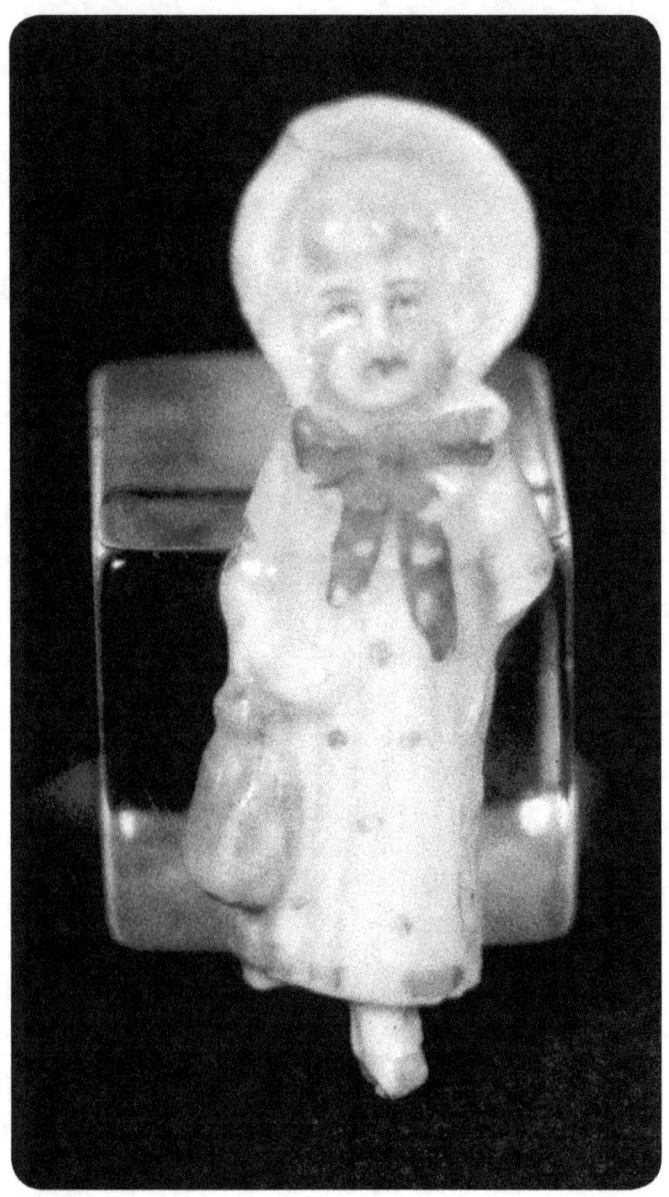

Figure 3. This figurine was recovered from a ca. 1890 deposit at the Maynard-Burgess House, an African American home in Annapolis, Maryland. The romanticized image of a peasant girl was relatively typical of sentimental bric-a-brac aesthetics that contrasted with urban industrial life in Victorian society. (Photograph by author, 2003).

visiting an African American's Georgia home where "the floors were carpeted, the white walls were hung with pictures, the mantels and tables held bric-a-brac. In one room was a parlor organ, in another a sewing machine, and in another a piano, where a girl sat at practice." Edwards (1906:213) divined in such apparently mundane household materiality a picture

that racial ideologues feared, arguing that "The happiness of home-owning strikes the American negro with peculiar force. The centuries have taught him that the people who command respect are the owners of lands and homes; and once in his own home, the home itself begins to teach him higher things.... It has become the home of a self-respecting American citizen. And having secured for himself a permanent home, the possessor adds himself to the higher class and demands that the public around him share the respect he feels for himself."

For African American consumers these prosaic household objects were significant as shows of class ambition in defiance of racism. The implications of such goods certainly were not lost on white observers. An 1890 novel by William Henry Holcombe (1890:84-85) told the story of a woman visiting an African American's home, where she "was ushered into the negro's little parlor. ... Nicely papered walls, carpeted floors, comfortable sofa and chairs, centre-table bearing a big family Bible and a large album for family photographs, chromos over the mantel, and a profusion of china bric-a-brac everywhere, all told the story of ambitious and successful imitation of the white man. Given a race with the imitative faculty, conscious of its deficiencies, anxious to overcome them, and with a good model before it, and its future progress is certain." The commentary reduced African American consumption to "imitation" and inelegantly maintained white genteel superiority, but it acknowledged the power of such commonplace things to forge domesticity. African American consumers were always positioned in relation to racist representations that constructed black identity in particular ideological forms, and commodities provided a lived and concrete materiality that eroded if not defied those racist narrative conventions.

The ideological appeal of a proper genteel home was wide-ranging across class, color, and international lines alike. For example, Eleanor Casella and Sarah Croucher's (2010) analysis of farm cottages near Manchester, England illuminates how modest rural households were quite active participants in late 19th and early 20th-century consumer culture, seizing on commodities that fabricated particular ideological notions of domestic space. One of the working-class cottages Casella and Croucher (2010:123) examined even had a piano in their modest parlor, and many of the neighbors' homes included Victorian goods like floor coverings, furniture, souvenirs, and decorative bric-a-brac that collectively materialized the ideological picture of a Victorian home. What such objects truly meant to the households who acquired them was inevitably idiosyncratic, dynamic, and highly contextualized, but bric-a-brac is less about concrete reflections of consumer identity and material symbolism than it is about desire; that is, figurines illuminate how consumers imagined themselves in relation to both their concrete experiences and the ideological notion of a Victorian social mainstream. Figurines positioned consumers within (and sometimes against) the dominant ideological vision of genteel Victorian society, and that position and the desires projected onto bric-a-brac reflected both consumers' distinctive lived experiences and their socially specific visions of broader social structure.

The symbolic richness of knick knacks is perhaps marked, but the mechanics of everyday material desire for bric-a-brac are not radically different from those projected onto any commodity. The symbolism of prosaic things is rarely articulate, and it typically has much less to do with function, the confirmation of narrowly defined identity or economic status, or the adherence to dominant styles than archaeological analysis suggests. Material assemblages are often indications of who consumers imagined themselves to be, rather than especially clear illustrations of an essential identity or dominant symbolism. Consumers do not normally have particularly instrumental understandings of how any given commodity will paint its possessor as wealthy, knowledgeable, cultured, or ideologically desirable. This does not mean that consumer desire is simply unfettered creativity disconnected from broader social contexts and dominant ideology (Wurst and McGuire 1999). Instead, it tends to be inchoate, idiosyncratic, and spontaneously negotiate and resist dominant practices even as it reproduces some of their underlying ideologies. Michael Dietler (2005:64-65) argues that consumption is "a process of structured improvisation that continually materializes cultural order by also dealing with alien objects and practices through either transformative appropriation and assimilation or rejection." In this sense, consumer desire is a dynamic, creative process that is socially, culturally, and historically positioned.

The politics of bric-a-brac took complicated forms, even when portraying partisan motifs. For instance, a tin silhouette of President Grover Cleveland was recovered from an African American home in Montgomery County, Maryland whose residents outside Washington DC held modest jobs as domestic laborers (Furgerson 2011; Schablitsky, this volume) (Figure 4). The home's rich assemblage of decorative goods was sealed by a fire in about 1916, leaving an unusually complete assemblage that included 96 artifacts the excavators identified as knick knacks (which included flower pots and broadly defined decorative goods as well as figurines). The political artifacts in the assemblage paint an interesting picture of African American political ambition and optimism in the wake of Emancipation. The assemblage included an 1860 Lincoln-Hamlin campaign medallion, which was from an election in which African Americans could not even vote, but free blacks and captives alike certainly recognized their stake in partisan politics, and the African American household's attraction to Lincoln would not have been uncommon. In contrast, the Grover Cleveland silhouette is somewhat more problematic as a partisan political statement. Cleveland was a Democrat who carried Maryland and the South in 1884, 1888, and 1892, winning the national election in 1884 and 1892—Cleveland always carried the South while the Republicans always carried the North, and his undistinguished record on race and deference to Southerners' re-established racist codes in the wake of the Civil War certainly boosted his popularity in the South. If they had been recovered individually, the two objects might be interpreted in quite different ways linking the position of African Americans to contrasting sets of partisan, social, and color line politics. Alongside each other the Lincoln and Cleveland artifacts could be narrowly construed as conflicting statements of partisan affiliation, but they instead underscore African American investment in politics: African Americans had hopes in the potential of democracy, if not in its late 19th century practice or in the specific candidates political parties offered. It is perhaps telling as well that the 1860 medallion was still in the household over 50 years after the Lincoln election, and the Cleveland bust

40

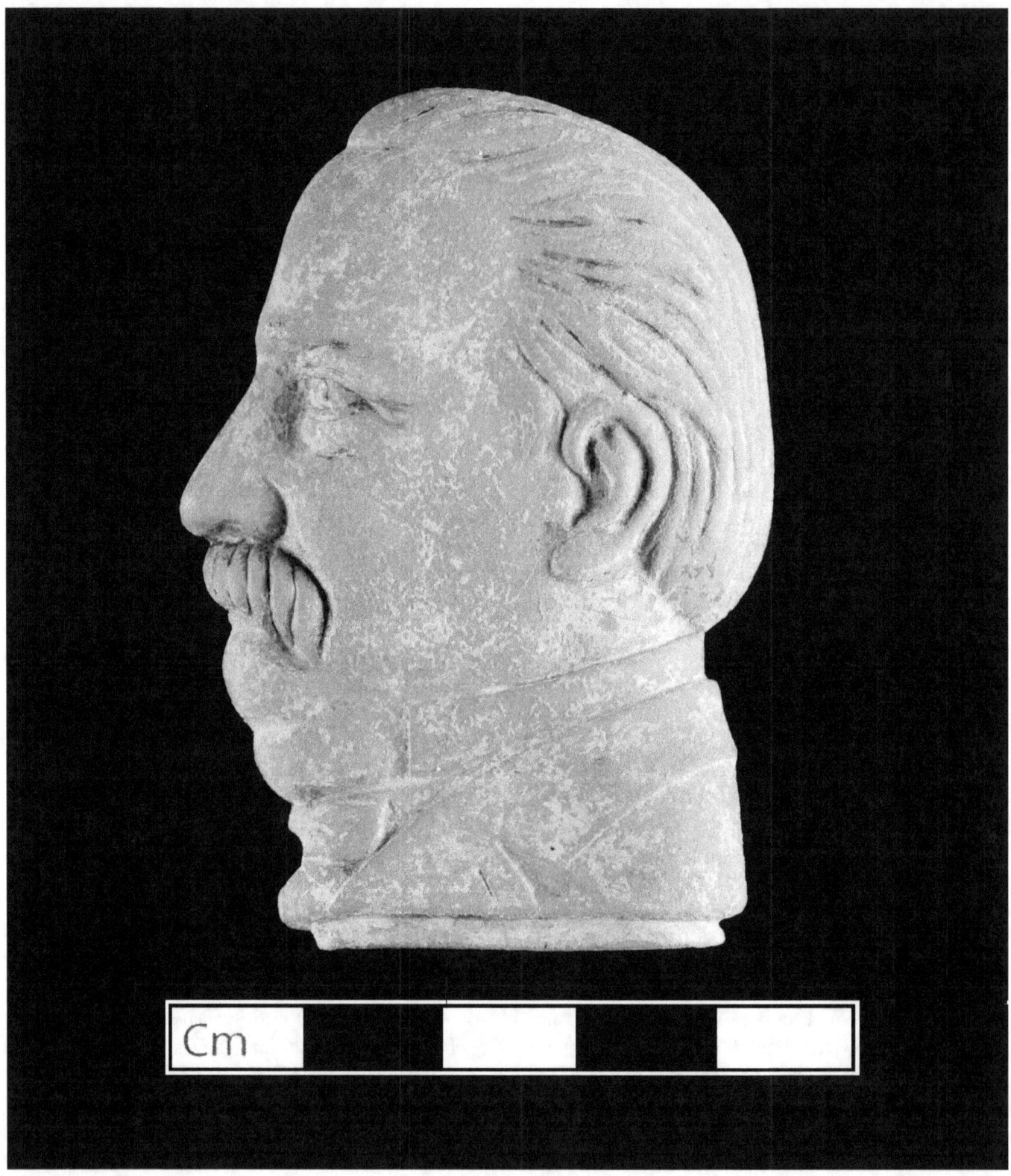

Figure 4. This tin silhouette of Grover Cleveland was recovered from a late 19th century African American deposit in Montgomery County, Maryland. Cleveland was a Democrat who carried Maryland and the South in 1884, 1888, and 1892, but he never supported positions that favored African Americans. (Photograph by Kathy Furgerson; courtesy of Maryland State Highway Administration, 2010).

was over 20 years old. Their long-term curation in the household suggests that they evoked the ideal potential of democracy more than any particular adherence to the platforms of a specific politician or party.

Certainly many consumers invested political and social ambitions in things, but like most everyday materiality the politics was tactical, relatively spontaneous, and ever-emergent, so it breaks significantly from the strategic politics of goal-oriented ambitions that unfold over time. Bric-a-brac underscores the social and political meaningfulness of banal and apparently trivial material culture, at once stressing the inchoate politics of desire projected onto everyday materiality while it compels archaeologists to rethink inherited notions of material significance and symbolism. Bric-a-brac consumption is not an especially powerful challenge to the ideological foundations of consumer capitalism, but if we take the notion of everyday desire seriously, it is significantly more meaningful and does hold the seeds of radical critique, if not intervention. The imaginative and spontaneous desire projected onto seemingly innocuous things illuminates consumer culture's power to subordinate consumers even as it risks embracing everyday desires that challenge the roles, ideologies, and structural alienation at the heart of that very society. Vaneigem (1979:91-92) hinted at the revolutionary potential of consumer desire, indicating that "the consumption of goods—which comes down always, in the present state of things, to the consumption of power—carries within itself the seeds of its own destruction and the conditions of its own transcendence." Yet he was skeptical of consumer revolution and wary "that, as they gradually free themselves from the imperatives of production, people should be trapped by the newer obligations of the consumer. By opening up the wasteland of `leisure' to a creativity liberated at long last thanks to reduced working hours, our kindly apostles of humanism are really only raising an army suitable for training on the parade ground of a consumption-based economy" (Vaneigem 1979:111). In this vein an archaeology of consumer desire would circumspectly view the freedoms promised by consumption yet take seriously the highly contextual if not individual symbolism of things, stressing spontaneity, pleasure, and lived immediacy. Rather than frame consumer symbolism only in terms of its relationship to dominant material meanings or societal identities, an archaeology of consumer desire would examine how people essentially lose themselves in things, always seeking a subjectivity based in their own experience and desires. Archaeology is of necessity a methodologically systematic analysis a step removed from such everyday experience and prone to distortions by dominant rationalized frameworks for knowledge, but Vaneigem (1979:113) counsels scholars to "try to incorporate an element of constant self-criticism, so as to make the work of co-optation a little harder than usual."

Historical archaeology has enormous power to dissect the details of everyday material life, those patterns that have become invisible yet are packed with social and cultural symbolism. Nevertheless, a fixation on the most prevalent patterns and processes, an arbitrary elimination of some materiality, and reluctance to embrace the inchoate but consequential politics of the everyday risk undercutting the rich picture of everyday life that archaeology can paint. Like all material goods, figurines were mechanisms of desire and not simply reflections of function and narrowly defined social position, so their consumption potentially holds insights into essential dimensions of everyday desire that ideology shapes profoundly yet can never utterly control or contain. A distinctive disciplinary niche has been carved out by archaeologists crafting highly focused pictures of commonplace material patterns, but like life itself those pictures risk being dull and irrelevant without clearly argued linkages to structural and global influences that simultaneously dissect the idiosyncrasies within every material assemblage. *The Importance of Material Things* most firmly underscored the richness archaeology can produce when its attention encompasses a vast range of material culture that is critically, rigorously, and creatively interpreted, and it is that expansive albeit long-ignored notion of materiality that may still harbor historical archaeology's most interesting insights.

Acknowledgements

Thanks to Julie Schablitsky and Mark Leone for inviting me to contribute to the volume and providing comments on several drafts. Chris Matthews and Joe Joseph provided thoughtful guidance on a late draft. Thanks to the many colleagues who have shared their bric-a-brac data and discussed these ideas, including Richard Affleck, Varna Boyd, Geoff Carver, Gerda Coetzee, Pete Connelly, Jake Crockett, Sarah Croucher, Emma Dwyer, Jack Eastman, Kathy Furgerson, Erica Gibson, Ryan Gray, Amanda Haught, Lori Lee, Ralph Mills, Jeff Oliver, Jim Symonds, John Triggs, Mark Warner, Jane Webster, and Timo Ylimaunu. Preliminary versions of this paper were presented at and benefited significantly from comments at the 2010 Contemporary and Historical Archaeology in Theory (CHAT) conference; the University of Aberdeen Northern Archaeology Research Seminar Series; the University of York Department of Archaeology Seminar; and the Newcastle University School of Historical Studies Seminar. Funding for those presentations was provided by an Overseas Conference Fund Grant from the Indiana University Office of the Vice President of International Affairs. Any shortcomings of the paper are entirely my own fault despite so much good advice.

References

AFFLECK, RICHARD M., MERA KAKTINS, META JANOWITZ, PATRICIA MILLER, AND INGRID WUEBBER

2010   *At the Road's Edge: Final Archaeological Investigations of the Wilson Farm Tenancy Site (7NC-F-94), Middletown, New Castle County, Delaware.* URS Corporation, Burlington, NJ.

THE ALBION

1867   Bric-a-Brac Hunting. *The Albion* 45(19):218.

BARBER, EDWIN ATLEE

1893   *The Pottery and Porcelain of the United States.* G.P. Putnam's Sons, New York, NY.

BAUDRILLARD, JEAN

1988   *Jean Baudrillard: Selected Writings.* Stanford University Press, Stanford, CA.

BLANCHOT, MAURICE

1993   *The Infinite Conversation.* Originally published 1969. Translated by Susan Hanson. University of Minnesota Press, Minneapolis.

CAMPBELL, COLIN

1987   *The Romantic Ethic and the Spirit of Modern Consumerism.* Basil Blackwell, Cambridge, MA.

CASELLA, ELEANOR CONLIN AND SARAH K. CROUCHER

2010   *The Alderley Sandhills Project: An Archaeology of Community Life in (Post-) Industrial England.* Manchester University Press, Manchester, UK.

CLELAND, CHARLES E.

2001   Historical Archaeology Adrift? *Historical Archaeology* 35(2):1-8.

COETZEE, GERDA C.J.

2011   Settlement patterns and material culture: A Historical Archaeological study of the farm Vaale Krans in the Venterstad district. Unpublished Master's Thesis, University of South Africa.

DE CERTEAU, MICHEL

1984   *The Practice of Everyday Life*. University of California Press, Berkeley.

DEETZ, JAMES

1977   Material Culture and Archaeology—What's the Difference? In *Historical Archaeology and the Importance of Material Things*, Leland Ferguson, editor, pp.9-12. The Society for Historical Archaeology, Special Publication Series No.2.

DIETLER, MICHAEL

2005   The Archaeology of Colonization and the Colonization of Archaeology: Theoretical Challenges from an Ancient Mediterranean Colonial Encounter. In *The Archaeology of Colonial Encounters: Comparative Perspectives,* Gil J. Stein, editor, pp.33-68. School of American Research Press, Santa Fe, NM.

EDWARDS, HARRY STILLWELL

1906   The Negro and the South. *The Century* 72(1):212-215.

FERGUSON, LELAND

1977   Historical Archaeology and the Importance of Material Things. In *Historical Archaeology and the Importance of Material Things*, Leland Ferguson, editor, pp.5-8. The Society for Historical Archaeology, Special Publication Series No.2.

FURGERSON, KATHLEEN, VARNA BOYD, CAREY O'REILLY, JUSTIN BEDARD, TRACY FORMICA, AND ANTHONY RANDOLPH, JR.

2011   Phase II and III Archaeological Investigations of the Fairland Branch Site and the Jackson Homestead Site (18MO609), Montgomery County, Maryland. Report to Maryland State Highway Administration, Baltimore, from URS Corporation, Gaithersburg, MD.

GAINES, W.J.

1897   *The Negro and the White Man*. A.M.E. Publishing House, Philadelphia, PA.

GARDINER, MICHAEL E.

2000   *Critiques of Everyday Life*. Routledge, New York, NY.

GAZIN-SCHWARTZ, AMY

2001   Archaeology and Folklore of Material Culture, Ritual, and Everyday Life. *International Journal of Historical Archaeology* 5(4):263-280.

GLASSIE, HENRY

1977   Archaeology and Folklore: Common Anxieties, Common Hopes. In *Historical Archaeology and the Importance of Material Things*, Leland Ferguson, editor, pp.23-35. The Society for Historical Archaeology, Special Publication Series No.2.

HALL, H. BYNG

1875   *The Bric-a-Brac Hunter*. Chatto and Windus, London, England.

HIGHMORE, BEN

2006   *Michel de Certeau: Analysing Culture*. Continuum Books, London, England.

HOLCOMBE, WILLIAM H.

1890   *A Mystery of New Orleans: Solved by New Methods*. JB Lipincott, Philadelphia, PA.

KAPLAN, ALICE AND KRISTIN ROSS

1987   Introduction. *Yale French Studies* 73:1-4.

KIRBY, THOMAS E.

1887   *Catalogue of the Bric-a-Brac, Rare Oriental Rugs, Oil Paintings, Furniture, Fine Curtains, Large Collection of Fine Old Engravings and Etchings and the Valuable Library Belonging to the Estate of the Late Rev. Henry Ward Beecher*. American Art Association, New York, NY.

LEFEBVRE, HENRI

1987   The Everyday and Everydayness. *Yale French Studies* 73:7-11.

1991   *The Critique of Everyday Life*. 2nd ed. Verso, London, England.

MICHAEL, MIKE

2006   *Technoscience and Everyday Life: The Complex Simplicities of the Mundane*. Open University Press, New York, NY.

44

MILLS, RALPH

2010   Miniatures in Historical Archaeology: Toys, Trifles, and
           Trinkets Re-Examined. Master's Dissertation, School of
           Archaeology and Ancient History, University of Leicester,
           Leicester, UK.

OWENS, ALASTAIR, NIGEL JEFFRIES, KAREN WEHNER, AND RUPERT FEATHERBY

2010   Fragments of the Modern City: Material Culture and the
           Rhythms of Everyday Life in Victorian London. *Journal
           of Victorian Culture* 15(2):215-225.

PLANT, SADIE

1992   *The Most Radical Gesture: The Situationist International
           in the Postmodern Age*. Routledge, New York, NY.

POSTER, MARK

2002   Everyday (Virtual) Life. *New Literary History* 33(4):743-
           760.

RICHARDS, WILLIAM C.

1853   *A Day in the New York Crystal Palace*. G.P. Putnam and
           Company, New York, NY.

SOUTH, STANLEY

1977   Foreword. In *Historical Archaeology and the Importance
           of Material Things*, Leland Ferguson, editor, pp.1-2. The
           Society for Historical Archaeology, Special Publication
           Series No.2.
1988   Whither Pattern? *Historical Archaeology* 22(1):25-28.

THE ROYAL COMMISSION

1851   *Great Exhibition of the Works of Industry of all Nations,
           1851, Official Descriptive and Illustrated Catalogue*.
           Volume 2. Spicer Brothers, London, England.

UPTON, DELL

2002   Architecture in Everyday Life. *New Literary History*
           33(4):707-723.

VANEIGEM, RAOUL

1979   *The Revolution of Everyday Life*. Originally published
           1967. Translated by John Fullerton and Paul Sieveking.
           Rising Free Collective, London, England.

WURST, LOUUANN AND RANDALL H. MCGUIRE

1999   Immaculate Consumption: A Critique of the "Shop till you
           Drop" School of Human Behavior. *International Journal
           of Historical Archaeology* 3(3):191-199.

Paul R. Mullins
Department of Anthropology
Indiana University-Purdue University, Indianapolis
Cavanaugh Hall 413B
Indianapolis, Indiana 46202

Julie M. Schablitsky

Meanings and Motivations Behind the Use of West African Spirit Practices

Men communicate by means of symbols and signs; for anthropology, which is a conversation of man with man, everything is symbol and sign, when it acts as intermediary between 2 subjects.

-Levi Strauss (1966:115)

ABSTRACT

Over 30 years ago, historical archaeologists began to recognize signs of Africa in their sites as they studied cosmograms in colonoware bowls and etched lines in the concave bowls of spoons. These findings, along with ritually placed caches composed of everyday objects in curious contexts, stimulated discussions on the survival of African religion. Recognizing an archaeological record that speaks to enduring African traditions has changed the way archaeologists think about African American sites in significant ways. These spiritually inspired objects and practices have provided ways of understanding power relations, spiritual life, and social interactions. In addition to these studies lies the opportunity to recognize emotionally motivated behavior stimulated by interactions between individuals. Using the burned remains of a 19th century home, I examine the reasons behind the use of concealed material culture by an African American family. Furthermore, I discuss how interpretations of caches and objects of conjure can expose emotion at the household level and how these human responses can advance our understanding of not just the past but, the people who lived it.

Introduction

In a wooded lot nestled between U.S. Highway 29 and several automobile dealerships lay the burned remains of an African American home. Historical research and archaeological excavations revealed that either Ann Downs or her father, Zachariah, directed the construction of a slave[1] quarter on this property sometime between the 1820s and 1840s (Furgerson et al. 2011:47). Through an examination of population and slave censuses, we learned that Malinda Jackson, her children,[2] and perhaps at one time her mother Rachel Adams, lived in this small cabin. In 1830, Zachariah died and willed Rachel and her children to his daughter Ann with the direction that his male and female slaves be granted freedom at 37 years of age and that their children be released from bondage at 35 years of age (MCRW 1826).

Once they were emancipated, the formerly enslaved, including Malinda and her family, needed to consider whether they would continue to work for their former owner under a different arrangement or if they would leave to seek economic and educational freedom elsewhere (Hucles 1993:34). Not surprisingly, Malinda remained on the Downs' estate and married Thomas Jackson, a local farm laborer and probable father to her three youngest sons and daughters. In Maryland, it was quite common for former slaves to stay in their quarters and be paid a wage of about $5 a day (Fuke 1999:10,199). In all probability, Malinda did just this. By 1869, she saved enough money to purchase 8.75 acres of land along with the old slave cabin from Ann Downs. For an African American woman, owning property in the reconstruction South was a significant accomplishment. By 1870, just 116 blacks (out of 7,434 blacks enumerated in the U.S. Census) owned land in Montgomery County (Fuke 1999:49). Fuke (1999:62) further underscores the implication of land ownership for African Americans during this time, stating:

> ...even the smallest plots of land served a vital individual and community function by providing rural blacks, not with prosperity or wealth, but with a modicum of autonomy amidst a generally discouraging environment. Land, even in one- or –two-acre plots, provided an alternative to the close supervision of whites and permitted black families to dispose of some of their resources as they chose.

Despite attempts to live as free citizens in post-emancipation Maryland, African Americans continued to be violently reminded of their place in society thereby exposing the true meaning of *their* freedom— whites consistently disrupted gatherings, burned black churches and schools, and delivered beatings for the most minor of infractions or for no apparent reason at all. For example, the sight of Union African American veterans marching home after the war was enough to cause violence to spring from the hands of former Confederate soldiers on the eastern shore of Maryland. These acts of intimidation resulted in Union soldier's venturing out only in daylight, lest they be beaten and their weapons stolen (Fuke 1999:206-207). The reaction of certain whites to black soldiers wearing symbols of the United States government is a powerful statement and sends a message that African Americans were not even worthy to fight or die for their country. The anger incited in some Marylanders by blacks in military dress is especially poignant here since archaeologists recovered three ca. 1860 Maryland military coat buttons and a hard rubber U.S. Navy button from the Jackson's home.

During the reconstruction years, Jim Crow moved into Maryland and disseminated a list of segregation statues that affected every aspect of public life including transportation, education, and entertainment (Johnson 1943; Franklin 1956:7; Fuke 1999:195). Although being "separate and unequal" was part of black society's mantra ever since their arrival on this continent, these statutes simply made the familiar yoke of oppression legal, and perhaps worse, prominent in their daily life. African Americans could not step out of their front doors without being reminded of their second-class status and that the men who governed their country deemed them an "inferior race." The only physical space that they could gather, learn, and live without the guillotine of racism raised over their head was their home. Although the shelter of family could deflect some aspects of intimidation, African Americans continued to live under the threat of potential home invasions and the destruction of their property. Consider then, the extreme precautions that a southern black family would take to ensure the safety and protection, and ultimately the survival, of their home.

Malinda Jackson passed away in the late 1870s, but her children inherited the home and property and constructed a 20 x 13 ft., two-story addition onto the west side of the 10 x 13 ft. log cabin during the late 19th century. The financial freedom to triple the size of their home is a prime example of what land ownership enabled free African Americans to accomplish within a few decades. Around 1915, a fire burned the Jackson family home to the ground; it was never rebuilt. The property left family ownership in 1944, when Perry Eli Johnson, the husband of Malinda's granddaughter, sold the acreage to Marshall and Ethel D. Lehman (U.S. Bureau of Census 1910; Furgerson et al. 2011:66-74). In 1983, the property was acquired by the state for the construction of the Intercounty Connector (ICC) project, a beltway linking Prince George's and Montgomery counties around Washington DC.

The Archaeology of West African Spirit Practices

The charred remains of the Jackson Homestead were found by archaeologists surveying for the proposed ICC project in 2004. After coordination with project engineers, the Maryland Historical Trust, and consulting parties, the Maryland State Highway Administration determined the project could not be designed to avoid the site. As part of the mitigation for the destruction of the eligible property, the state commissioned the archaeological excavation of the entire house remains and portions of the surrounding site in the fall of 2007. The deadline for construction was nigh and therefore, the State Highway

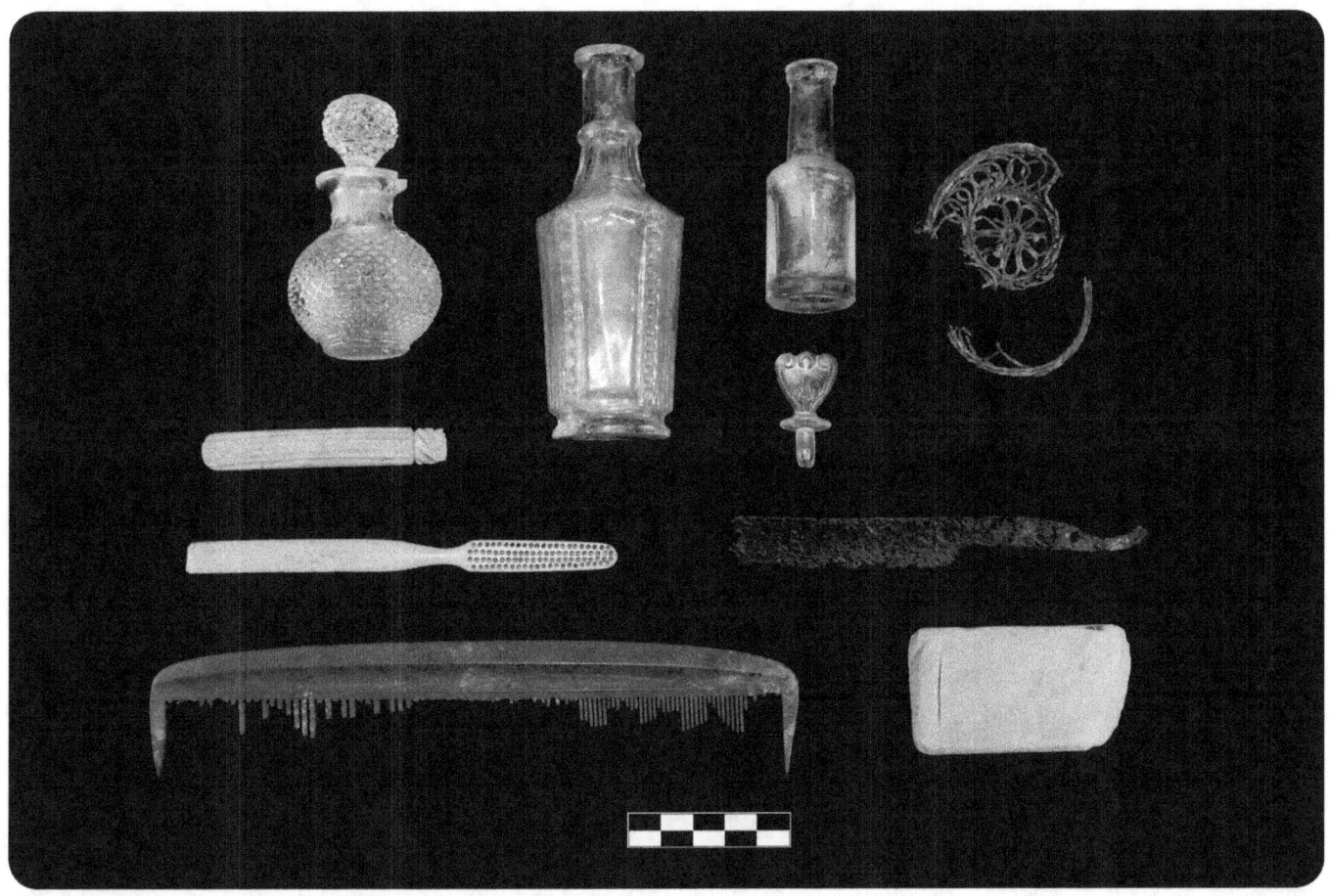

Figure 1. Toiletry items recovered from the Jackson Homestead site. (Photograph by Lisa Guerre, 2010; courtesy of Maryland State Highway Administration).

Administration rented large tents, lights, and heaters to keep the dedicated archaeologists working through the winter.

The site yielded an artifact assemblage consistent with a working class household. Artifacts recovered included personal belongings (clothing fasteners, jewelry, bric-a-brac [Mullins this volume], and harmonicas), inexpensive whiteware plates, and food remains (animal bone, jelly jars, and beverage bottles) (Furgerson et al. 2011) (Figure 1). In addition to these everyday objects discarded over time and lost in the fire, we also recovered ritually placed objects, or caches, including a collection of quartz crystals and pierced silver coins. Depending on the context of the discovery, quartz crystals may be recognized as an artifact type that alerts archaeologists to the potential for ritually concealed objects and caches (Schablitsky 2009).

While the crew excavated through the winter, I turned my attention to numerous books and articles published on African religion, ethnographic accounts of hoodoo, and African American sites with ritual components (Puckett 1925; Wing 1941; Thompson 1983; Klingelhofer 1987; Thomspon 1993; Wilke 1995; Chireau 1997; Wilke 1997; Jones 1999; Leone and Fry 1999; Brown 2001; Leone and Fry 2001; Raboteau 2004; Leone 2005; Fennell 2007). This topic has intrigued anthropologists since the 19th century, yet we continue to wrestle with the origins, meanings, and composition of these spirit practices. I quickly learned that we don't even know how to properly refer to these African-based rituals. The most popular terms captured in ethnographic and contemporary accounts include provocative words such as: "hoodoo," "conjure," "root work," and "folk magic" (Puckett 1926; McQuillar 2003; Bird 2007). Although archaeologists are known to use these same names, they also incorporate words such as "African American Magic," "West African spirit practices," and "spiritual beliefs" (Wilkie 1997; Leone

2005; Fennell 2007). In order to ensure consistency with other writings on the Chesapeake region (Jones 1999; Leone and Fry 1999; Leone 2005), and to acknowledge that many (although not all) captives were taken from West Africa (Fennell 2011:5), I primarily use the term West African spirit practices.[3]

Archaeologists working in the Midatlantic and in the South had already navigated their way through the thick cultural history of African religion and recognized a relationship with their own sites (Wilke 1997; Thomas 1998; Leone 2005; Fennell 2007). Although they had not yet settled on a contemporary name for the incorporation of African culture into American material, these scholars knew this was not just a "slave religion" (c.f. Raboteau 2004); both enslaved and free African Americans concealed objects and/or caches within and outside of their home for ritual purposes. In fact, the items and context of material culture found on archaeological sites are familiar to contemporary African Americans. Similar rituals are still performed today, but many are warned to avoid the practice citing it as witchcraft and contradictory to Christian beliefs (L'Keisha Markley pers. comm. 2010). While discussing our archaeological findings with Reverend Spencer Jackson, Malinda Jackson's great-great grandson, I asked if his family ever used or discussed such spirit practices. Reverend Jackson stated that he only heard "root work" mentioned a few times, and only in negative contexts and was told to stay away from it. Many formerly enslaved African Americans also viewed these practices as negative, and some even denied the effectiveness of hoodoo (Bruce 1897:52). These perspectives appear to conflict with earlier, general views of African inspired spirit practices among the southern black community, and may be interpreted as a temporal and perhaps even a generational shift in attitude about such folk traditions. Although the knowledge of these spiritual beliefs survived, the general contemporary attitude towards this practice appears to be one of fear and avoidance, particularly in the case of the Jackson family.

Based on archaeological findings and current regional African American memory of these spirit practices, there is no doubt that a "religion" of African gods, iconography, and beliefs survived the passage to America. Although in bondage, the enslaved still carried their songs, rituals, and respect for their ancestors in their hearts and minds. Once they arrived here, those feelings and that identity transferred itself onto objects and into behavior that can be read today in artifact assemblages throughout the south and eastern United States. One of the oldest West African symbols is the Kongo cosmogram, or the *dikenga dia Kongo,* and it can appear in ritually touched African American sites. The dikenga sign is a simple cosmogram symbol with complex meaning drawn with a circle encompassing a cross with smaller circles on the ends of the cross. The vertical axis connects God and the dead while the horizontal axis delineates the water boundary between the living and the dead; the circles on the ends of the cross represent the four stages of the soul (Thompson 1993:49). This symbol is significant since we can encounter it in ritual contexts on African American sites.

Archaeologists in Annapolis, for example, found a starburst-patterned pearlware bowl placed over a cache containing other artifacts, including several buttons. Buttons transform nicely into small, yet three-dimensional, cosmograms given their round form and four holes that can be joined to form a cross (Vlach 1978, 1987; Leone 2005:203). Cosmograms may also assume the shape of a room or an entire home with caches demarcating the four points and center (Brown 2001:102; Leone 2005:217). The creation of caches is BaKongo in origin and they are usually assembled with the assistance of ritual specialists and placed at significant locations to invoke the help of spirits for many reasons including protection and health (Fennell 2007:56-57). The items in caches recovered archaeologically often include: crystals, straight pins, buttons, beads, glass, ceramic, bone, and cut nails (Brown 2001; Leone 2005; Schablitsky 2009). The object's metaphoric meaning rather than the function of the button, nail, or pane glass, for example, is what empowers the cache.

Within the same cities and even at the same site, we can sometimes detect a multi-cultural absorption of African beliefs. In other words, when material culture and its context are dissected, it is possible to see individual representations, for example, from the BaKongo but also expressions of Yoruba culture. I am not the first to observe this. Leone (2005:214) states, "...when African spirit traditions appear archaeologically in the early eighteenth century, they are African, but are probably also American, and they may be the beginning of an amalgam of several African traditions, such as the BaKongo, Fan, Ifa, and Yoruba traditions."

In addition to archaeologists' efforts to produce cohesive interpretations and connections back to Africa from this spiritually charged material culture, we continue to consider how visible these practices were in public and private settings as well as how the rituals evolved over time. In some cases, particularly those associated with the early arrival of enslaved people of African descent, homogenous manifestations of African spirit practices (whether those be Kongo or Yoruba or others) may have been captured and preserved in the archaeological record as early as ca. 1700 (Leone 2005:222; Wilford 2008). Some of the earliest artifacts include colonoware bowls etched with cosmograms and possibly African-inspired clay pipes (Deetz 1993; Wilke 1997:99; Ferguson 1999; Mouer et al. 1999:112-113; Monroe and Mallios 2004). We know that early European folk magic was entrenched in colonial society, but were African-based rituals also publicly tolerated? Did the slave-holding community overlook open displays of African rituals, dismissing them as manifestations of typical "savage" behavior? Fennell (2007:68) suggests the public acceptance of African religion was unlikely, stating:

> ...only private and covert forms of ritual were undertaken, each employing instrumental and abbreviated forms of the dikenga to obtain protection and well-being for the individuals involved. The institution of slavery and the dominant religion of Christianity had pushed the BaKongo beliefs off the stage of publicly displayed group rituals.

In other words, unlike in Africa, those who were enslaved could not openly display deity shrines or publicly practice their beliefs for fear of intolerance and punishment by those in power. True, it is unlikely a ritually charged public display by a marginalized group would have been tolerated, especially during and after the Enlightenment. But perhaps this was not the case in the very beginning of African enslavement.

Annapolis archaeologists discovered a mass of clay holding lead shot, brass pins, ferrous nails and a stone axe in a ca. 1700 gutter feature (Wilford 2008). The discovery is African in origin and if this was indeed displayed above ground in a public area it may suggest young Annapolis tolerated open displays of African magic. Of course, it is also possible someone placed the bundle in an inconspicuous arrangement under the cover of night, thereby supporting the argument that those practicing such spiritual practices did so in secret. Another interesting point to consider on this matter is that many whites were quite aware of enslaved populations practicing African religion; these captured moments of intolerance in the written record insinuates such behavior was not entirely hidden from view. In 1779, a publication on the progress of the colonies in South Carolina reported slaves to be strangers to Christianity and "...under the influence of Pagan darkness, idoltry and superstition, as they were at their first arrival from Africa" (Hewatt 1779:100; Berlin 1996:285). Others suggest that initially, European Americans felt indifferent about the spiritual paths of their slaves, discouraging their adoption of Christianity for fear that it could result in "instances of solidarity and defiance" or worse, "weaken the argument for slavery" (Fennell 2011:36). Indeed, a fuller and deeper understanding of how the colonies reacted to African spirit practices is pivotal in learning how and why the contexts and manifestations of these rituals evolved over time. Until such research is complete, we can at least comment on later archaeological discoveries and ethnographies. We know that expressions of African culture would not have been acceptable in public or in the white homes where enslaved African Americans lived and worked. Archaeology also tells us that African spirit practices survived by becoming a set of secret and hidden rituals.

Separate or Syncretic Ritual Behavior?

In order for their identity to survive, those of African descent adapted European-made material culture and American grown roots and animals into their caches, bundles, and protective pieces. Ritually created caches and spiritually placed artifacts incorporated everyday items. Archaeology has already demonstrated the reciprocal exchange of ideas between cultures regarding the decoration of pottery and possibly tobacco pipes. Therefore, it is not outside the realm of possibility that Native Americans shared the medicinal properties of roots and plants with enslaved Africans who in turn, incorporated them into their own religious and healing practices (Tantaquidgeon 2001).

West African spirit practices also share some similarities with European magic thereby confounding the problem of determining a specific object's significance or a ritual's origin. Hoodoo conjurers, for example, often filled bundles and bottles with a variety of objects and then secreted the container (bottle or cloth ball) under steps, a floor, or in a path where the intended person would walk. "A black bottle containing a liquid mixture, and nine pins and nine needles, is a favorite charm. Sometimes the charm is a bundle containing salt, pepper, and silver five-cent pieces; sometimes needles pins, hairs, snake heads" (Herron and Bacon 1896:145). The use of bottles to contain and bury "liquid" and pins is very similar to the use of European witch bottles during the 17th and 18th centuries. This ritual consisted of concealing a bottle filled with urine, pins, and bent nails in a wall, under the floor, in the yard, or beneath a fire hearth in an attempt to throw back the evil believed to have been cast by a witch (Merrifield 1988: 167-168; King 1996:28-29).

Another possible incorporation of European practices into conjure may be the wearing of silver coins for luck and/or protection. One of the greatest fears of those who believe in magic is to be "conjured" or to have someone direct evil or ill will towards you. Often, those who believed in West African spirit practices wore protection such as a small bag filled with roots, bone, and other items around their neck or a coin around their ankle or in their shoe. The Jacksons may have used silver coins to protect themselves from evil. Archaeologists recovered three pierced silver coins that were either lost and/or recycled for ritual concealment (Figure 2).[4] The coins include an 1859 three-cent piece, an 1884 half dime, and another mid-19th century half dime with an illegible date. The coins are so heavily worn that devotional wear (continual rubbing or holding) is suspected (Randolf 2009).

In 1935, Hyatt (1970:1619) interviewed a conjure doctor's wife who revealed the reason behind wearing silver dimes:

Figure 2. Three silver coins discovered within the late 19th century addition. (Photograph by Lisa Guerre, 2010; courtesy of Maryland State Highway Administration).

Take a little small nail an' stick a hole in de dime. Dey put it round on a piece of cord, but most of dem use a string. But de proper way is to fix have a piece of copper wire-jes a little thin copper wire. An' yo' wraps it around near de ankle of yore laig, on yore left left leg, an' if anybody do's yo' harm-or if anybody put anything down fo' yo' dat deime will turn dark and dat will give you a signal.

What is significant in this description is the location of the charm and the mention of copper wire. Although the practice of wearing a silver coin is not known in Africa, Senegambians wore copper coins around their neck while those in the Kongo culture strung round seeds or light wood around the neck and ankle, "close to the foot, and to the unfolding of one's path" (Thompson 1993:59). At this time, there is no direct evidence that wearing silver coins traces back to Africa (Wilkinson 1851:55; Merrifield 1988:25-26; Davidson 2004: 26-27). Instead, we should consider the possibility that African Americans incorporated the use of silver coins from Europeans, but kept the placement of the charm around the ankle, and in some cases the use of copper, from Africa. Here, we see flexibility in the object used, but the location or context retains its African origin. Whether the roots of this protective piece were African, European, or both, African Americans readily welcomed the silver coin into their spiritual toolkit. The "flash" of the silver and the cross and circle relief of a 16th century three-pence, for example, likely made silver coins an attractive charm (Davidson 2004:28, 34).

Although similarities to these African inspired spirit practices can be found cross culturally and within many religions, I believe the core is African with flexibility to absorb rituals and symbols that appear congruous with their own beliefs. In fact, many African Americans were Christians and did not see "rootwork" to be in conflict with these beliefs. Despite the incorporation of prayers and scriptures into African spirit practices by the late 19th century, some scholars suggest that the absence of Christian objects in caches is evidence that these practices are African in origin (Leone and Fry 1999:384). One alternative explanation for the absence of such paraphernalia is that Protestants own very few if any religious items since their beliefs do not

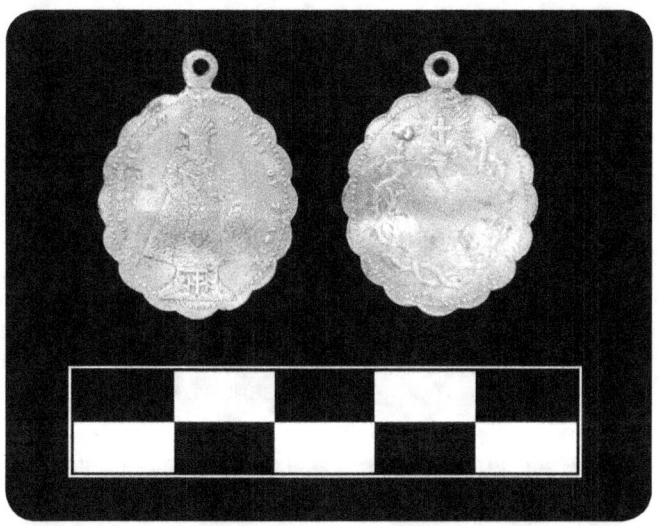

Figure 3. Infant of Prague medallion discovered adjacent to the front of the home. (Photograph by Lisa Guerre, 2010; courtesy of Maryland State Highway Administration).

encourage the creation or possession of graven items as warned in Exodus (The Holy Bible 20:3-5), "Thou shalt not make unto thee any graven image, or any likeness of any thing that is in heaven above or that is in the earth beneath, or that is in the water under the earth." Unlike the Protestants, Catholics do incorporate rosaries, medallions of saints, and small statues of the Virgin Mary into their worship. In fact, archaeologists commonly find broken rosaries and the occasional saint medallion on domestic sites. What remains curious to us is the use of Catholic paraphernalia by those who engage in African spirit practices.

One of the archaeologists at the Jackson Homestead site showed me a Roman Catholic Infant of Prague medallion they found near what would have been the front of the house, in a location that would once have been beneath a covered porch (Figure 3). To the Roman Catholic, this image is linked with blessings, miracles, and healings (Furgerson et al. 2011:371). The Jackson family had been Protestant and the presence of this infant Jesus was a surprise. One interpretation is that someone in the family, or perhaps a visitor, was Catholic and simply lost their sacred medallion. Further research revealed that similar African American sites produced a St. Christopher's medal and rosaries from contexts without a strong Catholic link (Orser 1994:38; Deagan and MacMahon 1995:23-35; Wilkie 1997:95-96). Ethnographies suggest, and now archaeology confirms, that by the 19th century many Christian practices and objects had been incorporated into the material culture of West African spirit practices. Indeed, Catholic paraphernalia may have even played a role in African religion as early as the late 1700s since the BaKongo had been exposed to, and in some cases embraced, Catholicism (Thornton 1998:259; Fennell 2007:62-63). At a minimum, the recovery of sacramentals in such contexts suggests a belief by individuals who respected the power of all things spiritual. Furthermore, the presence of these items demonstrates the flexibility of African spirit practices to incorporate another religion's iconography into its own (Puckett 1926:563-565). Although we will never know who lost the medallion, it is probable someone in the Jackson family considered the piece sacred and used the Infant of Prague medallion for luck, protection, or conjure.

Archaeology of the Jackson Homestead

While the field crew was finishing the excavation on the Jackson Homestead, I was back in my office in Baltimore surrounded by books, scratching my own cosmogram symbols next to important sections in journal articles trying to absorb the complexities of African spirit practices. I read about the ways Mark Leone (2005:221) and Jane Cox worked together to come up with a predictive model for finding ritually placed caches in buildings. The results of their research suggested archaeologists should investigate three locations: (1)

Figure 4. View towards the east of Jackson home with foundation and chimney base. (Photograph by Kathy Furgerson, 2008; courtesy of Maryland State Highway Administration).

Figure 5. View towards south of chimney base that contained four caches. (Photograph by Kathy Furgerson, 2008; courtesy of Maryland State Highway Administration).

northeast corners, (2) hearths, or chimney bases, and (3) thresholds or bottoms of staircases or steps. Although caches could include a variety of objects, the most common items included pins, buttons, coins, glass bits, rings, bone pieces, and stones. Roots are also a key element in African spirit practices; however, they rarely survive in an archaeological context. In most cases, people placed caches in their homes in order to control the movement of spirits and protect the people who lived inside (Leone and Fry 1999:377-378). Those who believed in these rituals saw any opening, including windows, doors, and chimney flues, as a potential entrance for spirits. Placement of objects such as crystals could prevent unwanted energy from entering the home.

As soon as I learned that one could predict where caches may be hidden, I knew we were not done excavating the Jackson Homestead. I drove back out to the site and spoke with the field director to find out when they expected to dismantle the foundation and chimney base. Since the entire interior of the home and adjacent exterior had been excavated, the plan was to leave the foundation and hearth in place (Figure 4).

Typically, we want to leave something behind for the future and not completely destroy a site through total excavation; but, the construction contract had been signed and if we did not disassemble the foundation and chimney base, the heavy equipment operators would happily obliterate it for us in preparation for the new highway. In this case, we had nothing to lose and everything to gain-I wanted to know if someone had placed a cache and/or concealed objects within the home during construction. So, in the name of science, we restrung the units over the foundation and chimney base and began to dig.

Home Protection with Caches

Leone and Cox inspired us to disassemble the chimney, stone by stone, to determine if members of the Jackson family had concealed caches within their home. First, we dismantled the four-course stone chimney base and

TABLE 1. Description of artifacts, flora, and fauna discovered in each of the four caches.

COURSE 1
Artifacts: Brick, metal button, glass and quartzite burned conglomerate, whiteware, glass (aqua, colorless, green, and window), lead shot, mica, and cut nails. *Flora:* Poke berry seeds and grape seeds. *Fauna:* Eggshell, teeth (squirrel and rabbit), mouse (deer and house), medium-large mammal, unidentified bird, catfish, pheasant/partridge, and a cardinal wing.
COURSE 2
Artifacts: lead shot, cut nails, straight pins, glass (aqua, colorless, and window), round metal lid, brick fragments, ferrous pressed lattice jewelry, ferrous mesh, fence staple, copper alloy wire, copper alloy shoe grommet, copper alloy shoe grommets, shoe screw, cut tack, whiteware, gray stoneware, mica, black hexagonal glass beads, clay tobacco pipe stem, pencil lead, buttons (shell, bone, black glass/metal, Prosser porcelain), white glass collar stud with bulls eye pattern. *Flora:* Poke berry seeds. *Fauna:* Rabbit, squirrel, teeth (pig), chicken wing, flicker wing, frog/toad, hispid cotton rat, eastern harvest mouse, deer mouse, vole, rat, perch-like fish, snake, and venomous snake.
COURSE 3
Artifacts: Ferrous wire mesh, cut nails, percussion cap, colorless glass (heat altered), black hexagonal bead, copper alloy rivet, gray hexagonal bead (heat altered), white bead, brick fragment, and round and oval ferrous lids. *Flora:* Poke berry seeds and grape seeds. *Fauna:* Turkey wing, snake, house mouse, opossum, Bobwhite quail, squirrel, rabbit, fish, bird, eggshell, and teeth (pig, rabbit, squirrel, and opossum).
COURSE 4
Artifacts: Gray cylindrical bead (heat altered). *Flora:* Poke berry seeds. *Fauna:* Fish, bird, rabbit, squirrel, turtle, eggshell, and tooth (squirrel).

kept the artifacts horizontally controlled (Figure 5). The rock was solid and with some effort, easily removed from the decomposing mortared joints. I observed the mortar that cemented the stones together and it appeared to be a simple mixture of lime and sand. Our collection methods included picking out any obvious artifacts and removing the thin layer of soil between the courses of stone for flotation. I realized that any roots had likely decomposed, but seeds or other botanical remains may have survived in this sealed context. When we removed the first layer of stone, I saw several animal bones. The bone was well preserved and not calcined, nor was it part of the mortar. While excavating beneath the second course of stone, I troweled back a thin layer of soil to reveal a cache of glass, brick, and nails. Within a few minutes, I saw the other associated objects-- straight pins, lead shot, and Prosser porcelain buttons. Although it can be dangerous to draw conclusions in the field, I felt certain we had a West African spirit cache. After several days of additional fieldwork, we determined that a cache of artifacts and bones had

been sealed between each of the four courses of stone during construction of the original home (Figure 6) (Table 1). The concentration of artifacts in the center of each course of stone, sealed by mortar, along with the variety and type of artifacts, reflected a typical hoodoo calling card. Since this slave cabin was the first building on the site, we could not explain away the artifact assemblage in the chimney base as accidental inclusion during this first phase of construction. The solid integrity of these caches demonstrated, perhaps for the first time in this region, that ritual objects were not just sealed under a loose board or brick–ancestral spirit practices were also being incorporated into, and assembled during, building construction.

Several months later, I sat down in the laboratory to examine the four separate sets of artifacts collected from between the courses of the chimney base. My questions were not unique, but important. Was it possible to identify an alternative ritual meaning behind each artifact? Did the artifacts, when viewed together, contain the right combination of items to be

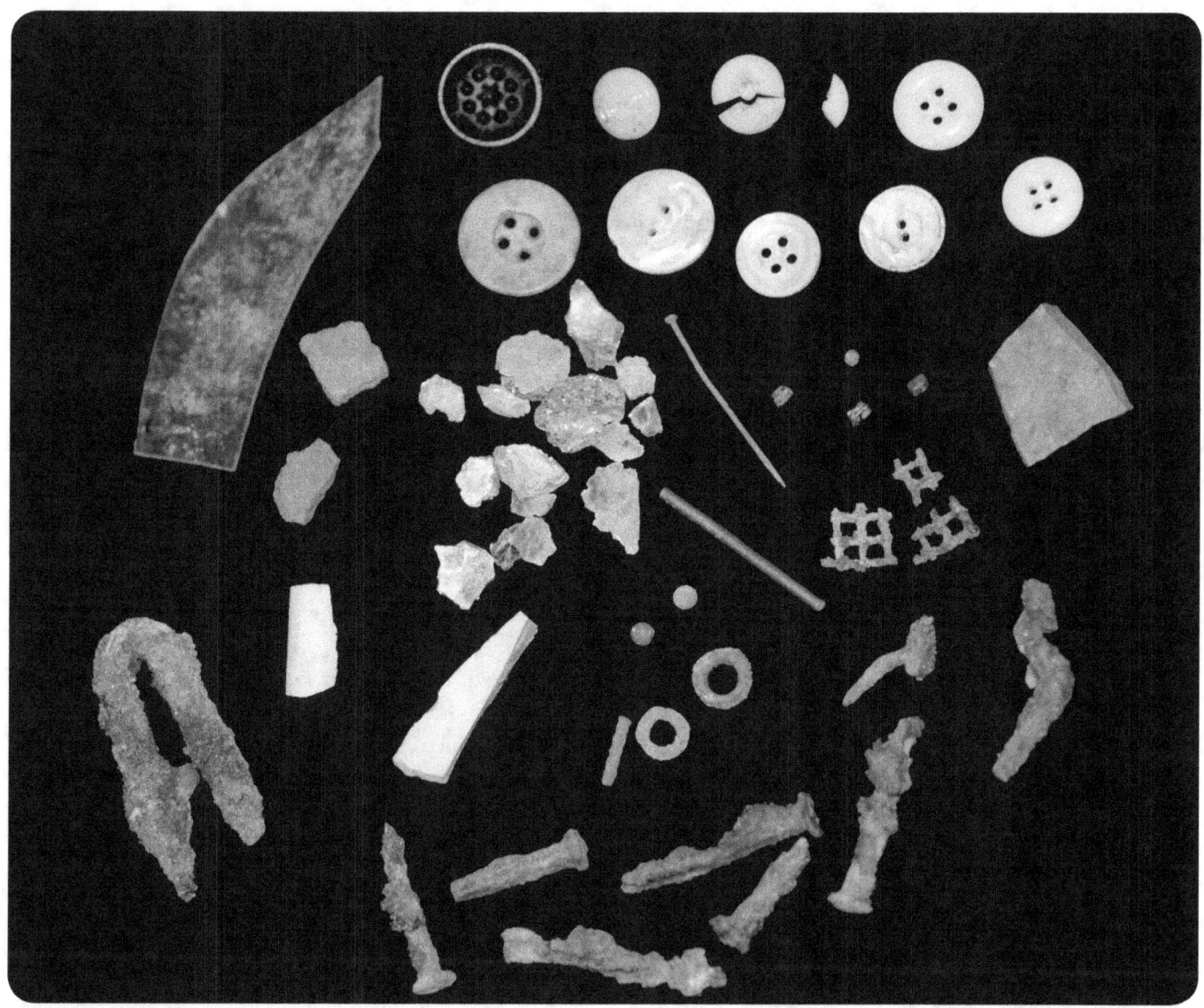

Figure 6. Cache discovered under the second course of stone in chimney base. Artifacts pictured include pane glass, buttons, brick, ferrous mesh, mica flakes, hexagonal beads, pencil lead, straight pin, lead shot, shoe grommets, shoe screw, stoneware, pipe stem fragment, whiteware fragment, fence stable, cut tack, and cut nails. (Photograph by author, 2009).

interpreted as a ritual cache? I considered both the finds of other archaeologists and interpretations of African scholars when observing the assemblages. The BaKongo name for bundles that contain and direct spirits that are concealed in the earth or worn on the person are minkisi (nkisi is singular) (Thompson 1983:117). I learned that color and material rather than the original use of the object was important in understanding the function of a nkisi. Although it was

not possible to ascertain the meaning behind all of the objects, many items could be interpreted and linked to African beliefs. The white ceramic sherds and pipe stems, for example, may have been added to these caches because of their white color and even their clay material that symbolizes the spiritual realm (Thompson 1993:57). The buttons made from shell, bone, and Prosser porcelain may have been attractive for the same reasons, but also for the potential use as a cosmogram. Unlike the Annapolis caches, the Jackson's chimney base only contained bits of mica and glass rather than crystals, however, these still would have functioned to capture the "flash" of the spirit and the body of water that exists between the living and the dead (Thompson 1983:117).

Cut nails, straight and bent, are encountered in many caches and three of the four courses of stone in the chimney base also held ferrous nails. Some interpret the presence of nails and/or pins as objects related to the function of the cache (Leone 2005:235). What should also be considered is a possible influence from the Yoruban god called Ogun, a deity of war and iron. It is believed that Ogun's spirit "…lives in the piercing or slashing action of iron" and is honored by iron or brass (Thompson 1983:53). The influence of Ogun has also been considered in the interpretation of cast iron pots, bayonets, and chain among other artifacts, in a mid-19th century slave cabin in Texas (Brown 2001:102).

Late 19th and early 20th century ethnographic interviews with African Americans revealed regular use of bones in their spiritual practices. Some practitioners incorporated bones into charms and bundles that they wore around their neck for protection while others collected wild fauna to be used in rituals for curing and harming (Herron and Bacon 1896:143; Deane 1937). Wings from birds, jaws from rodents, and parts of poisonous snakes were usually one ingredient in a charm bundle recipe that held other items such as pins and hair (Puckett 1926:232). The faunal assemblage from the Jackson's chimney base included a variety of rodents, squirrel, rabbit, opossum, and pig along with Bob White quail, chicken, turkey, pheasant, a Common flicker and fish. Reptiles were also sealed in the chimney and included a venomous snake and frog/toad along with 700 shell fragments from bird eggs (Table 1). Although only pieces of the larger mammals were found between the courses of stone, complete bodies of the smaller rodents appear to have been deposited. The bone fragments were not part of the mortar nor did small rodents drag them into the crevices of the stone; out of the over 1,200 bone fragments, only three exhibited rodent gnaw marks (Windham 2009). One rabbit tibia showed evidence of carnivore gnawing while seven rabbit and bird long bones were disarticulated from the body through twisting that resulted in a spiral fracture. The presence of animal chewed bone as well as butchering patterns suggest that bone used in ritual caches could be freshly caught or collected from carcasses.

At the center of African spirit practices is the use of roots. Because roots seldom survive in typical archaeological contexts we can only minimally address their use; however, nuts, seeds and wood can be found during the flotation of soil. Since we did not want to miss one seed, pin, or bead, all of the soil found in the caches was collected, floated, and analyzed by an archaeobotanist. Of course, small quantities of walnut shell, grass seeds, and grape seed appeared to be accidental inclusions. But, the discovery of over 8,000 poke berry seeds (*Phytolacca americana*) in a single cache feature was a different story, especially since such a high number of seeds equated to approximately 800 berries. Although it would be possible to dump a bucket full of berries between the courses of stone, it seemed just as probable that the Jacksons poured the red, seed filled pulp from processed berries onto the stone chimney base during construction.

Pokeweed is an edible plant that is prepared much like other southern greens after boiling and rinsing several times. The berries can be rendered down to produce a juice that can be used as a dye or to create jelly or color wine. Although the leaves and berries can be eaten after thorough preparation, the seeds are poisonous and only edible by birds. Pokeweed remains have also been found in extremely high numbers on other African American sites. At the King's Bay Plantation in Georgia over 75% of the 20,000 seeds recovered came from pokeweeds (Rock and Newsom 1987:441-442). African and Native Americans used pokeweed roots to make a tea to treat rheumatism (Puckett 1926: 364; Tantaquidgeon 2001:32). Rubbing with poke root tea was also believed to remove conjure (Bruce 1895:55; Puckett 1926:235). Since pokeweed can be used in various conjure related activities, it is possible that they served a similar purpose here.

In the end, I determined that at least one of the cabin occupants initiated the placement of four ritual caches between the stone layers that formed the base of a wood burning fire hearth. The objects included ferrous pieces, bits of glass, and other objects that may have been significant for their color, material, or as a personal belonging contributed to the cache for protection. The faunal remains represented a variety of small mammals, however, the discovery of teeth, bird wings, and snake vertebrae are interesting since they may be referenced back to more recent West African spirit practices. The use of poke berries in one of the caches may be significant because of their red color (for communication with the spirits) (Thompson 1993:59) and for the power to remove conjure. Since the concealment of these objects took place during the construction of the cabin sometime between the 1820s and 1840s, it is likely this ceremony was performed openly, at least in front of other African Americans. The context, rather than the items, suggests the caches were sealed in the chimney base to protect the Jackson family from spiritual harm. Any opening within the house, including flues of chimneys, can serve as a passageway for spirits. The first occupants of this small slave cabin believed that this multi-cache concealment in the chimney base was their insurance against malevolent magic entering their home.

Home Protection with Objects

Archaeologists have excavated few, if any, stone foundations to search for ritually placed objects. In most cases, the structural integrity of the foundation has been compromised from rodents and tree roots. The Jackson home's late 19th century foundation had been mortared; however, the southern wall and the cabin foundation were found partially collapsed. Despite the marginal integrity of some areas of the foundation, careful excavation of the northern and southern stone foundation revealed a number of artifacts. Twenty buttons were found in the south wall of the late 19th century addition and five buttons were pulled from the north wall, four of which were white Prosser porcelain. Archaeologists also removed numerous bones, as well as a bat leg (femur) and a cat's lower leg (metapodial) from between these stones. Although some of these bones and artifacts may have been placed between and underneath the foundation stones through natural means or as accidental inclusions, other objects appear to have been consciously sealed during construction. While dismantling part of the southern stone foundation, I observed an archaeologist lift one stone up to reveal a porcelain doll's arm nestled beneath it. This object was perfectly encased between two intact stones.

In the southwest corner of the original slave cabin, incorporated within the foundation, we also found a prehistoric siltstone ax (Figure 7). The ax was not part

Figure 7. Stone ax found under southwest corner of original cabin. (Photograph by author, 2009).

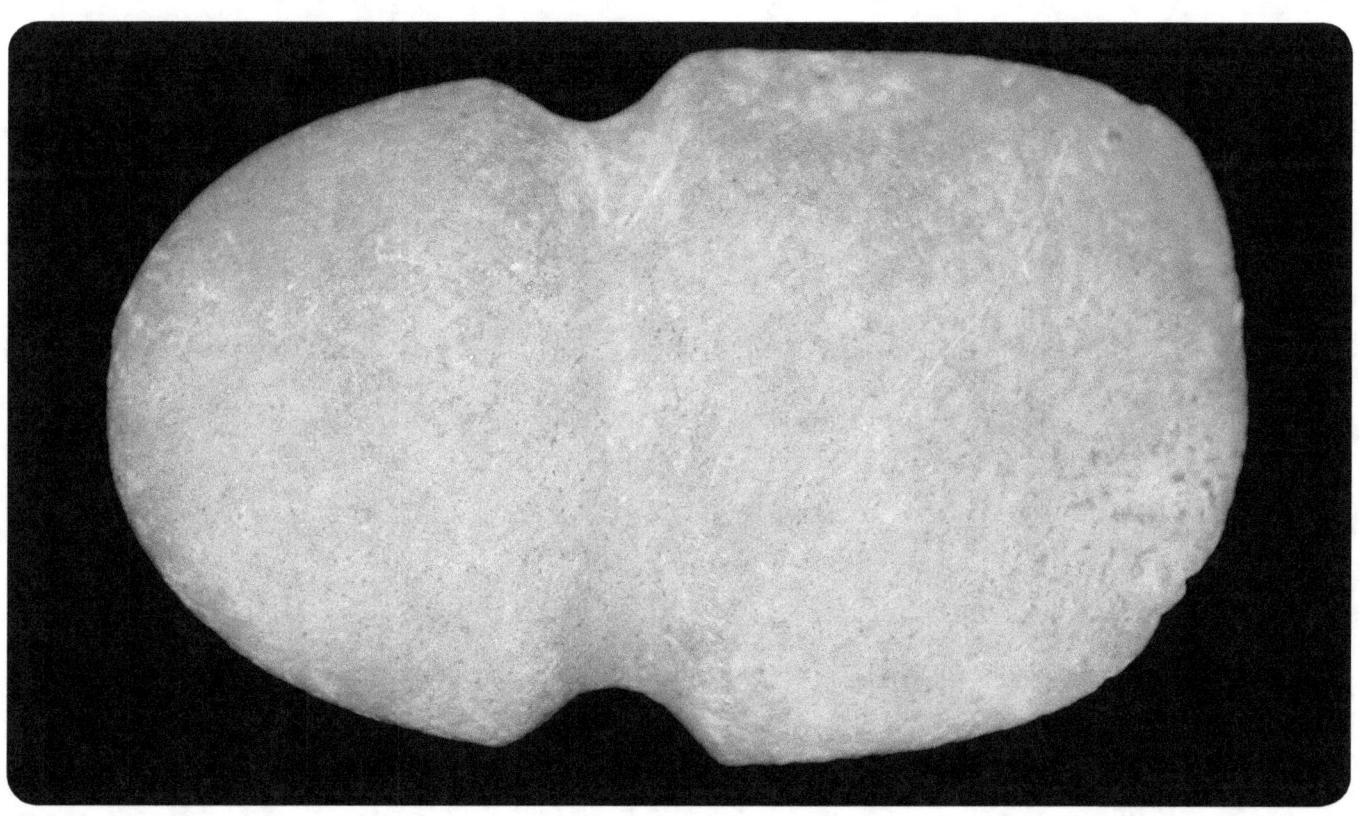

of a prehistoric component of the site. Instead, this stone tool appeared to have been found, collected, and incorporated into the foundation during initial construction. Ethnographic accounts reveal that axes were believed to chase storms away. To turn away the driving wind, rain, and lightening, one could take an ax and wave it in the air, chop up the ground with it, or simply "place an ax in the corner of the house" (Puckett 1926:320; Raboteau 2004:81). In addition to this stone ax, we collected eight quartzite projectile points primarily placed within the home along the exterior walls in both the cabin and late 19th century addition (Figure 8). Prehistoric tools, including scrapers and projectile points, have been found on several African American sites across the south and southeastern United States (Adams 1987; Patten 1992; Wilke 1995; Brown 2001). In most cases, these prehistoric stone artifacts have

been interpreted as an item picked up out of curiosity, while others insinuate the points may have been used for other purposes (Wilke 1995:143). Interestingly, an interview with a conjure doctor in Mississippi revealed "…that the Indian arrowheads often found in the locality were not made by man at all, but were fashioned by God out of thunder and lightening" (Puckett 1926:315). Thompson revealed this belief likely has roots in Africa. Shango, a god depicted balancing a doubled edged ax on his head, rules thunder and lightening–his power "…streaks down in meteorites and thunder stones, stones both symbolic and real" (Thompson 1983:86).

Fear of loss of their home by fire through lightning and severe storm events likely motivated the Jackson family to place a siltstone ax in the southwest corner of their log home. It is not possible to know unequivocally why they tucked quartzite projectile points along their foundation, but it is possible these artifacts were used to protect the family from harm either from spirits and/or lightening. It is also probable that the quartz material was seen as significant, but not the sole reason for

Figure 8. Footprint of home displaying location of quartz/quartzite projectile points and siltstone ax. (Map by Kathy Furgerson, 2010; courtesy of Maryland State Highway Administration).

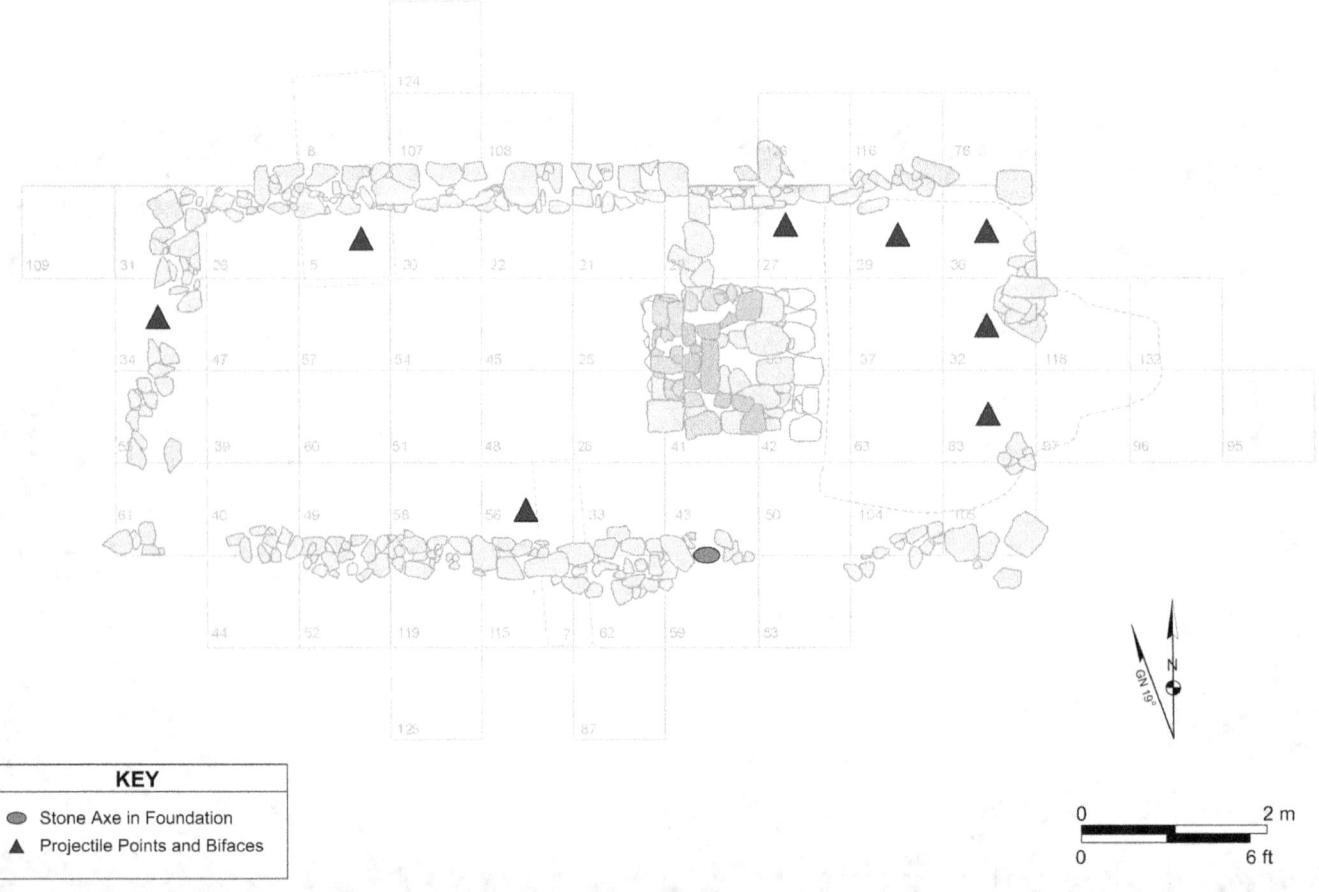

KEY

⬬ Stone Axe in Foundation
▲ Projectile Points and Bifaces

| 0 | | | 2 m |
| 0 | | | 6 ft |

collection and use in this context.[5] The fear of loss of a home by fire was a real fear among those who cooked, heated, and lived by open flames. In order to abate these feelings of anxiety, the Jacksons sought out methods of protection. Since the men in the family worked as farm laborers on property with a prehistoric site, the acquisition and eventual incorporation of quartz projectile points into the home was easily accomplished.

In sum, the Jacksons' home received protection during the **construction** of the original cabin and again during the formation of the 19th century addition. This is different from many similar sites that have caches and/or objects concealed during occupation. Like other places yielding expressions of African based spirit practices, this home, and perhaps even the yard space, continued to receive offerings throughout time. After I received the results of the faunal analysis, I knew the discovery of some of the artifacts in the late 19th century foundation, perhaps even the bat wing and cat paw (among other animal bone), may not have been the result of coincidence or natural depositional events. These multiple episodes of ritual concealment began when the builder laid the first course of stone on the property and continued through at least the late 19th century. The concealment of caches and individual objects within, around, and under the structure suggest the entire home was ritually managed as a conceptual whole. It is also important to understand that the Jackson's concept of "safe space" was not necessarily confined to the area between the walls of their house. The surrounding yard area, including the trees, paths, and fence lines, were also likely manipulated and incorporated into their use of spiritual space (Upton 1988:367; Gundaker 1993:60-61).

Symbols of Emotion

Some scholars interpret the meaning of African spirit practices in the context of slavery, stating it was the only way those enslaved could hold on to their African identity, preserve their community, and exert some control over their life while in bondage (Wilke 1995:138; Thomas 1998:534,546; Leone and Fry 1999:381). Some may be impressed by the perseverance of any manifestation of African religion in the face of such terror, but in truth, there was little choice-ritual provided a mechanism for an emotional release from acculturation, bondage, and loss (Harkin 2003:276). Although these African-based religious traditions were not created to mitigate the stress of enslavement, participation in these rites did provide an outlet for everything born of slavery. Most archaeological discoveries and observations about these practices have come to us from enslaved contexts where the people remain unnamed and the population is discussed as a whole. The institution of slavery and lack of detailed records is to blame for these broad interpretations. Consequently, we have not fully considered the meaning of conjure to the individual nor the way it can be used by one family.

Reflecting back to the ethnographic accounts of "hoodoo," it is apparent African Americans invoked the spirit world in an attempt to control areas of their lives in which they felt powerless and as a means to mitigate the violent tendencies and acts of intimidation manifested by racism. Indeed, enslavement was one facet of their life, but it was not the only or necessarily the most common ailment treated by African spirit practices. Sickness, loss of a loved one, and various other tragedies were the types of daily problems negotiated by everyone, including the enslaved—and those experiences stimulated emotions such as fear, anger, revenge, desire, among others. If we consider for a moment the person or even a family unit occupying the same space, and forego the larger consideration of an enslaved population, it facilitates our appreciation of the range of reasons those of African descent engaged in spirit practices—it moves beyond the plantation and considers the individual. If, as archaeologists, we are to properly interpret the placement of such material culture, sometimes we must narrow our focus.

During artifact analysis in the laboratory, an archaeologist noticed that a simple hard rubber overcoat button dating to the latter half of the 19th century had been inscribed with the initials M and A with an X on the back and again on the rim (Figures 9a and 9b). U.S. Census records revealed that Malinda's 27-year old daughter in law, Mary J. Walker Adams and 10-year old granddaughter Mary Ida Adams lived in the home in 1880. After we identified occupants with those

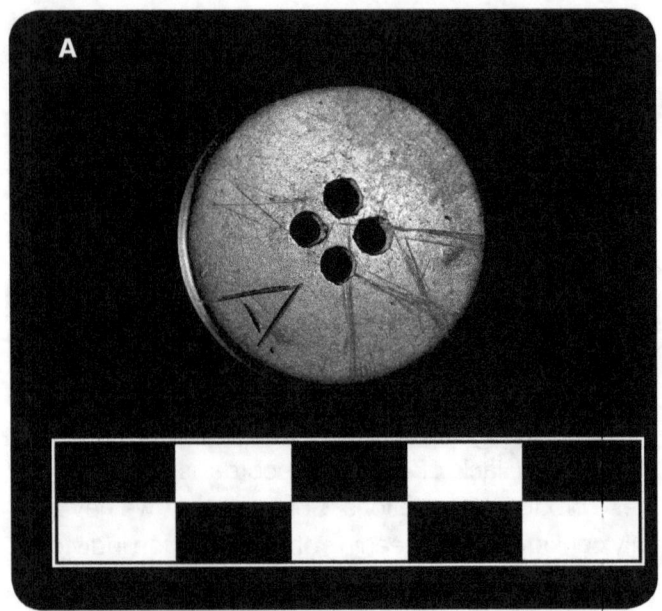

Figure 9a and b. Hard rubber coat button with incised M, A, and X on back and side. (Photograph by Lisa Guerre, 2010; courtesy of Maryland State Highway Administration).

initials, we considered the possibility that the letters may have been etched on the button by the owner of the coat to communicate possession; however, the scratches were placed on the back and side of the button. In close proximity to the button, archaeologists also recovered three fragments of pane glass; one was scratched with an X, another with parallel lines with a perpendicular line, and a third with the letter A. The button and glass shards were recovered from the upper levels of the cellar fill associated with an area under the floor and just in front of the fire hearth. Unlike the chimney base caches that served to protect the family inside of the home, the button and pane glass

may have been concealed in secret. Ethnographic accounts relate many ways to bring harm to a person, to control their actions, or to throw back conjure. One of the most common methods involves scratching an item with an X and the name of the person to be conjured. This now powerful object would then be hidden beneath the floorboards or doorway just under the path of the person chosen to be affected (Hyatt 1970:760-761; Leone and Fry 1999:381; Fennell 2007: 23-24).

Considering the context of the coat button and possible association with the scratched pane glass, I now understood these objects to have been incorporated into a conscious and ritual effort intended to bring harm upon an individual or to control someone's actions. The placement of the button within the home suggests that the person to be conjured was most likely a family member or at least someone who frequented the home and spent time in the public part of the house, the kitchen. The possibility that someone within the home engaged in conjuring provided an opportunity to consider the dynamics of the household. We know that conjuring can be performed on anyone for any reason, so it is not surprising that it also takes place within the home. What is interesting is that this ritual behavior, caught in the archaeological record, allows us to reflect upon actions steeped in emotions. Whoever secreted these objects under the kitchen floor in front of the fire hearth was actively replacing feelings of powerlessness, fear, and perhaps even anger, with feelings of hope and control. Although the exact identity of the conjurer or the intended victim, and the reason behind this conjure, cannot be unequivocally determined, we now know it is possible to identify the presence of family or familiar relationship tensions within the archaeological record. Indeed, these types of findings urge us to further explore the possibility of considering emotions in archaeology.

Recognizing emotionally influenced behavior in archaeology, for the most part, has been overlooked except in cases of mortuary behavior, death, and burial (Trinkaus and Zimmerman 1982; Meskell 1994, 1998). The homogenous and small number of publications is to be expected since the more temporal and cultural distance that exists between ourselves and the people we study, the more uncomfortable we become using our emotional understanding as a template for analysis.

Tarlow (2000:723) states there is a question regarding "how far the perceptions, experiences, and emotions of modern individuals can be considered the same as the perceptions, experiences, and emotions of people in the past." I believe historical archaeologists are at an advantage here since we can receive, recognize, and sometimes even empathize with emotional responses to past life experiences through oral histories, journals, ethnographies, and other written records—they are us. In the case of West African spirit practices, we know that individuals concealed objects, bundles, and bottles in the ground or under steps and floors to influence spirits and control an individual's behavior or to reverse an assumed spell. The concealment of a coat button with the initials M and A along with an X under the floor is an expression of fear and not necessarily from a stranger, but fear from conjure or fear regarding the outcome from the perceived actions of an individual. Tarlow (2000:728-729) argues such detection and understanding of individual emotions is outside the purview of archaeology and she believes we will be most successful studying the social rather than individual emotional experience. In many cases, this may be true, but with single component sites, tight integrity, and a solid written record it is possible to recognize expressions of emotion in an archaeological site and tie those back to an individual family. If it is possible to identify activities driven by necessity (for example, food consumption and home construction) why would it not be possible with emotionally driven behavior (such as ritual caches and erection of a monument)?

Concluding Thoughts

In the early 1930s, Harry Middleton Hyatt conducted countless interviews with African Americans and whites[6] concerning their spiritual beliefs and practices. He published four volumes containing a range of interviews with practitioners and "root doctors" who shared "recipes" one could use to control the spirit world and in turn, affect your life or the lives of others. When trying to understand and interpret a ritually-placed artifact cache, unusual animal bones, or modified artifacts, it is logical to search these interviews for similar objects in an attempt to "break

the code." Although there may be similarities between artifacts recovered from archaeological contexts and those items used in ethnographic accounts and contemporary practice, caution must be exercised during the interpretation of these objects–African spirit practices are flexible. These rituals constantly evolve and the items used in practice also change due to simple reasons such as the availability of objects, roots, and bones. The incorporation of Catholic saints into African spirit practices is another unique example, and a cautionary note to archaeologists, of how *any* object can become empowered in the eyes of the practitioner.

Spirit management practices in North America vary regionally due to a variety of factors, such as the availability of items to be used in caches, influences of different European traditions, and by different interpretations that evolved in locally-specific ways. Wilke (1997) urges archaeologists to incorporate a diachronic approach to our study of these spiritual practices so that we may recognize changes that occurred within African American communities as communicated through expressions in their ritual practices. What complicates this approach is that these practices "shape shift" over time, across regions, within communities, and between individuals. Hyatt (1973:XV) observed:

> Hoodoo is a religion for many believers…not every believer in hoodoo believes the same thing, or believes with the same intensity. This of course is also true of Christians. Furthermore, hoodoo is an amorphous body of rites and substances continually changing. Not all of the matter I discovered more than a generation ago would be found today…

As archaeologists, our aim should not be to match artifact assemblage with a known recipe in a hoodoo cookbook to understand the significance of the object(s) and the meaning behind a cache. The variation on the individual level is too great. Instead, our focus should be to recognize the belief system as revealed to us in the archaeological record, and to determine the intensity and duration in which the individual or group adhered to such beliefs. This approach would allow us to recognize conflict at the household or community level, and to determine if the archaeological context can communicate the emotion(s) behind the behavior and if that relates to fear regarding the activity of an individual (e.g. control of lover), simple protection of self or household (e.g. wearing of silver coins and use of stone projectile points), or others.

Family is a very important aspect of African American life and the preservation of these ritual traditions protected those relationships (Wilke 1995:138). All families endure periods of harmony and conflict at the household and community level. Since the late 1800s, the Jacksons' home supported several family members, as well as transient laborers who lived on the property in separate residences. Admittedly, it is risky for an archaeologist to attempt to resurrect expressions of family conflict from the archaeological record. However, I believe it is possible to peer into their past lives and recognize the presence of fear, anger, and conflict in the behaviors that resulted in the creation of these caches.

The attempt to protect yourself, your family, or your things from natural (e.g. weather events and fire), spiritual, and human forces is a response that can be triggered on a daily basis. Fear is one of the strongest human emotions that we possess and that sentiment manifests itself in behavior and those actions can and do incorporate objects. Malinda Jackson and her children knew slavery, and the opportunity to own their house and a small parcel of land was significant to them in ways we can never appreciate. Despite freedom from enslavement, the Jackson family continued to struggle with each other as well as their antebellum community. They clearly communicated the presence of conflict that manifested itself as fear and expressed itself as ritual behavior and desires through the caches and objects they tucked within their home. West African spirit practices served as a private outlet for such basic emotions as fear and even anger.

In many publications, archaeologists have assigned the internment of complete animal skeletons, pierced silver coins, and discovery of crystals on African American sites as an attempt by people to control their environment and/or the actions of others, in particular, those in power. The interpretation of these caches as ritually-related usually stops here and the reader either accepts or rejects this unconventional proposition. Although the identification of human behavior from the archaeological record is a cornerstone of our discipline, it is also important to understand the motivation behind a specific action—the use of West African spirit practices was not always performed to maintain family ties, to counteract oppression, or to direct harm upon their captors. In many instances, conjure was used to control relationships within the home and within the immediate African American community.

I argue that it is within household contexts (domestic space occupied by any number of related individuals) using emotionally charged archaeological evidence that we can identify expressions of fear that have been directed at friends or family who occupy and encounter the same space. In other words, there is often an emotional response behind a ritualistic act that expresses itself as the grouping, hiding, or even wearing of specific objects believed to help influence the spirit world. By recognizing the emotion behind the ritual we can advance our understanding of past human behavior that is related to control of the environment that can be stimulated by conflict, either at the individual, household, or community level. Although I focused on the detection of fear-motivated behavior, archaeologists should also consider other emotions such as joy, pride, hope, denial, and anger when the integrity of the site allows for such interpretations. At the root of many forms of ritual behavior is an emotion that has been triggered by an external stimulant and/or internally derived stressor. When an individual charges that emotion with spirituality, their response to that particular situation, ailment, or person may be heightened and even exaggerated. As archaeologists, we will not be able to detect most emotions expressed by the people we study. Admittedly emotions can be internally processed and often are not manifested as behavior that would be captured and preserved in an archaeological context. But, when the opportunity presents itself, we should be ready to recognize and consider the potential.

Acknowledgements

I would first like to acknowledge Mark P. Leone and Joe Joseph for their inspiration, comments, and edits on this essay. My appreciation is also extended to Chris Fennell for his insightful observations and sensitive comments. Thank you to Lisa Kraus for her thorough edits and for her intellectual conversations with me that helped solidify this essay. The following archaeologists are commended for their research and presentations on aspects of the Jackson Homestead Site at the 2009 Society for Historical and Underwater Archaeology Conference in Toronto, Canada: Varna Boyd, April Fehr, Kathy Furgerson, Tara Giuliano, Kristen Heasley, Mechelle Kerns, Sharon Moose, Nichole Mutchie, Carey O'Reilley, Brian Ostahowski, and Anthony Randolf. Recognition and gratitude is also imparted to Kathy Furgerson who directed the excavation of the Jackson Homestead site. I would also like to thank Reverend Spencer Jackson, Malinda's great-great grandson, and the Jackson relatives for their involvement and participation in the journey to learn more about their family. I am so glad we found you.

References

ADAMS, WILLIAM HAMPTON (EDITOR)

1987   *Historical Archaeology of Plantations at Kings Bay, Camden County, Georgia.* Reports of Investigation 5. Department of Anthropology, University of Florida, Gainesville.

BERLIN, IRA

1996   From Creole to African: Atlantic Creoles and the Origins of African-American Society in Mainland North America. *The William and Mary Quarterly*, Third Series, Vol. L111, No. 2, April, 251-288.

BIRD, STEPHANIE ROSE

2007   *Sticks, Stones, Roots and Bones, Hoodoo, Mojo and Conjuring with Herbs.* Llewellyn Publications, Woodbury, MN.

BROWN, KENNETH L.

2001   Interwoven Traditions: Archaeology of the Conjurer's Cabins and the African American Cemetery at the Jordan and Frogmore Manor Plantations. In *Places of Cultural Memory: African Reflections on the American Landscape*, 99-114. Conference Proceedings, National Park Service, Washington DC http://www.nps.gov/history/crdi/conferences/AFR_99-114_KBrown.pdf.

BRUCE, HENRY CLAY

1895   *The New Man. Twenty-Nine Years as a Slave Twenty-Nine Years a Free Man.* P. Anstadt and Sons, York, PA.

CHIREAU, YVONNE

1997   Conjure and Christianity in the Nineteenth Century: Religious Elements in African American Magic. *Religion and American Culture* 7(2):225-246.

DAVIDSON, JAMES M.

2004   Rituals Captured in Context and Time: Charm Use in North Dallas Freedman's Town (1869-1907), Dallas, Texas. *Historical Archaeology* 38(2):22-54.

DEAGAN, KATHLEEN AND DARCIE MACMAHON

1995   *Fort Mose: Colonial America's Black Fortress of Freedom.* University of Florida Press, Gainesville.

64

DEANE, JAMES
1937   Personal interview with James V. Deane, ex-slave on
        September, 1937 at his home 1514 Druid Hill Ave.,
        Baltimore. Born in Slavery: Slave Narratives from
        the Federal Writers' Project, 1936-1938, Maryland
        Narratives Volume VIII. http://memory.loc.gov/cgi-bin/
        ampage?collId=mesn&fileName=080/mesn080.db&recNu
        m=8&itemLink=D?mesnbib:9:./temp/~ammem_0g9F.

DEETZ, JAMES
1993   Flowerdew Hundred: The Archaeology of a Virginia
        Plantation, 1619-1864. University of Virginia Press,
        Charlottesville.

FENNELL, CHRISTOPHER C.
2007   Crossroads and Cosmologies, Diasporas and
        Ethnogenesis in the New World. University Press Florida,
        Tallahassee.
2011   Early African America: Archaeological Studies of
        Significance and Diversity. Journal of Archaeological
        Research 19:1-49.

FERGUSON, LELAND G.
1999   The Cross Is a Magic Sign: Marks on Eighteenth-Century
        Bowls from South Carolina. In I, Too, Am America:
        Archaeological studies of African American Life, Theresa
        A. Singleton, editor, pp.116-131. University Press of
        Virginia, Charlottesville.

FRANKLIN, JOHN HOPE
1956   History of Racial Segregation in the United States. Annals
        of the American Academy of Political and Social Science
        304 (March):1-9.

FRANKLIN, MARIA
2004   An Archaeological Study of the Richneck Slave Quarter
        and Enslaved Domestic Life. Colonial Williamsburg
        Research Publications, Colonial Williamsburg Foundation,
        VA.

FRATPIETRO, STEPHEN
2009   Genetic Analysis using nuclear DNA (nDNA) to determine
        ethnic background, the number of individuals present
        on each sample and the sex of the individual. Report to
        Julie Schablitsky, Maryland State Highway Administration,
        Baltimore, from Paleo DNA Laboratory, Thuder Bay,
        Ontario, Canada.

FUKE, RICHARD PAUL
1999   Imperfect Equality, African Americans and Confines of
        White Racial Attitudes in Post-Emancipation Maryland,
        Fordham University Press, New York, NY.

FURGERSON, KATHLEEN, VARNA BOYD, CAREY O'REILLY, JUSTIN BEDARD,
TRACY FORMICA, AND ANTHONY RANDOLPH, JR.
2011   Phase II and III Archaeological Investigations of the
        Fairland Branch Site and the Jackson Homestead (Site
        18MO609), Montgomery County, Maryland. Report to
        Maryland State Highway Administration, Baltimore, from
        URS Corporation, Gaithersburg, Maryland.

GUNDAKER, GREY
1993   Tradition and Innovation in African-American Yards.
        African Arts 26(2):58-71, 94-96.

HARKIN, MICHAEL E.
2003   Feeling and Thinking in Memory and Forgetting: Towards
        an Ethnohistory of the Emotions. Ethnohistory 50(2):261-
        284.

HERRON, LEONORA AND ALICE M. BACON
1896   Conjure and Conjure-Doctors in the Southern United
        States. The Journal of American Folklore 9(33):143-147.

HEWATT, ALEXANDER
1779   An Historical Account of the Rise and Progress of the
        Colonies of South Carolina and Georgia, Vol. 2, London,
        England.

HUCLES, MICHAEL
1993   Emancipation's Impact on African-American Education in
        Norfolk, Virginia, 1862-1880. Organization of American
        Historians Magazine of History 7(4)32-35.

HYATT, HARRY MIDDLETON
1970   Hoodoo-Conuration-Witchcraft-Rootwork, Vol. 2, Western
        Publishing Co., Inc., Cambridge, MD.
1973   Hoodoo-Conuration-Witchcraft-Rootwork, Vol. 3, Western
        Publishing Co., Inc., Cambridge, MD.

1978   *Hoodoo-Conuration-Witchcraft-Rootwork*, Vol. 5, Western Publishing Co., Inc., Cambridge, MD.

JOHNSON, CHARLES S.
1943   *Patterns of Negro Segregation*, Harper and Brothers, New York, NY.

JONES, LYNN D.
1999   Crystals and Conjuring in an Annapolis Household. *Maryland Archeology* 35(2):1-8.

KING, JULIA A.
1996   The Patuxent Point Site. In *Living and Dying on the 17th Century Patuxent Frontier*, Julia A. King and Douglas H. Ubelaker, editors, pp.15-46. Maryland Historical Trust Press, Crownsville.

KLINGELHOFER, ERIC
1987   Aspects of Early Afro-American Material Culture: Artifacts from the Slave Quarters at Garrison Plantation, Maryland. *Historical Archaeology* 21(2):112-119.

LEONE, MARK P.
2005   The Archaeology of Liberty in an American Capital, Excavations in Annapolis. University of California Press, Los Angeles, CA.

LEONE, MARK P. AND GLADYS-MARIE FRY
1999   Conjuring in the Big House Kitchen, An Interpretation of African American Belief Systems Based on the Uses of Archaeology and Folklore Sources. *Journal of American Folklore* 112(445):372-403.

LEONE, MARK P. AND GLADYS-MARIE FRY, WITH ASSISTANCE FROM TIMOTHY RUPPEL
2001   Spirit Management among Americans of African Descent. In *Race and the Archaeology of Identity*. Charles E. Orser Jr., editor, pp.143-157. University of Utah Press, Salt Lake City.

LEVI-STRAUSS, CLAUDE
1966   The Scope of Anthropology. *Current Anthropology* 7(2):112-123.

McQUILLAR, TAYANNAH LEE
2003   *Rootwork, Using the Folk Magick of Black America for Love, Money, and Success.* Fireside, New York, NY.

MERRIFIELD, RALPH
1988   *The Archaeology of Ritual and Magic.* New Amsterdam Books, New York, NY.

MESKELL, LYNN
1994   Dying Young: The Experience of Death at Deir el Medina. *Archaeological Review from Cambridge* 13:35-46.

1998   The Irresistible Body and the Seduction of Archaeology. In *Changing Bodies, Changing Meanings: Studies on the Human Body in Antiquity*, Dominic Monstserrat, editor, pp. 139-161. Routledge, New York, NY.

MONROE, J. CAMERON AND SETH MALLIOS
2004   A Seventeenth-Century Colonial Cottage Industry: New Evidene and Dating Formula for Colono Tobacco pipes in the Chesapeake. *Historical Archaeology* 38(2):68-82.

MONTGOMERY COUNTY REGISTER OF WILLS (MCRW)
1826   Will of Zachariah Downs, Liber 3, Folio 451, Appendix C, Maryland State Archives, Annapolis.

MOUER, L. DANIEL, MARY ELLEN N. HODGES, STEPHEN R. POTTER, SUSAN L. HENRY RENAUD, IVOR NOEL HUME, DENNIS J. POGUE, MARTHA W. McCARTNEY, AND THOMAS E. DAVIDSON
1999   Colonoware Pottery, Chesapeake Pipes, and "Uncritical Assumptions". In *"I, Too, Am America,"* Theresa A. Singleton, editor, pp. 83-115. University Press of Virginia, Charlottesville.

ORSER, CHARLES E., JR.
1994   The Archaeology of African-American Slave Religion in the Antebellum South. *Cambridge Archaeological Review Journal* 4(1):33-45.

PATTEN, M. DRAKE
1992   Mankala and Minkisi: Possible Evidence of African American Folk Beliefs and Practices. *African American Archaeology* 6:5-7.

PUCKETT, NEWBELL NILES
1926   *Folk Beliefs of the Southern Negro.* University of North Carolina Press, Chapel Hill.

RABOTEAU, ALBERT J.
2004   Slave Religion: The "Invisible Institution" in the Antebellum South, updated from 1980 edition. Oxford University Press, New York, NY.

RANDOLPH, ANTHONY
2009   The Conservation of the Jackson Homestead Assemblage: A Study in the Condition and Treatment of Burned Material Culture. Paper presented at the 42nd Annual Meeting of the The Society for Historical Archaeology, Toronto, Ontario, Canada.

ROCK, CAROLYN AND LEE NEWSOM
1987   Botanical Analysis of the Privy Pits, Kings Bay Plantation. In *Historical Archaeology of Plantations at Kings Bay, Camden County, Georgia*, William H. Adams, editor, pp. 441-442. Department of Anthropology, University of Florida, Gainesville. Submitted to the Naval Submarine Base, United States Department of the Navy, Kings Bay, GA.

SCHABLITSKY, JULIE M.
2009   No Stone Unturned: African American Spiritual Practices within the Jackson Homestead, Montgomery County, Maryland. Paper presented at the 42nd Annual Meeting of the The Society for Historical Archaeology, Toronto, Ontario, Canada.

TANTAQUIDGEON, GLADYS
2001   *Folk Medicine of the Delaware and Related Algonkian Indians.* Anthropological Series No. 3, Commonwealth of Pennsylvania, Harrisburg.

TARLOW, SARAH
2000   Emotion in Archaeology. *Current Anthropology* 41(5):713-746.

THE HOLY BIBLE, ENGLISH STANDARD VERSION
2007   Good News Publishers/Crossway Books, Wheaton, IL.

THOMAS, BRIAN W.
1998   Power and Community: The Archaeology of Slavery at the Hermitage Plantation. *American Antiquity* 63(4):531-551.

THOMPSON, ROBERT FARRIS
1983   *Flash of the Spirit, African and Afro-American Art and Philosophy.* Random House, Inc., New York, NY.
1993   *Face of the Gods, Art and Altars of Africa and the African Americas.* Museum of African Art, New York, NY.

THORNTON, JOHN K.
1998   *Africa and Africans in the Making of the Atlantic World, 1400-1800.* 2nd edition Cambridge University Press, England.

TRINKAUS, E. AND M.R. ZIMMERMAN
1982   Trauma among the Shanidar Neanderthals. *American Journal of Physical Anthropology* 57:61-76.

U.S. BUREAU OF THE CENSUS
1860   Population Schedules of the Eighth Census of the United States, 1860. U.S. Bureau of the Census.
1870   Population Schedules of the Ninth Census of the United States, 1870. U.S. Bureau of the Census.
1880   Population Schedules of the Tenth Census of the United States, 1880. U.S. Bureau of the Census.
1910   Population Schedules of the Twelfth Census of the United States, 1910. U.S. Bureau of the Census.

UPTON, DELL
1988   White and Black Landscapes in Eighteenth Century Virginia. In *Material Life in America*, Robert Blair St. George, editor, pp. 357-369. Northeastern University Press, Boston, MA.

VLACH, JOHN M.
1978   *The Afro-American Tradition in the Decorative Arts.* Cleveland Museum of Art, OH.
1987   Afro American Domestic Artifacts in Eighteenth-Century Virginia. *Material Culture* 19(1):3-23.

WILFORD, JOHN NOBLE
2008   Under Maryland Street, Ties to African Past. *The New York Times* 21 October. http://www.nytimes.com/2008/10/21/science/21arch.html?_r=1.

WILKIE, LAURIE A.

1995   Magic and Empowerment on the Plantation: An
        Archaeological Consideration of African-American World
        View. *Southeastern Archaeology* 14(2):136-148.

1997   Secret and Sacred: Contextualizing the Artifacts of
        African-American Magic and Religion. *Historical
        Archaeology* 31(4):81-106.

WILKINSON, T.T.

1851   *Folklore of Lancashire*, No. 1. Notes and Querries
        3(65):55-56.

WINDHAM, R. JEANNINE

2009   Of Food and Ritual: Zooarchaeological Remains from the
        Jackson Homestead (18MO609), Montgomery County,
        Maryland. Report to URS Corporation, Gaithersburg,
        Maryland, from New South Associates, Stone Mountain,
        Georgia.

WING, J. VAN

1941   Bakongo Magic. The Journal of the Royal Anthropological
        Institute of Great Britain and Ireland 71(1/2):85-97.

Endnotes

1   On occasion, the term "slave" may precede and aid
     in the description of a type of structure, be used in
     reference to an historical document, or be used in an
     attempt to achieve temporal context; the term is only
     used when deemed essential. The term "enslaved"
     is used to describe people of African descent kept in
     bondage.

2   The 1860 US Slave Census documented four young
     boys aged 1, 3, 5, and 11, as "mulatto". DNA analysis
     revealed four degraded mtDNA profiles on four smoking
     pipe stems. All four samples were consistent with
     Haplogroup H which is common in North Africa, Europe,
     and the Middle East (Fratpiertro 2009).

3   When speaking in general, I may also use African spirit
     practices. Infrequently, I incorporate the terms hoodoo,
     conjure, and magic in an attempt to acknowledge the
     terminology employed by those who practiced these
     rituals in the recent past.

4   The silver coins were found in burned contexts and
     association with a cache is uncertain.

5   A large quartz quarry is only a few miles away with a
     prehistoric lithic component right below the Jackson
     site. Quartz and quartzite rock would have been easily
     obtained from nearby sources for the use in spiritual
     practices.

6   The interviews took place as far north as Baltimore,
     Maryland and as far south as Jacksonville, Florida.

Julie M. Schablitsky
Maryland State Highway Administration
707 North Calvert Street
Baltimore, MD 21202

Christopher N. Matthews

Emancipation Landscapes: Archaeologies of Racial Modernity and the Public Sphere in Early New York

The public sphere was a space of opportunity as well as of danger, a space of abysmal voicelessness as well as of unexpected opportunities for expression.... Consequently, freedom was broadly experienced not as a natural or inherent state of being but as a profoundly discontinuous and contingent condition that required constant vigilance.

- Brooks (2005:92)

ABSTRACT

This paper examines the creation of the public sphere as a key context for understanding early 19th century New York. The focus is on the struggles and conflicts that came with emancipation as whites and African Americans negotiated their place on the same landscape. Whites took advantage of their superior position to subtly designate public space as white. This segregation was absorbed into the landscape so that it can be recognized in new settlement patterns and changes in domestic landscapes. African Americans countered white claims to urban space in varied ways, with a special emphasis placed on inserting themselves in publicly visible positions. African American attempts to racially integrate the public sphere ultimately failed leading to the development of more formalized forms of segregation that helped to underwrite more damaging assumptions about African American racial inferiority in the antebellum era.

Introduction

It is context that makes material things important. Where things come from, what they were part of and found with, how they were made and used, and by and for whom constitute the basic questions archaeologists must answer in order to understand their material findings. Building proper interpretive contexts, however, is not straightforward. As the field of historical archaeology continues to grow, the process of placing people in the recent past has received serious critiques from mainstream theorists writing from feminist, postcolonial, post-structural, and Marxist standpoints. While interested in different issues, all of these critical perspectives call for a greater sensitivity to the multiple contexts that past actors and present researchers negotiate every day. Moreover, these perspectives highlight that the contextual intersections of nation, class, race, gender, sexuality, knowledge, power, and authority are always fluid and poised for change. Proper contextualization thus requires flexibility on our part encouraging us to ask diverse questions simultaneously about the possible meanings of recovered histories and the way these meanings change through time and across the social spectrum. We also require a deeper understanding of the historical and material contexts of how past actors, as well as their descendents, positioned themselves within, and at times against, their contexts. These contexts are thus defined by a two-way process in which historical actors should be seen in dialogue with their material, social, and cultural conditions, neither producing nor being produced by these conditions exclusively.

The key in this for archaeology is the need for a nuanced sense of the work that material things "do" in the constitution and criticism of social discourse, or the way persons use things to actively engage in and make sense of their relationships with others. As others have noted, things were indeed components of past lives and their materiality permitted and delimited certain expressions and meanings (Olsen 2003, Brown 2004, Miller 2005). Yet, thinking contextually, the function we need most to understand is how things embodied statements about persons, relationships, and social formations, as well as the cultural sensibilities and expectations of past people and groups. To address social discourse calls for well-defined contexts that help us to conceptualize and thus question the foundations of identity and belonging in past societies. Since most historical archaeologists study plural and divisive settings, understanding the conflicted discourses of identity and belonging is vital to the process of interpreting and explaining the importance of material things. To explain this further, I propose we think of how contexts operate in two distinct yet overlapping categories, the historical and the material.

The Historical Context

Building a historical context requires an understanding of the social discourse engaged in by historical actors. We can begin this process by listing familiar national, racial, class and gendered contexts in which past people can be placed. For example, one of the main characters in this paper, Rufus King, was a wealthy, white American man from New York. In order to truly understand the material culture from King Manor, his home in Jamaica, Queens, we need more than just King's vital statistics—we need his life history. Certainly, I can add that he lived in the late 18th and early 19th century (1755-1827), the era of the American Revolution and the subsequent phase of American state formation where he served as a Federalist politician, United States Senator, delegate to the Constitutional convention, and minister to England. We can also gather that he came from a prominent Massachusetts merchant family and married a wealthy New Yorker, Mary Alsop, with whom he had several children. All of these descriptions begin to flesh out the traditional social contextual background typically gathered in historical archaeology, which for the most part focuses on domestic activities and a professional portfolio. Indeed, these are significant aspects of his life, but they alienate rather than connect Rufus King to his daily life at King Manor--we need more of the social context before we can even begin to understand the domestic sphere and the meanings behind the artifacts and features discovered in archaeology. Most

important, we need to understand King's relations with those who moved in and out of his daily life. In this case, these people include the range of laborers, domestic servants, and supervisors who found employment on his property.

King Manor was a farm involved with raising animals, field crops, and fruit orchards. The farm produced goods for the household as well as for sale locally and in nearby New York City. Thus, the historical and material record of the site documents not the just activities of the King family but also their employees. Notably, before the Kings, the site was owned by the Colgan-Smith family who also operated a farm on the property from the 1760s until the Kings obtained it in 1805. The Colgan-Smiths differed from the Kings in that their laborers included as many as 10 enslaved Africans (US Federal Census 1790, 1800). While the archaeology of American slavery has produced many invaluable insights and understandings about enslavement and African American life (Ferguson 1992; LaRoche and Blakey 1997; Edwards 1998; Singleton 1999; Fennell 2007), these contexts cannot function as a template for understanding Rufus King, who did not own slaves while living at King Manor. In fact, King was an anti-slavery advocate throughout his political career (Ernst 1968).

My discussion thus far indicates the sort of contextual richness that most well documented sites contain and which should be considered. However, we should not stop here. More is needed to fully understand the archaeology. Specifically, we need to recognize the social context of Rufus King's life and how he was "seen" by not just his peers but, his subordinates. What was the meaning of being wealthy, prominent, Federalist, white, and anti-slavery in early 19th-century New York? In other words, how did these various contexts that intersect at King Manor produce the meaning of being Rufus King during the years he lived there?

The Material Context

The material context provides this framework. At the center of the site is the manor house (Figure 1), the home of the King family as well as the Colgan-Smiths who preceded them. The

Figure 1. King Manor Museum, Jamaica, Queens. The house depicted is a final architectural permutation after several modifications to earlier structures that are now largely incorporated within it. (Photograph by the author).

house is a modified Georgian "Long Island Half-house" that was expanded by the Kings around 1810 to produce the unified, full-framed federalist façade seen today. The Kings expanded the service ell (Figure 2) immediately after moving in by adding a new kitchen with a lean-to shed addition in the rear. The new kitchen complemented an existing kitchen that was not actually removed. Rather, the new King-era kitchen was distinguished by a larger workspace and a very large beehive bread oven, the body of which extended under the lean-to shed. It seems the Kings required both a household kitchen and a separate working kitchen for the farm.

Beyond the house, King Manor also contained a series of outbuildings and facilities (Figure 3). Some of these date to the 18th-century Colgan-Smith ownership,

including a privy and a structure later designated as Building K (Figure 2), a stone walled outbuilding adjacent to the kitchen ell that was likely a dairy, smokehouse, and/or barracks. The other buildings shown to the north of the manor house were barns and sheds built by the Kings. Thus, while both the Kings and the Colgan-Smiths used the property for farming, only the Kings erected a substantial service landscape to support this work. Not knowing exactly what sort of farming the Colgan-Smiths undertook, this may reflect different practices, but the question of the shift from the use of enslaved versus free laborers nevertheless lies waiting to be explored.

Before considering this aspect of the material context, however, the site must be further situated in the surrounding material world of Jamaica, Queens,

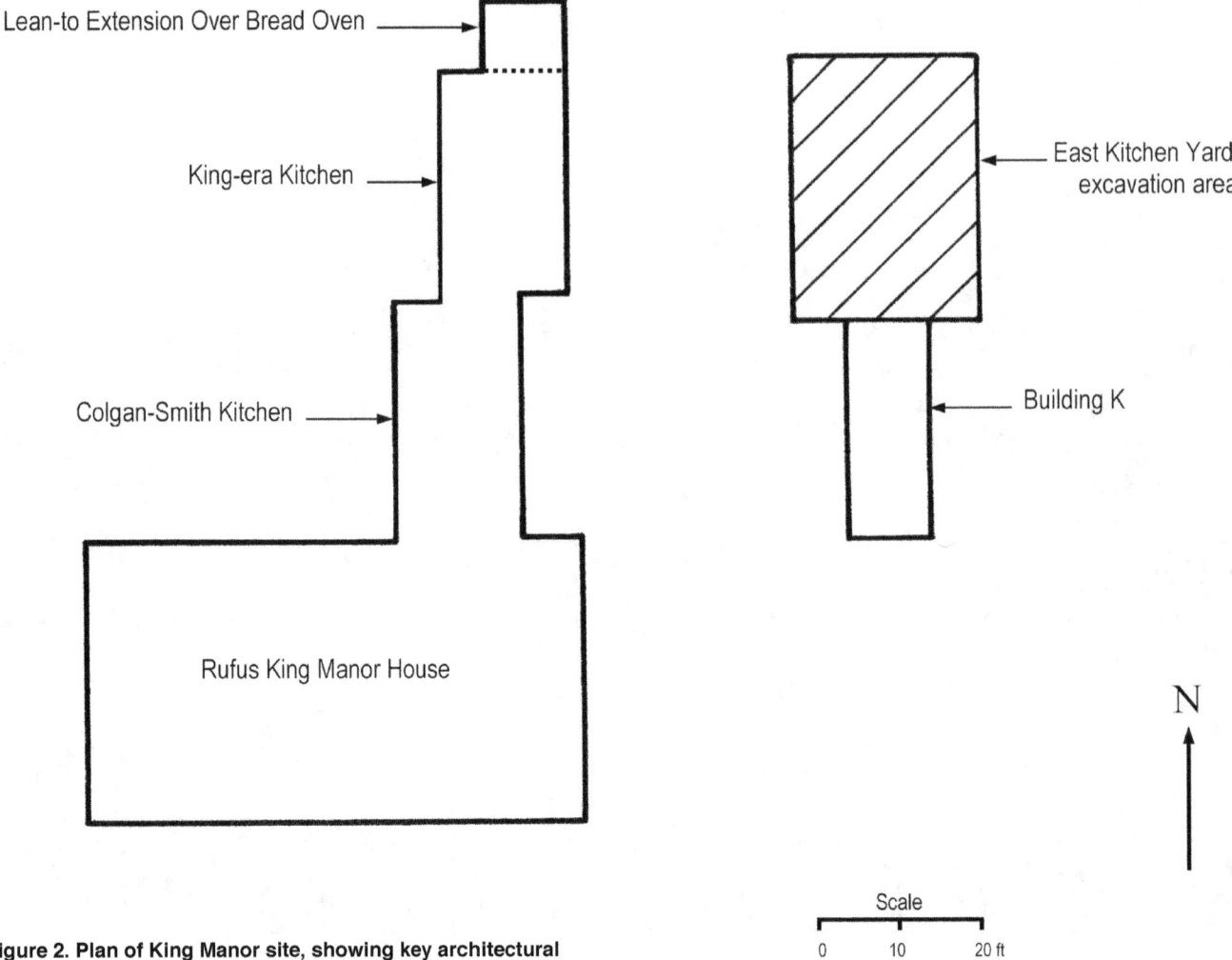

Lean-to Extension Over Bread Oven

King-era Kitchen

Colgan-Smith Kitchen

Rufus King Manor House

East Kitchen Yard excavation area

Building K

N

Scale

0   10   20 ft

Figure 2. Plan of King Manor site, showing key architectural elements and excavated areas (Drawing by Ross Rava, 2011).

and early New York. While Jamaica was a small rural village when the Kings moved there, it was a political center for the county and thus held some prominence in the region. Nearby New York City, then confined solely to lower Manhattan, was fast rising to international commercial significance as a port of trade in the north Atlantic basin. Working New Yorkers were also undergoing a shift from a skilled craft-base to an unskilled industrial productive economy. Given these factors, the material context of the early 19th century in New York was primarily marked by a great deal of significant change and modernization that overturned long-held norms and introduced new ideas about work, the creation of urban space, and its peopling.

These particular data refer to one of the most basic components of the material context: the body in social space. During times of great change, bodies,

as basic units of experience, become beacons for conceptualizing and understanding new practices and interpretive orders (Foucault 1976, 1979; Joyce 2009). Furthermore, placing the body in its proper material and historical context presents a useful way to record and understand the meanings of social change to the people who experienced them. It is this topic, in particular, that I pursue by exploring the way bodies became engaged with historical contexts during transition from slavery to freedom at King Manor and in the New York area. I have introduced the basic transformation of the dominant system of production in early New York, but other factors and historical data need to be considered in order to contextualize the record of how bodies changed in the making of a free New York. It is the connections between people, spaces, artifacts, and ideas that give objects importance, and illustrating

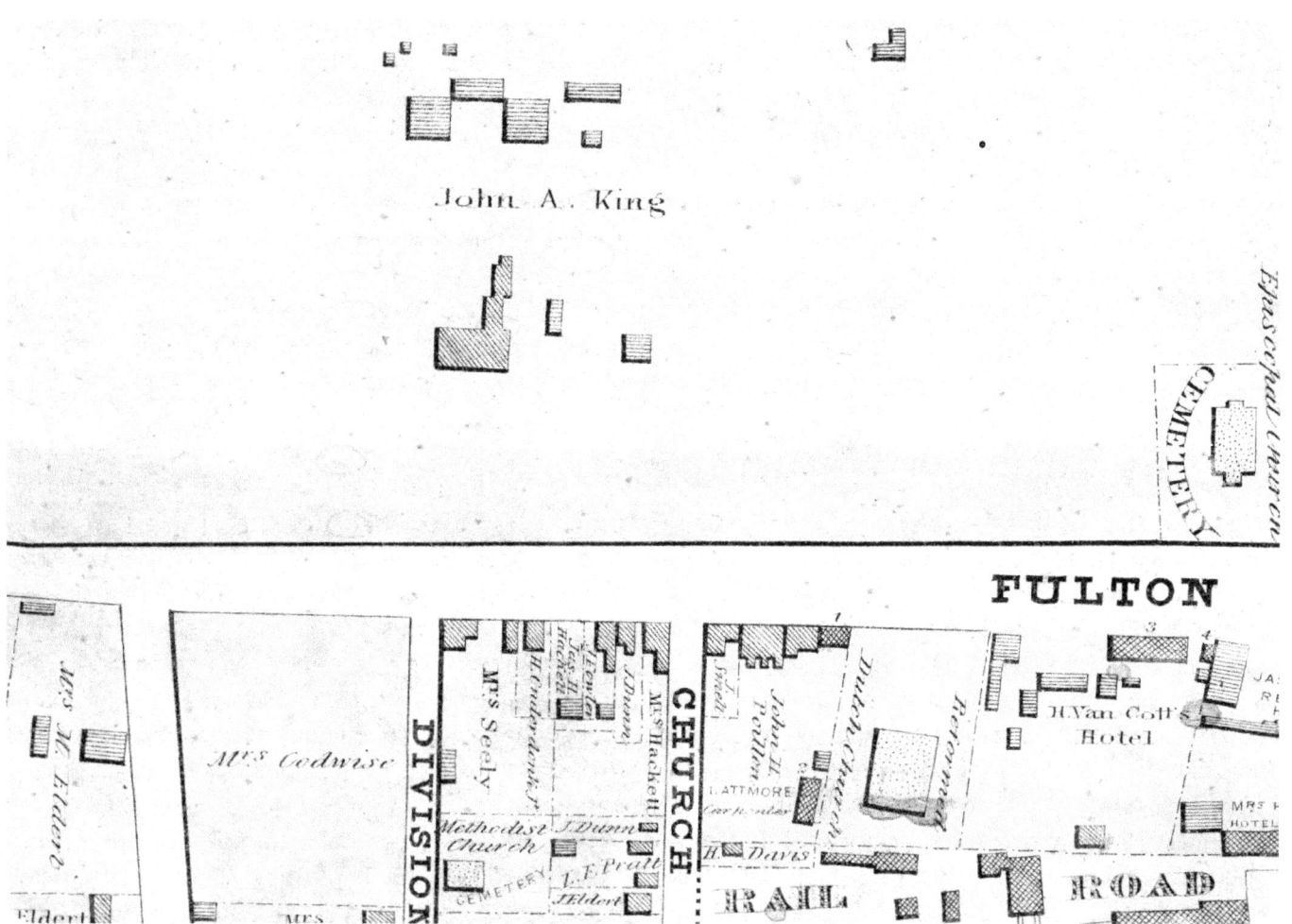

Figure 3. Map of the village of Jamaica, Queens County, Long Island, 1842 Q-1842.FI; Martin G. Johnson. (Courtesy of the Brooklyn Historical Society).

a broader and more nuanced contextualization of material things—whether excavated, above ground, and/or reconstructed from historical documents—is the central purpose of this paper.

Landscapes of Slavery and Freedom in New York

While a northern state, slavery was widespread in New York prior to the state's gradual emancipation act of 1799, which led to the end of slavery in 1827 (White 1991; Gellman 2006). During the 18th century, New York City contained the largest population of urban captives north of Charleston, South Carolina. African New Yorkers worked as domestic servants, in the shops of craftsmen, and as laborers on the docks and on farms near the city. African labor was vital to the success of the colony, and slave ownership grew with each decade of the colonial period. In fact, many historians agree that New York was becoming more like a "slave society" (Berlin 1998) leading up the American Revolution, such that not only did the number of captives grow but ancillary businesses like auction houses, printers, lawyers and scriveners became more closely tied to the practice of slavery for their livelihood (McManus 1966). Even after the Revolutionary War, when the tide of liberty held strong in the north and many states promptly enacted emancipation legislation in the 1770s and 1780s, New York failed to follow suit. Nevertheless, after the state's 1799 gradual emancipation act, and for some even before, slavery wound down relatively quickly in New York and a free black community of some significance emerged in the city. For example, while the number of enslaved Africans fell from more than 2,000 in 1790 to 1,440 in 1810, the community of free blacks grew substantially from just over 1,000 to 7,470 (White 1991:26, 156).

The rapid growth of the free black community, which is accounted for as much by a rural to urban migration as local emancipation, was a major part of the changes that marked the emergence of modern New York, though other important parts of society also changed during this era. For most New Yorkers, the nature of work shifted. While in the 18th century, trades were dominated by skilled masters who owned and operated private shops, the mechanization of production shifted work increasingly towards wage-based industrial factory systems. One result was the deskilling of labor, a process that unified members of different trade guilds and fostered a consciousness of their shared class standing (Wilentz 1984). Another outcome was the removal of non-family members from the combined homes and workplaces of master craftsmen and brokers. Instead, early factory-owners, commercial agents, and other members of the middle class moved to new homes on the city's edge that were kept separate from work places downtown. By 1840, most household heads in New York (70%) lived in homes separate from where they worked (Wall 1994). The early 19th century was thus not only a time of emancipation but also of class formation and settlement change that dramatically changed the landscape of New York.

I propose that we regard these changes as the material context for American freedom—meaning both the underlying principles of liberty that emerged in the Revolution as well as the simultaneous end of northern slavery and the articulation of new relations between masters and workers. To document freedom in early New York, I use an archaeological perspective to describe how the way life was articulated within the imagined ideals of liberty that drove so much of social discourse, a process that puts the material and historical contexts in close dialogue. To describe and interpret the material context of American freedom in New York I consider the period from roughly 1785 to 1830, or what I call the "emancipation era." Here, I draw from excavated data at King Manor and other sites as well as a broader reaching set of landscape data that

reference the materiality of the city and position how it was experienced during this time of great change.

The main goal is to examine and explain the essential context of the emancipation landscape: "the public sphere." During the colonial period, deferential paternalistic norms and a moral economy (Thompson 1963) constrained the emergence of "the public" (cf. Fraser 1990; Habermas 1991; Brooks 2005). Yet, during the emancipation-era, diverse claims made on the emerging public sphere reveal an array of circumstances and negotiations that arose with American democracy and new ideas and practices of liberty and citizenship (Leone 2005). Debates over who was actually free in early America were actually conflicts over the right to have a legitimate stake in the public sphere where this freedom materialized. The first pattern I discuss is how the public sphere in New York came to be designated as a "white" space. The second is the way the free black community challenged this designation through temporary, yet regular and visibly spectacular, occupations of the public sphere, especially through participation in commemorative parades.

To integrate these data, I employ James Brewer Stewart's (1998; 1999) notion of "racial modernity." Racial modernity describes the new "race relations" that emerged during the emancipation era as free African Americans and whites sought, for the first time, to occupy the same landscape. Racial modernity emerged in the way whites resisted African American claims on almost every front. Whether in the labor market or on the open street, whites of all ranks regularly expressed their disapproval of emancipation. Ensuing conflicts were sometimes violent, yet, whether passive or aggressive, white resistance consistently asserted the illegitimacy of a visible black freedom. Whites ultimately embraced the "racially modern" idea of blacks as permanently inferior and at odds with the image of American citizenship. As a concept, racial modernity captures the sedimentation of social difference and segregation in the immutability of race such that, at least in the opinion of most "modern" whites, blacks and whites were inherently separate and unequal races. My goal is to elaborate how racial modernity was built in a truly material sense and to explore how to use archaeology to develop a sense of the materiality of the racially modern experience. While I draw from traditional sources such as settlement patterns and excavated archaeological data, the evidence is not handled in standard ways. That is, I do not seek solely to explain what was found as much as to use these findings to create a contextualized sense of the dynamics that fostered racial modernity in the public sphere. I key materiality to performance such that artifacts, bodies, spaces, buildings, and streets are employed as necessary props in the difficult racial discourse that came with emancipation. As things, artifacts and features of the landscape were present, entangled, integral, and debated, and they speak to the making of past lives. Yet, in this story, it is less the meaning of things that was in debate than the ability of some to certify their preferred meanings in the public sphere and thus force others to accept these meanings (and whether they did so) that is the focus of my discussion.

The Invisibility of White Public Space

Research on white public space highlights the making of an "invisible normal[ity]" (Page and Thomas 1994) through indirect rather than direct action such that whites less often claim spaces for themselves than monitor and control others' access (Hage 2000). While the dominant position of whites in public space supports this claim, restrictions are not like the images we have of the "whites only" Jim Crow American South. Rather, they are the result of subtle boundary enforcements such as assumptions and homogenizations that define some actions as different and disorderly despite the same actions being defined as "colloquially normal" when performed by members of the dominant group (Hill 1998; 2008). This interpretive distinction reveals a broad acceptance of diversity within social groups combined with strict policing of the boundaries between them. Linguist Jane Hill (1998:682) suggests that we think of white public space as an "indirect [racial] indexicality" such that "disorder on the part of whites is rendered invisible and normative" thereby making minority disorder even more visible; so visible, Hill argues, that

it can become the "object of expensive campaigns and nationwide 'moral panics'." As an example, Hill cites the 1990s movement for English-only education in the United States based on highly visible and supposedly threatening non-English (predominantly Spanish) language use by non-whites. She contrasts this movement with whites' use of "mock-Spanish" (for example, the well-known line from *Terminator*: "hasta la vista, baby") that is instead seen as humorous and politically neutral. I make a similar case suggesting that what we see in the crystallization of modern racial communities in emancipation-era New York reflects a moral campaign to normalize white authority. This authority rested on emergent modern foundations of race and was formed in the face of an insistent black freedom, which was regarded as threatening because of its difference and because of the interpretation of African Americans' attempts to express their rightful place on the American landscape as confrontational. A key factor that underwrites the success of indirect racial indexicality is homogenization, a process that the concept of race exemplifies so well (that all blacks or all whites are the same).

Evidence of the emergence white public space in early New York is found in settlement pattern data that show that whites actively cultivated structural changes to the way lived social space was defined in the city. Tracking data from city directories, Diana Wall (1994:21) shows by 1840 that the majority of New Yorkers shifted from living in combined homes and workplaces to living in homes separated from work (Blackmar 1991). This new settlement pattern elicited new ideas embraced especially by middle class households regarding domesticity and respectability. A proper life highlighted the moral purity of the family, an idea that was simultaneously a spatial construct that characterized the workplace and the market more generally as an immoral sphere to be isolated from the home. Wall's archaeological study of several of these new households in Greenwich Village documents a diversity of strategies employed by middle-class women to ensure their homes met the respectable standards of modern domesticity. Both etiquette manuals and excavated ceramic assemblages, for example, indicate an increasing ritualization of family meals. The service of multiple courses with specialized vessels to present and contain food as well as the use of increasingly decorated and expensive wares through time record the growing investment families put into the meaning and significance of the activities defining a modern and separate "home" (Wall 1994: 136-47, Appendix E). That most household members spent significant time away from home at work or at school, further intensified the ritual aspects of family meals, which came to be seen as "a constant and familiar reunion" (Frederick Law Olmstead in Wall 1994:113) through which the family—as both a collective *and* as a modern idea—was reproduced.

Wall's study offers insight into the gendered aspects of this process, and shows how the family home created a separate female sphere in the city especially as women took control of the moral authority of the household. The process of isolating and symbolizing certain bodies in social space is key to her analysis. Both through the location of women and their actions as household managers, the separate home served a middle class seeking to publicly demonstrate a highly gendered sense of respectability. While Wall does not consider race in her study, she nevertheless describes a white pattern of settlement in the context of a multi-racial city. African Americans, New York's most visible minority, did not follow their more well-off white neighbors to the city's fringe, nor were they invited. As such, a next step is to ask how separate homes and workplaces speak to the racial as well as the class and gendered concerns of those who adopted this new life during the emancipation era.

In fact, this settlement pattern was elaborated at King Manor and because the site has a history of slavery, I consider the settlement transformation there in light of the racial dynamics of emancipation. I mentioned previously that Rufus King was known for his Federalist anti-slavery politics (Ernst 1968). Specifically, he is credited with leading the effort to ban the expansion of slavery to the Northwest Territories in 1785, and later in his career he became famous for his anti-slavery speeches in 1820 during the Senate's Missouri Compromise debates. Still, while his politics were anti-slavery, King grew up with slaves in his childhood home in Massachusetts and owned slaves as an adult prior to moving to Jamaica (Ernst 1968). Additionally, many of his neighbors, friends, and peers

in Queens and elsewhere in New York remained slave owners during the era of gradual emancipation. As such, prior to their arrival at the site, the Kings knew well the landscapes of northern slavery (Fitts 1996). Looking at how they altered their property shows the differences that their embrace of freedom looked like, and also how they envisioned the world after slavery should be.

Archaeology shows that the Kings' created an emancipation landscape at the site by shifting the locations for household labor (Figure 2). Excavations in several areas around the manor house as well as in the fields where the barns and service sheds once stood show a distinct pattern of change through time. The area most intensively used during the period of slavery was located adjacent to the original kitchen and behind Building K. This area contained a buried living surface layer with a large number of crushed late 18th century creamware and pearlware ceramics as well as a collection of large olive green wine bottle fragments found in sheet deposits located directly behind Building K. The crushed ceramics indicate a frequently used work yard during the time of slavery while the larger glass shards may indicate the illicit consumption of alcohol by enslaved laborers in what was then a hidden space (Matthews 2008; 2010). Based on the distinct lack of early 19th century artifacts in this area, this space ceased to be used with any regularity after the Kings moved to the site. Building the new kitchen at the rear of the service ell, which included the covered lean-to rear addition, they provided instead indoor space for household work. Excavation in the lean-to space in fact produced early and mid-19th century ceramics as well as a large collection of other artifacts indicating an intensively used domestic workspace during the King-era. Archaeological testing in the area of the barns and other service buildings in the north field show that this area was also used only in the 19th century (Grossman 1991). The sum of this evidence indicates that the Kings deliberately created distinct areas for work through new construction that enclosed work spaces near the house and designated other areas for work in the back fields, a lengthy distance from the house.

These findings establish the Kings' embrace of the same settlement idea of separating the home from the workplace found in the city discussed by Wall

(1994). During the time of slavery, African laborers at King Manor worked near the house in view of their master and others in the neighborhood. In the Kings' landscape, by contrast, free laborers worked either inside the new kitchen or lean-to addition or in spaces in and near new barns far removed from the manor house itself. This landscape arguably made the laborers and by extension the labor they performed on behalf of the Kings largely invisible to the public eye and certainly distinct from home space that people would have visually associated solely with the Kings. Like in the city, emancipation at King Manor involved the creation of a home clearly separated from areas at the site devoted to work, but this was a home that was as much the result of the era's racial discourse as it was about class and gender.

Additional meanings of the landscape emerge by tying it to King's federalist politics, which rested on a theory of a competent and autonomous political subject who could navigate the political spheres of federal, state, and local authorities. The new landscape projects this democratic ideal and materializes for the Kings' laborers and peers the idea that the home *should* be separate from work and that all citizens should have a home to return to at the end of the workday. In this light, emancipation was not only about freeing the slaves but also about freeing masters (now more broadly construed as citizens) from a direct association with work and those who did it. This process effectively transformed the workplace—whether a workshop, factory, counting house, or farm—into a politically neutral site where those coming together arrived on their own "free" will as equivalent parties in the production process. Against the backdrop of slavery, this Federalist conception of separation and equivalence was a powerful break from the past, which had integrated political and legal power with the way work was done. After emancipation, masters and laborers were no longer qualitatively distinct by their legal or class status but equivalent except for their quantitative wealth differences at the given moment.

The landscape was also integral to the federalists' racial ideals. One interesting aspect of Rufus King's political career was his support of the American Colonization Society after its founding in 1817 (Burin 2005:18). Colonization was a pseudo-abolitionist effort to create new settlements in West Africa for enslaved African Americans to occupy after their emancipation. Despite a long record of vehemently resisting the spread of slavery to new territories, King seemingly had no trouble joining with others in thinking that free blacks were a threat to America's democracy and thus better removed from, rather than folded into, American society. He offered his assessment on this matter during the contentious New York State constitutional convention in 1821: "As certainly as the children of any white man are citizens, so the children of the black men are citizens; and they, may in time, raise up progeny, which will be disastrous to the other races of this country" (Gellman and Quigly 2003:126-7). The issue, colonizationists believed, was a racially modern sense that African Americans were degraded beyond recovery and that their natural inferiority put the security of the nation as a whole at risk. Adding further justification, King and others likened emancipation and colonization to other early 19th century "internal improvements" like the national bank, turnpikes, canals, and railroads (Burin 2005:17-18). Clearly, emancipation was tied to an imagined landscape that many elites sought to construct.

Documents suggest that the Kings hired both black and white laborers in Jamaica, so his new landscape was not solely for enclosing and hiding black bodies from view. However, the message of the separated home was aimed only at whites, or those that King felt capable of reaching his expectations for citizenship. His support for colonization illustrates a similar approach to space and the emancipation landscape. As African American's racial difference was more than he imagined the system could handle, removing black bodies from view or altogether through colonization simplified his desire for creating a nation of actually equivalent persons.

Yet, while colonization ultimately failed, King also embraced another proposal, whose legacy still colors many popular conceptions about slavery in America. At the same convention in 1821 he argued:

It is now the proud boast of England, that the moment a slave stands upon her soil, breathes her air, he becomes a free man. Yet, we are informed that time was, when England sold

English men into foreign bondage; and that so great was the number of English youths sent for sale to the Irish market, that Ireland passed a non-importation law to keep them out. If this practice of ancient times be almost sunk in oblivion, does not the circumstance encourage us to hope that the enslaving of black men hereafter be forgotten? (in Gellman and Quigley 2003:198).

This wishful sentiment that slavery might be put behind Americans and that racial divisions could be whisked away reveals King's limited recognition of the racism that marked his imagined American future. On the one hand he feared the "disaster" of a black America and on the other he found solace in the absurd idea of forgetting slavery. It is notable that his statement came the same day that another convention delegate claimed quite to the contrary that "the provisions designed to deny black men the right to vote in New York had indelibly imprinted the legacy of slavery on the new constitution" (Gelmann 2006:213). King's statement nevertheless foreshadows northern practice of "disowning slavery," which, as Joanne Melish shows, helped white Northerners to forget their slavery by inventing a history of a "free" North set in opposition to the "slave" South. Notably, this distinction rested on and praised the widespread evidence of white property ownership in the north as the proper basis of a free society as opposed to southern practices that founded a society on human chattel, which not only degraded African Americans but their masters as well. A society of northern white freeholders was an ideal embraced by King since the 1780s and the foundation of the voting franchise established in most northern states after emancipation that excluded the majority of blacks from civic society. It is my contention that we owe modern conflations of "whiteness as property" (Harris 1993; Roediger 1999) to King and his social contemporaries who prized the values of private property and failed to address the problems and legacies of slavery for black citizenship due to a persistent denial of a full black humanity that was, after all, visible before them almost every day.

African Americans in White Public Space

To understand black humanity during the emancipation era we need to ask where African Americans in the early 19th century, many of whom as ex-slaves embodied freedom in its most fundamental way, ended up in the new city of the separate spheres. The problem is that being a minority in a propertied landscape, African Americans are not so easy to find: some remained enslaved and even some of those set free continued to live with their masters; others were recent migrants and lived wherever they could; and as a whole African Americans were much more transient than whites who have to date typically been the *de facto* focus of archaeological study (Wall 1994; Yamin 2001; White 2002). This is why we gain so much by looking at African American public actions, especially parades. But, we need to look to the public sphere not only because that is where we can find them, but also because that is where African Americans put themselves in order that they may be found. Parades reveal a consciousness among African Americans about their marginal, transient, dismissed and invisible presence in early New York, and a *strategic* program of visibility to assert—as black Americans—the legitimacy of their freedom and rightful place on the landscape.

An excellent example of the free black emancipation era landscape relates to the New York Manumission Society (NYMS), a group of elite whites organized to assist African Americans in the transition to freedom. Among the NYMS accomplishments was the founding of the New York African Free School in 1787 (Figure 4). Emphasizing that it was slavery that caused black degradation, the NYMS argued that proper instruction in core white values would naturally bring about black improvement. This paternalistic rationale alienated the black community who naturally rejected assumptions of their inferiority. Most African Americans agreed that education was essential for their improvement and achievement in New York, but they disagreed that an education in white norms best suited their interests. For them the values of the NYMS reflected the very racism that they claimed was the true source of their degradation, more so than slavery ever was. Evidence

Figure 4. New York African Free School Number 2, drawn by P. Reason, 1822. (Courtesy of the General Research & Reference Division, Schomburg Center for Research in Black Culture, the New York Public Library, Astor, Lenox, and Tilden Foundations).

of this racism was documented by a 1788 NYMS committee formed to "consider ways and means to prevent the irregular behavior of free negroes" in order that they remain in the good graces of NYMS "patronage" (Swan 1992:339). It was proposed that:

- All negroes under the society's patronage be registered in a book containing names of the negroes, their ages, places of abode, occupations, and number of male and female children.
- Negroes should report every change of abode and birth and death in their families.

- Trustees can refuse admission to school of children of unregistered negroes.
- That negroes when registered be informed of the benefits derived from the society [and] are not to be extended to any except such as maintain good characters for sobriety and honesty and peaceable and orderly living— and that they be particularly cautioned against admitting servants or slaves to their houses— receiving or purchasing anything from them and against allowing fiddling, dancing, or any noisy entertainment in their houses whereby the tranquility of the neighborhood may be disturbed.

- The committee thinks that a negro should forfeit patronage of the society if some mode of informing others could be devised. Suggests committing the case to writing and placing it in a conspicuous place in the school as a measure that would ... be a warning to the scholars and tend to impress their minds with sentiments of respect for the society. (Swan 1992:339-40).

With these points, we may expand the black landscape from one defined solely by the contrast of transience and shoddy housing with the inspired institutional buildings to one actively framed and experienced as racial subjugation in public space. For one, by seeking to create a register of the city's black population, the NYMS clearly entrusted itself with the surveillance of the community on behalf of all whites. Moreover, the register was tied to the control of everyday public and even private actions. Black sobriety was their concern but so was black celebration and, effectively, happiness, which was to be found in isolated and quiet households that reinforce "the tranquility of the neighborhood" rather than in communal "noisy" celebrations. Finally, we also see how the school buildings meant to inspire learning also served as spaces of social control where warnings to students about the consequences of misbehavior could be posted and instilled.

Accordingly, as historian Robert Swan argues, the failures of the African Free Schools to promote a just space for black education cultivated a racial consciousness especially among free black youth about the depths of their marginality. Because of their frustrations and disappointments with the African Free School, they created a more organized and racially defined activist black New York community consisting of both free and enslaved members. As whites failed to respect black achievement and ignored clamors for statewide manumission after 1785, blacks coalesced and started to act more than ever on their own behalf at the end of the 18th century (Gellman 2006).

The landscape of the city during this period contains increasing evidence of this African American agency. For example, after learning the NYMS would not support a separate black religious society under their auspices, blacks formed their own: the African Methodist Episcopal Zion church in 1796 (Rael 2005:135). Benevolent and mutual aid societies also formed. One of the earliest, the African Society in New York, hosted the enslaved poet and speaker Jupiter Hammon in 1787 who delivered his famous "Address to the Negroes of the State of New York" (Ransom 1970; Swan 1992:341). While these earliest societies did not survive, the African Society for Mutual Relief founded in 1808 remained active until 1945. The African Society was highly concerned with the black image in the white mind requiring of "its members 'upright' deportment and a solid reputation" (Rael 2005:136). Still, its cofounder, William Hamilton (1809), offers a different perspective on the substance of the black community than we get from NYMS:

But my Brethren, mere socialities [sic] is not the object of our formation, but to improve the mind, soften the couch of the sick, to administer an elixir to the afflicted, to befriend the widow, and become the orphan's guardian, and is this not a noble employment, can there be found a better, you ought to be proud to be engaged in such an exercise. It is employment of this kind that raises the man up to the emperium, or highest heaven.

Rather than solely a concern with social control and an interest in the black future, the black community emerges here as interested *and* capable of providing for itself, by providing for its members in need now.

Related to both the early black church and mutual aid societies was a concern for finding a proper place to respect black New Yorkers at death. Having long used what is now known as the "African Burial Ground" along lower Broadway, the community sought out a new space after that land was subdivided in 1790s and built over. A petition from the African Society to establish a cemetery on Christie Street was accepted in 1795. The city agreed to provide £100 towards the £450 purchase price, which the African Society raised on its own. Obviously, building over the African Burial Ground stands as a powerful example of how white power made the black landscape disappear. Moreover, the call for the new cemetery followed soon after a rather torrid compliant in 1788 in which African petitioners accused doctors and students of robbing graves for the purpose of collecting cadavers to study. Obviously, the lack of respect for the dead, both in the past and future, would have angered the black community and further led them to take matters into their own hands (Perry et al. 2006:62-8).

While we see a free black landscape start to emerge in schools, churches, mutual aid societies and a new cemetery, the landscape was also a site for a more active discourse of racial conflict in the city. For example, the 1788 grave robbing complaint was tied to the landscape by a violent social action known now as the Doctor's Riot (Bell 1971). The violence started with the discovery of disturbed graves and dismembered cadavers in medical student labs, which caused public outrage and spurred a riot that terrorized the city for three days. In the end the medical labs were destroyed and three rioters were killed by the militia. While the mob is not described, nor were the abuses perpetrated in the African Burial Ground, it would be surprising if the mob was not interracial. The riot also puts the landscape into motion through the choreographies of street violence. It was the **streets** where the politics of this issue were played out and where some members of the community lost their lives and others restored order. Thus, to fully understand the emancipation landscape, we have to consider both the sites and the connecting tissues that peopled those sites, or the streets—the home of the public sphere.

In order to find early New York's free blacks, one should look to the streets rather than in traditional household archaeological studies. Shane White (2002:35-6) records that before 1820 pockets of black settlement began to appear in the city. However, he also notes that most free blacks lived in deplorable, crowded mixed-race slum neighborhoods in "cellars that filled with filth when it rained" and "back-alley shanties that lacked any amenities." Lacking fair access to property ownership, African Americans have not yet been found in household archaeological collections from emancipation-era New York. This is not to deny that an archaeology of black households in early New York is possible, only that this data does not yet exist. With the good fortune that accompanies much of New York City's historical archaeology, emancipation era

African American sites may yet come to light. In fact, archaeologists have produced some very compelling and important studies of African Americans in New York from the periods before and after the emancipation era. For example, we have learned a great deal about African New Yorkers from the findings of the African Burial Ground project (Blakey and Rankin-Hill 2004; Perry et al. 2006) as well as a study of Africanisms by Wall (2000). New research by Diana Wall and Anne-Marie Cantwell (2010) also explores evidence associated with Africans in New Amsterdam. For later periods, archaeology has researched the late 19th century African American communities of Weeksville in Brooklyn (Henn 1981; Geismar 2010) and Sandy Ground in Staten Island (Askins 1985). Diana Wall and Nan Rothschild have also laid the groundwork for upcoming excavations at the site of Seneca Village, a mixed-race mid-19th century community formerly located in what is now Central Park (Wall et al. 2004). As of yet, however, emancipation-era African American life remains archaeologically unknown.

The written record of African American public actions is very rich and provides a fine sense of their political and cultural lives as an oppressed yet emergent minority community. The city streets provided black New Yorkers the opportunity to express themselves in parades and other public events held in view of the white majority, and they did so regularly. Moreover, parades helped to further establish their African and black identities and equally their claim to belonging and ultimately citizenship in America. Parades also reveal the underlying racial animus African Americans negotiated every day.

The earliest recorded African American parade was on July 5th, 1800 to celebrate the one-year anniversary of the 1799 gradual emancipation act. With "grand marshals, uniforms, banners, and music" (Swan 1992:343), the large parade had the same material trappings and pomp and thus appeared the same as any white parade already known to New Yorkers. The effort and expense put into a parade that stood equal to those of the whites demonstrated the substance of the black community, challenging dominant assumptions about their degraded condition. Aspects of this parade emphasize the confrontational politics that parades produced. First, the organizers of the 1800 parade asked the well-known Pierre Toussaint to be grand marshal, and though Toussaint declined, the invitation is telling. Toussaint was an enslaved Haitian who had come to New York with his master, Jean Berard, in 1787. After later losing their fortune in the Haitian Revolution, the Berards remained in New York. To support themselves they apprenticed Toussiant to a hairdresser, where he learned the trade and rapidly became quite well-known and wealthy while still enslaved (S.V.D.P. Management, Inc. 2004). As Toussaint was not freed until 1807, the request for him to be grand marshal was a call to put a slave at the head of the emancipation commemoration parade. Perhaps the organizers wanted to put a black Haitian on public display, and they certainly sought to put up a slave as someone capable of leading the community. With Toussaint as an example, they hoped to use the parade to make the public statement that it was less slavery than racism that degraded blacks.

The second part of the 1800 parade that stands out is the date: July 5th. The parade followed after a series of July 4th Independence Day activities held by whites in the city. With the streets dominated by the Tammany Society and other white merchant and mechanic organization parades, July 4th festivities were declared unsuitable for African American celebrations. So, African American revelers seized the very next day to celebrate their freedom. In so doing 5 July became a traditional "Black Independence Day" and set black New Yorkers to creating their own ritual calendar for marking the passing achievements of their lives. The date also put forward the awkward juxtaposition of having two freedoms in American life, one black and one white, a declaration that thoroughly criticized assimilationist efforts to make them adhere to white norms and exclusionary efforts to deny them—as black Americans—a legitimate place on the landscape (Sweet 1976:265-66).

The decision to parade in 1800 was informed by other factors as well, some of which reflect African American heritage. It was common for northern enslaved communities in the 18th century to celebrate at festivals such as Negro Elections, Pinkster, and Negro Militia or Training Days, which brought African Americans together on specific days for rituals, performances, contests, and other pleasurable activities (Wade 1981,

Piersen 1988, Lott 1995, White 1994, Williams-Meyers 1994, Rael 2002, Kachun 2003). After emancipation rural slave festivals declined and were replaced by city parades led by free blacks (White 1994:15,33). The shift in part reflects the migration of free blacks to northern cities whereas the colonial festivals were typically held in the country. Yet, more than just adapting to a new place, emancipation era free blacks inhabited a new setting and lived in new circumstances increasingly framed by race. Denied fair access to the emancipation landscape African Americans sought ways to assert their presence and establish legitimacy to their lives through orderly public actions.

African Americans may also have played off of a related "tradition" of racial violence associated with black public actions in early America. Historian Shane White records that blacks enjoyed election day on the Boston Common as they were free to drink, gamble, and dance without trouble. This varied from other days where such visible enjoyments would have been cause for whites, as remembered by theater man Sol Smith, to "chase all the niggers off the common" (White 1994:17). The guarantee of open white hostility towards organized black visibility may have been a counter-intuitive reason to parade. African American parades were apt to bring out crowds of whites who verbally and physically assaulted black revelers. Parades were "followed by the rabble; hissed, hooted, and groaned at every turn, and one would suppose that Bedlam had broken loose" recollected *The Liberator* in 1847 (White 1994:38). Similarly, "coachmen and carters were notorious for mean-spiritedly and often dangerously driving their vehicles through black processions in order to disrupt them" (White 2002:64). Disorder, in other words, was part of the black parades even if those marching were orderly. This suggests an African American strategy to create a visible opposition between themselves as orderly ranks of marchers in military uniforms and regalia next to a crowd of jeering, disorderly whites. Even if onlookers were unsympathetic to black interests, no one would miss how the orderly black regiments made the white crowd look to be the problem.

Nevertheless, black celebrants were not always orderly. In at least one instance white harassment in Boston hit its mark and blacks broke rank to fight back

(White 1994:38). Evidence of other disorderly black behavior like drinking, gambling, and singing is also known indicating that parade days were seized by blacks as rare instances of public personal enjoyment. Referring to an upstate New York Pinkster celebration, James Fenimore Cooper described African Americans "beating banjoes, singing African songs, drinking and, worst of all, laughing in a way that seemed to set their very hearts rattling within their ribs" (Rael 2002:58). Such visible black celebrations were alarming to the sensibilities of the white elite. Still, we need to consider that frivolity and festivity in the face of oppressive power may have been one reason for their zeal. The fact that most parades, like the New York parade in 1800, were commemorative also explains their exuberance and celebration. The making of a black ritual calendar for parades commenced in earnest in the early years of the 19th century. Soon after establishing July 5th as emancipation day, in 1808 blacks adopted New Year's Day for parades commemorating the abolition of the foreign slave trade. Starting in 1834, the July 5th celebrations declined as African Americans embraced the celebration of West Indian emancipation on August 1st (Gravely 1982:303-4). It was in favor of the August celebrations that Frederick Douglass directed his famous July 5th, 1852 speech where he asked his Rochester audience: "What, to the American slave, is your 4th of July?" (Sweet 1981:248).

Despite good reasons to celebrate, the problem with any sign of black disorder was that it was essentially twice as visible as that of whites, and parades were closely monitored by both blacks and whites. Historian Patrick Rael (2005:136-7) reports that "In 1809, when New York blacks held such a parade, even their white 'friends' cautioned them against the move. Black New Yorkers would not be denied, however, and proceeded nonetheless." Additional examples of black political assertion through parading are plentiful. This richness is itself evidence that parades supported conceptions of black political agency. As parades occupied the landscape for long stretches in highly visible and politicized arrangements, they demanded recognition and commentary by New Yorkers. Some of these strategies and impressions were described in the 1827 Minutes of the Common Council of the City of New York:

A long procession of black men and boys in rows five or six wide marched behind the major men's associations. African Society members flew brightly colored silk banners and were 'splendidly dressed in scarfs of silk with gold edgings, and with colored bands of music, and the banners appropriately lettered and painted.' The main orator was on horseback with a scroll tightly clasped in his right hand. The grand marshal, Samuel Hardenbaugh, sat atop of white horse trotting beside the procession. Hardenbaugh drew his sword as he led the marchers to City Hall to meet the mayor. 'The sidewalks were crowded with the wives, daughters, sisters, and mothers of the celebrants' (in Wilder 2005:225-6).

Parades, though, were not just statements, they were actions that put black New Yorkers in view of those who found them threatening. Parading tempted fate, and, as parades were public claims by free African Americans to civic belonging, they contributed significantly to New York's developing emancipation era racial discourse. As historian Craig Steven Wilder (2005:225) writes:

It was in the very public spaces that white New Yorkers expressed themselves most violently in defense of the racial order. In 1807, a committee planning black New York's celebration of the impending end of the United States participation in the slave trade had to petition the city council for a 'sufficient number of peace officers' to protect the celebrants. An 1809 parade honoring the African Society for Mutual Relief's first anniversary and an 1810 celebration of its incorporation were met with threats of violence and warnings from city officials who refused to grant safety to the participants. 'Secure in their manhood and will,' wrote an antebellum member, 'they did parade.'

African American parades show that "the streets of New York City were every bit as important an arena for racial politics as were the statehouse and the courtroom. Public processions staged African Americans' demands for equality far more effectively than white abolitionists championed black rights" (Rael 2005:136-37). I suggest we take this further and see the streets as essential and integral to the workings of emancipation politics writ large. Streets were not just an alternate site for action, they also fostered a different form of expression of the same discourse and debate that was otherwise contained within the exclusionary walls of government. Walls at sites of power have two sides: one facing inward and enclosing those directly involved in political discussions and another facing outward towards the public whose lives will be effected by the decisions made within. There are times, however, when debate is less about what goes on inside spaces of power than about how the walls themselves are re-positioned and appropriated to create new spaces for social action. The results of legislative acts, court decisions, or presidential proclamations, that is, are not necessarily more empowering or constraining than the public actions that assert alternative and critical opinions, presences, and processes on the street. In this light, African American parades and other actions were constitutive of the emancipation landscape. Parades were neither sideshows nor merely symbolic performances, they constructed the political agency of an African American community who, collectively, demanded recognition. The streets, as the space where newly imagined public lives confronted public power, fostered new meanings and experiences of freedom and of racial modernity that have since driven actions supporting and rejecting an array of programs from Reconstruction to Civil Rights. The streets were not only used but also **made** into spatial crucibles of political and racial conflict. Archaeologists can read these spaces on maps, measure their remains on the ground, and reconstruct them in their interpretations to document how landscapes created the politics that drove history.

Conclusion: Regarding the Noise of Capitalism

By way of conclusion, I want to discuss a final set of examples from New York's emancipation landscape to show the racially modern distinctions that emerged in the antebellum era. In 1859, for example, Frederick Douglass drew on a landscape experience that typified African Americans' emancipation struggle: "No one idea has given rise to more oppression and persecution toward the colored people of this country, than that which makes Africa, not America, their home. It is that wolfish idea that *elbows us off the sidewalk*, and denies us the rights of citizenship [emphasis added]" (Douglass 1859). A key component of the public sphere, sidewalks absorbed the conflicts of emancipation in New York, and in turn became a space that marked America's racially modern resolutions. The 19th century sidewalk was a busy urban space, filled with people moving and socializing as well as the goods merchants and shopkeepers displayed for sale. It was also where one stood to watch African American parades, and it was the space that some stepped down from in order to harass them. The sidewalk was also the space where blacks and whites came into close and at times unwanted contact, as described in the exasperated words from a black woman in 1822, who "wished the yellow fever would kill all the whites, so that [the blacks] might have the sidewalks to themselves" (White 2002:58). In Providence, Rhode Island, in fact, an 1824 race riot ensued when blacks refused to step down from the sidewalk to make way for whites (Gilje 1995:89). The sidewalk also marked the proper space from which to witness the association of private property and the autonomous dignities of citizenship, as at King Manor, and equally the supposed folly of the blacks who claimed a public right to a citizen's dignity on the street. In contrast, for Douglass and other African Americans, the sidewalk was a space of citizenship for all Americans. It was where one could walk as a free person while witnessing the spectacles and experiencing the turmoil of a free society that any citizen could claim as their own. Access to and removal from the sidewalk, in other words, was a significant part of the emerging American democracy.

It is notable that Douglass's criticism was of the African Civilization Society (ACS), a colonization group based in Brooklyn's African American Weeksville community (Bernstein 2005:302). The founding of a black led colonization group illustrates the depths that modern racial differentiation reached in the minds of both whites and blacks by the antebellum era. For members of both races, racial separation was the solution to racial conflict, and thus, we have to interpret that racial mixing, in both its social and sexual senses, lay at the root of the problem. Douglass rejected this as he consistently criticized his exclusion (Stauffer 2004). Yet, there were others who, albeit less politically notable than Douglass, were equally ambivalent about segregation. These were the ones whose livelihood counted on the commerce of amalgamation in places far from the dignities of street or the citizen's home.

The way into these hidden landscapes is to follow the path of Charles Dickens, one of antebellum New York's most famous observers. When Dickens toured the city in 1842 he wrote about lower Broadway. "How quiet the streets are ... are there no punches, fantoccinis, dancing-dogs, jugglers, conjurers, orchestrinas, or even barrel-organs?" (Cook 2003:I:1). Unlike in London, downtown New York after emancipation took on qualities of a segregated urban landscape, which valued privacy over access, separation over integration, quiet over liveliness, and an unmarked dominant whiteness over a visible subordinate blackness. The distinctions Dickens discovered between the New York and London streets show the peculiarity of the American landscape and describe the impact of emancipation and racial modernity that was not known in England. In New York, the struggle to make ends meet and to find a niche for making a living and a life were removed from view. Whether in the new factories or the quiet suburbs, the noise of capitalism in New York seemed orderly or at least kept at bay. Unsatisfied with such a distorted view of urban life, Dickens grew "increasingly impatient" and "quit Broadway above City Hall, 'plunging' himself into an east-side neighborhood known for its amusement of another sort—the infamous Five Points" (Cook 2003:I:1). This amusement was interracial amalgamation.

Five Points presented Dickens with "squalid streets," "wretched beds," "fevered brains," and "heaps of negro women" who force the "rats to move away in search of better lodgings." It also presented Almack's, a renowned black-owned dance cellar whose "welcoming mulatto 'landlady' with 'sparkling eyes' and a 'daintily ornamented' handkerchief [and a] 'landlord' ... with a 'smart blue jacket' and a gleaming gold 'watchguard'" (Cook 2003:I:3) inspired Dickens. His descriptions in *American Notes* made Almack's world famous along with its leading dancer, William Henry Lane, also known as Master Juba (Master Juba 2010) (Figure 5).

Figure 5. Engraving of William Henry Lane, a.k.a. Master Juba, performing at Almack's in New York City. Note the several "sporting men" looking on. (Dickens 1842).

While Dickens' description of Almack's and Lane's rise to fame as a black minstrel are well documented, historian James W. Cook's recent contextual interpretation provides an important perspective for understanding the emancipation landscape. Five Points and other mixed-race poor urban neighborhoods in the United States had taken on part of their aura less because they contained vice, poverty, and crime, all of which were in fact quite obvious, but also because they hid the principle patrons of Almack's and other interracial public houses from view. This was a new sort of urban American: young, white, single, white-collar "sporting men," whose gender, race, income, and desires sustained poor neighborhoods who in turn helped to support the modern basis for an emergent white invisibility.

Pious and licentious, sunshine and shadow, innocent and vulgar, high and low–antebellum sporting culture took root between and across the binary distinctions represented by middle-class conduct manuals as natural and fixed. In this way, sporting men put themselves in close proximity to the "rougher" social worlds of the emerging urban proletariat, and even identified with some of its causes. But the milieux were never simply equivalent. More accurately, they overlapped and intersected–temporarily–in particular urban sites: brothels, saloons, boxing arenas, cockpits, gambling dens, theaters, and dance halls–places, in short, like Almack's (Cook 2003:II:3).

For sporting men, their travels to Five Points were a rite of passage on the way to a respectable middle-class manhood (Stewart 1998:190). For others, the slum was their home, a space in part of their own making but one from which they were increasingly hard pressed to escape. Five Points was the antithesis of the removed and isolated middle class landscapes of the Kings and their protégés in Greenwich Village, but it was a home for the working class nonetheless. The problem was that the interests and activities of sporting men sustained many livelihoods in Five Points. Since sporting men were intentionally hidden from view, reformers and critics found it difficult to fault anyone other than Five Points' visible residents for the spectacles of poverty and vice that characterized the slum (Yamin 2001; Mayne and Murray 2002; Reckner 2002). I have tried to reconnect these communities in order that Five Points is seen not only as a home for landless laborers and racial amalgamators but a place where sporting men—those the system most subsidized by virtue of their race, gender, and aspirations—could enjoy the fruits of their privilege. The key is that their pleasure and patronage came with an expectation of privacy or invisibility that demanded others be positioned in public view.

Because of a tendency to see some actions and actors and not others, this essay has in part used a deep reading of the contexts of the emancipation era to rearticulate the city's neighborhoods, events, and actors with one another in order to see them in dialogue and, more so, as opposite sides of the same coin. This was the coin of American freedom, which defined freedom as being self-contained or self-possessed and, because of wealth and privilege, of being invisible to the eyes of power. In addition, it is against the dominant drive to ignore black visibility that African American parades must be placed. The public positioning of black bodies, in an orderly procession and in the face of disorderly white assault, put on display the issue of emancipation and how African Americans might fit into the public landscape. In contrast, whiteness was expressed by a withdrawal into the private home and away from the active or at least *visibly* active use of public space. This withdrawal did not leave the streets un-signified but established that the whole of the urban landscape was under white surveillance. Whites were free to walk anywhere, even into interracial brothels, yet, they were also free to stay at home where they nonetheless remained visible as the standard of American morality and citizenship. Lacking this legitimate basis for what may be called an invisible-visibility, African Americans struggled to participate in the social discourse and establish their rightful belonging. Bearing the doubled burden of being both formerly enslaved and racially distinct, of being highly visible and at the same time politically invisible, African Americans turned to the streets to perform their presence in the city.

Acknowledgements

I would like to thank Julie Schablitsky, Mark Leone, and Joe Joseph for the invitation to contribute to this collection. In addition to their comments, I also thank Paul Mullins, Jim Moore, Whitney Battle-Baptiste, Robert Paynter, Zoë Burkholder, and Kurt Jordan for the helpful advice on the content and structure of the paper. All shortcomings are of course my own responsibility. My research at King Manor was supported by the Hofstra University Department of Anthropology. I thank Mary Anne Mrozinksi, Kathy Forestall, Roy Fox, David Gary, Jenna Coplin, and Ross Rava for their contributions to this project.

References

ANDREWS, CHARLES C.

1969 [1830]   The History of the New-York African Free Schools, From Their Establishment in 1787, to the Present Time; Embracing a Period of More than Forty Years: Also a Brief Account of the Successful Labors of the New-York Manumission Society. Mahlon Day, New York. Reprint, Negro Universities Press, New York, NY.

ASKINS, WILLIAM.

1991   Oysters and Equality: Nineteenth Century Cultural Resistance in Sandy Ground, Staten Island, New York. Anthropology of Work Review 12(2):7-13.

BELL, WHITFIELD J. JR.

1971   Doctors' Riot, New York, 1788. Bulletin of the New York Academy of Medicine. 47(12):1501-3.

BERLIN, IRA

1998   Many Thousands Gone: The First Two Centuries of Slavery in North America. Belknap Press, Cambridge, MA.

BERNSTEIN, IVER

2005   Securing Freedom: The Challenges of Black Life in Civil War New York. In Slavery in New York, Ira Berlin and Leslie M. Harris, eds., pp. 289-324. The New Press, New York, NY.

BLACKMAR, ELIZABETH

1991   Manhattan for Rent, 1785-1850. Cornell University Press, Ithaca, NY.

BLAKEY, MICHAEL L. AND LESLEY M. RANKIN-HILL (EDITORS)

2004   The New York African Burial Ground Skeletal Biology Final Report. Prepared by Howard University, Washington, D.C. for The United States General Services Administration Northeastern And Caribbean Region.

BROOKS, JOANNA

2005   The Early American Public Sphere and the Emergence of a Black Print Counterpublic. The William and Mary Quarterly 62(1):67-92.

BROWN, BILL (EDITOR)

2004   Things. University of Chicago Press, IL.

BURIN, ERIC

2005   Slavery and the Peculiar Solution: A History of the American Colonization Society. University Press of Florida, Gainesville.

COOK, JAMES W.

2003   Dancing Across the Color Line. Common Place 4(1). http://www.common-place.org/vol-04/no-01/cook/. Accessed 7 Jan. 2011.

DOUGLASS, FREDERICK

1859   African Civilization Society. http://teachingamericanhistory.org/library/index.asp?document=1031. Accessed 7 Jan. 2011.

DUANE, ANNA MAE AND THOMAS THURSTON

2010   The History of the School, Bricks and Mortar. Examination Days: The New York African Free School Collection. New York Historical Society. Available online at https://www.nyhistory.org/web/afs/history/history.html. Accessed 7 Jan. 2011.

EDWARDS, YWONE

1998   "Trash" Revisited: A Comparative Approach to Historical Descriptions and Archaeological Analysis of Slave Houses and Yards. In Keep Your Head to the Sky: Interpreting African American Home Ground, Grey Gundaker, ed. pp. 245-272. University of Virginia Press, Charlottesville, VA.

ERNST, ROBERT

1968   Rufus King: American Federalist. University of North Carolina Press, Chapel Hill.

FENNELL, CHRISTOPHER C.

2007   Crossroads and Cosmologies: Diasporas and Ethnogenesis in the New World. Univeristy Press of Florida, Gainesville, FL.

FERGUSON, LELAND G.

1992   Uncommon Ground: Archaeology and Early African America, 1650-1800. Smithsonian Institution Press, Washington, D.C.

FITTS, ROBERT K

1996   The Landscapes of Northern Bondage. *Historical Archaeology* 32(2):54-73.

FOUCAULT, MICHEL

1976   T*he History of Sexuality Vol. 1: The Will to Knowledge.* Penguin, London, England.

1979   *Discipline and Punish: The Birth of the Prison.* Vintage, New York, NY.

FRASER, NANCY

1990   Rethinking the Public Sphere: A Contribution to the Critique of Actually Existing Democracy. *Social Text* 25/26:56-80.

GEISMAR, JOAN E

2010   Archaeology at Weeksville's Historic Hunterfly Road Houses. Presentation at the Museum of the City of New York, April 24, 2010.

GELLMAN, DAVID N.

2006   *Emancipating New York: The Politics of Slavery and Freedom, 1777-1827.* Louisiana State University Press, Baton Rouge.

GELLMAN, DAVID N. AND DAVID QUIGLEY (EDITORS)

2003   *Jim Crow New York: A Documentary History of Race and Citizenship, 1777-1877.* New York University Press, NY.

GILJE, PAUL A.

1987   *The Road to Mobocracy: Popular Disorder in New York City, 1763-1834.* University of North Carolina Press, Chapel Hill.

GRAVELY, WILLIAM B.

1982   The Dialectic of Double-Consciousness in Black American Freedom Celebrations, 1808-1863. *The Journal of Negro History* 67(4):302-317.

GROSSMAN, JOEL W.

1991   Archaeological Tests and Artifact Analysis Results from Rufus King Park, Jamaica, Queens, New York. Prepared for Land-Site Contracting Corp. On File, King Manor Museum, New York, NY.

HABERMAS, JURGEN

1991   *The Structural Transformation of the Public Sphere: An Inquiry into a Category of Bourgeois Society.* MIT Press, Cambridge, MA.

HAGE, GHASSON

2000   *White Nation: Fantasies of White Supremacy in a Multicultural Society.* Routledge, New York, NY.

HAMILTON, WILLIAM

1809   Address to the New York African Mutual Relief Society. Available online at http://nationalhumanities.center.org/pds/maai/community/text5/hamiltonmutualbenefit.pdf. Accessed 7 Jan. 2011.

HARRIS, CHERYL I.

1993   Whiteness as Property. *Harvard Law Review* 106(8):1707-1791.

HENN, ROSELLE

1981   The Weeksville Historical Archaeological Research Project: A Progress Report and Proposal for Future Research. Manuscript. The City College of New York/Weeksville Heritage Center.

HILL, JANE H.

1998   Language, race, and white public space. *American Anthropologist* 100 (3):680-689.

2008   *The Everyday Language of White Racism.* Wiley-Blackwell, New York, NY.

JOYCE, ROSEMARY

2009   *Ancient Bodies, Ancient Lives: Sex, Gender, and Archaeology.* Thames and Hudson, New York, NY.

KACHUN, MITCH

2003   *Festivals of Freedom: Memory and Meaning in African American Emancipation Celebrations, 1808-1915.* University of Massachusetts Press, Amherst.

LA ROCHE, CHERYL J. AND MICHAEL L. BLAKEY

1997   Seizing Intellectual Power: The Dialogue at the New York African Burial Ground. *Historical Archaeology* 31(3):84-106.

LEONE, MARK P.
2005   *The Archaeology of Liberty in an American Capital: Excavations in Annapolis*. University of California Press, Berkeley.

LOTT, ERIC
1995   *Love and Theft: Blackface Minstrelsy and the American Working Class*. Oxford University Press, New York.

MASTER JUBA
2010   Master Juba: The Inventor of Tap Dancing. http://www.masterjuba.com/. Accessed 7 Jan. 2011.

MATTHEWS, CHRISTOPHER N.
2008   Report of 2004-2006 Archaeological Investigations at the Rufus King Manor Site (81.01.11) in Jamaica, Queens, New York. Report on file, Center for Public Archaeology, Hofstra University, NY.
2010   Freedom as Negotiated History, Or an Alternative Sort of Event: The Transformation of Home, Work, and Self in Early New York. In *Eventful Archaeologies*. Douglas Bolender, ed., pp. 199-215, SUNY Press, NY.

MAYNE, ALAN AND TIM MURRAY (EDITORS)
2002   *The Archaeology of Urban Landscapes: Explorations in Slumland*. Cambridge University Press, MA.

McMANUS, EDWARD J.
1966   *A History of Negro Slavery in New York*. Syracuse University Press, NY.

MELISH, JOANNE POPE
1998   *Disowning Slavery: Gradual Emancipation and Race in New England, 1780-1860*. Cornell University Press, Ithaca, NY.

MILLER, DANIEL (EDITOR)
2005   *Materiality*. Duke University Press, Durham, NC.

OLSEN, BJØRNAR
2003   Material Culture After Text: Remembering Things. *Norwegian Archaeological Review* 36(3):87-104.

PAGE, HELAN AND R. BROOK THOMAS
1994   White Public Space and the Construction of White Privilege in U.S. Health Care: Fresh Concepts and a New Model of Analysis. *Medical Anthropology Quarterly* 8:109-116.

PERRY, WARREN R., JEAN HOWSON, AND BARBARA A. BIANCO (EDITORS)
2006   New York African Burial Ground Archaeology Final Report. Prepared by Howard University, Washington, D.C. for The United States General Services Administration Northeastern And Caribbean Region.

PIERSEN, WILLIAM D.
1988   *Black Yankees: The Development of an Afro-American Subculture in Eighteenth-Century New England*. University of Massachusetts Press, Amherst.

RAEL, PATRICK
2002   *Black Identity and Black Protest in the Antebellum North*. University of North Carolina Press, Chapel Hill.
2005   The Long Death of Slavery. In *Slavery in New York*, Ira Berlin and Leslie M. Harris, eds., pp. 111-146. The New Press, NY.

RANSOM, STANLEY A. (EDITOR)
1970   *America's First Negro Poet, The Complete Works of Jupiter Hammon of Long Island*. Kennikat Press, Port Washington, NY.

RECKNER, PAUL
2002   Remembering Gotham: Urban Legends, Public History, and Representations of Poverty, Crime, and Race in New York City. *International Journal of Historical Archaeology* 6(2):95–112.

ROEDIGER, DAVID R.
1999   The Pursuit of Whiteness: Property, Terror, and Expansion, 1790-1860. *Journal of the Early Republic* 19(4): 579-600.

S.V.D.P. MANAGEMENT, INC.
2004   Venerable Pierre Toussaint. http://www.toussaintacademy.org/pierretoussaint.html. Accessed 7 Jan. 2011.

SINGLETON, THERESA A. (EDITOR)
1999   *"I, too, am America": Archaeological Studies of African-American Life*. University of Virginia Press, Charlottesville.

STAUFFER, JOHN
2004 *The Black Hearts of Men: Radical Abolitionists and the Transformation of Race.* Harvard University Press, Cambridge, MA.

STEWART, JAMES BREWER
1998 The Emergence of Racial Modernity and the Rise of the White North, 1790-1840. *Journal of the Early Republic* 18(2): 181-217.
1999 Modernizing "Difference": The Political Meanings of Color in the Free United States, 1776-1840. *Journal of the Early Republic* 19(4): 691-712.

SWAN, ROBERT J.
1992 John Teasman: African-American Educator and the Emergence of Community in Early Black New York City, 1787-1815. *Journal of the Early Republic* 12(3):331-356.

SWEET, LEONARD I.
1976 The Fourth of July and Black Americans in the Nineteenth Century: Northern Leadership Opinion Within the Context of the Black Experience. *Journal of Negro History* 61(3):256-275.
1981 *Black Images of America, 1784-1870.* W. W. Norton, New York.

THOMPSON, EDWARD P.
1963 *The Making of the English Working Class.* Vintage, New York, NY.

U.S. FEDERAL CENSUS
1790 Jamaica, Queens, New York, Roll M637_6, Page 28, Image 380; Family History Library Film 0568146.
1800 Jamaica, Queens, New York, Roll 25, Page 544, Image 137; Family History Library Film 193713.

WADE, MELVIN
1981 "Shining in Borrowed Plumage": Affirmation of Community in the Black Coronation Festivals of New England (c. 1750-c. 1850). *Western Folklore* 40(3): 211-231.

WALL, DIANA DIZEREGA
1994 *The Archaeology of Gender: Separating the Spheres in Urban America.* Plenum Press, New York, NY.

2000 Twenty Years After: Re-examining Archaeological Collections for Evidence of New York City's Colonial African Past. *African-American Archaeology*, Number 28. http://www.diaspora.uiuc.edu/A-AAnewsletter/newsletter28.html#anchor14439436. Accessed, 7 Jan. 2011.

WALL, DIANA DIZEREGA AND ANNE-MARIE CANTWELL
2010 Africans in 17th Century New York. Paper presented at the 2010 meetings of the Council for Northeast Historical Archaeology. Lancaster, PA.

WALL, DIANA DIZEREGA, NAN A. ROTHSCHILD, CYNTHIA COPELAND, AND HERBERT SEIGNORET
2004 The Seneca Village Project: Working with Modern Communities in Creating the Past. In *Places in Mind: Public Archaeology as Applied Anthropology*, Paul A. Shackel and Erve J. Chambers, eds., pp.101-118. Routledge, NY.

WHITE, SHANE
1991 *Somewhat More Independent: The End of Slavery in New York City, 1770-1810.* University of Georgia, Press, Athens.
1994 "It Was a Proud Day": African Americans, Festivals, and Parades in the North, 1741-1834. *Journal of American History* 81(1):13-50.
2002 *Stories of Freedom in Black New York.* Harvard University Press, Cambridge, MA.
2005 Black Life in Freedom: Creating a Popular Culture. In *Slavery in New York,* Ira Berlin and Leslie M. Harris, eds., pp. 147-180. The New Press, New York, NY.

WILDER, CRAIG STEVEN
2005 Black Life in Freedom: Creating a Civic Culture. In *Slavery in New York,* Ira Berlin and Leslie M. Harris, eds., pp. 215-238. The New Press, New York, NY.

WILENTZ, SEAN
1984 *Chants Democratic: New York City and the Rise of the American Working Class, 1788-1850.* Oxford University Press, New York, NY.

WILLIAMS-MEYERS, A. J.

1994   *Long Hammering: Essays on the Forging of an African*
            American Presence in the Hudson River Valley to the
            Early Twentieth Century. Africa World Press, Trenton.

YAMIN, REBECCA (EDITOR)

2001   Becoming New York: The Five Points Neighborhood.
            Historical Archaeology 35(3).

Christopher N. Matthews
Department of Anthropology
Hofstra University
Hempstead, NY 11549 USA

Matthew M. Palus

Networked Infrastructure as the Material Culture of Liberal Government

...the finality of government resides in the things it manages and in the pursuit of the perfection and intensification of the processes which it directs; and the instruments of government, instead of being laws, now come to be a range of multiform tactics...
-Foucault (1991:95)

ABSTRACT

Foucault's theory of governmentality describes the emergence of economic liberalism, from the Enlightenment to its most modern expressions. In governmentality Foucault brings together seemingly opposed historical trends, specifically the conditions for liberalization of the political economy, but also the expansion and intensification of governmental authority and instrumentation. These concepts and tensions provide a useful framework for approaching the archaeology of networked infrastructure. Infrastructure is central to the operation of government, and its history coincides with the history of capitalism and the engagement between democracy and liberalism. Using historical archaeological data, I explore these themes in the context of infrastructural expansion in and around the city of Annapolis, Maryland, during the later 19th and early 20th centuries.

Introduction

Michel Foucault (1991) and others writing on "governmentality" have defined the elements of classical liberalism as it emerged in Western Europe and in the United States, and as it manifests in present-day society.

Archaeological evidence for the installation of infrastructural networks in Annapolis, Maryland reveals a transition from patronage towards liberalism as distinct styles of municipal government. Furthermore, it shows clear inequalities in access to services, and therefore the uneven application of governmental power across different neighborhoods and racially bounded communities. It is difficult to reconcile the understanding of liberalism that is promoted by Foucault's notion of governmentality from discussions of neoliberal policies in the contemporary globalizing economy (Ferguson and Gupta 2002; McCarthy and Prudham 2004; Castree 2006; Jeffrey 2007; Harris 2009). For Foucault, liberalism signifies a pervading governmental apparatus of knowledge and control that is directed at sustaining economic growth. Neoliberalism, in contrast, references the privatization of once public assets, among other things. David Harvey (2007:65) has recently written that under neoliberal theory, economic growth and general prosperity "can best be secured through free markets and free trade. Neoliberals are particularly assiduous in seeking the privatization of assets... Sectors formerly run or regulated by the state must be turned over to the private sphere and be deregulated [or] freed from any state interference". At the same time, Harvey (2007:69) writes that "neoliberals have put strong limits on democratic governance," creating "the paradox of intense state interventions and government by elites and 'experts' in a world where the state is supposed not to be interventionist [emphasis in original]."

This aspect of governmentality is as important as any other, in that the historical trend towards liberalism may run counter to democracy. The manner in which government expands and intensifies tends to separate the operations of government from democratic processes, and instead isolates them amidst policies and apparatuses that are ultimately the product of technical knowledge and expertise. Harvey sees the trend towards liberalism, or neoliberalism in the present moment of capitalism, as a trend away from democratic governance; liberalism promotes the rule of experts, and constrains and confines democratic processes by replacing those processes with technical ones. In this sense, inquiry into 20th century governmentality is simultaneously an inquiry into the historical condition of, and outlook for, democracy.

Our contemporary experiences with privatization, deregulation, and capital mobility underscore the paradox that David Harvey presents in the passage above: between the expansion of state apparatuses, and the pursuit of an economic theory that favors a market free from overt regulation. Foucault actually describes an historical origin for this state of intensive interventions, micro-scale regulation, and authority vested in the expertise of social scientists, chiefly statisticians and economists. I believe that the paradox Harvey identifies is not a new one; rather it is one of the contradictory conditions that is underpinned by liberal thought and new techniques for governing a modern capitalist society. Over the later 19th and early 20th centuries, infrastructural development yields an opportunity for archaeologists to describe the materialization of government under economic liberalism. In this way we can use archaeology to reconnect these seemingly separate moments in the historical advance of capitalism, seeing continuity between the development of classical liberalism during the 19th century and the emergence of neoliberalism in recent decades.

The term "infrastructure" can describe most of the built environment, and includes structures and networks that are owned publicly, or owned privately and operated for profit, such as railroads, ports, highways, and other aspects of transportation, facilities for the generation and transmission of power, communications, water, sanitation, and so forth. Economic growth and the very organization of modern industrial society rely on these systems. We can also speak of a "soft infrastructure" (Niskanen 1991), referring to the legal and discursive frameworks that support the economy in ways that are homologous to the physical infrastructure: codes and courts, accounting functions, and certain cultural dispositions and social forms that are no less central to production. In this essay, I primarily discuss municipal services as "networked infrastructure" (Graham and Marvin 2001; Neuman 2006): technical systems that connect people to utilities, like electricity, gas, telecommunications, clean water, sanitary sewers, and other public services. This infrastructure is an artifact; there are social forms that assemble in and around these networks, and I am particularly interested in those routines that are implicated in governance. My objective is to situate networked infrastructure as a component of government, and show how it reflects a transformation of government in the United States.

Specifically, I focus on the expansion of sanitary systems in Annapolis following the Civil War and throughout the first half of the 20th century. I then discuss the expansion of sewer and water infrastructure into a neighboring community called Eastport, located just outside of the historical jurisdiction of Annapolis, on a peninsula to the south called Horn Point (Figure 1). The village of Eastport was part of a nearly five square mile area that was annexed into Annapolis in 1951 (*Evening Capital* 1951a), and I argue that water and sanitary infrastructures were material components of Eastport's annexation. In this perspective, annexation was not simply the result of a referendum vote, but rather an extended process of embedding the Eastport community within the infrastructural network of Annapolis.

Students participating in the Archaeology in Annapolis field school excavated at the homes of immigrants, African Americans, and white families in Eastport from 2001 to 2004. There are clear differences in the development of infrastructure in Eastport and Annapolis. The disparity between these two areas provides evidence of deepening governmentality in Annapolis and the dramatic expansion of the apparatuses for governing during the decades preceding Eastport's annexation. Further, these data show how different segments of the Eastport community engaged the infrastructure as material connections to Annapolis government. Sanitary infrastructure introduced to the Eastport neighborhood was clearly racialized, and at mid-century a significant proportion of African American households in the neighborhood were not connected to municipal water or sewers (Palus 2011).

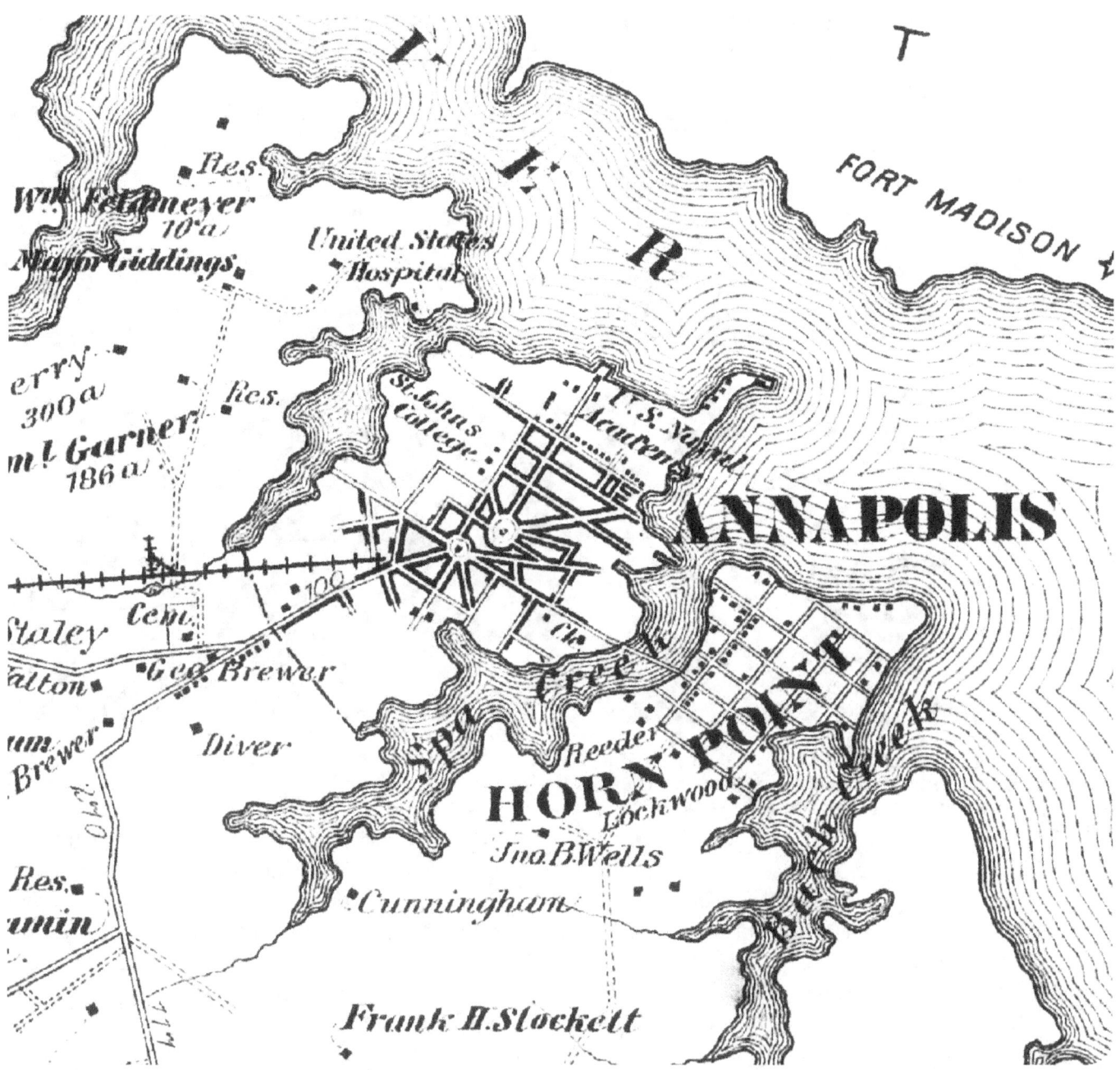

Figure 1. Detail from 1878 atlas showing relative development in Annapolis and Eastport, then called Horn Point (Hopkins 1878).

Archaeological Approaches to Sanitation Infrastructure

Although always anticipated, urban archaeologists consider buried utility lines as sources of disturbance, rather than as significant archaeological data. In fact, some of these utilities are known and identified for us before we dig in order to protect this infrastructure from damage. I say some, because there are always unexpected finds, precisely because the historical infrastructure is not well documented. Most of the utilities we find beneath the ground are a cipher, and we often have no way of knowing precisely what they once accomplished, where they come from, or where they go. Their relevance to the sites we investigate is not always clear, and despite growing interest in 20th century archaeological contexts, utility lines are frequently dismissed out of

Figure 2. View of stratigraphy associated with terra cotta sewer pipes exposed during excavation on Market Space in Annapolis in 2008. (Photograph by the author; courtesy of Archaeology in Annapolis).

hand, as inconvenient and unfortunate disturbances to older strata. Active infrastructural networks lay alongside abandoned, derelict networks that remain from the earliest efforts at modernization, such as 19th century sanitation reform, or street lighting. These are truly archaeological (sometimes the in-use networks are so decayed and antiquated that they too should be called archaeological), and yet none of it means anything to us, except in its stratigraphic associations and terminus post quem markers (Myers 2010) (Figure 2). In most cases, our real objective lies between and underneath these features. There are many reasons why underground utilities evoke such limited interest. Ubiquity is one, and the sense that these features are too recent to trouble over, but another more subtle explanation is the absence of a conceptual framework that places utilities in an interesting and data-producing context.

Sanitation Reform

One of the most significant accomplishments of North American urban archaeology is the production of a compelling contextual framework for understanding the historical campaign of sanitation reformers during the 19th and early 20th centuries to eradicate cesspools, fill privies, cap contaminated wells, and pursue similar measures that would ultimately contribute to improvements in public health. Volumes have been written addressing the historical movements for urban improvement and reform (Geismar and Janowitz 1993; Wheeler 2000b). In broad strokes, the apparent relationship between "miasma" or filth, and diseases like cholera, yellow fever, and typhoid prompted municipal governments to regulate the method of privy construction and maintenance during the mid-19th century, and later to enact proscriptions against privies, sinks, and cesspools (Melosi 2000:58). These steps were initially taken to prevent contamination of well water, but wells themselves were soon seen as dangers to public health. Subscriptions to municipal water and sewer services were made mandatory during the early 20th century in many U.S. cities. Wells were filled or capped to prevent them from being packed with waste, completing a reorganization of the metabolism of the city. Inspection and surveillance by health officials became commonplace, and local, regional, and state governments collected data that reinscribed perceptions of public health and its maintenance (Mrozowski et al. 1989; Howson 1992/1993; Geismar and Janowitz 1993; Demeter 1994; Ford 1994; Stottman 1995, 2000; Rosenswig 1999; Carnes-McNaughton and Harper 2000; Crane 2000; McCarthy and Ward 2000; Peña and Denmon 2000; Wheeler 2000a; Meyer 2004). Health and sanitation also have ideological importance, and public health discourse became a field for underscoring class, race, and ethnic differences and legitimizing discrimination on those bases. Indeed, there is a direct relationship between unequal investment in infrastructure and the displacements of powerless people associated with urban renewal later in the 20th century (Schuyler 2002; Mullins 2003, 2006).

Urban archaeology has been in part defined by the rediscovery of these historical improvement projects, as well as the processes of renewal and redevelopment. Our chronologically sensitive excavation methods, combined with nuanced readings of municipal ordinances and the broader historical discourses on public health and hygiene, have provided a sturdy framework for thinking about the infrastructure, especially sanitation infrastructure. This framework has not come from direct analysis of the apparatuses that manifested reformers' ideals of sanitation, but from reviewing the historical infrastructure that is abandoned in the face of sanitation reform. In zones of disinvestment where well and privy features are abandoned much later, our traditional methods and frameworks for studying 19th-century sites still work. But, 20th century contexts are still waiting for a framework that will make sense of networked infrastructure, something that will make these features more than a conclusion to the urban archaeological record, not a punchline that comes at the end of the 19th century, but a research problem that will produce new interest in the 20th century. Geographers Stephen Graham and Simon Martin (2001:34) write:

Because much of contemporary urban life is precisely about the widening and intensifying use of networked infrastructures to extend social power, the study of the configuration, management and use of such networks needs to be at the centre, not the periphery, of our theories and analyses of the city and the metropolis.

I agree with their perspective, that networks are a dominant characteristic of cities, perhaps even definitive of cities, and that urban history is "punctuated" by a series of attempts to expand infrastructural networks both within and between cities (Graham and Marvin 2001:9). The suggestion that networked infrastructure embeds social power into substantive technical systems is also an important one, a suggestion that will lead me again to Foucault and his ideas about governmental power in the context of liberal economic thought.

Infrastructural Expansion and Exclusion

Any theory addressing the historical expansion of infrastructure must also treat the fact that some people are excluded or significantly delayed from connecting to these networks. My own interest in public utilities and their meaning formed around a historic dwelling in Annapolis that was condemned by the city around 1957, primarily because it was not connected with municipal sewers. Today the dwelling is called Shiplap House, named for the style of the wood siding on the early 18th century structure. The Shiplap House was not razed, but rather restored by the Historic Annapolis Foundation (HAF) soon after the group was founded in 1954, and before it became the premier preservation advocacy group in the city (*Sunday Star* 1957). I learned about Shiplap House from the staff of HAF and also from my own research on the early historic preservation movement in Annapolis. When the house was acquired by HAF it was occupied by four families dwelling in separate apartments. Within months, the building was condemned, the families were moved out, and the restoration of Shiplap House became a demonstration project for historic preservationists in the city (*Evening*

Capital 1958). As I learned about the history of Shiplap House, I wondered how it was possible to be "off the grid" in a mid-20th century city. I initially neglected to consider structuring factors like race or class, social constructs that clearly effect access to public services in complicated ways even today. I reasoned that public services infrastructure was an expression of power, and that the "powers at work" would not permit anyone to opt out of the infrastructure. The condemnation of Shiplap House expresses another aspect of power, which also rests on the authority of municipal government. But, how was Shiplap House left disconnected from the sanitary infrastructure for so long (Palus 2009:10-13)?

The literature on privy construction and abandonment typically presents individuals who either consciously postpone compliance with new sanitation ordinances, or are prevented from accessing sanitary infrastructure as a dimension of their poverty. Indeed, poverty and powerlessness are real conditions of urban life, yet seeing infrastructural connections only as a relative measure of wealth and poverty is problematic (Palus 2011). The sophisticated approaches to consumption in historical archaeology should apply to this question: we can no longer interpret an assemblage of artifacts as a direct indication of economic status, or see individuals consuming to the utmost of their capability (Cook et al. 1996; Wurst and McGuire 1999). Ford (1994) stands out for his recognition of the possibility that disconnection might signal distancing from social control and regulation. In his study of sanitation reform and its archaeological traces in the Lower Town of Harpers Ferry, West Virginia, Ford reads sanitary infrastructure as an active engagement with new social norms that emerged from 19th century health reform movements. This framework leads Ford towards two interpretations. First, he argues that improved sanitation reinscribed class boundaries and created a new stage for social competition among the town's elite and middle class (1994:57-58). Second, while Ford recognizes that embracing new sanitary infrastructure in Harpers Ferry signaled economic prosperity, he rejects the notion that economic factors were central in determining the pace of infrastructural expansion, that making connections to the infrastructure is primarily about what it costs (1994:59).

Historic Context for Sewer Infrastructure in Annapolis

Annapolis is a medium-sized city on the Severn River, one of seven rivers flowing east that contribute to the vast estuary of the Chesapeake Bay. The city was settled during the 17th century, and became the capital for the Maryland colony in 1694. During the 18th century this port town was considered an economic power as well as a political center for the colony. By the early 19th century Maryland's capital city was overshadowed economically by Baltimore to the north, a city then known for its industrial development and deep water port (Leone 2005:5-6). Events in Annapolis during the 19th and early 20th centuries, including its reconfiguration as a historic city and a showcase for Maryland's colonial heritage, even its eventual gentrification, occur against a backdrop of deep economic fretfulness. Matthews (2002) describes the earliest efforts to modernize Annapolis as explicit attempts to tie the city more securely into the political economy for the region, in terms of transit and shipping, but also in the construction of urban infrastructure to attract industry. Elites in Annapolis invested in the industrialization of light and water, with the establishment of gas light and municipal water utilities during the mid 19th century (Matthews 2002:23-25, 99-113). An extensive infrastructural network developed in Annapolis over the second half of the 19th century and the first part of the 20th, but on a much smaller scale than neighboring Baltimore or Washington DC (Figure 3).

In my research on public utilities in Annapolis I have worked to promote a framework that sees infrastructural expansion as a register for governmentalization, interpreting these networks as vehicles for the intensification of governance, a kind of social control that lives both at the point of articulation with the network, but also in the discursive products and the kinds of knowledge that support the operations of this infrastructure. Municipal government in Annapolis as well as other U.S. cities transformed over the period of infrastructural expansion, roughly from the 1850s to the 1930s, and it shifts incrementally from a patronage system to a more bureaucratic and technical mode of

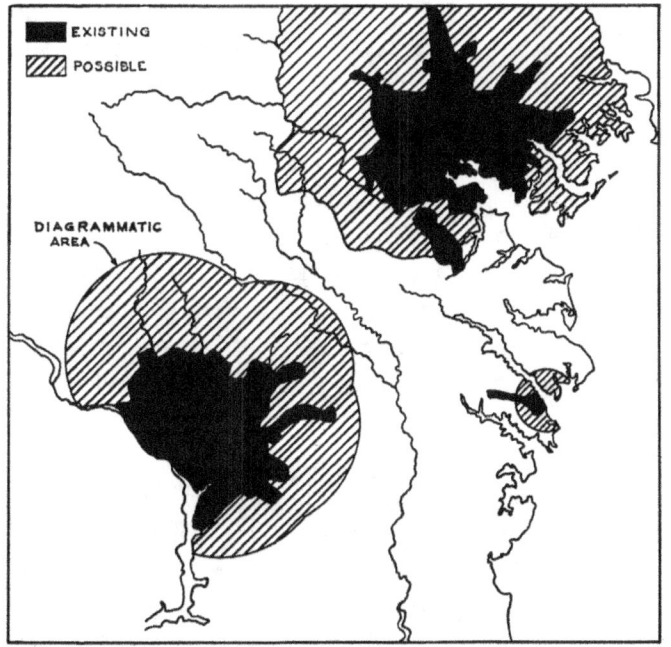
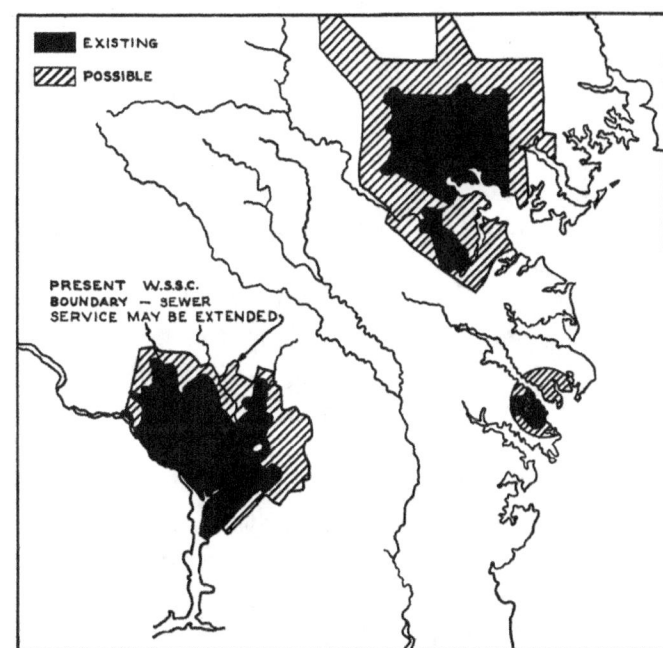

WATER SERVICE AREAS　　　　　**SEWER SERVICE AREAS**

Figure 3. Detail of a regional plan published in 1937, depicting networked water and sewer infrastructure for Annapolis (lower right), Baltimore (upper right), and Washington DC (lower left) (Maryland State Planning Commission 1937:52).

governance. In turn, archaeological and documentary evidence has captured engagements with these governmental forms at different scales of analysis, from households, to neighborhoods, and to the political economy of the region.

The operation of patronage in Annapolis during the later 19th century is in some ways subtle. Because there were no large factories, party politics did not have the same machine-like quality that was seen in Baltimore (Arnold 1978; Euchner 1991). Annapolis does not match Shackel's (1996) vivid accounts of the political *junta* that controlled the town of Harpers Ferry in West Virginia (Shackel and Palus 2010), though certainly many Annapolis elites had financial dealings with one another, invested their money in common, and also served on the city council (Matthews 2002). Still, I stress the paternalistic character of government in Annapolis during the 19th century and even see it expressed in the minutes of the city council's regular meetings.

Euchner (1991) writes that the development of sewerage in Baltimore between 1859 and 1905 was

checked and slowed because patronage produced decentralized decision making in the city government. Each member of the city council promoted the concerns of their ward, improvement projects carried out were local in scale, and no agency existed to promote a wider scope of government until after the city's charter and governing structure were reorganized in 1898. In Annapolis, the minutes of the city council also describe periodic appeals from residents for specific improvements to be made, such as the installation of new sewers or street lighting. Street lighting in particular was apportioned according to the dictates of the city council, which located each lamp and sustained the local electric utility during its early operation (Palus 2005). Sometimes these appeals were presented by residents on their own behalf, and at others, they were offered to the city council by one representative on behalf of an influential constituent from their ward of the city. All such requests were generally referred to the city council's "Committee on Streets," meaning that the outcome would be determined off record. In this way, the infrastructure developed in piecemeal fashion through a series of intercessions and non-intercessions by the city council (Hertzfeld 1992), in contrast with more comprehensively planned improvement projects of the early 20th century.

The corporate proceedings for the city show the creation of a Committee on Streets in 1803, "to superintend the repairs of the streets, the public wharfes (sic), the cleaning of the dock, purchasing of oil and directing the watchmen and lamplighters in their duty subsequently" (Mayor and City Council of Annapolis [MCCA] 1811:162). This committee persisted throughout the 19th and 20th centuries. Corporate proceedings show that most inquiries pertaining to infrastructure were referred to the Street Committee during this period, typically "with power to act". The Street Committee was thus empowered to let contracts, supervise construction, and expend funds from the city coffers. In this capacity it came to anchor the power of the historical patriarchy that gave city government its paternalistic character (Matthews 2002). The Street Committee left no meeting minutes, and only a few construction estimates, receipts and bills, and other minutia are archived with the proceedings of the city council at the Maryland State Archive.

Activities of the Street Committee described in the City Council proceedings during the first half of the 19th century include construction at the city dock, channeling or bridging streams and watercourses within the city, grading streets, laying pavements, curbs and sidewalks, planting shade trees, and similar improvements (Russo 1988, 1991). The earliest effort at sewer building recorded in the proceedings came in 1867. In June of that year, the committee on streets gathered two bids to construct a sewer along Main Street, also known as Church Street, which runs downhill from Church Circle to the city dock (Figure 4). One contractor bid $1,295 to complete a sewer of approximately 300 yds. in length and 18 in. square in section, predominantly built from mortared stone with paving brick for a base. A second bid was submitted to construct a similar sewer of brick with flagstone forming the top of the conduit for $1,125. The proceedings note that a sewer constructed from brick is easier to connect with lateral pipes, while being as durable and secure as stone (MCCA 1869:123). The Main Street sewer was completed by ca.1870. In 1869, amidst this construction, the city's health officer advised that the Main Street sewer be routed away from the city dock; the proceedings specify an outlet within several yards of an oyster packing house on Spa Creek to the south (MCCA 1869:239). It is not known whether the sewer builders accepted this advice, or if they followed the most direct route to the water.

The few municipal sewers that were built in the first decades following the Civil War were added to untold private sewer lines that served individual houses and drained into dry wells, disused privies, or waterways where possible. After the Main Street sewer was completed, a second sewer line was undertaken entirely by property-owning citizens on Hanover Street, which runs along the boundary line between the city and the U.S. Naval Academy (Figure 4). In 1872 the City Council authorized property owners to lay a sewer in the public right-of-way on Hanover Street at their own expense so long as the work was completed before the street was next paved (MCCA 1877:129). However, in 1880 the city sought new powers to levy taxes in the name of infrastructural improvements, which severed this sort of public-private partnership and solidified the city's jurisdiction over public thoroughfares. The city's counselor was directed to draft an act for the Maryland Assembly to amend the city charter, in order to allow the corporation to levy taxes specifically to pay for new sewer construction (MCCA 1886:page illeg.). In 1900 the city obtained further powers from the Maryland Assembly to take on a bond debt to finance infrastructure projects (MCCA 1901:210). The Maryland Assembly passed an act to allow the city to issue $120,000 in bonds to pay off floating debt and raise a fund "for the permanent improvement of said city" (State of Maryland 1900).This large fund created an outlet for patronage relations within the city to express themselves. Like electric street lighting (Palus 2005), new sewer construction followed requests made to the city government, continuing in the pattern established earlier in the 19th century.

The beginnings of sewer construction – and the provisioning of clean water from a municipal reservoir beginning at around the same time – interrupted the traditional metabolism of the city that drew water out of the ground and put waste back into it. The urgent reason to interrupt this cycle is revealed by the mayor's

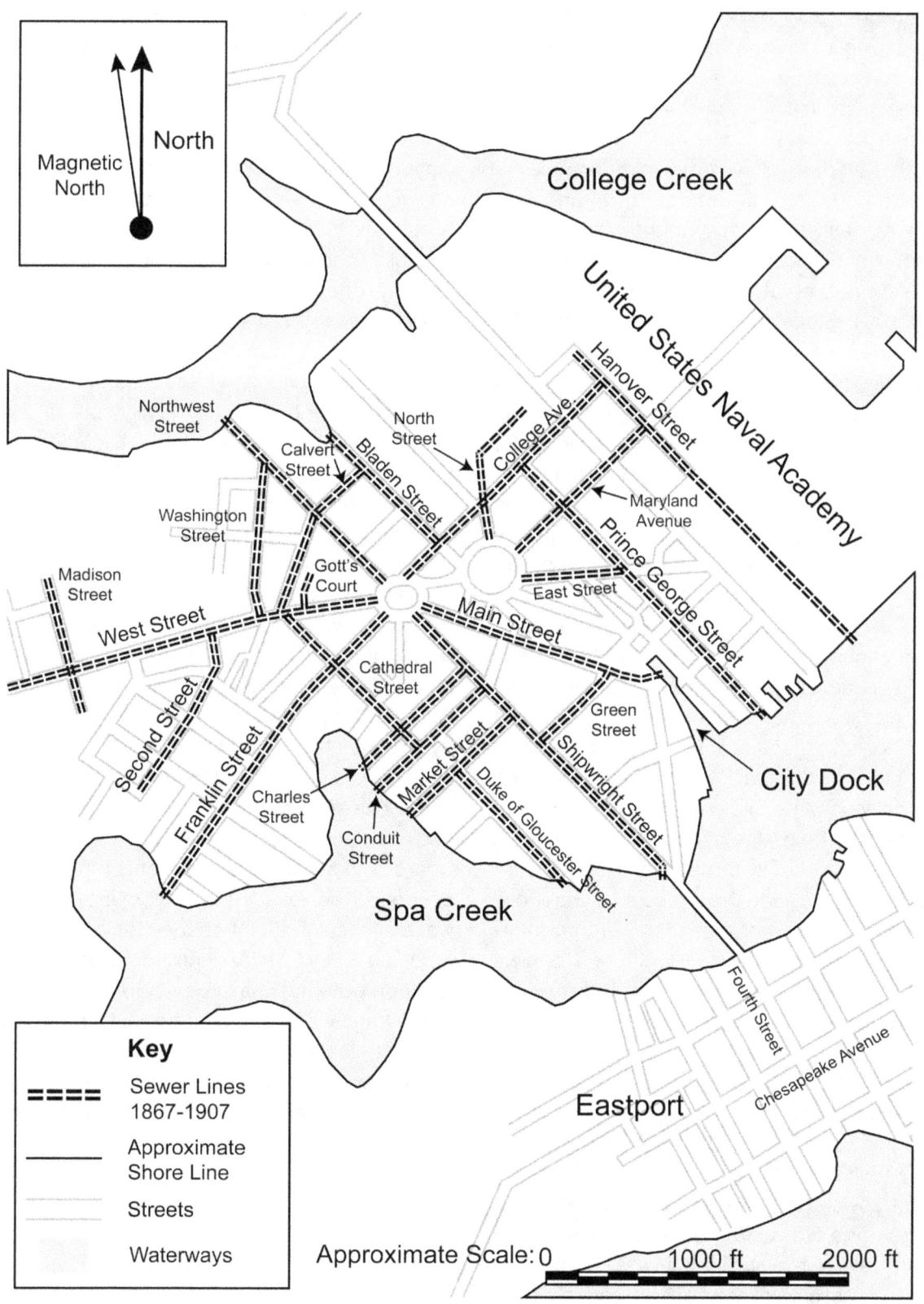

Figure 4. Conjectural plan of public sewers constructed in Annapolis from 1867-1907 (Sanborn Map Company 1913:sheet 1).

report issued on 1 July 1880: "A continuation of the plan of permitting cesspools to honeycomb our city must be discontinued...from the porous nature of our soil and the indiscriminate use of privy sinks, the water in our pumps has become poisoned and unfit for use" (Warren 1990:xviii). This and similar complaints occurring in reports from the mayor, and especially from the city's health officer early in the 20th century, are reminiscent of previous archaeological accounts of privy regulation and sewer construction in other U.S. cities (Ford 1994; Stottman 1995, 2000). Despite the 1880 pronouncement, well water remained necessary as the reservoir for the city began to fail towards the end of the 19th century. The first water reservoir was completed by the Annapolis Water Company in 1866, and collected surface water from several streams into a partially lined earthen containment pond (Annapolis Water Company 1867); expansion of the reservoir's capacity in later years seems to have compromised water quality. The last public well in the city was constructed in 1887, and reached potable artesian water from an aquifer almost 300 ft. below the surface (MCCA 1892; referenced in McWilliams 2009). Public wells drawing ground water rather than artesian water seem to have operated in the city through at least 1900. Large public wells have been discovered archaeologically on State Circle (Stabler 1990) and on Cornhill Street (Cochran et al. 2008), which runs from State Circle towards the City Dock in Annapolis.

Between 1885 and 1910 the city council undertook the responsibility to build or extend sewers on many streets in the city's center (Table 1). Figure 4 depicts the conjectural arrangement of sewers approved for construction by the city council between 1867 and 1907 (Russo 1988, 1991) into several networks, indicating the most likely direction of drainage. In nearly every instance, sewers constructed in Annapolis before 1937 discharged into the waterways that surrounded the city, certainly offsetting the public health benefits of underground sewerage. Initial sewer lines extending to the water's edge created the possibility of installing sewers on streets where no right-of-way to the water existed. The earliest sewer lines became central drains for numerous adjoining sewers. In this way, piecemeal sewers accreted gradually and with little evidence of planning into several branching networks to drain the city. The most common sewers were individual pipes that ran down residential streets dead-ending at the water, discharging into College Creek to the north, or Spa Creek to the south (Figure 4). The city council records mention sewers built from various materials, including wood, mortared stone and brick, concrete, and terra cotta pipes (see Figure 2). Sewer construction followed citizens' petitions to the city council, producing an "ask-and-receive" rhythm to the city council's proceedings. Some areas of the city did not see sewer construction amidst this boom of infrastructural expansion, a probable indication of the amount of influence each area of the city enjoyed with respective patrons on the city council. Suburbs of the city were also, by and large, excluded from these improvements.

My fieldwork in Eastport showed that residents in this neighborhood were using 19th-century infrastructure – privies, wells, cisterns, and other improvisations – well after sanitary sewers and reservoir water were widely accessible in Annapolis. There are occasional dwellings or areas of Annapolis that were without service early in the 20th century, such as the Shiplap House. Except for a few electric street lights paid for by the county, Eastport was entirely without service, until developments that occurred during the 1920s and 1930s. Eastport was also home to an established and economically secure African American community, where landowning was prevalent. The ultimate rate of connection achieved by this community once sewer and water services were introduced is significantly different from adjacent white-identified households. Finally, Eastport was part of a large annexation that took place in 1951 and was passed by a popular referendum vote. I propose that Eastport was annexed with infrastructure before it was annexed politically. This claim relies on an understanding of infrastructure as a material culture of government.

A Theory of Government for Historical Archaeology

The classical view of networked infrastructure is that it is integrative. Indeed, geographers Stephen Graham and Simon Marvin

TABLE 1. Sewer Construction Authorized by Annapolis City Council, 1867-1907, By Street, Year, and Proposed Terminus (Source: City Council Meeting Minutes in Russo 1988).

Street	Year Authorized by City Council	Proposed Terminus
Lower Main Street	1867	To deep water, Spa Creek
Upper Main Street	1868	To deep water, Spa Creek
Hanover Street	1872	Spa Creek
East Street	1885	Prince George Street sewer
Water Street	1885	City Dock
Charles Street	1885	Spa Creek
Prince George Street	1885	Spa Creek, wharf area
Northwest Street, County Jail	1886	College Creek
Market Street	1887	Spa Creek
Maryland Avenue	1888	Prince George Street sewer
Green Street	1890	Main Street sewer or Spa Creek
Conduit Street	1891	Spa Creek
Duke of Gloucester Street	1891	Spa Creek
College Avenue	1892	Prince George Street sewer
North Street	1897	College Avenue sewer
Bladen Street catch basin	1897	College Avenue sewer
Cathedral Street	1898	Spa Creek
Calvert Street	1898	College Creek
West Street	1898	City Limits?
Bladen Street	1903	St. John's Street and College Creek
Calvert Street extension	1906	College Creek
Market Street	1906	Spa Creek
Shipwright Street	1906	Spa Creek
Washington Street	1906	College Creek
Franklin Street	1906	Spa Creek
Madison Street	1906	West Street sewer?
Second Street	1906	Spa Creek
Gott's Court	1907	West Street sewer?

(2001:8) argue that networked utilities are analytically transparent, because they are assumed to be universal and equitable in their cost and application. They write:

...street, power, water, waste or communications networks are usually imagined to deliver broadly similar, essential, services to (virtually) everyone at similar cost across cities and regions... Fundamentally, infrastructure networks are thus widely assumed to be integrators of urban spaces. They are believed to bind cities, regions and nations into functioning geographical or political wholes.

We may adopt this notion for a foil. Because these networks are imagined to be everywhere, they have no geography (Graham and Marvin 2001). And yet, we know that networked infrastructure is not universal or equitable in its cost, nor in its application. Therefore it does have its own pattern and geography. Access to public services is a privilege, and at present we are ill prepared to understand what it costs to connect with new infrastructure across different racial, ethnic, or class divisions. Based on what archaeology tells us, we cannot accept that "access" or the "presence or absence" of utilities is solely or even primarily dependent on the financial capabilities or limitations of a household. Rather than placing pipes, privies, and other utilities immediately into the interpretive context of sanitation, or improvement (Tarlow 2007), I propose a framework where the different services are interpreted as the material culture of governing a population. Sewers are indeed about sanitation, but they are also about governing, and archaeologists can use their materiality to address the relationship between these technologies and new expressions of power that arise from them:

> Technologies can transform governing processes in unanticipated ways. Further, technologies which arise in other domains may precipitate transformations in government through the emergence, growth and solidification of new discourses and practices and thus the very conceptualisation of government. In short, the technical construction of government may transform its social/discursive construction (Henman 2006:209).

Infrastructural networks can thus be situated within a chain of consequences that transforms and intensifies the action of government, and shifts the basis for government's operation towards the technical, apparatus-like quality of bureaucracy.

The concept of governmentality is one that Foucault develops in his later scholarship, as an extension, if not culmination, of his research into personal discipline (1977) and bio-power (1990:140-144) as complementary techniques of power that are crucial to the development of capitalism. The core elements marking the historical emergence of governmentality are first, the invention and institution of political economy, which resituates the source of wealth from land or territory to production, and makes the minute management of the economy a part of the "art of government" (Foucault 1991:92). Second is the emergence of statistics as the "science of the state" (Foucault 1991:96; Pels 1997:165) and

the broadening statistical representation of both the populations under governance, and also the functioning of political economy according to certain measurable parameters. Third is the state's instrumentation, through which it detects, records, and orders the social, but also expresses its power and acts upon populations. This instrumentation is bracketed as the apparatus of security, which includes police power, but also the apparatuses of economic regulation and fields of policy and knowledge production (Foucault 1991; Gordon 1991; Dean 1999:9-39; Hannah 2000:17-25). The realization of political economy and the application of statistics to statecraft are 17th century developments that progress towards more sophisticated forms through later centuries. There is a close relationship between the generation of statistical knowledge – what Ferguson and Gupta (2002:981) might call representations of population – and the apparatus of security, which produces knowledge about population and the economy, and carries out projects based upon that knowledge. This complex comprises the instrumentation of the state (Dean 1999:59), and is something that archaeologists can access via our customary evidentiary sources. We can describe a historical progression in this instrumentation that marks ongoing governmentalization at different scales and at different locations, both archaeological and discursive. These three elements, the discovery, inscription, and regulation of population, can be assembled into an "analytics of government" (Dean 1999:9) that provides for critical analysis of specific, historical projects of governing.

Governance is carried out through the economy, but population is the object of governmental rule (Foucault 1991:99-100; Dean 1999:19). For Foucault, social statistics create new awareness of the citizenry as a population, and define the points of contact between populations and the schemes of governing institutions. Colin Gordon (1991:10) describes this imperative as "an omnivorous espousal of governed reality" and it is the very same imperative that generated many of the documentary sources that historical archaeologists rely upon. The accumulation of social statistics and the broadening availability of these data to archaeologists reveals ongoing governmentalization in specific historical contexts. How the state knows, its instrumentation for knowing, is also how it governs: "The finitude of the state's power to act is an immediate consequence of the limitation of its power to know" (Dean 1999:16).

Another materialization of government must therefore be texts. For example, the limitation of the state's power to know figures prominently in the following narrative about the Parole neighborhood of Annapolis, a predominantly African American community that grew outside of the city's western limits after the Civil War, and like Eastport was annexed in 1951. The speaker (identified as WB) and his son (identified as AB) described events that took place outside of a store called Herndon's. Herndon's store was the only African American owned general store in the Parole community, selling ice, wood, coal and kerosene, food and cold drinks; "They had everything," is how WB describes it, before offering the following story:

> **MP:** *What was it like in Parole during the war years [World War II]?*
>
> **AB:** *Lotta men were gone (laughs).*
>
> **WB:** *Another story...[This man] was in charge of the draft board. He had a cornfield, someplace, out in the country. ...Anyway, he stepped out on the Herndon's porch. And there was some youngsters, and a fellow by the name of "Nip" Jones, we called him Nip Jones, Milton Jones was his right name. This guy was in charge of the draft, you know.*
>
> **AB:** *Draft board.*
>
> **WB:** *He asked them about going down country to cut some corn. So Nip said, "Oh you bring your corn field up here! We'll cut your corn!" (laughter). And evidently, Nip he had no social security [number], he had nothing. 'Cause everybody was on that porch was drafted within a week or so! And Nip he never was drafted.*
>
> **AB:** *They cleaned Parole out. Even drafted some old people!*
>
> **WB:** *Yeah, my uncle, he was 40 years old. But they didn't get Nip!*
>
> **AB:** *The guy who started the trouble, he didn't have identification, he didn't have a birth certificate I guess (Brown 2006).*

Scott (2010:228; 220) writes in *The Art of Not Being Governed* that "The elementary form of statecraft is the population list and household census: the basis for taxation and conscription," and yet, "the absence of writing and texts provides a freedom of maneuver in history, genealogy, and legibility that frustrates state routines."

Several efforts recorded in the proceedings of the Annapolis City Council during the 1890s reflect the council's desire to establish greater legibility or what might be termed scriptural control over public works, and to fix and assess the state of the city's infrastructure. In December of 1894, the Street Committee was directed by the City Council to determine the feasibility and propriety of working jointly with the Annapolis Gas and Electric Light Company, and the Annapolis Water Company to produce a map of the city identifying pertinent infrastructure. This map was to locate existing fire hydrants, electric street lights, sewer lines, water and gas mains, and identify street grades (MCCA 1898:179). What is striking about this directive is the suggestion that much of the city's infrastructure was undocumented at the end of the 19th century, calling its integration, effective administration, and systematicity into question. Furthermore, it belies the style of government that implemented these networks, which permitted a degree of improvisation in the installation of critical infrastructure. Uncharted is to a degree ungoverned.

By 1898 the City Council had created a Permanent Improvement Commission that was closely related, or possibly located within the Committee on Streets. Late in 1898 the City Council ordered a census to determine which houses were connected to sewers and which were not, if houses without sewer service could reasonably be connected, what streets were not paved and curbed, and what sidewalks needed repair. In June of 1900 the City Council also advertised for bids to create a topographical map of the city for use in laying additional sewers (MCCA 1901:227-232). Like the map issue raised in 1894, this census and the complementary effort to map the contours and drainages of the city again bring to light the scriptural life of Annapolis infrastructure, revealing that this network was only partially documented, and therefore only partly governed and administered, which is not to imply that it could ever be completely documented, nor completely governed (de Certeau 1984).

Sanitary Infrastructure in the Eastport Community

Annapolis experienced considerable problems stemming from the deterioration of its water and sewer infrastructure during the first decades of the 20th century (Jones 1905; 1922:13-14; Strange 1914:9; Smith 1925:15-16). The city's water reservoir was enlarged over the decades to meet demand, but the ponds were not properly lined and typically filled with mud. The original 1866 reservoir was constructed with a simple sand filtration system that was actually quite sophisticated for its day (Annapolis Water Company 1867:16; Melosi 2000:85-87), but the water that reached Annapolis during later years was effectively unfiltered. By the 1920s the city's water infrastructure was in desperate need of investment, and significant improvements were completed around 1927, including construction of a filtration plant at the city's reservoir, a million-gallon stand pipe within Annapolis, and new water mains throughout the downtown. At this time water service was also delivered to the Eastport neighborhood for the first time, drawing from the same reservoir that provided water to Annapolis; however, water infrastructure was not installed in any other suburb of the city (Sanborn Map Company 1930).

The practice of discharging sewage directly into the waterways surrounding Annapolis also became untenable during the first decades of the 20th century. In a peninsular, maritime community this practice put many people into direct contact with human wastes. A public bath called the Eastport Bath House opened in 1895 on Spa Creek near the bridge to Annapolis, and advertised that the baths were "free from all sewerage and filth, in a strong tide" (*Evening Capital* 1895; in McWilliams 2009). This statement hints that contaminated conditions prevailed in other waters around Annapolis, while Eastport, a neighborhood without sewers, may have been host to cleaner waters or perceived that way though a short distance away. Early in the 20th century the health officer for Annapolis included a recommendation in his annual report, to

...respectfully urge a complete revision of our sewerage system. Our once beautiful creeks are polluted by poisonous matters, unquestionably deleterious to health, which have for some years been flowing into them from many sources, and they must inevitably at some time, if they have not already, become breeding places for disease (Strange 1914:9).

Dilution of sewage in waterways was a common and inexpensive approach to disposing of liquid waste in U.S. cities before 1920. It was not until the mid-1930s that collection and treatment of sewage with mechanical and chemical measures for purification became increasingly common, an outcome of New Deal investment in public works (Melosi 2000:162-163, 210-211).

Towards the end of the 1920s, the State of Maryland supported a plan to extend municipal sewers to a large area beyond the historical boundaries of Annapolis. In essence, the state government offered funding for an entirely new, modern sanitary sewer system, with a sewage treatment plant and separation of rainwater, on the condition that service be extended to virtually all suburbs surrounding the city. A redesignation of governmental authority in and around Annapolis was necessary for the provision of municipal sewer services to neighboring communities in the county. The vehicle for this change was the creation of a large special purpose district in 1931 that was administered by a new commission in Annapolis, and encompassed a significant area of the county's jurisdiction outside of the city's corporate limits (Burwell 1931). I think it is significant that this process culminated in the annexation of a number of neighboring communities, including the village of Eastport and the entire area of the 1931 sanitation district, into the City of Annapolis in 1951 (*Evening Capital* 1950, 1951a, 1951b; Warren 1990).

Wells and Cisterns in the Eastport Neighborhood During the Early 20th Century

Excavations in Eastport from 2001 to 2004 were directed at understanding the neighborhood's historical trajectory towards annexation. Infrastructural connections between the two communities trace out immaterial social and economic connections that bound Eastport and Annapolis starting in the later 19th century. Several features discovered at domestic sites in Eastport that pertain to the provisioning of household water prior to and after the introduction of municipal water in the neighborhood. These include a large concrete cistern at 201 Chesapeake Avenue (18AP101), and a brick-lined well at 113 Chester Avenue (18AP90). Together these features represent tactics for mitigating the lack of public services in Eastport during the early 20th century, and also continued the 19th-century pattern of provisioning and containing water.

The cistern at Site 18AP101 is associated with the household of German immigrants Adolph and Pauline Braun who acquired this property in 1910; however the property at 201 Chesapeake Avenue was occupied by a sequence of German immigrants between 1885 and 1944. By 1910, there were approximately 40 German immigrants scattered throughout Eastport (U.S. Bureau of the Census 1910). The Brauns sold the property to other German immigrants and then re-acquired it three times during the first half of the 20th century. In 1910 the Brauns actually had two mortgages on the property at 201 Chesapeake Avenue (Anne Arundel County Circuit Court 1910), and this strain on their equity may reflect their significant investments in the community. Adolph Braun operated a slaughterhouse, sausage factory, and meat-packing plant at the former site of a 19th century glass factory on Spa Creek, approximately one block away from his home. The Brauns boarded three German men at the time of the 1910 census, and the three of them – two butchers who immigrated during the 1890s and a meat-wagon driver who immigrated in 1909 – worked at the slaughterhouse (U.S. Bureau of the Census 1910). The buildings at Site 18AP101 were arranged into a compound so that the boarders resided in a separate dwelling from the Braun family. When the Brauns purchased the property in 1910, they moved a small wood-frame dwelling that had stood on the property since at least 1885 to the rear of the lot facing onto a different street. The relocation of this building was to accommodate the construction of a new home with a poured concrete foundation (Sanborn Map Company 1891, 1913).

The cistern that was discovered at Site 18AP101 is situated in the yard between these two residences, and all three structures are still extant. One corner of the cistern was uncovered within a five-ft. square excavation unit, and the cistern measures around 10 by 12 ft. with a depth of 5.8 ft. below the current ground surface (Figure 5). The upper portion of the cistern was demolished slightly below the ground leaving the lower portion of the cistern walls intact. Given those approximate dimensions, this feature would contain 2,250 gallons of water to a depth of 2.5 ft., or upwards of 5,000 gallons when filled completely.

Figure 5. Detail of 1921 Sanborn map showing primary dwelling and outbuildings at 201 Chesapeake Avenue (Site 18AP100), identified as House No. 404. The cistern is depicted at the center of the property (Sanborn Map Company 1921: sheet 22, courtesy of the Library of Congress).

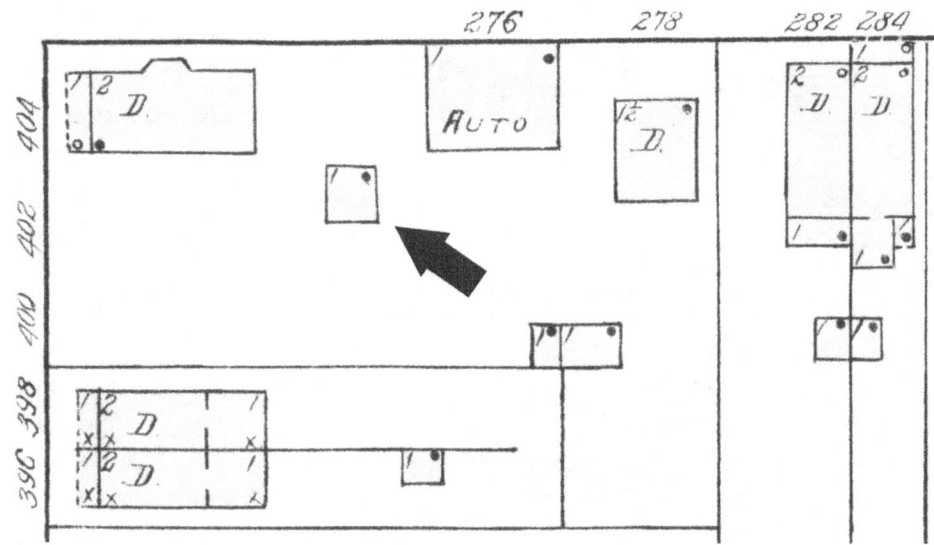

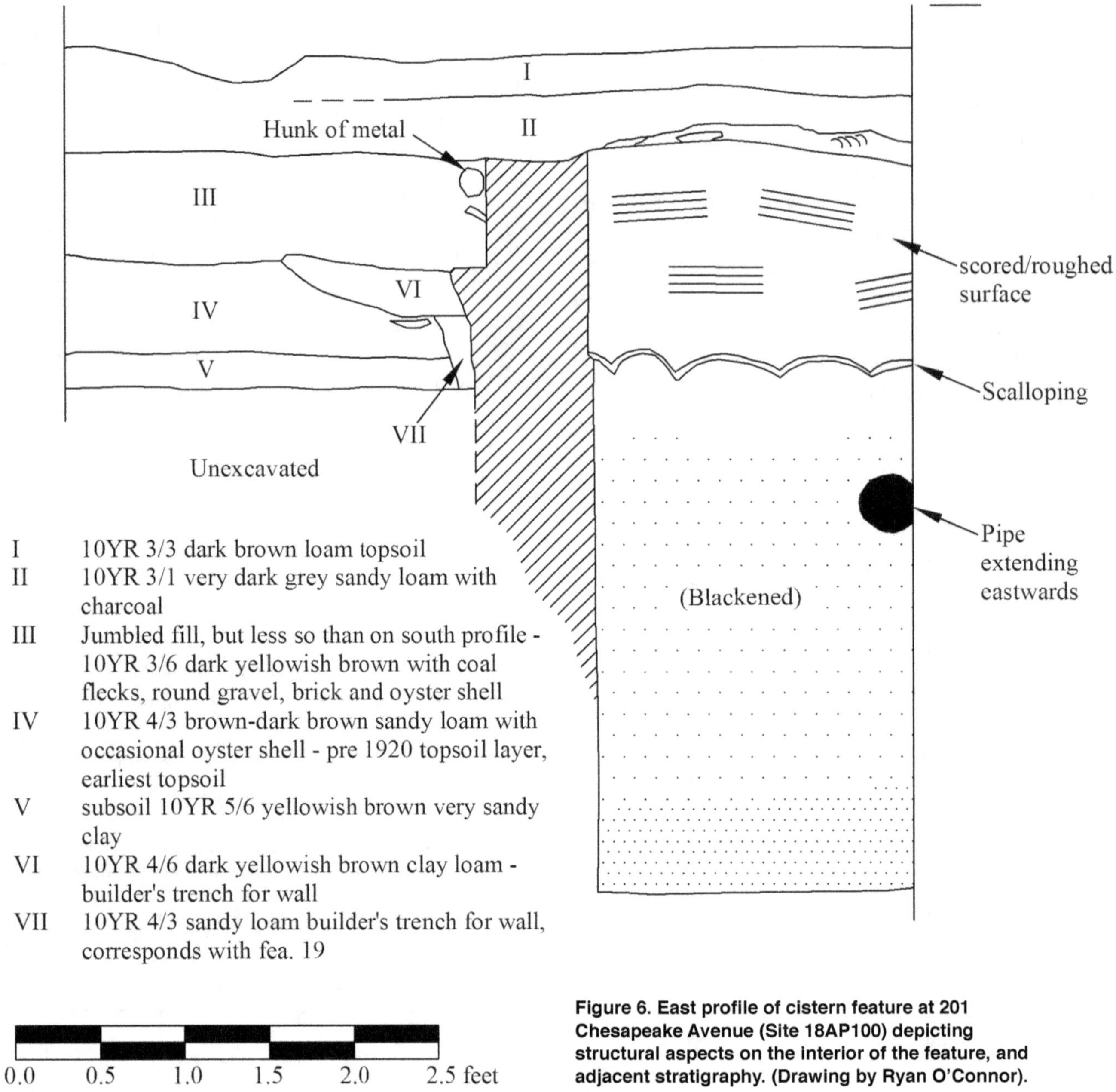

Hunk of metal

I

II

III

IV

VI

V

VII

Unexcavated

scored/roughed surface

Scalloping

(Blackened)

Pipe extending eastwards

I   10YR 3/3 dark brown loam topsoil
II   10YR 3/1 very dark grey sandy loam with charcoal
III Jumbled fill, but less so than on south profile - 10YR 3/6 dark yellowish brown with coal flecks, round gravel, brick and oyster shell
IV 10YR 4/3 brown-dark brown sandy loam with occasional oyster shell - pre 1920 topsoil layer, earliest topsoil
V   subsoil 10YR 5/6 yellowish brown very sandy clay
VI   10YR 4/6 dark yellowish brown clay loam - builder's trench for wall
VII 10YR 4/3 sandy loam builder's trench for wall, corresponds with fea. 19

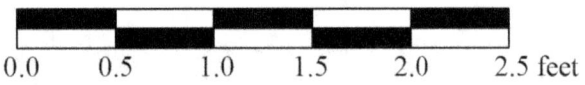

0.0   0.5   1.0   1.5   2.0   2.5 feet

Figure 6. East profile of cistern feature at 201 Chesapeake Avenue (Site 18AP100) depicting structural aspects on the interior of the feature, and adjacent stratigraphy. (Drawing by Ryan O'Connor).

This structure was constructed from poured concrete, with oyster shell mixed into the mortar to bind and stretch the concrete material. The feature is water tight and flooded somewhat during excavation in 2003. It is fed (or drained) by at least one underground pipe, which entered from the direction of the Braun family dwelling at approximately 2.6 ft. above the floor of the cistern. A decorative scalloped motif was formed into the concrete running around the interior of the cistern

around 3.5 ft. above the floor of the feature, perhaps marking the anticipated fill line (Figure 6).

The Braun's cistern was probably abandoned soon after the dwelling was connected with municipal sewers after 1937. The upper fill of the feature contains a large quantity of butchered beef bones, and lower fill layers consisted of stratified deposits of coal, cinders, and lens-shaped deposits of ash. The lowermost fill, which was only sampled, is a waterlogged, black,

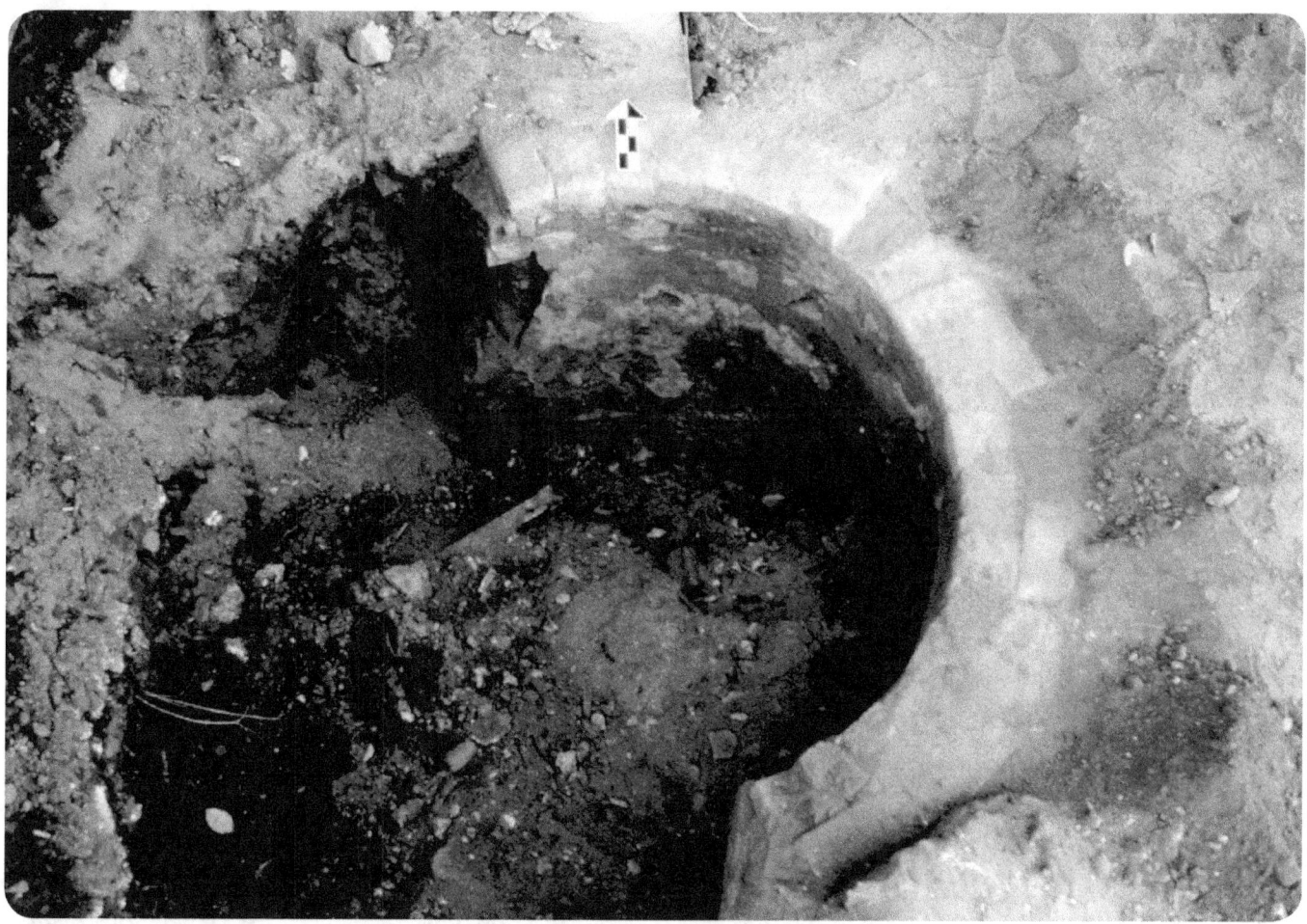

Figure 7. Abandoned Well Uncovered in 2001 at 113 Chester Avenue (Site 18AP90) in Eastport. (Photograph by James Gibb).

rubbery-textured loam that resembles night soil. This loam contained preserved wood, egg shells, straw, and other organic material. The character of this fill raises the probability that at some point during its use this substantial concrete feature was the underground vault for a latrine or privy rather than a cistern. Whether interpreted as a cistern, a privy vault, or both, this feature indicates the steps that were taken in Eastport during the early 20th century to maintain a functioning residence in absence of water and/or sewer infrastructure.

Another compelling feature is a well that was exposed during renovations to a wood-frame dwelling in 2001 (Figure 7), and is the only archaeological well feature recorded in Eastport (Gibb 2001). The associated dwelling was occupied during the early 20th century by a middle class white family native to Maryland, and is larger than neighboring homes on the same block (U.S. Bureau of the Census 1920, 1930). At least one other well is described in the deed to a different residential property nearby. The well at Site 18AP90 measures approximately 4 ft. in diameter on the interior, and is lined with hand-made or early machine-made bricks. The bricks are set in Portland cement in an irregular pattern, either in a header bond pattern or lengthwise with two rows extending side-by-side. This irregularity speaks of modification and repair. There is a plaster-like parging over the interior of the brick lining, which continues down into the shaft of the feature. Gibb (2001) notes that the feature had not been filled upon abandonment, but contained debris from demolition work conducted at the site concurrently with his investigation. Large voids suggested that the well shaft below is at least partially open. The depth of the feature was not determined, but 20 ft. would probably be sufficient to provide adequate ground water in most areas on the low-elevation peninsula. A news item ran in the *Evening Capital* (1884) stating that a well excavated by a speculator at another location on Horn Point had reached fresh water 25 ft. beneath the surface. The well at 18AP90 was located immediately behind the dwelling on the property, and had been covered over by a rear addition. If this was the pattern for well construction in Eastport, then numerous abandoned or functioning wells may remain intact underneath the dozens of rear building additions in this neighborhood.

What is striking about the well at Site 18AP90 is that the feature is tapped by lead water pipes, which exit the well in four directions. The implication is that four pumps, and potentially four households were drawing water from his well before its abandonment. In that sense, the well was a shared resource. At the same time, the well would have produced a drastically different relationship between neighbors than public wells that remained in use in Annapolis until the first decade of the 20th century, or public wells found in other urban archaeological contexts. For instance, excavations conducted by New South Associates at James City, North Carolina uncovered a communal well, at the center of an urban block that was occupied by African Americans from the end of the Civil War until the 1940s. The well was abandoned after the 1920s (Wheaton et al. 1990:35, 85). Wheaton et al. argue that the shared well was a daily meeting place, which promoted a sense of community and cultivated a "communal, egalitarian lifestyle" among the emancipated African Americans occupying James City (1990:247-248). In contrast, neighbors on Chester Avenue in Eastport did not visit the well at Site 18AP90 for water, but rather pumped it to their adjacent properties. From this we interpret there was little opportunity for neighbors to encounter one another when securing water for their households, at least following the well's modification for plumbing. In that sense this well expresses a certain degree of alienation and individuation of those households drawing from it, in simulation of the social form dictated by central-supply services like electricity or municipal water. Further, this relation seems to be based in legal definitions of ownership and access to water from the well, rather than some communal or mutual relation. These definitions of rights of access may have arisen from conflicts over how limited supplies of well water should be shared, and periodic shortages resulting

from over-use. Households drawing water from the well at site 18AP90 were still connected socially, the water lines tracing out these connections in a material way.

The sale in 1969 of a home and property nearby at 119 Chester Avenue (18AP93) specifically mentioned *another* shared well, and gives a sense for how the use of the well at Site 18AP90 was structured. The deed instrument stipulated that the lot at 119 Chester Avenue was conveyed "SUBJECT, nevertheless, to the use in common of the well, now located on the lot hereby conveyed, with the owner of the eastern half of said lot No. 165," (Anne Arundel County Circuit Court 1969) which would be the house currently located next door at 121 Chester Avenue. The first mention of this well appears on a 1920 deed to the property at 119 Chester Avenue. For a period of time the adjacent homes at 119 and 121 Chester Avenue were owned by members of one white family, and the right of access to the well at 119 Chester Avenue seems to have been fixed for the occupants of the neighboring residence at that time.

The location of the well at Site 18AP93 was not ascertained during archaeological investigations conducted in 2001-2002. It could remain beneath the extant rear addition on the existing house, which is where the well at Site 18AP90 was discovered during the renovation of that structure, and where other Eastport residents have reported finding similar though undocumented features. The pattern set at Sites 18AP90 and 18AP93 is of one functioning well for every few households.

Finally, it is interesting to consider that the persistence of legal assertions of the right of access until 1969 may signify that a shared well at Site 18AP93 was still in use more than 40 years after the Eastport neighborhood was provided with water from the Annapolis Water Company reservoir. Municipal utility plans produced during the 1930s, discussed in more detail below, depict the lot at Site 18AP93 as an empty lot, although it was certainly improved and occupied. This would indicate that the dwelling extant at Site 18AP93 was almost certainly without water or sewer service until at least 1954, when these plans were archived by the city. A water well maintained for use helps to explain how this household managed without making use of municipal services.

Differential Access to Municipal Water and Sewers in Eastport

If well, cistern, and privy features in the Eastport neighborhood represent archaeological evidence for the general absence of municipal services, or redundancy with sanitary services that were introduced during the early 20th century, what can be said about the sanitation networks that were introduced to the Eastport community? Detailed plans depicting water, sewer, and storm drain networks installed in Eastport were drawn under the authority of the Annapolis Metropolitan Sewerage Commission (AMSC 1932-1937a). These plans charted the location of main and service lines for municipal water, installed in Eastport in ca. 1927, and sanitary sewers, as well as a pumping station that drained the entire system and delivered sewage to a treatment plant some distance south of Annapolis. The sewer lines, pumping station, and treatment plant were constructed between ca. 1933-1937, and photographs of sewer mains being installed in Eastport are dated 1934 (Figure 8). The plans are detailed and present another example of the inscription or representation of population. Each lot depicted on the plans is numbered, and individual water and sewer connections at dwellings and other structures are identified with serial numbers or customer numbers. Additionally the relevant structures are drawn to scale, including outbuildings such as privies where these structures are sometimes connected to sanitary infrastructure rather than the dwelling itself. Property

Figure 8. Sewer Construction on Chester Avenue in Eastport, Photographed in November 1934. (AMSC 1933-1937; courtesy of Tom and Pamela Dawson, Stevensville, MD).

112

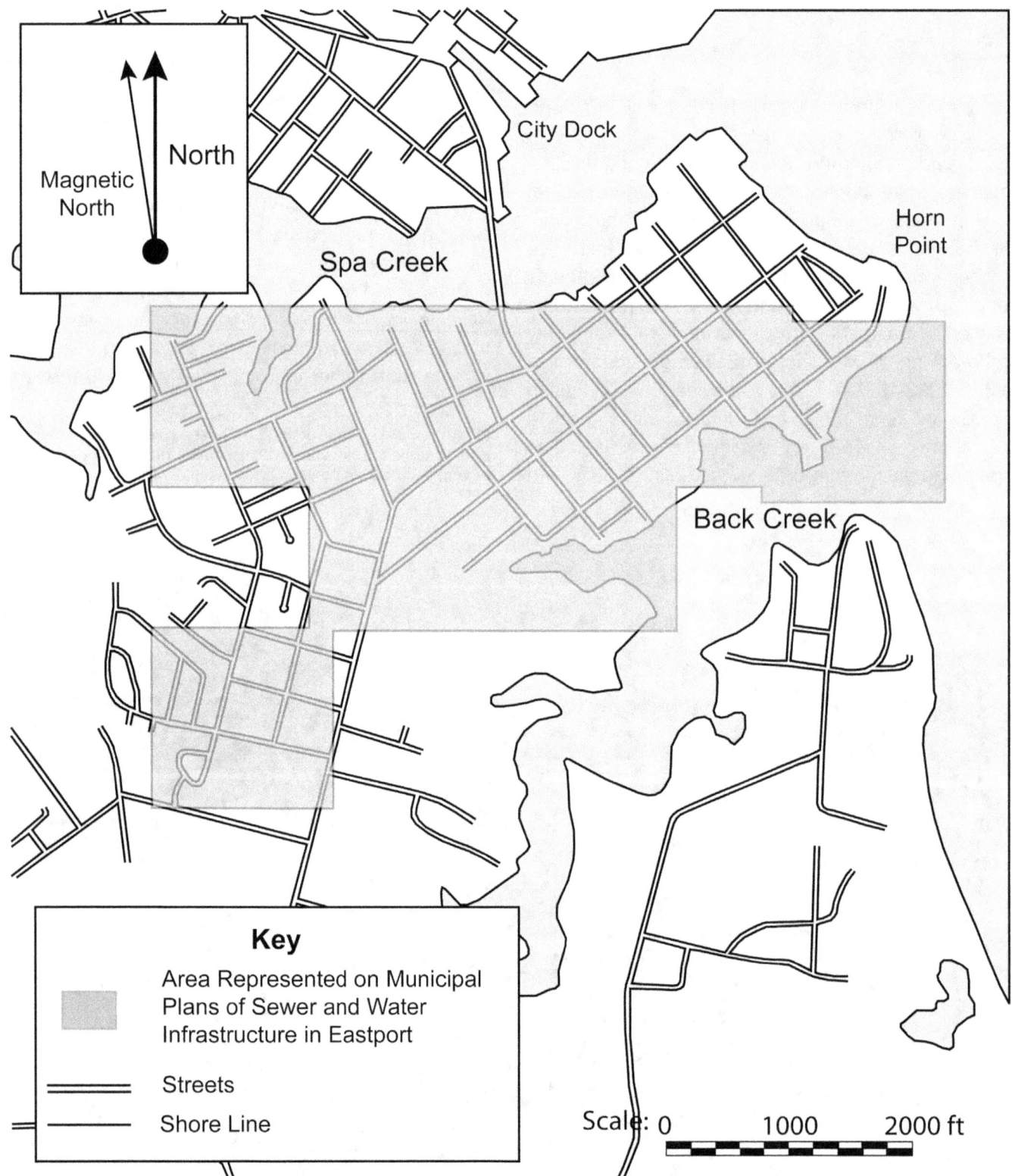

North

Magnetic
North

City Dock

Horn
Point

Spa Creek

Back Creek

Key

Area Represented on Municipal
Plans of Sewer and Water
Infrastructure in Eastport

Streets

Shore Line

Scale: 0   1000   2000 ft

Figure 9. Plan of Area Covered by Municipal Sewer
and Water Plans for Eastport Used in This Study (Base
Map: United States Geological Survey 1978).

owners are named on the plans, and a book-and-page deed reference is also entered for each property. As such, the plans collate a terrific volume of information, which hints at the knowledge that was produced by the responsible authority in Annapolis. Figure 9 depicts the area covered by the 14 sheets examined during this study.

Comparison of plans of the water and sewer infrastructure in Eastport and demographic data presented in the 1930 U.S. census reveals patterns in the provision and use of municipal services by individual households. Not all homes in Eastport were connected to municipal services introduced from Annapolis. But which homes were making use of city services, and which ones were not? Who lived in the homes that were disconnected, presumably continuing with earlier, traditional, sometimes ingenious solutions to the problems of securing water for their household and managing waste? What is the relationship between these variables and racial and socioeconomic data recorded during the 1930 census? Can distinct practices of incorporation and use of city services be identified for African American and white identified households, or for dwellings that were rented versus those that were owner-occupied? These questions present some salient measures that address the themes of governmentalization and annexation, and also explore the limitations of the project of liberal government at this metropolitan scale. If some households and some proportion of Eastport's population is left out of the "apparatus of security" that is put in place there early in the 20th century, does that reveal gaps and spaces in the governmentalization of Annapolis over the same period? Does it reveal that Eastport's annexation is also incomplete, or that some were secured – and therefore governed – to a lesser degree than others?

Out of 594 households enumerated in Eastport during the 1930 U.S. Federal Census, 244 households could be linked to dwellings depicted on the Annapolis Metropolitan Sewerage Commission plans. Cross-tabulating data from the sewer and water plans with the race variable in the 1930 census suggests these services were racialized, in that they were more greatly accessible to white households. The 244 enumerated households in the sample include 66 African American families and 177 households coded as "white," including a small number of European immigrants. One-third of these African American households were not connected to municipal sewer or water, irrespective of whether those structures were rented or owner-occupied. A much smaller proportion of white-identified households were without service; 8 ½ % were not connected to city sewer (n=15), and a little more than 12% were without running water (n=22). Several plumbed privies occur at both African American and white-identified households (Palus 2009:277-284; 2011).

Because municipal water and sewers define the color line in a new way, we can consider these technologies as racial materialities, by looking at how municipal services were apportioned and how these services identified people more clearly to their racial categories. The sanitary system as an apparatus of security becomes a part of the ongoing construction of race, despite the changes in how Annapolis was governed at the end of the 19th century and early in the 20th. Furthermore, if services like municipal sewers can be described as the material culture of government, what does the relative rate of connection and disconnection signal about how communities of different races in Eastport were governed? How is the relationship between each household and the municipal infrastructure the work of agency?

In the context of this research – which sees a convergence of government and public services infrastructure – the lack of coverage in public services may suggest a curious gap in the governance of this community, and the racialization of government. Importantly, the rate of home ownership among African Americans in Eastport is approximately equal to that of white households in the community at the time of the 1930 census, around 60%, far above what is seen historically in Annapolis and across the state (Palus 2009:300-320; Schweninger 1990:180). This helps us to interpret the disparity in service. African Americans in Eastport wielded substantial economic power. Rather than representing a neglected population, the void may just as well indicate an exit from the multiform tactics of governance that are implied by service. Interpretation of the racialization of utilities and the partiality of the program of governing becomes one of the most crucial elements of this history.

Conclusion

In Annapolis it is possible to chart the transition from patronage as a mode of government towards something that very much resembles liberalism, or governmentality as Foucault and others define it. The transition is clear but it is not sudden, and patronage is probably never eliminated completely from municipal government, though its questionable legality drove it into back rooms later in the 20th century. The historic preservation movement in Annapolis essentially operated through channels of patronage in the city during the 1960s, by providing sound advice to an especially progressive mayor in office at that time (Palus 2008). The contrast between patronage and liberalism as styles of government tells in the execution of infrastructural projects. Where in earlier contexts infrastructural improvements such as sewers or electric lights are granted to those possessing adequate influence with the city council, and are minimally planned and poorly documented, a shift in practice produced a very different infrastructure after the first decades of the 20th century. The sanitation apparatus installed throughout the Annapolis Metropolitan Sewerage District reveals the apparatus-like quality of government itself. Annapolis became a metropolitan area and the focus of improvements that created benefits – and extended local government – beyond the city's corporate limits. The Eastport community was effectively governed by the city of Annapolis before it was annexed politically, not only by the services that Annapolis provided, but also by the administrative apparatus that accompanied service. Infrastructure becomes an expression of power, and perhaps even subordination to what is ultimately an apparatus for economic growth, at the same time that infrastructure becomes an expression of governmentalization.

The metropolitan sewerage project of the 1930s created the first cohesive sanitation network in Annapolis that worked properly. It is this same system that still serves Annapolis today. Though the sewerage treatment plant completed in 1937 is now abandoned and in ruins, much of the network remains intact. It is this apparatus, designed and installed after the Great Depression was underway, tinkered with and modified over the years, upon which the contemporary city depends. Finding one small portion of this system, the individual lines, provokes disappointment and disinterest, even with plans of the network on hand. And yet, as archaeologists we must have something to say about these systems, because such networks completely color urban life after the end of the 19th century, even in contexts where service is uneven or absent.

I offer two areas where advancing governmentality registers, and these can be used to interpret aspects of the infrastructure in other contexts. First, the historical documentation of the infrastructure grows more elaborate over the period of this study. We can differentiate utility lines that are largely improvised and piecemeal from those that result from deliberate improvement projects, and we can consider evidence for planning in different scopes and scales in the execution of these projects. We can also consider how infrastructural networks produce data about population in an ongoing sense, in maps, subscriptions, taxes, fines, photographs, and other records that result from their implementation. This is central to seeing these networks as instruments of government. Second, we can describe the extent of infrastructural networks and identify who they serve and who they exclude, which relates to the question of who is governed, and how. The vastness of these networks presents a special analytical challenge and diverse data must be collated to address this question clearly.

These data can show how networked infrastructure manifests class or race-based privileges, and heightened the meaning of these racial identities, not only through discourse, but through material culture. To me, it is the blank spaces on the plans that are especially intriguing, and challenging. These voids read one way when the infrastructure is taken at face value – and such things as waste, water, and light are loaded with meaning in present society – but they can also be read as spaces open to a different kind of citizenship. That interpretation is impossible to reconcile with the view that networked infrastructure only conveys something that is of utility. A governmentality framework shows that networked infrastructure conveys other things as well, and thus has its own distinctive meaning for urban archaeology.

Acknowledgements

I am grateful to Mark Leone and Julie Schablitsky for inviting me to contribute to this volume, and for providing insightful criticism and feedback as this essay progressed. Both were generous with their time, as was journal editor Joe Joseph. This essay draws on research for my doctoral dissertation completed under the supervision of Nan Rothschild at Columbia University. Research on the history of infrastructure in Annapolis and the Eastport neighborhood was supported by historians Jean Russo and Jane McWillaims, who shared data continually and have been long supporters of Archaeology in Annapolis. The same can be said of archaeologist James Gibb. Detailed plans of the water and sewer infrastructure installed in Eastport during the 1930s are archived at the Department of Public Works in Annapolis, and were provided by Paul Lackey. Homeowners Greg Barranco and Allison Porter permitted field school excavations on their property on Chesapeake Avenue in Eastport in 2003, as did numerous others across several summers. This research was supported in critical ways by these homeowners, students participating in the field school program, and by the Mayor and City Council of Annapolis.

References

ANNAPOLIS METROPOLITAN SEWERAGE COMMISSION [AMSC]

1932-1937 a Eastport Sewer, Water and Storm Drains, Detail Drawings. On File, Department of Public Works, Annapolis, MD.

1933-1937b Annapolis Metropolitan Sewerage Commission Photographic Record. Howard G. Hayman, Sr., photographer. Original photographs in possession of Thomas and Pamela Dawson, Edgewater, MD.

ANNAPOLIS WATER COMPANY

1867   The First Report of the President and Directors of the Annapolis Water Company to the Stockholders; and the Report of the Engineer, Annapolis, February 12, 1867. On file, Annapolis Department of Public Works, Annapolis, MD.

ARNOLD, JOSEPH L.

1978   Suburban Growth and Municipal Annexation in Baltimore, 1745-1918. *Maryland Historical Magazine* 73(2):109-128.

BROWN, WILLIAM A.

2006   Oral History Interview with William A. Brown of Parole, March 3, 2006. Archaeology in Annapolis, University of Maryland College Park, College Park, MD.

BURWELL, ROBERT L.

1931   Plan of Annapolis Metropolitan Sewerage District, Annapolis. On file, Maryland State Archive, Annapolis.

CARNES-MCNAUGHTON, LINDA F. AND TERRY M .HARPER

2000   The Parity of Privies: Summary of Research on Privies in North America. *Historical Archaeology* 34(1):97-110.

CASTREE, NOEL

2006   Commentary: From Neoliberalism to Neoliberalisation: Consolations, Confusions, and Necessary Illusions. *Environment and Planning A* 38(1):1-6.

COCHRAN, MATTHEW D., MATTHEW M. PALUS, STEPHANIE N. DUENSING, JOHN E. BLAIR, JR., JOCELYN E. KNAUF AND JESSICA LEIGH MUNDT

2008   Phase II Archaeological Testing on Fleet Street (18AP111), Cornhill Street (18AP112), and 26 Market Space (18AP109), Annapolis, Maryland, 2008.

Prepared for the City of Annapolis, Public Works Bureau of Engineering and Construction. Archaeology in Annapolis, University of Maryland College Park, College Park, MD.

COOK, LAUREN, REBECCA YAMIN, AND JOHN P. McCARTHY
1996   Shopping as Meaningful Action: Toward a Redefinition of Consumption in Historical Archaeology. *Historical Archaeology* 30(4):50-65.

CRANE, BRIAN D.
2000   Filth, Garbage, and Rubbish: Refuse Disposal, Sanitary Reform, and Nineteenth-Century Yard Deposits in Washington D.C. *Historical Archaeology* 34(1):20-38.

DE CERTEAU, MICHEL
1984   *The Practice of Everyday Life*. University of California Press, Berkeley.

DEAN, MITCHELL
1999   *Governmentality: Power and Rule in Modern Society*. Sage Publications, London, UK.

DEMETER, STEPHEN C.
1994   Nineteenth-Century Sanitation Technology in Urban Detroit. *Michigan Archaeologist* 40(1):1-24.

EUCHNER, CHARLES C.
1991   The Politics of Urban Expansion: Baltimore and the Sewerage Question, 1859-1905. *Maryland Historical Magazine* 86(86):270-291.

EVENING CAPITAL
1884   "Artesian Well," *Evening Capital*, 8/30/1884(93):1. Annapolis, MD.
1895   Eastport Bath House Open, *Evening Capital*, 06/11/1895. Annapolis, MD.
1950   Greater Annapolis Voted; City to Become Fourth Largest in Maryland. *Evening Capital*, 05/24/1950, 71(120). Annapolis, MD.
1951a   New Year Rings In Greater Annapolis. *Evening Capital*, 01/02/1951, 72(1). Annapolis, MD.
1951b   Population of Greater Annapolis Set at 25,104; Federal Bureau of Census Informs Mayor Rowe; Figure As of April, 1950. *Evening Capital*, 01/16/1951, 72(13). Annapolis, MD.

1958   Weigle Envisions Shaded Parking Space Around Slicer House After Restoration; Cites Tourist Business Aid to City in Talk. *Evening Capital*, August 1958. Annapolis, MD.

FERGUSON, JAMES AND AKHIL GUPTA
2002   Spatializing States: Toward an Ethnography of Neoliberal Governmentality. *American Ethnologist* 29(4):981-1002.

FORD, BENJAMIN
1994   Health and Sanitation in Postbellum Harpers Ferry. *Historical Archaeology* 28(4):49-61.

FOUCAULT, MICHEL
1977   *Discipline and Punish: The Birth of the Prison*. Penguin, London, UK.
1990   *The History of Sexuality Volume 1: An Introduction*. Translated by Robert Hurley. Vintage Books, New York, NY.
1991   Governmentality. In *The Foucault Effect: Studies in Governmentality*, Graham Burchell, Colin Gordon and Peter Miller, editors, pp. 87-104. University of Chicago Press, Chicago, IL.

GEISMAR, JOAN H. AND META F. JANOWITZ
1993   Health, Sanitation, and Foodways in Historical Archaeology. *Historical Archaeology* 27(2).

GIBB, JAMES G.
2001   Memorandum to Chair and Members of the Annapolis Historic Preservation Committee regarding 111/113 Chester Avenue, November 26, 2001. Department of Planning and Zoning, City of Annapolis, MD.

GORDON, COLIN
1991   Governmental Rationality: An Introduction. In *The Foucault Effect: Studies in Governmentality*, edited by Graham Burchell, Colin Gordon and Peter Miller, pp. 1-51. University of Chicago Press, Chicago, IL.

GRAHAM, STEPHEN AND SIMON MARVIN
2001   *Splintering Urbanism: Networked Infrastructures, Technological Mobilities and the Urban Condition*. Routledge, London, UK.

HANNAH, MATTHEW G.

2000   *Governmentality and Mastering Territory in Nineteenth-Century America.* Cambridge University Press, Cambridge, UK.

HARRIS, LEILA M.

2009   Gender and Emergent Water Governance: Comparative Overview of Neoliberalized Natures and Gender Dimensions of Privatization, Devolution and Marketization. *Gender, Place & Culture* 16(4):387-408.

HARVEY, DAVID

2007   *A Brief History of Neoliberalism.* Oxford University Press, Oxford, UK.

HENMAN, PAUL

2006   Segmentation and Conditionality: Technological Reconfigurations of Social Policy. In *Analysing Social Policy: A Governmental Approach,* edited by Greg Marston and Catherine McDonald, pp. 205-222. Edward Elgar, Cheltenham, UK.

HERZFELD, MICHAEL

1992   *The Social Production of Indifference: Exploring the Symbolic Roots of Western Bureaucracy.* University of Chicago Press, Chicago, IL.

HOPKINS, GRIFFITH MORGAN

1878   *Atlas of Fifteen Miles Around Baltimore, Including Anne Arundel County, Maryland.* G. M. Hopkins and Company, Philadelphia, PA.

HOWSON, JEAN

1992/1993   The Archaeology of 19th-Century Health and Hygiene at the Sullivan Street Site in New York City. *Northeast Historical Archaeology* 21/22:137-160.

JEFFREY, CRAIG

2007   Introduction: Seeing the State - Governance and Governmentality in India. *Geoforum* 38(4):597-598.

JONES, SAMUEL

1905   *Report of the Mayor of Annapolis on the State of its Finances from July 1st, 1903 to December 21, 1904, with the Treasurer's Exhibit and Health Reports.* Printed in Annapolis by the Annapolis Chronicle. Maryland Room, University of Maryland College Park, College Park, MD.

1922   *Report of the Mayor of Annapolis on the State of the City's Finances from July 1, 1921 to June 30, 1922. With Statement of Sinking Fund.* Capital Gazette Press, Annapolis. Maryland Room, University of Maryland College Park, College Park, MD.

LEONE, MARK P.

2005   *The Archaeology of Liberty in an American Capital: Excavations in Annapolis.* University of California Press, Berkeley.

MARYLAND STATE PLANNING COMMISSION

1937   *Regional Planning Part IV: Baltimore-Washington-Annapolis Area.* Johns Hopkins University, Baltimore, MD.

MATTHEWS, CHRISTOPHER N.

2002   *An Archaeology of History and Tradition: Moments of Danger in the Annapolis Landscape.* Kluwer Academic/Plenum Publishers, New York, NY.

MAYOR AND CITY COUNCIL OF ANNAPOLIS [MCCA]

1811   *Mayor, Council and Aldermen Proceedings, 1801-1811.* Annapolis Records section 8, On file, Maryland State Archives M47-13 (01/22/01/052) Original Municipal Records, Mayor and City Council of Annapolis. Annapolis, MD.

1869   *Proceedings of the Mayor and Aldermen of Annapolis, Volume 26, 1863-1869.* On file, Maryland State Archives M49-10 (01/22/01/062) Original Municipal Records, Mayor and City Council of Annapolis. Annapolis, MD.

1877   *Proceedings of the Mayor and Aldermen of Annapolis, Volume 27, 1869-1877.* On file, Maryland State Archives M49-11 (01/22/01/063) Original Municipal Records, Mayor and City Council of Annapolis. Annapolis, MD.

1886   *Proceedings of the Mayor and Aldermen of Annapolis, Volume 28, 1877-1886.* On file, Maryland State Archives M49-12 (01/22/01/064) Original Municipal Records, Mayor and City Council of Annapolis. Annapolis, MD.

1892   *Proceedings of the Mayor and Aldermen of Annapolis, Volume 29, 1886-1892.* On file, Maryland State Archives M49-13 (01/22/01/065) Original Municipal Records, Mayor and City Council of Annapolis. Annapolis, MD.

1898 *Proceedings of the Mayor and Aldermen of Annapolis, Volume 30, 1892-1898.* On file, Maryland State Archives M49-14 (01/22/01/066) Original Municipal Records, Mayor and City Council of Annapolis. Annapolis, MD.

1901 *Proceedings of the Mayor and Aldermen of Annapolis, Volume 31, 1898-1901.* On file, Maryland State Archives M49-15 (01/22/01/067) Original Municipal Records, Mayor and City Council of Annapolis. Annapolis, MD.

McCARTHY, JAMES AND SCOTT PRUDHAM

2004 Neoliberal Nature and the Nature of Neoliberalism. *Geoforum* 35(3):2004.

McCARTHY, JOHN P. AND JEANNE A. WARD

2000 Sanitation Practices, Depositional Processes, and Interpretive Contexts of Minneapolis Privies. *Historical Archaeology* 34(1):111-129.

McWILLIAMS, JANE W.

2009 Annapolis History Chronology (Electronic File). Jane W. McWillams, Annapolis, MD.

MELOSI, MARTIN V.

2000 *The Sanitary City: Urban Infrastructure in America from Colonial Times to the Present.* Johns Hopkins University Press, Baltimore, MD.

MEYER, MICHAEL D.

2004 Sidebar: From Chamber Pots to Privies that Flush. In *Putting the "There" There: Historical Archaeologies of West Oakland (I-880 Cypress Freeway Replacement Project, Interpretive Report No. 2),* edited by Mary Praetzellis and Adrian Praetzellis, pp. 164-166. Anthropological Studies Center, Sonoma State University, Rohnert Park, CA.

MROZOWSKI, STEPHEN A, E. L. BELL, M. C. BEAUDRY, D. B. LANDON AND G. K. KELSO

1989 Living on the Boott: Health and Well Being in a Boardinghouse Population. Theme Issue, The Archaeology of Public Health. *World Archaeology* 21(2):298-319.

MULLINS, PAUL R.

2003 Engagement and the Color Line: Race, Renewal, and Public Archaeology in the Urban Midwest. *Urban Anthropology* 32(3):205-230.

2006 Racializing the Commonplace Landscape: An Archaeology of Urban Renewal Along the Color Line. *World Archaeology* 38(1):60-71.

MYERS, ADRIAN T.

2010 Telling Time for the Electrified: An Introduction to Porcelain Insulators and the Electrification of the American Home. *Technical Briefs in Historical Archaeology* 5:31-42.

NEUMAN, MICHAEL

2006 Infiltrating Infrastructures: On the Nature of Networked Infrastructure. *Journal of Urban Technology* 13(1):3-31.

NISKANEN, WILLIAM A.

1991 The Soft Infrastructure of a Market Economy. *Cato Journal* 11(2):233-238.

PALUS, MATTHEW M.

2005 Building an Architecture of Power: Electricity in Annapolis, Maryland in the 19th and 20th Centuries. In *Archaeologies of Materiality,* edited by Lynn M Meskell, pp. 162-189. Blackwell Publishing, Oxford, UK.

2008 "Preservation was a Fight!": An Oral History of Historic Preservation and Progressive Reform in the Annapolis City Government. In Looking Closer: 300 Years of Annapolis History, a public symposium for the 300th anniversary of the charter of the City of Annapolis, St. John's College, Annapolis, MD.

2009 *Materialities of Government: A Historical Archaeology of Infrastructure in Annapolis and Eastport, 1865-1951.* Ph.D. Dissertation, Columbia University, New York. University Microfilms International, Ann Arbor, MI.

2011 Infrastructure and African American Achievement in Annapolis, Maryland During the Early 20th Century. In *The Materiality of Freedom,* edited by Jodi Barnes. University of South Carolina Press, Columbia, SC.

PARRINGTON, MICHAEL

1983 The History and Archaeology of Philadelphia Roads, Streets, and Utility Lines. *Pennsylvania Archaeologist* 53(3):15-31.

PELS, PETER

1997   The Anthropology of Colonialism: Culture, History, and
        the Emergence of Western Governmentality. *Annual
        Review of Anthropology* 26:163-183.

PEÑA, ELIZABETH S. AND JAQUELINE DENMON

2000   The Social Organization of a Boardinghouse:
        Archaeological Evidence from the Buffalo Waterfront.
        Historical Archaeology 34(1):79-96.

ROSENSWIG, ROBERT M.

1999   Nineteenth Century Urbanism and Public Health:
        The Evidence of Twelve Privies in Albany, New York.
        Northeast Anthropology 58:27-45.

RUSSO, JEAN B.

1988   Encouraging Authenticity and Excellence of Urban
        Design. National Endowment for the Arts Grant-related
        research. Historic Annapolis Foundation, Annapolis,
        MD.

1991   The Public Thoroughfares of Annapolis. *Maryland
        Historical Magazine* 86(1):66-76.

SANBORN MAP COMPANY

1891   *Annapolis, Maryland.* Map accessed through ProQuest,
        LLC, copyright held by Environmental Data Resources,
        Inc., Milford, CT.

1913   *Annapolis, Maryland.* Map accessed through ProQuest,
        LLC, copyright held by Environmental Data Resources,
        Inc., Milford, CT.

1921   *Annapolis, Maryland.* Map accessed through ProQuest,
        LLC, copyright held by Environmental Data Resources,
        Inc., Milford, CT.

1930   *Annapolis, Maryland.* Map accessed through ProQuest,
        LLC, copyright held by Environmental Data Resources,
        Inc., Milford, CT.

SCHUYLER, DAVID

2002   *A City Transformed: Redevelopment, Race, and
        Suburbanization in Lancaster, Pennsylvania, 1940-
        1980.* Pennsylvania University Press, University Park,
        PA.

SCHWENINGER, LOREN

1990   *Black Property Owners in the South, 1790-1915.* Blacks
        in the New World. University of Illinois Press, Urbana,
        IL.

SCOTT, JAMES C.

2010   *The Art of Not Being Governed: An Anarchist History
        of Upland Southeast Asia.* Yale Agrarian Studies. Yale
        University Press, New Yaven, CT.

SMITH, CHARLES W.

1925   *Report of the Mayor of Annapolis on the State of the
        City's Finances from July 1, 1924 to June 30, 1925,
        with Statement of the Sinking Fund.* City of Annapolis,
        Annapolis Mayor & Aldermen, Reports and Minutes
        (Mayor's Report, 1894-1959). Maryland State Archive,
        Annapolis, MD.

SHACKEL, PAUL A.

1996   *Cultural Change and the New Technology: An
        Archaeology of the Early American Industrial Era.*
        Plenum, New York, NY.

SHACKEL, PAUL A. AND MATTHEW M. PALUS

2010   Industry, Entrepreneurship, and Patronage: Lewis
        Wernwag and the Development of Virginius Island.
        Historical Archaeology 44(2):97-112.

STATE OF MARYLAND

1900   Chapter 188: An Act to Authorize the Mayor, Counsellor
        and Aldermen of the City of Annapolis to Issue Bonds to
        the Amount of One Hundred and Twenty-One Thousand
        Dollars to Pay Off the Present Floating Indebtedness
        of the City of Annapolis, and to Provide a Fund for the
        Permanent Improvement of Said City, Approved April
        5, 1900. Laws of the State of Maryland, Made and
        Passed at the Session of the General Assembly Made
        and Held at the City of Annapolis on the Third Day of
        January, 1900, and Ended on the Second Day of April,
        1900. Accessed through Archives of Maryland Online,
        11/11/2008. William J. C. Dulaney Co., State Printers,
        Baltimore, MD.

STABLER, JENNIFER

1990   *Archaeological Investigation of the State Circle Public
        Well, 18AP61, #40 and #42 State Circle, Annapolis,
        Maryland* Barbara J. Little, Principal Investigator.
        Archaeology in Annapolis. University of Maryland
        College Park, College Park, MD.

STOTTMAN, M. JAY

1995   Towards a Greater Understanding of Privy Vault Architecture. In *Historical Archaeology in Kentucky*, edited by Kim A. McBride, Stephen W. McBride and David Pollack, pp 316-335. Kentucky Heritage Council, Frankfort, KY.

2000   Out of Sight, Out of Mind: Privy Architecture and the Perception of Sanitation. *Historical Archaeology* 34(1):39-61.

STRANGE, JAMES F.

1914   *Report of the Mayor of Annapolis on the State of its Finances from July 1 1913, to June 30, 1914.* With Statement of Sinking Fund. Maryland Room, University of Maryland College Park, College Park, MD.

SUNDAY STAR

1957   Society Seeks to Save 234-Year-Old House. *Sunday Star*, May 19, 1957. Washington, D.C.

TARLOW, SARAH

2007   *The Archaeology of Improvement in Britain, 1750-1850.* Cambridge University Press, Cambridge, UK.

UNITED STATES BUREAU OF THE CENSUS

1910   *Thirteenth Census of the United States: 1910 Population. Anne Arundel County, Maryland.* Special Collections, McKeldin Library, University of Maryland College Park, College Park, MD.

UNITED STATES GEOLOGICAL SURVEY

1978   *Annapolis, Maryland.* U.S. Geological Survey, Reston, VA.

WARREN, MAME

1990   *Then Again... Annapolis, 1900-1965.* Time Exposures Ltd, Annapolis, MD.

WHEATON, THOMAS R., JR., MARY BETH REED, RITA FOLSE ELLIOTT, MARK S. Frank and Leslie E. Raymer

1990   James City North Carolina: Archaeological and Historical Study of an African-American Urban Village. Technical Report No. 9. New South Associates, Stone Mountain, GA.

WHEELER, KATHLEEN

2000a   View from the Outhouse: What We Can Learn from the Excavation of Privies. *Historical Archaeology* 34(1):1-2.

WHEELER, KATHLEEN (EDITOR)

2000b   View from the Outhouse: What We Can Learn from the Excavation of Privies. *Historical Archaeology* 34 (1).

WURST, LOUANN AND RANDALL H. McGUIRE

1999   Immaculate Consumption: A Critique of the "Shop till you drop" School of Human Behavior. *International Journal of Historical Archaeology* 3(3):191-199.

Matthew M. Palus
Department of Anthropology
University of Maryland College Park
1111 Woods Hall
College Park, MD 20742

Adam Heinrich and Carmel Schrire

Colonial Fauna at the Cape of Good Hope: A Proxy for Colonial Impact on Indigenous People

As archaeologists our first responsibility is pattern recognition. We must then ask why the patterns are distinct, why there is this regularity, why there is this variability.

-South (2002:43)

ABSTRACT

This study of faunal remains shows how power operated within a mercantile capitalist trade network in the 17th and 18th centuries. A large data set of bones from colonial sites of the Dutch East India Company (VOC) at the Cape of Good Hope was analyzed using experimental and comparative methods of faunal analysis. Results reveal how a European global trading company established a meat industry by hybridizing indigenous herds, imposing European breeding patterns, and butchering stock, all to satisfy the meat trade within the settlement and for the calling trade ships. Ultimately, these practices dispossessed and impoverished the indigenous Khoekhoen, forcing them to become an underclass within the new colonial settler society.

Introduction

Zooarchaeologists use patterns in faunal assemblages to reconstruct the human exploitation of animals and their environment (Klein and Cruz-Uribe 1984:1,3; Reitz and Scarry 1985:1; Davis 1987:19; Reitz and Wing 1999:3; O'Connor 2000:173). Historical archaeologists have access to written sources, and replete though they may be with biases and omissions, they nevertheless provide a contextual background to help evaluate archaeological findings and a foundation for broader questions about the past. Lewis Binford (1977:21), whose insistence on inferring behavior from patterns in archaeological residues gave rise to the "New Archaeology" paradigm, conceded that although the written historical record is one of the best tools available to archaeologists it often lacks the details that archaeologists need regarding diet. Yet, the analysis of faunal remains can provide us with a rich and objective record of the past. With this understanding, James Deetz (1996:73-79,168-171) stressed the value of thinking about the wider issue of foodways, to integrate bones, ceramics and utensils with documentary sources. Over the past few decades, researchers have used faunal residues to address questions that reach beyond the identification of species consumed at the household level; these include topics such as the evolution of hybrid breeds, adaptation of animals to new environments, social status based on cost of type and cut of meat, ethnicity (e.g. species preference and butchering patterns), and the development of rural and urban markets (Landon 2005, 2009).

The processual approach is intrinsic to faunal analysis where the patterns in the collection can reveal systematic husbandry, slaughter, consumption behaviors, and environmental influences. Within this approach, a strong taphonomic perspective affords more confident comparative interpretations across sites (e.g. Lyman 1994). Close examination of bones under slight magnification (Blumenshine et al. 1996) together with actualistic taphonomic experiments are commonplace in prehistoric zooarchaeology (e.g. Gifford 1981, Lyman 1994), but with few exceptions, they have not been applied to historic period sites (e.g. Reitz 1987; Landon 1992, 1996, 1997; Heinrich 2010a, 2010b). Analyses of faunal collections from five sites are presented here to help infer the consequences of the establishment of a colonial meat industry at the colonial Cape of Good Hope. We combine a taphonomic perspective with inferences drawn from the official records of the ruling Dutch East India Company, observations of international callers and settlers, as well as scholarly syntheses. Together these sources allow the patterns identified in the bones to be incorporated into an understanding of how this meat industry affected the indigenous people and the colonizers of the Cape.

Historical Background

The *Verenigde Oost-Indische Compagnie* (VOC), or the Dutch East India Company, was chartered in 1602 to develop profitable trading partnerships in Asia and they eventually grew to be a major player in the Euro-Asiatic trade networks during the 17th and 18th centuries (Israel 1989). In a period of high mortality and illness at sea due to malnutrition, the VOC, under the command of Jan van Riebeeck, established a node at the Cape of Good Hope at the southern tip of Africa in 1652 to support their seaborne mercantile trade networks by provisioning their ships with fresh water, vegetables, fruits, and meat (Robertson 1945a:3; Sleigh 1980:49; Schrire and Merwick 1991:12; Grove 1997:128; Schrire 1995:13; De Vries and Van der Woude 1997:429; Israel 1998:938).

The rationale for VOC settlement at the Cape arose from glowing testimonies of many sailors that spoke of the fertile soil, fresh water, and bright trading prospects with the Khoekhoe pastoralists who led a transhumant lifestyle with their herds of sheep (*Ovis aries*) and cattle (*Bos taurus*) (Raven-Hart 1967:174-180; Elphick 1977:58, 1985:58; Penn 1986:63; Elphick and Malherbe 1988:8-10; Klein and Cruz-Uribe 1989:92; Boonzaier et al. 1996:29; Balasse and Ambrose 2002:927-928; Smith 2006:13). The local Khoekhoe pastoralists who regarded their stock as wealth traded them for the usual European goods that included beads, copper, iron tools, tobacco, and alcohol (Kolben 1731a:262-263, 1731b:65; Mentzel 1921:53; Robertson 1945b:84; Raven-Hart 1970a:103,217; Elphick 1977:57, 1985:38,57; Boonzaier et al. 1988:42,44-47; Schrire 1995:52,57-58,111-112). Immediately upon settlement, the Dutch interbred the indigenous sheep with imported Bengali and Persian breeds in order to create a larger, meatier hybrid that was well-adapted to the

arid Cape environment (Mentzel 1921:56, 1944:210; Thom 1936:246, 249; Raven-Hart 1970b:381; Guelke 1988:71; Cruz-Uribe and Schrire 1991:97). As the Cape settlement on the beach at Table Bay expanded from an original mud fort to a stone castle surrounded by a small town, the VOC fulfilled their provisioning obligations with immense herds of sheep and cattle.

Jan van Riebeeck, the Commander of the first settlement, intended that each calling ship would receive eight cattle and eight sheep (Elphick 1985:152). Sheep were always more plentiful in the Dutch holdings partly because they bred faster than cattle and because the Khoekhoen were reluctant to trade their more esteemed cattle (Elphick and Malherbe 1988:21; Ross 1988:251-254). A mere decade after the first landing in 1652, nine times as many sheep as originally envisaged by Van Riebeeck was slaughtered for the ships whose reliance on mutton grew steadily into the later 17th century (Elphick 1985:153). Even as the stock trade with the Khoekhoen fell off over time, sheep continued to outnumber cattle in the Dutch herds at a "living ratio" of about 2.5 sheep to each cow in 1720, and about 4:1 by 1770 (Elphick 1985:153; Ross 1988:253). The high demand for meat created difficulties for the VOC during the first 50-75 years of the settlement; however, as time went on and the Dutch developed their own herds, the meat industry became a predominant component of the Cape economy (Templin 1984:19; Elphick 1985:151-161; Penn 2005:29). By the early 18th century, the VOC required a total of 390,000 pounds of slaughtered meat annually for ships, with much of this being mutton (Mentzel 1925:56).

Although the VOC were meticulous record keepers, complete details of their meat industry are lacking in the archival collections, possibly because it was such a mundane aspect of their overall workings, and possibly because it operated in both private and distant sectors. For whatever reason, the summary of work presented below tries to fill this gap in colonial Cape economic and social history (Heinrich 2010a).

The Faunal Collections

Seven faunal samples from five sites were analyzed in order to evaluate the VOC meat industry at the Cape of Good Hope.

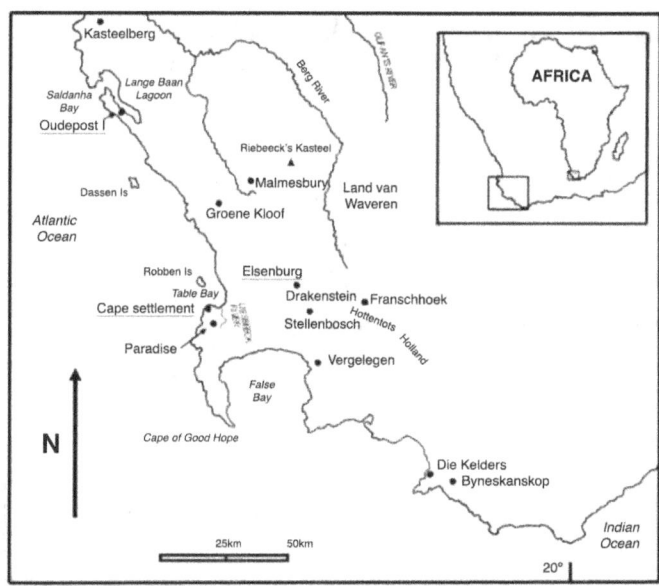

Figure 1. Map showing landmarks of the Western Cape with the locations of the sites highlighted (Heinrich 2010a:2).

Figure 2. View of Table Bay with a plan of the Castle of Good Hope (N. de Fer, Paris, 1705 in Schrire collection). The historic jetty is visible in the upper panel. The location of the Moat excavation is between the right ravelin and the right seaward bastion.

Three sites are located in the political and military headquarters of the Castle of Good Hope at the main Cape settlement and include the Van der Stel Moat and two structures within the Castle, namely the Granary and a supposed torture chamber called *Donkergat* (DKG). The other two sites lay beyond the main settlement: a VOC farm called Elsenburg, lying about 50 km east of the Cape settlement, and Oudepost I, an outpost on the frontier of Dutch penetration about 120 km north of the Castle (Figure 1). Site descriptions are present for the Castle sites (Hall n.d.b, 1989), Elsenburg (Hart and Halkett 1993), and Oudepost I (Cruz-Uribe and Schrire 1991; Schrire et al. 1993; Schrire 1995, 2010).

Castle of Good Hope: Van der Stel Moat

Construction of the pentagonal and moated Castle of Good Hope began in 1666, with an original seaward-facing entranceway. This was relocated in 1682 to face the town. Although minor

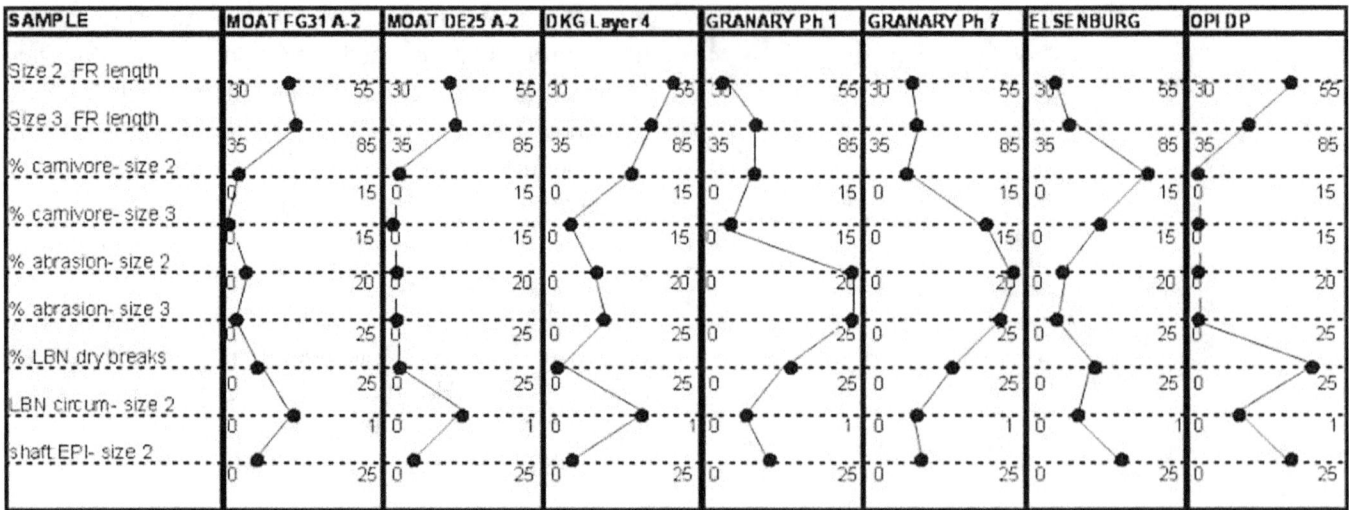

Figure 3. Diagram summarizing and comparing the taphonomic details of the major faunal samples (Heinrich 2010a:286). Lower proportions of post-depositional taphonomic damage (carnivore or abrasion) correlate with larger bone fragment sizes and greater preservation of diagnostic bone portions such as epiphyses, which therefore allows for increased fragment identifiability. Higher proportions of post-depositional damage and dry breaks are indicative of bones being exposed on ground surfaces which affect preservation and identifiability. Note: FR= fragment, size 2= sheep-sized mammal, size 3=cow-sized mammal, LBN= long bone, shaft:EPI= long bone midshaft fragment to epiphysis ratio, and lengths are in millimeters.

deposition occurred in the Moat during the late 17th century, the depression was rapidly filled in ca. 1720-1725 with a mixture of construction debris, discarded tobacco pipes, ceramics, glass, in addition to bones from kitchen and provisioning waste to provide an earthen approach to the new entranceway (Hall 1989:7; Fitchett 1996:143-144; Jordan 2005:7; Klose 2005:26; Yates et al. n.d.:23). Two faunal samples were analyzed from the Moat; both came from the main level (called A-2) from a southern column (called DE25) located near the entrance, and a northern column (called FG31) near the historic jetty where animals were slaughtered (Raven-Hart 1970b:346) (Figure 2).

The faunal remains are well preserved with larger than average fragment sizes as compared to the other samples presented here (Figure 3). Long bone shaft circumferences are relatively complete and midshaft:epiphyses fragment ratios are low, suggesting that destructive processes did not fracture the bones and render them unidentifiable. This is supported by

the observation that trampling and carnivore chewing traces are rare. Breakage patterns are mainly oblique showing that fragmentation occurred while the bones were fresh. The low frequency of postmortem damage on the faunal remains suggests that the bones were not left exposed on the ground surface for an extended period of time and instead, were quickly deposited into the Moat as part of a quick fill event.

Castle of Good Hope: Donkergat

*D*onkergat (DKG), or "dark hole" is a small 4 x 8m room located along the seaward curtain wall in the interior courtyard of the Castle that is thought to have served as a torture chamber. A thick, bone-rich fill stratum was excavated (called Layer 4) around 40 cm below the surface and dates to the end of the VOC occupation, around the 1790s.

The taphonomic details of the DKG bones reveal a very well-preserved collection (Figure 3). The average bone fragment sizes are the largest average sizes for any of the VOC period sites. Long bone breakage patterns are predominately oblique and suggest fragmentation occurred when the bones were fresh. Epiphyses are well represented and long bone shafts are also the most complete of the sites described here. Carnivore damage is rare and trampling damage is moderate. Though the abrasion traces are observed in moderate frequencies, the abrasive processes did not render the bones into smaller, unidentifiable fragments.

Castle of Good Hope: Granary

A long vaulted Granary was completed within the Castle's interior courtyard along an internal dividing wall by 1691. The Castle was built on ill-drained ground and suffered repeated water damage, so in order to keep grain dry, the floor of the Granary was raised with multiple fill events (Fitchett 1996:164). Seven Phases of stratigraphic fill were excavated, of which two - Phase 1 and Phase 7 - were chosen for faunal analyses. Phase 1 is the earliest deposit from the Castle and dates to 1666-1691, before the dividing wall was constructed. Phase 7 is the last deposit and dates roughly to the mid-18th century (Hall n.d.b:7-8).

The bones from both samples were heavily affected by taphonomic processes (Figure 3). Average bone fragment sizes are amongst the smallest of the VOC sites discussed here and this is echoed in low long bone shaft circumference completeness and the very low numbers of long bone epiphyses. This fragmentation was partly caused by heavy carnivore and trampling involvement. Fragmentation occurred at two times: a high proportion (72.39 % in Phase 1, 70.69% in Phase 7) occurred while the bones were fresh, but a moderate 14.82% of the long bones from each Phase were broken when they were dry. These timing of fragmentation suggests ground surface exposure that allowed trampling and scavenging as well as subsequent breakage. Together with the fact that no refitting of bone fragments was possible, it seems the bones were brought in with secondary fills from outside the Granary, and they did not derive from slave meals eaten *in situ* as was originally argued (Hall n.d.a:3, 1992:389-390, 1999:196, 2000:18, 2008:128-130).

Elsenburg

Elsenburg was a large farmstead located about 50 km east of the Castle near the early frontier settlement of Stellenbosch. Originally granted to the VOC Secunde Samuel Elsevier in 1698, Elsenburg changed ownership through sales and inheritance after Elsevier was recalled in 1707 for inappropriate usage of VOC funds (Mentzel 1921:19; Fairbridge 1931:138; Valentyn 1971:151; Fransen and Cook 1980:166; Schutte 1988:304; Markell et al. 1995:10). Being a large farm, the numbers of stock were recorded in regular tax surveys. They show sheep outnumbering cattle in ratios from 4:1 to 9:1 in the 1740s and 1750s at the farm (VOC 1741,1742,1746-1753). The main archaeological collection comes from a thick, rich deposit of kitchen and household debris called the "Dump" that accumulated in a natural ground surface depression that was eventually sealed by the foundations of the current manor house in 1761 (Hart and Halkett 1993:25-26) (Figure 4). Deposition may have begun as early as the 1730s, but it mainly accumulated in the 1740-1750s (Hart and Halkett 1993:32; Klose 1997:126).

Figure 4. The manor house at Elsenburg built in 1761. (Photograph by Heinrich, 2005).

The faunal collection from Elsenburg is very well-preserved, though it was highly fragmented (Figure 3). Most of the fragmentation occurred when the bones were fresh, though 11.27% of the long bones were fragmented after experiencing some drying. As expected in a surface deposit, carnivore damage is high and trampling damage is observed in moderate frequencies. Low long bone shaft completeness and low numbers of epiphyses further demonstrate high degrees of fragmentation.

Oudepost I

Oudepost I was a VOC frontier outpost on Saldanha Bay about 120 km north of the Cape settlement. The outpost included a rectangular lodge, a small fort, and several unidentified structures. It was manned by a small contingent of four to ten soldiers between 1669 and 1732, except for a period from 1673 to 1684/6 when it was abandoned after a Khoekhoe attack. Due to their distance from the main VOC stock farms, the garrison supplemented their rations by hunting, fishing and trading with the local Khoekhoen. Archaeological residues include a rich faunal collection derived from the terrestrial site around the structures, and an additional dump of bones from an intertidal zone (hereafter DP, for "Dump") where butchery waste was apparently dumped into the lagoon (Cruz-Uribe and Schrire 1991; Schrire et al. 1993; Schrire 1995:108-109) (Figure 5).

The taphonomic history of the terrestrial sample was not systematically studied, though the bones are reported to be fragmentary with most large bovid postcranial material unidentifiable to the species taxon (Cruz-Uribe and Schrire 1991:94,96). The composition of DP is the product of winnowing from the tidal actions that dissolved or washed away the softer portions of the skeleton leaving behind isolated teeth and less diagnostic long bone midshaft fragments. For example, 69.51% of sheep-sized and 76.25% of cow-sized specimens are midshaft fragments. The winnowing away of softer and smaller bone fragments allowed DP's bone fragments to be amongst the largest in the VOC samples presented here (Figure 3). Due to the brackish, tidal environment, only four bone fragments (0.38%) retain their original condition while the rest are heavily rounded or exhibit surface exfoliation which did not allow for the investigation of taphonomic traces from butchery, carnivore scavenging, and trampling.

Figure 5. The fort at Oudepost I on the shore of Langebaan Lagoon, Saldanha Bay. The DP deposit is just beyond the walls of the fort in the intertidal zone. Scale in 20 cm increments. (Photograph by Schrire, 1986).

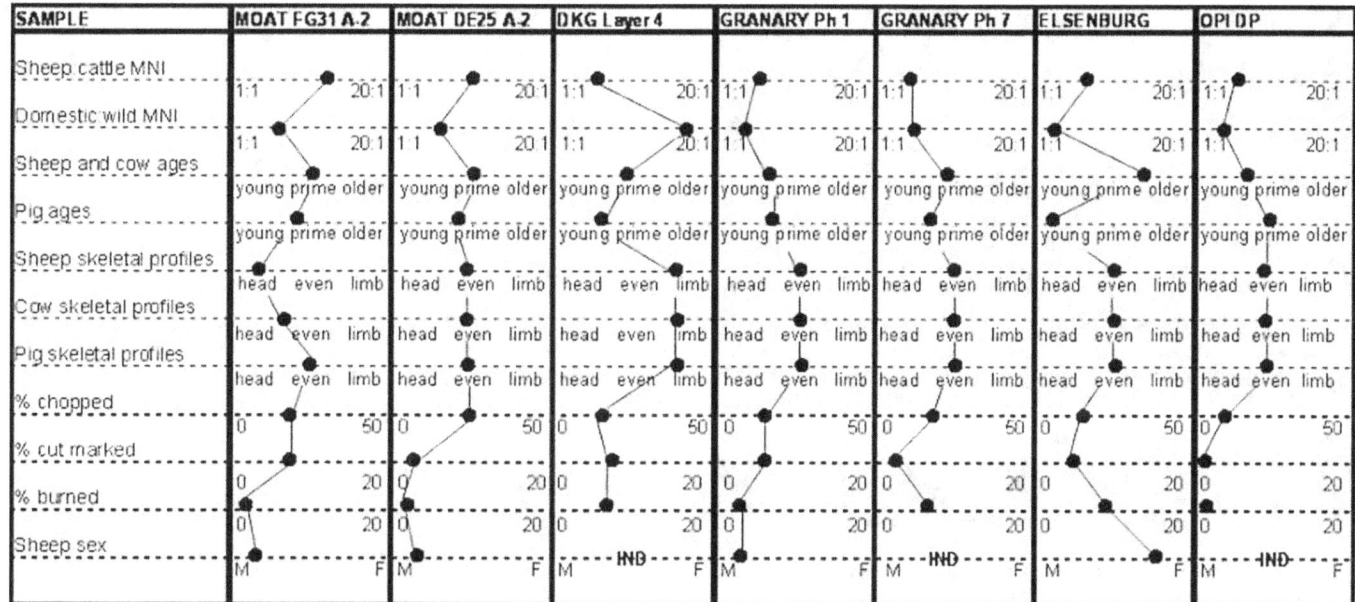

Characteristics of the VOC Meat Industry

An economic system incorporates a variety of individual units that work together to meet the demands of the consumers (Braudel 1979:138-230; Wallerstein 1980:38-39; Johnson 1999:220-226; Orser 2005:77-80). In the case of the VOC meat industry, the major units include livestock producers, slaughterers, and consumers whose interplay is apparent in the results of the faunal analyses tabulated in Figure 6.

Meat Consumption

Butchery marks reveal consumption and marketing practices. All sites show that animals were initially reduced in similar manners before the portions were sent onto ships, to markets, or to kitchens for further processing. The samples from all sites were dominated by chop marks aimed at dismembering the carcasses and rendering them into more manageable segments (Figure 6). Initial chops were in predictable locales such as near major joints and distal limb midshafts above the foot. Secondary chopping divided the vertebral columns into sagittal halves as well as into smaller segments (such as between lumbar and thoracic vertebrae)

Figure 6. Diagram summarizing and comparing the details of the major faunal samples (Heinrich 2010a:287). Urban sites contain fewer wild animals compared to those in the frontier and the stock was generally slaughtered at prime ages. The Moat shows that a disproportionate number of sheep were slaughtered compared to cattle due to provisioning activities. Sheep and cattle were kept older at the production site of Elsenburg. The early sites (Granary's Phase 1 and Oudepost I) show that a higher proportion of sheep were slaughtered younger. Pigs, which were not used for provisioning, were slaughtered at their prime ages, except at Elsenburg where they were predominately very young and raised at the farm for personal consumption. Sites where kitchen/table refuse was dumped exhibit moderate proportions of butchery and cooking evidence.

and separating ribs from thoracic vertebrae and then further into smaller segments (Figure 7). Chopping that split the crania into sagittal halves is well represented in the Moat and Elsenburg samples (Figure 8).

Figure 7. Sheep lumbar vertebrae from the Castle of Good Hope's Moat showing sagittal chopping splitting the carcass into halves. The two right examples also show transverse chopping that divided the vertebral column into shorter segments. (Photograph by Heinrich, 2005).

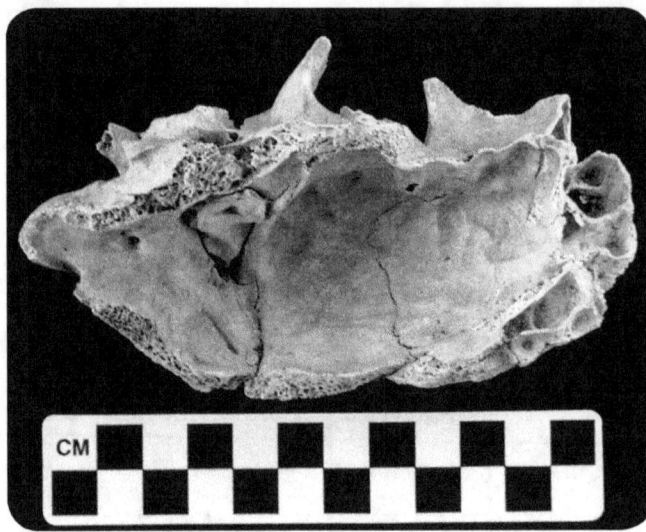

Figure 8. Sheep cranium from the Castle of Good Hope's Moat showing sagittal chopping that was aimed at accessing the brain (Photograph by Heinrich, 2005).

Knife processing, seen as cut or scrape marks, is generally less common than chop marks (Figure 6). These marks are observed on limb shafts where meat was removed, near joints where ligaments and tendons were severed, and on crania and distal foot elements where carcasses were skinned (The Hide, Leather, and Allied Trades Improvement Society 1928:7; Landon 1996:67). Moderate frequencies of cut marks are found in food consumption residues from DKG (8.93%), both Phases of the Granary (6.00% in Phase 1, 2.30% in Phase 7), Elsenburg (4.07%), and the terrestrial sample from Oudepost I (5.16%) (Cruz-Uribe and Schrire 1991:100). The Moat samples have fewer knife marks, suggesting that most of these bones derive from an early stage of butchery. Bones from both ends of the Moat excavation produced different proportions of knife cut marks: those from the northern end near the historical jetty did show moderate amounts (6.91% in A-2) while those from the southern end, closer to the Castle gateway, have few cut marks (1.69% in A-2). While the northern sample has a moderate amount of knife cutting, the disproportionately high numbers of sheep cranial, hyoid, and mandibular fragments contain 52.27% of the observed cut marks, which suggests heavy skinning and tongue removal. A low frequency of knife marks can be indicative of primary butchery done at an abattoir (Reitz 2007:98; Zierden and Reitz 2009:346,349).

Evidence of table refuse can be identified in the Moat, DKG, the Granary, and Elsenburg. Roasts were allegedly common in the Cape diet and they are often mentioned in historical documents (Fouche 1914:75; Gerber 1959:65; Botha 1970:57; Coetzee 1977:87,89,91,92,94; Robinson 1994:181; Abrahams 1996:226-227). Burned bone confirms the presence of meat roasted on the bone in the archaeological contexts (Figure 6). DKG shows the clearest evidence for kitchen/table refuse due to the dominance of large bone fragments from meat-bearing elements together with a high incidence of burning (6.82%). The characteristic purplish color of the burnt bones suggests cooking of greasy or meat laden bones so that their presence in DKG reflects consumption of roasted meat (David 1989:74). In addition, isolated burnt spots and/or burning inside long bone shafts also suggest exposure of bones to flame or very high heat while portions of the bones were protected by meat (Figure 9 and 10). Burning in DKG is moderate and comparable to frequencies from Elsenburg (9.06%), Phase 7 from the Granary (5.80%), and higher than that found in the terrestrial sample from Oudepost I (2.60%). These frequencies contrast with the Moat where burning is rare (0.00-1.17%), though a charred gray duiker (*Sylvicapra grimmia*) bone suggests that some wild fauna was roasted. This confirms that the Moat was not a major deposit for kitchen refuse, at

FIGURE 9. A proximal cow tibia from DKG showing burning on the interior shaft. (Photograph by Heinrich, 2005).

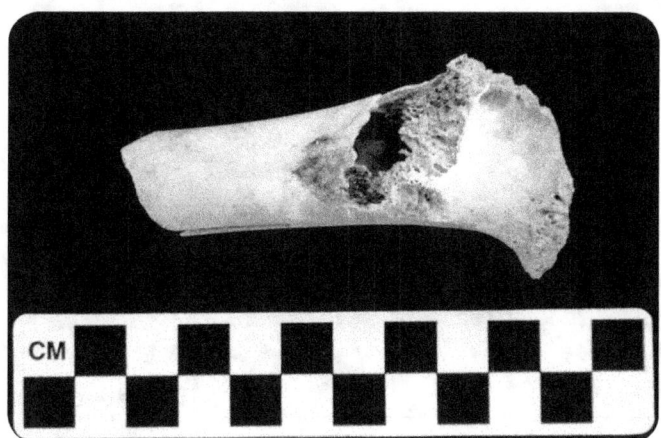

Figure 10. A proximal sheep femur from DKG showing isolated burning spots where meat did not protect the bone during roasting. (Photograph by Heinrich, 2005).

least not roasts. The Moat's associated collection of coarse earthenware cooking vessels is dominated by food preparation vessels that may have been used to make stews instead of, or as well as, roasts (Jordan 2000:136).

Stews are not readily identifiable in the VOC faunal samples. It is believed that meat prepared for stews was customarily chopped into small pieces with the bones so the most grease can be extracted through simmering (e.g. Baker 1980:34; Crader 1984:548, 1989:230-231; 1990:710; Otto 1984:172). Actualistic studies have shown that this is not necessary, but the traditional idea has persisted (Church and Lyman 2003). Documentary sources record the popularity of stews made by Malay and Asian cooks at the Cape in the mid-18th century (Mentzel 1921:112; Gerber 1959: 10; Botha 1970:49; Coetzee 1977:28,44-47; Elphick and Malherbe 1988:28-35; Elphick and Shell 1988:225; Abrahams 1998:6-8). Hall (n.d.a:3, 1992:389-390, 1999:196, 2000:18, 2008:128-130) and Thackerey (1989) originally interpreted the high fragmentation levels in the Granary deposits as evidence of stews made by slaves trying to extract as much nutrition as possible from the bones, but taphonomic investigations contradict this inference. Stews or wet dishes might have been an important component of the evolving creolized Cape diet, but the confirmation is not visible on bones. In the Dutch and the Cape cuisine, boiled meats were generally removed from the bone and cut into manageable sizes before being placed in the pot

(Gerber 1959; Rose 1989). Some of this meat may be represented through cut marks such as those on femora or humeri, though these marks cannot be confidently attributed to the filleting of meat for stews or being cut from roasts.

The types of animals present in the deposits also speak to local diet. The Moat contrasts with the other sites due to the fact most of the sample strongly represents primary, *en masse* slaughter for calling ships or other markets before reaching a kitchen, but portions of the Moat collection do not fit an expected provisioning model. There is a small number of burnt bones derived from kitchen refuse, probably from inside the adjacent Castle. In addition, animals that would not fit provisioning needs but instead met the needs of the elite include lamb, wild animals, and birds. These animals represent a diet where the people ate according to their taste and/or to acquire exotic wild animals that were illegal except for those hunted for the Governor's table (i.e. Mentzel 1925:101; Thackeray 1989:1; Cruz-Uribe and Schrire 1991:95; Hall n.d.a:3, 1992:389-390). Birds used for provisioning were minimally processed and sent nearly complete and therefore the bones would have been removed away from the sites.

In 16th century Spanish Florida, where diverse wild fauna was available, a low diversity of taxa was characteristic of military diets since rations were normally derived from regularly suppliable domestic meat (Reitz and Scarry 1985:88). At the Cape, this pattern is evident at DKG and Phase 7 of the Granary where only one or two wild mammal individuals are present (Figure 6). These sites inside the Castle contrast markedly with the terrestrial sample from the distant, and earlier dated Oudepost I where hunting supplemented the meat rations and where the domestic sheep, cow, and pig only make up about 25-29% of the individuals (Schrire 1990:15; Cruz-Uribe and Schrire 1991:96-97).

Fulfilling Livestock Demands

Whether the site was at the consumption or the production end of the system, each faunal sample provides clues about how the stock was raised for the market. For the most part,

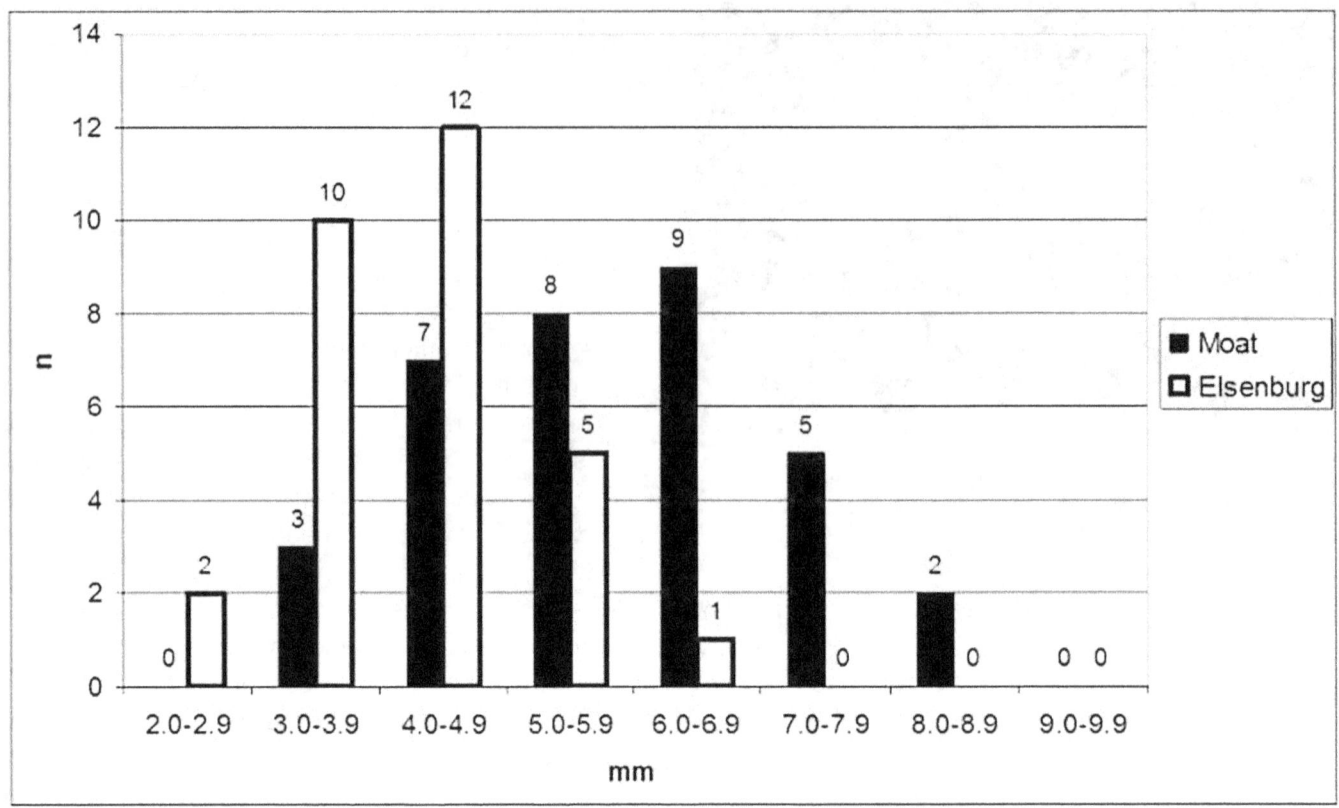

Figure 11. Histogram illustrating the distribution of medial acetabular measurements for sheep in the Moat and how they compare to those from Elsenburg (Heinrich 2010a:111). The Moat mainly contains males or wethers while Elsenburg is dominated by females.

these clues are the demographic categories of age and sex.

Age provides two different patterns. Sites from the late 17th and first quarter of the 18th centuries (Phase 1 in the Granary, the terrestrial sample and DP from Oudepost I) show a predominance of younger sheep slaughtered around 12 to 18 months of age. At Oudepost I, the terrestrial sample shows that a high proportion of sheep were slaughtered between 6 weeks and 2 years of age (Cruz-Uribe and Schrire 1991:98), and in the DP sample from the intertidal zone shows that a large proportion of sheep were slaughtered between 9 months and 18 months of age. The postcranial specimens from all contexts confirm the dental findings with a large proportion of unfused elements that typically fuse around one to three years of age. In contrast to these earlier contexts, sheep from the mid to later 18th century (Moat, DKG, and Phase 7 from the Granary) show that almost all sheep were slaughtered

in their prime (two to six years). Similar findings appear in the Grand Parade in the Cape settlement (Abrahams 1996:244-245) and Paradise, a forestry outpost about 10 km from the Cape (Avery 1989:115).

In contrast to the urban situation, most of the sheep from the farm Elsenburg were slaughtered slightly older between four to six years of age with some even older. Cattle, though relatively rare in VOC sites, conform to the patterns seen with the sheep, with slaughter in the urban areas at prime ages, and those slaughtered at Elsenburg were beyond their prime such as one cow whose worn dentition would have hardly been effective for food processing. These findings from both the urban and rural sites contradict the documentary sources, namely Otto Mentzel (1921:56, 1944:212), describing between 1733-41 after the Moat was filled, who stated that wethers were slaughtered between one and two years of age.

Turning to sex, the two largest samples (Moat and Elsenburg) provided measurable acetabulae, whose medial acetabular walls are among the best indicators of sex in osteological bovid materials (Figure 11) (Greenfield 2002). The Moat sample was dominated by larger sheep, most likely male wethers (Leibbrandt

1905:130-131; Mentzel 1921:56, 1944:212), while Elsenburg was dominated by smaller sheep, mostly females ($t = 3.58$, $P = 0.0008$). Measurements of distal humeri and tibiae, though less pronounced, support this finding. The humeri and tibiae from the terrestrial sample from Oudepost I indicate a more even split between male and female sheep.

In summary, the patterns of slaughter define meat production strategies at the Cape. The samples from the 17th and early 18th centuries (Phase 1 from the Granary, Oudepost I) show that sheep were often slaughtered younger than what seemed to be ideal in the mid to later 18th century. In addition, the sex data gleaned from Oudepost I also suggests that a higher proportion of females were being slaughtered alongside males during this earlier period. In contrast, the established herds drawn on for the samples from Elsenburg, the Moat, DKG, and the Granary samples show that prime-aged males/wethers were preferred for slaughter, while useful females were kept on the farms until they exceeded their reproductively fit ages. Together, the age and sex information point to tension between the desire to develop the herds and the obligation to slaughter for the VOC meat market. The VOC had difficulties keeping up with the demands for meat during the first 50-75 years of the settlement's establishment, which required continual trading and raiding expeditions into the interior to obtain even more stock from the Khoekhoen (Elphick 1985:151,154; Penn 2005:29). When indigenous herders went broke or moved north, the VOC established their own meat posts at places like Groene Kloof (today's Mamre) and then cashed in on official VOC contracts given to farmers. Stock holders might have preferred to breed the animals that they were forced to market for meat (Fouche 1914:xix; Mentzel 1921:171, 1925:55-56; Robertson 1945b:79-80; Elphick and Malherbe 1988:11; Ross 1988:247; Van der Merwe 1995:1). A similar pattern is observed in the Chesapeake, where the English colonists experienced initial difficulties in establishing their herds. Cattle and pigs were slaughtered younger in the 1620-1660 period than during the 1660-1700s when better established stock was slaughtered at prime ages (Bowen 1999:362-363). Likewise, Spanish colonists in Florida and Dutch colonists in New Amsterdam initially slaughtered their cattle younger than what was typical

in later periods (Reitz and Scarry 1985:80,96-97; Reitz 1991:65,69; Janowitz 1993:16; Cantwell and DiZerega Wall 2001:179).

Once the Cape meat system was established, husbandry then grew to resemble the trends seen in other colonial period meat production systems. This contrast between the rural producers and urban consumers is a product of animal husbandry that is focused on large scale meat production for high-demand systems like those seen for large urban centers, exports, or ship provisioning instead of diversified products such as dairy, draught, and wool (Trow-Smith 1957:172-173,239, 1959:199; Pennington 1989:61; Wilson 1994:111; Landon 1996:114,123; Davis 1997:416; Sykes 2006:63). In this system, urban sites generally exhibit an incomplete demographic since the breeding portion of the herd would have remained at the production sites, like that seen at Elsenburg, until the animals were past their reproductive value (Allison 1958:101-102; Zeder 1984:285; Landon 1996:8,123, 1997:57,61; Sykes 2006:62). At the Cape, sites at the consumption end of the system, like the Granary, DKG, the Moat, Paradise, and the Grand Parade from the Cape settlement, are dominated by prime-aged animals that are usually male (Avery 1989:115; Abrahams 1996:244-245).

The Impact of the VOC Meat Industry on the Indigenous People and Landscape

Once the VOC settled at the Cape, the future of the indigenous Khoekhoe pastoralists became bleak. The Cape settlement needed to produce sufficient amounts of vegetables and meat for the calling ships, and eventually for the expanding colonial population. As early as 1657, European farmers set up grain growing operations, but they soon realized that large scale, labor-intensive grain production would never work in the labile Cape climate, so many moved to stock rearing. Meat was a valuable commodity in continual demand. In order to meet this challenge, settlers commandeered vast farms in the frontier thereby competing brutally with the indigenous stock owners (Fisher 1969:9; Templin 1984:18-19;

Geulke 1988:70-71,80,86; Schutte 1988:288-291; Van der Merwe 1995:1-11,14,19; Giliomee 2003:7). The Khoekhoen did not take the arrival of the VOC lying down (Marks 1972; Elphick 1985). They resisted repeatedly in covert acts like setting fire to the thatched roofs of the settlers, and in more overt acts of aggression like murder (Schrire 1995:87). Their leaders are even recorded as asking exactly how equitably the Dutch might tolerate a Khoekhoe invasion of Holland. But in the end guns, horses, and a seemingly endless stream of new settlers won out over the stone age technology of the pre-colonial Cape. Khoekhoe leadership was subverted in the face of brandy, tobacco and brass-knobbed sticks of office (Schrire 1995:68). Their leadership eventually disintegrated, leaving them nothing but petty theft in order to recoup stock. Settlers retaliated with institutionalized plunder and more formal wars carried out by excursions of official VOC soldiers as well as commando groups from nearby outposts. The Khoekhoen were dubbed "bandits," "Bushmen," and worse (Elphick 1985:225-227; Elphick and Malherbe 1989:18-21,26). Dispossessed Cape Khoekhoen, who retreated north with their depleted flocks found themselves outgunned by the settlers called *trekboer*, tied to a market economy (Penn 2005).

The process of dispossession was complex. While the acquisition of stock from the VOC and other local European farmers was difficult and expensive during the first 50-75 years after settlement (Templin 1984:19; Elphick 1985:151-161; Penn 2005:29), the Khoekhoen presented both an opportunity and an obstacle to stock farming. The VOC tried to control the stock trade but after years of trading, the indigenous market became glutted with imported trinkets like copper and beads. Trading expeditions to the interior Khoekhoen became less productive and VOC officials feared that unregulated freelance colonial farmers would undercut their control by paying higher prices or by committing violent theft. These fears were realized when the farmers' mistreatment of the Khoekhoen led to retaliation and restricted markets (Penn 1986:66; 2005:38-39,41,52-55; Guelke 1988:77; Legassick 1988:359-363; Schrire 1990:17-18; Van der Merwe 1995:25).

In the late 17th century, Governor Simon van der Stel's (1679-1699) efforts were ineffectual at defining and protecting the frontiers as well as stopping freelance stock trading beyond them. In 1700, his successor, Willem Adriaan van der Stel (1699-1707), promoted frontier settlement and opened free trade with the Khoekhoen (Elphick 1985:155-161; Elphick and Malherbe 1988:21 Guelke 1988:79; Van der Merwe 1995:21-22,35-38; Penn 2005:27-30). By 1708, the open trade devastated the Khoekhoe herds probably taking an under-recorded 35,562 sheep and 8,871 cattle (Elphick and Malherbe 1988:21).

Between trade, theft, and natural breeding, the VOC herds increased in number. To avoid over-grazing, the **trekboeren** adopted a Khoekhoe-like lifestyle of seasonally transhumant pastoralism and spread inland into arid areas where the stock required large tracts of land around suitable water sources. When a smallpox outbreak in 1713 further reduced the Khoekhoen to about 1/10th of their already diminished strength, there was little to impede the farmers from incorporating the grazing lands and water sources of the Khoekhoen (Mentzel 1925:36; Elphick 1977:229-233, 1985:233; Penn 1986:65, 2005:42; Elphick and Malherbe 1988:21-22; Guelke and Shell 1992:823-824; Ross 1998:307). Further loss of the Khoekhoe identity continued when the desperate and dispossessed had to give up their ancestral transhumant stock herding independence to become servants of the farmers in order to survive (Elphick 1985:217-219; Penn 1986:66; Elphick and Malherbe 1989: 20; Ross 1998:308-311).

The inference drawn from the earliest faunal samples from Oudepost I and Phase 1 from the Granary speaks to the efforts of the VOC to meet the demands of the ship's provisioning market. This required sheep to be slaughtered younger and in disproportionate sex ratios than what was seen as ideal in the mid to later 18th century. This management style forced farmers into continual accumulation of stock through trade and capture from the dwindling Khoekhoe holdings. The success of this strategy is seen in the later samples from the Moat, Phase 7 from the Granary, Elsenburg, and DKG, when there were self-replenishing herds, large enough for wethers to be slaughtered in their prime ages. This achievement is also seen in the collections from Oudepost I and especially the Moat (with a much higher than "living ratio" of sheep outnumbering cattle 10-14:1 in the larger contexts)(Figure 6), where sheep and sometimes cattle were slaughtered in great numbers to meet demands which had multiplied significantly since Van Riebeeck's original mid-17th century plan for eight sheep and eight cattle per ship (Elphick 1985:152).

The price of settler success in the meat market was paid by the Khoekhoe herders. Their dispossession follows the same patterns of transformation that probably preceded, and certainly followed, European colonial ventures in their new worlds (Crosby 1986:275; Grove 1997:126; Wolf 1997; Mann 2005). In the Southwest Cape, prehistoric hunter-gatherers, foragers, and pastoralists lived in low density groups that moved with the availability of resources. When the VOC settlement was established in 1652, an estimated 50,000 Khoekhoen, including about 8,000 Peninsular Khoekhoen, lived in the diverse, rich ecozone of the Western Cape (Theal 1897:126; Skead 1980, 1987:813-855; Elphick 1985:23,92; Avery and Underhill 1986; Cruz-Uribe 1988:184; Cruz-Uribe and Schrire 1991:93,96). By the mid-18th century, a European population that slowly increased to a maximum of about 5,000 settlers had so markedly modified the landscape that wild fauna was rare within 24 German (120 English) miles of the Castle (Mentzel 1925:101, 1944:77,102; Spilhaus 1966:99; Raven-Hart 1970b:270; Skead 1987:813-855; Guelke 1988:66). The faunal collection from Oudepost I illustrates the hunting effectiveness of a small garrison with European technology where a large proportion of wild mammals and birds were hunted, shot, and trapped, and where seals were obtained from offshore islands with boats, guns, and knives (Schrire 1988:214-225, 1990:15-17, 1995:107; Cruz-Uribe and Schrire 1991:96). The process was a direct outcome of the commercial success of the meat trade.

Archaeological data presented here confirms the historic accounts of depletion of wild fauna (Figure 6). Wild fauna is rare in all the urban sites not necessarily because it was illegal and reserved for official meals, but because it had all been hunted out! Mid-18th century Elsenburg, situated further into the inland frontier, included a greater amount and diversity of wild fauna compared to the urban sites, but this pales in comparison to the earlier Oudepost I terrestrial fauna. Oudepost I relied on the wild fauna to supplement rations (Cruz-Uribe and Schrire 1991:96; Schrire 1995:107);

Elsenburg was a well-established stock farm where wild fauna would have served as a dietary change. Most of the wild fauna at Elsenburg and the Moat are those that were less affected by human actions. The wild birds are generally migratory and live in marine environments, and the smallest bovids are relatively solitary and they have survived in settled areas even until the present day (Skead 1980:448-449,456; Estes 1991).

Conclusion

This study shows how diasporic Europeans transplanted and adapted their husbandry practices to a new environment. A question here is why it took so long for the impact of European colonization to decimate the indigenous Khoekhoe people? After all, their first contact went back 155 years before the 1652 settlement when the Portuguese captain Vasco da Gama landed at the Cape in 1497 (Raven-Hart 1967:3-7).

It seems obvious that the Khoekhoen might have survived better had they simply jogged along as casual traders on the margins of the European enterprise. After all, one thing they had going for them was an epidemiological immunity to the infectious disease pool shared by all stock farmers. Instead of being hit by the kind of devastating pandemics that ravaged the indigenous Americans in waves since first contact, the Cape Khoekhoen were salted against a slew of zoonotic diseases like smallpox, scrapie, anthrax, and tuberculosis by millennia of intimate coexistence with their flocks and herds (e.g. Diamond 1999; Mann 2005). It took until 1713 for a major epidemic to hit the Khoekhoen. This epidemic, traced to laundry from a calling ship, must have been a new strain of the disease as it killed Europeans and slaves and proved most devastating of all to the native people (Elphick 1977:231-233).

What fractured and decimated Khoekhoe society was not so much illness or trade, or even finding themselves at the end of the barrel of a gun. All of these outrages might have been negotiated in one way or another, if not for the meat trade where "the disappearance of livestock must be counted the prime feature of the erosion of traditional [Khoekhoe] society…" (Elphick 1977:164). The VOC set its sights on Khoekhoe herds and sucked them and their owners into the maw of the colonial enterprise. Khoekhoe capital became the foundation of a global meat trade. Their sheep were hybridized; their cattle were inspanned in wagons. Sheep fat traditionally rubbed into Khoekhoe bodies was rendered into colonial soap and candles (Wilkens 1901:85; Botha 1970:87). Their nauseating curdled milk mixed with hair in skin bags now became European butter (Kolben 1731b:65; Wilkens 1901:74; Mentzel 1921:56, 1925:101; Botha 1970:50,86; Coetzee 1977:65,94). Instead of quietly drawing, drying, and inserting seeds into the intestines of sheep for use as rattling anklets and bracelets, the Khoekhoen now scavenged for guts at the VOC shambles on the beach, presenting a contemptible spectacle for visiting dignitaries, most of whom themselves had never taken a bath all year (Georg Meister in Raven-Hart 1970b: 346).

The Khoekhoen paid the price of the meat trade in their loss of capital, land, and life. Colonial Cape farmers set up shop in the meat business, some on wealthy plantations like Elsenburg, others on hardscrabble acreages in the arid frontier zones. Some married wealthy widows and strutted into the Castle on occasion; others lived in rough thatched huts and bred with local Khoekhoe girls to form the "Bastard" societies along the Great Orange River. The elements of their economy lie buried in the broken bone residues of the meat trade, waiting for archaeologists to explain exactly how it went down so many years ago.

Future Direction of Historic Period Zooarchaeology

The future of historic zooarchaeology has recently been reviewed by Landon (2005, 2009). Broadly, its future is tied to a paradigm shift that more fully relates the value of faunal studies to archaeological interpretations of the recent past (Landon 2009:94). The ability to integrate a range of sites calls for historic zooarchaeology to mature as a science with repeatable methodologies that incorporate a close investigation of taphonomic processes. This analysis of the development and impact of the colonial VOC meat industry shows how faunal residues from synchronic and diachronic contexts can be used to provide an objective set of data that can address questions that go beyond the site-level analysis. Analyzing the depositional environment of faunal collections helps connect them to human consumption and production strategies that lay at the heart of the mercantile trade empires.

Historic zooarchaeology has already adopted its analytical methods from prehistoric faunal studies (Jolley 1983:64-66), so it would be perfectly reasonable to incorporate their extensive experimental and applied taphonomic studies. Due to uniformitarian principles, i.e. assuming that the physical properties of today's bones are affected by taphonomic forces just as those in the past, the methods and findings from the prehistoric sphere can be reliably transferred to the historic material and even open avenues of historic period-specific taphonomic studies (Gifford 1981:397; Landon 2005:5-6). As has been demonstrated here, taphonomically-affected faunal collections can still provide valuable cultural information, though one must be aware of patterns that confuse those which are the results of subsistence practices and those that are the result of depositional environments. By understanding how the depositional environment affected the faunal collections, the patterns observed in these collections can be more confidently connected to human behavior and serve as a basis for future research.

References

ABRAHAMS, GABEBA
1996   Foodways of the Mid-18th Century Cape: Archaeological Ceramics from the Grand Parade in Central Cape Town. Doctoral Dissertation, Department of Archaeology, University of Cape Town, South Africa.

ALLISON, K. J.
1958   Flock Management in the Sixteenth and Seventeenth Centuries. *The Economic History Review* 11:98-112.

AVERY, D. MARGARET
1989   Remarks Concerning Vertebrate Faunal Remains from the Main House at Paradise. *South African Archaeological Bulletin* 44:114-116.

AVERY, GRAHAM AND L. G. UNDERHILL
1986   Seasonal Exploitation of Seabirds by Late Holocene Coastal Foragers: Analysis of Modern and Archaeological data from the Western Cape, South Africa. *Journal of Archaeological Science* 13:339-360.

BAKER, VERNON
1980   Afro-American Culture History. In *Archaeological Perspectives on Ethnicity in America*. Robert Schuyler, editor, pp. 29-37. Baywood Publishing Company, New York, NY.

BALASSE, MARIE AND STANLEY AMBROSE
2002   The Seasonality Mobility Model for Prehistoric Herders in the South-Western Cape of South Africa Assessed by Isotopic Analysis of Sheep Tooth Enamel. *Journal of Archaeological Science* 29:917-932.

BINFORD, LEWIS
1977   Historical Archaeology- Is it Historical or Archaeological. In *Historical Archaeology and the Importance of Material Things, Special Publication Series, Number 2*. Leland Ferguson, editor, pp. 13-21.

BLUMENSCHINE, ROBERT, CURTIS MAREAN, AND SALVATORE CAPALDO
1996   Blind Tests of Inter-analyst Correspondence and Accuracy in the Identification of Cut Marks, Percussion Marks, and Carnivore Tooth Marks on Bone Surfaces. *Journal of Archaeological Science* (23):493-507.

BOONZAIER, EMILE, CANDY MALHERBE, ANDY SMITH, AND PENNY BERENS
1996   *The Cape Herders: A History of the Khoikhoi of South Africa*. David Philip, Cape Town, South Africa.

BOTHA, C. GRAHAM
1970   *Social Life at the Cape Colony with "Social Customs in South Africa" in the 18th Century*. C. Struik Ltd, Cape Town, South Africa.

BOWEN, JOANNE
1999   The Chesapeake Landscape and the Ecology of Animal Husbandry. In *Old and New Worlds: Historical/Post Medieval Archaeology Papers from the Societies' Joint Conferences at Williamsburg and London 1997 to Mark Thirty Years of Work and Achievement*. Geoff Egan and R. L. Michael, editors, pp. 358-367. Oxbow Books, Oxford, England.

BRAUDEL, FERNAND
1979   *The Structures of Everyday Life: Civilization and Capitalism, 15th-18th Century Volume 1*. Siân Reynolds, translator. Harper and Row, New York, NY.

CANTWELL, ANNE-MARIE AND DIANA DIZEREGA WALL
2001   *Unearthing Gotham: The Archaeology of New York City*. Yale University Press, New Haven, CT.

CHURCH, ROBERT AND R. LEE LYMAN
2003   Small Fragments Make Small Difference in Efficiency When Rendering Grease from Fractured Artiodactyla Bones by Boiling. *Journal of Archaeological Science* 30:1077-1084.

COETZEE, RENATA
1977   *The South African Culinary Tradition: The Origin of South Africa's Culinary Arts during the 17th and 18th Centuries, and 167 Authentic Recipes of this Period*. C. Struik Publishers, Cape Town: South Africa.

CRADER, DIANA
1984   The Zooarchaeology of the Storehouse and the Dry Well at Monticello. *American Antiquity* 49:542-558.
1989   Faunal Remains from Slave Quarter Sites at Monticello, Charlottesville, Virginia. *Archaeozoologia* III/1, 2:229-236.
1990   Slave Diet at Monticello. *American Antiquity* 55:690-717.

136

CROSBY, ALFRED

1987   *Ecological Imperialism, the Biological Expansion of Europe, 900-1900*. Cambridge University Press, Cambridge, United Kingdom.

CRUZ-URIBE, KATHRYN

1988   The Use and Meaning of Species Diversity and Richness in Archaeological Faunas. *Journal of Archaeological Science* 15:179-196.

CRUZ-URIBE, KATHRYN AND CARMEL SCHRIRE

1991   Analysis of Faunal Remains from Oudepost I, an Early Outpost of the Dutch East India Company, Cape Province. *South African Archaeological Bulletin* 46:92-106.

DAVID, BRUNO

1989   How Was This Bone Burnt? In *Problem Solving in Taphonomy: Archaeological and Paleontological Studies from Europe, Africa, and Oceania*. Su Solomon, Iain Davidson, and Di Watson, editors, pp. 65-79. Anthropology Museum, University of Queensland, Queensland, Australia.

DAVIS, SIMON

1987   *The Archaeology of Animals*. Yale University Press, CT.

1997   The Agricultural Revolution in England: Some Zooarchaeological Evidence. *Anthropozoologica* 25/26:413-428.

DEETZ, JAMES

1996   *In Small Things Forgotten: An Archaeology of Early American Life*. Anchor Books, New York, NY.

DEVRIES, JAN AND AD VAN DER WOUDE

1997   *The First Modern Economy: Success, Failure, and Perseverance of the Dutch Economy, 1500-1815*. Cambridge University Press, England.

DIAMOND, JARED

1999   *Guns, Germs, and Steel: The Fates of Human Societies*. W. W. Norton and Company, New York, NY.

ELPHICK, RICHARD

1977   *Kraal and Castle*. New Haven. Yale University Press, CT.

1985   *Khoikhoi and the Founding of White South Africa*. Ravan Press, Johannesburg, South Africa.

ELPHICK, RICHARD AND V. C. MALHERBE

1988   The Khoisan to 1828. In *The Shaping of South African Society, 1652-1840*. Richard Elphick and Hermann Giliomee, editors, 3-65. Wesleyan University Press, Middletown, CT.

ELPHICK, RICHARD AND ROBERT SHELL

1988   Intergroup Relations: Khoikhoi, Settlers, Slaves, and Free Blacks, 1652-1795. In The Shaping of South African Society, 1652-1840. Edited by Richard Elphick and Hermann Giliomee. Middletown, Connecticut: Wesleyan University Press. 184-242.

ESTES, RICHARD DESPARD

1991   *The Behavior Guide to African Mammals*. The University of California Press, Berkeley.

FAIRBRIDGE, DOROTHEA

1931   *Historic Farms of South Africa: The Wool, the Wheat, and the Wine of the 17th and 18th Centuries*. Oxford University Press, London, England.

FISHER, JOHN

1969   *The Afrikaners*. Cassell and Company, London, England.

FITCHETT, ROWALLAN HUGH

1996   *Early Architecture at the Cape under the VOC (1652-1710): The Characteristics and Influence of the Proto-Cape Dutch Period*. Doctoral Dissertation, Department of History, University of Witswatersrand, South Africa.

FOUCHE, LEO

1914   *The Diary of Adam Tas: With an Enquiry Into the Complaints of the Colonists Against the Governor Willem Adriaan van der Stel*. A. C. Paterson, translator. Longmans, Green and Co., London, England.

FRANSEN, HANS AND MARY ALEXANDER COOK

1980   *The Old Buildings of the Cape: A Survey and Description of Old Buildings in the Western Province Extending from Cape Town to Calvania in the North and to Graaff-Reinet, Colesburg and Uitenhage in the East; Covering Substantially the 18th and 19th Century Styles: Cape Dutch, Cape Regency, Georgian and Victorian*. A. A. Balkema Press, Cape Town, South Africa.

Gerber, Hilda

1959   *Traditional Cookery of the Cape Malays: Food Customs and 200 Old Cape Recipes*. A. A. Balkema, Cape Town, South Africa.

GIFFORD, DIANE

1981   Taphonomy and Paleoecology: A Critical Review of Archaeology's Sister Disciplines. In *Advances in Archaeological Method and Theory, Vol. 4*. Michael Schiffer, editor, pp. 365-438. Academic Press, New York, NY.

GILIOMEE, HERMANN

2003   *The Afrikaners: Biography of a People*. Hurst and Company, London, England.

GREENFIELD, HASKEL

2002   Sexing Fragmentary Ungulate Acetabulae. Paper presented at the 9th International Congress of Archaeozoology, Durham, England.

GROVE, RICHARD

1997   *Green Imperialism. Colonial Expansion, Tropical Island Edens and the Origin of Environmentalism, 1600-1860*. Cambridge University Press, MA.

GUELKE, LEONARD

1988   Freehold Farmers and Frontier Settlers, 1657-1780." In *The Shaping of South African Society, 1652-1840*. R. Elphick and H. Giliomee, editors, pp. 66-108. Wesleyan University Press, Middletown, CT.

GUELKE, LEONARD AND ROBERT SHELL

1992   Landscape of Conquest: Frontier Water Alienation and Khoikhoi Strategies of Survival, 1652-1780. *Journal of Southern African Studies* 18:803-824.

HALL, MARTIN

1989   *The Castle Moat: A Report*. Unpublished report. Archaeological Contracts Office, University of Cape Town, Cape Town, South Africa.

1992   Small Things and the Mobile, Conflictual Fusion of Power, Fear, and Desire. In *The Art and Mystery of Historical Archaeology: Essays in Honor of James Deetz*. Anne Yentsch and Mary Beaudry, editors, pp. 373-399. CRC Press, London, England.

1999   Subaltern Voices? Finding the Spaces Between Things and Words. In *Historical Archaeology: Back from the Edge*. Pedro Paulo, A. Funari, Martin Hall, and Sian Jones, editors, pp. 193-203. Routledge Press, New York, NY.

2000   *Archaeology and the Modern World. Colonial Transcripts in South Africa and the Chesapeake*. Routledge Press, London, England.

2008   Ambiguity and Contradiction in the Archaeology of Slavery. *Archaeological Dialogues* 15: 128-130.

n.d.a   *Towards an Archaeology of Slavery in the Cape: The Castle- Cape Town*. Historical Archaeology Research Group, University of Cape Town, Cape Town, South Africa.

n.d.b   *Establishing Sequences and Chronology*. Unpublished report on the excavations for F1, F2, F3 and TB. Archaeological Contracts Office, University of Cape Town, Cape Town, South Africa.

HART, TIMOTHY AND DAVE HALKETT

1993   *An Archaeological Investigation of the Elsenburg Herehuis*. Report prepared for the Department of Local Government, Housing and Works. Archaeology Contracts Office, University of Cape Town, Cape Town, South Africa.

HEINRICH, ADAM

2010a   A Zooarchaeological Investigation Into the Meat Industry Established at the Cape of Good Hope by the Dutch East India Company in the Seventeenth and Eighteenth Centuries. Doctoral Dissertation, Department of Anthropology, Rutgers University, New Brunswick, NJ.

2010b   Critiquing Slave Diet: The Importance of Taphonomy to Zooarchaeological Interpretations. Paper presented at the 43rd Annual Conference on Historical and Underwater Archaeology, Amelia Island Plantation, Jacksonville, FL.

ISRAEL, JONATHAN

1989   *Dutch Primacy in World Trade, 1585-1740*. Claredon Press, Oxford, England.

1998   *The Dutch Republic: Its Rise, Greatness, and Fall, 1477-1806*. Claredon Press, Oxford, England.

JANOWITZ, META

1993   Indian Corn and Dutch Pots: Seventeenth-Century Foodways in New Amsterdam/New York. *Historical Archaeology* 27:6-24.

138

JOHNSON, MATTHEW
1999   Historical, Archaeology, Capitalism. In *Historical Archaeologies of Capitalism*. Mark Leone and Parker Potter, editors, pp. 219-232. Kluwer Academic Plenum Publishers New York, NY.

JOLLEY, ROBERT
1983   Historical Sites Zooarchaeology. *Historical Archaeology* 17:64-79.

JORDAN, STACEY
2000   The 'Utility' of Coarse Earthenware: Potters, Pottery Production and Identity at the Dutch Colonial Cape of Good Hope, South Africa (1652-1795). Doctoral Dissertation, Department of Anthropology, Rutgers University, New Brunswick, NJ.
2005   Castle Moat M90: Stoneware. Unpublished catalogue. On file in Department of Anthropology, Rutgers University, New Brunswick, NJ.

KLEIN, RICHARD AND KATHRYN CRUZ-URIBE
1984   *The Analysis of Animal Bones from Archaeological Sites*. The University of Chicago Press, Chicago, IL.
1989   Faunal Evidence for Prehistoric Herder- Forager Activities at Kasteelberg, Western Cape Province, South Africa. *South African Archaeological Bulletin* 44:82-97.

KLOSE, JANE
1997   Analysis of Ceramics Assemblages from Four Cape Historical Sites Dating from the Late Seventeenth Century to the Mid-Nineteenth Century. Masters thesis, Department of Archaeology, University of Cape Town, Cape Town, South Africa.
2005   Castle Moat M90: Asian Wares. Unpublished catalogue. Department of Anthropology, Rutgers University, New Brunswick, NJ.

KOLBEN, PETER
1731a   *The Present State of the Cape of Good Hope: Volume I, Containing the Natural History of the Cape*. Mr. Medley, translator. Johnson Reprint Corporation, New York, NY.
1731b   *The Present State of the Cape of Good Hope: Volume II, Containing the Natural History of the Cape*. Mr. Medley, translator. Johnson Reprint Corporation, New York, NY.

LANDON, DAVID
1992   Taphonomic Evidence for Site Formation Processes at Fort Christanna. *International Journal of Osetoarchaeology* 2:351-359.
1996   Feeding Colonial Boston: A Zooarchaeological Study. *Historical Archaeology* 30:1-153.
1997   Interpreting Urban Food Supply and Distribution Systems from the Faunal Assemblages: An Example from Colonial Massachusetts. *International Journal of Osteoarchaeology* 7:51-64.
2005   Zooarchaeology and Historical Archaeology: Progress and Prospects. *Journal of Archaeological Method and Theory* 12(1):1-36.
2009   An Update on Zooarchaeology and Historical Archaeology: Progress and Prospects. In *International Handbook of Historical Archaeology*. Teresita Majewski and David Gaimster, editors, pp. 77-104. Springer, New York, NY.

LEGASSICK, MARTIN
1988   The Northern Frontier to c.1840: The Rise and Decline of the Griqua People. In *The Shaping of South African Society, 1652-1840*. Richard Elphick and Hermann Giliomee, editors, pp. 358-420. Wesleyan University Press, Middletown, CT.

LEIBBRANDT, H. C. V.
1905   *Precis of the Archives of the Cape of Good Hope. Letter Requestum (Memorials); 1715-1806*. Cape Time Limited, Government Printers, Cape Town: South Africa.

LYMAN, R. LEE
1994   *Vertebrate Taphonomy*. Cambridge University Press, Cambridge, MA.

MANN, CHARLES
2005   *1491: New Revelations of the Native Americans Before Columbus*. Knopf Publishers, New York, NY.

MARKELL, ANN, MARTIN HALL, AND CARMEL SCHRIRE
1995   The Historical Archaeology of Vergelegen, an Early Farmstead at the Cape of Good Hope. *Historical Archaeology* 29:10-34.

MARKS, SHULA
1972   Khoisan Resistance to the Dutch in the Seventeenth and Eighteenth Centuries. *Journal of African History* 13:55-80.

MENTZEL, OTTO

1921   *A Geographical and Topographical Description of the Cape of Good Hope, Part One.* H. J. Mandelbrote, translator. Van Riebeeck Society, Cape Town, South Africa.

1925   *A Geographical and Topographical Description of the Cape of Good Hope, Part Two.* H. J. Mandelbrote, translator. Van Riebeeck Society, Cape Town, South Africa.

1944   *A Geographical and Topographical Description of the Cape of Good Hope, Part Three.* G. V. Marias, J. Hoge, and H. J. Mandelbrote, translators. Van Riebeeck Society, Cape Town, South Africa.

O'CONNOR, TERRY

2000   *The Archaeology of Animal Bones.* Texas A&M University Press, TX.

ORSER, CHARLES

2005   Network Theory and the Archaeology of Modern History. In *Global Archaeological Theory: Contextual Voices and Contemporary Thoughts.* Pedro Paulo Funari, Andres Zarankin, and Emily Stovel, editors, pp. 77-96. Kluwer Academic Plenum Publishers New York, NY.

OTTO, JOHN SOLOMON

1984   *Cannon's Point Plantation, 1794-1860; Living Conditions and Status Patterns in the Old South.* Academic Press, New York, NY.

PENN, NIGEL

1986   Pastoralists and Pastoralism in the Northern Cape Frontier Zone During the Eighteenth Century. *South African Archaeological Society Goodwin Series* 5:62-68.

2005   *The Forgotten Frontier: Colonist and Khoisan on the Cape's Northern Frontier in the 18th Century.* Ohio University Press Athens, OH.

PENNINGTON, D. H.

1989   *Europe in the Seventeenth Century.* Longman, New York, NY.

RAVEN-HART, ROWLAND

1967   Before Van Riebeeck: Callers at South Africa from 1488-1652. C. Struik Limited, Cape Town, South Africa.

1970a   *Cape Good Hope 1652-1702: The First Fifty Years of Dutch Colonization as Seen by Callers, Volume I.* Balkema, Cape Town, South Africa.

1970b   *Cape Good Hope 1652-1702: The First Fifty Years of Dutch Colonization as Seen by Callers, Volume II.* Balkema, Cape Town, South Africa.

REITZ, ELIZABETH

1987   Vertebrate Fauna and Socioeconomic Status. In *Consumer Choice in Historical Archaeology.* Suzanne Spencer-Wood, editor, pp. 101-109, Plenum Press, New York, NY.

1991   Animal Use and Culture Change in Spanish Florida. In *MASCA Research Papers in Science and Archaeology; Supplement to Volume 8, 1991: Animal Use and Culture Change.* Pam Crabtree and Kathleen Ryan, editors, pp. 63-77. University of Pennsylvania, Philadelphia, PA.

REITZ, ELIZABETH AND MARGARET SCARRY

1985   *Reconstructing Historic Subsistence with an Example from Sixteenth-Century Spanish Florida, Special Publication Series, Number 3.* The Society for Historical Archaeology.

REITZ, ELIZABETH AND ELIZABETH WING

1999   *Zooarchaeology.* Cambridge University Press, England.

ROBERTSON, H. M.

1945a   The Economic Development of the Cape under Van Riebeeck. *The South African Journal of Economics* 13(1):1-17.

1945b   The Economic Development of the Cape under Van Riebeeck. *The South African Journal of Economics* 13(2):75-90.

ROBINSON, A. M. LEWIN (EDITOR)

1994   *The Cape Journals of Lady Anne Barnard, 1797- 1798.* Van Riebeeck Society Cape Town, South Africa.

ROSE, PETER (EDITOR)

1989   *The Sensible Cook: Dutch Foodways in the Old and New Worlds.* Syracuse University Press, Syracuse, NY.

ROSS, ROBERT

1988   The Cape of Good Hope and the World Economy, 1652-1835. In *The Shaping of South African Society, 1652-1840.* Richard Elphick and Hermann Giliomee, editors, pp. 243-280. Wesleyan University Press, Middletown, CT.

1998   The First Two Centuries of Colonial Agriculture in the Cape Colony: A Historiographical Review. In *Settlement Patterns in Early Modern Colonization, 16th-18th Centuries.* Joyce Lorimer, editor, pp. 301-316. Ashgate, Brookfield, WI.

SCHRIRE, CARMEL

1988   The Historical Archaeology of the Impact of Colonialism in 17th century South Africa. *Antiquity* 62:214-225.

1990   Excavating Archives at Oudepost I, Cape. *Social Dynamics* 16:11-21.

1995   *Digging through Darkness: Chronicles of an Archaeologist.* University of Virginia Press, Charlottesville, VA.

2010   The Material World of the English at Jamestown, Virginia and the Dutch at the Cape of Good Hope. In *Archaeology of Early European Colonial Settlement in the Emerging Atlantic World, Special Publication 8.* William Kelso, editor, pp. 75-86. The Society for Historical Archaeology.

SCHRIRE, CARMEL AND DONNA MERWICK

1991   Dutch Indigenous Relations In New Netherland and the Cape in the 17th Century. In *Historical Archeology in Global Perspective.* Lisa Falk, editor, pp. 11-20. Smithsonian Institution Press, Washington, D.C.

SCHRIRE, CARMEL, KATHRYN CRUZ-URIBE AND JANE KLOSE

1993   The Site History of the Historical Site at Oudepost I, Cape. *South African Archaeological Society Goodwin Series* 7:21-32.

SCHUTTE, GERRIT

1988   Company and Colonists at the Cape, 1652-1795. In *The Shaping of South African Society.* Richard Elphick and Hermann Giliomee, editors, pp. 283-323. Wesleyan University Press, Middletown, CT.

SKEAD, C. J.

1980   *Historical Mammal Incidence in the Cape Province Volume 1.* The Department of Nature and Environmental Conservation of the Provincial Administration of the Cape of Good Hope, Cape Town, South Africa.

1987   *Historical Mammal Incidences in the Cape Province Volume 2; The Eastern Half of the Cape Province, Including the Ciskei, Traskei, and East Griqualand.* The Chief Directorate Nature and Environmental Conservation of the Provincial Administration of the Cape of Good Hope, Cape Town, South Africa.

SLEIGH, DAN

1980   *Jan Compagnie: The World of the Dutch East India Company.* Tafelberg Press, Cape Town, South Africa.

SMITH, ANDREW

2006   *Excavations at Kasteelberg and the Origins of the Khoekhoen in the Western Cape, South Africa.* Cambridge Monographs in African Archaeology 66. BAR International Series 1537.

SOUTH, STANLEY

2002   *Method and Theory in Historical Archaeology.* Percheron Press, New York, NY.

SPILHAUS, M. WHITING

1966   *South Africa in the Making, 1652-1806.* Juta and Company. Cape Town, South Africa.

SYKES, N. J.

2006   From *Cu* and *Sceap* to *Beffe* and *Motton*: The Management, Distribution, and Consumption of Cattle and Sheep in Medieval England. In *Food in Medieval England.* C. M Woolgar, D Sarjeantson, and T. Waldron, editors, pp. 56-71. Oxford University Press, England.

TEMPLIN, J. ALTON

1984   *Ideology on a Frontier: The Theological Foundation of Afrikaner Nationalism, 1652-1910.* Greenwood Press, Westport, CT.

THACKERAY, FRANCIS

1989   Report on Analysis of Mammalian Fauna from Excavations at the Cape Castle (CA88, F1 and F2). Report to Martin Hall, University of Cape Town, Cape Town, South Africa.

THEAL, GEORGE MCCALL

1897   *History of South Africa Under the Dutch East India Company, 1652-1795.* Swan Sonnenschein and Company, London, England.

THE HIDE, LEATHER AND ALLIED TRADES IMPROVEMENT SOCIETY

1928   *The Flaying of Hides and Skins and Their Preservation.* Cape Town, South Africa.

THOM, HENDRIK BERNARDUS
1936 *Die Geskiedenis van die Skaapsboerdery in Sud-Afrika.* Swets and Zeitlinger, Amsterdam, Netherlands.

TROW-SMITH, ROBERT
1957 *A History of British Livestock Husbandry to 1700.* Routledge and Kegan Paul, London, England.
1959 *A History of British Livestock Husbandry 1700-1900.* Routledge and Kegan Paul London, England.

VALENTYN, FRANCOIS
1971 *Description of the Cape of Good Hope with the Matters Concerning It: Amsterdam 1726, Part I.* P. Serton, Roland Raven-Hart, and W. J. de Kock, editors, Roland Raven-Hart, translator. Van Riebeeck Society, Cape Town, South Africa.

VAN DER MERWE, P. J.
1995 *The Migrant Farmer in the History of the Cape Colony; 1657-1842.* Roger Beck, translator. Ohio University Press, Athens, Ohio.

VOC (DUTCH EAST INDIA COMPANY)
1741 J188 Census Records, Cape Archives Depot, Cape Town, South Africa.
1742 J189 Census Records, Cape Archives Depot, Cape Town, South Africa.
1746 J193 Census Records, Cape Archives Depot, Cape Town, South Africa.
1747 J194 Census Records, Cape Archives Depot, Cape Town, South Africa.
1748 J195 Census Records, Cape Archives Depot, Cape Town, South Africa.
1749 J196 Census Records, Cape Archives Depot, Cape Town, South Africa.
1750 J197 Census Records, Cape Archives Depot, Cape Town, South Africa.
1751 J198 Census Records, Cape Archives Depot, Cape Town, South Africa.
1752 J199 Census Records, Cape Archives Depot, Cape Town, South Africa.
1753 J200 Census Records, Cape Archives Depot, Cape Town, South Africa.

WALLERSTEIN, IMMANUEL
1980 *The Modern World-System II: Mercantilism and the Consolidation of the European World-Economy, 1600-1750.* Academic Press, New York, NY.

WILKENS, W. H. (EDITOR)
1901 *South Africa a Century Ago: Letter Written from the Cape of Good Hope (1797-1801).* Dodd, Mead, and Company, New York.

WILSON, BOB
1994 Mortality Patterns, Animal Husbandry, and Marketing in and Around Medieval and Post-Medieval Oxford. In *Urban and Rural Connexions: Perspectives from Environmental Archaeology: Symposia of the Association for Environmental Archaeology No. 12.* A. R. Hall and H. K. Kenward, editors, 103-116. Oxbow Books Oxford, United Kingdom.

WOLF, ERIC
1997 *Europe and the People Without History.* University of California Press, Berkeley.

YATES, ROYDEN, STEFAN WOODBORNE, AND MARTIN HALL
n.d. *The Chronology of Colonial Settlement at the Cape of Good Hope: Clay Tobacco Pipes.* Report to the Department of Archaeology, University of Cape Town, Cape Town, South Africa.

ZEDER, MELINDA
1984 Meat Distribution at the Highland Iranian Urban Center of Tal-E Malyan. In *Animals and Archaeology: Early Herders and Their Flocks.* Juliet Clutton-Brock and Caroline Grigson, editors, pp. 279-307. BAR International Series, British Archaeological Reports. Oxford, England.

Adam Heinrich
Department of Anthropology
Rutgers, the State University of New Jersey
131 George Street
New Brunswick, NJ 08901-1414
Carmel Schrire
Department of Anthropology
Rutgers, the State University of New Jersey
131 George Street
New Brunswick, NJ 08901-1414

Martin Gibbs

Beyond the New World – Exploring the Failed Spanish Colonies of the Solomon Islands

The question "When" was but one of many: Why were there so many sites in so small an area? Who had lived there, and why? What happened to cause them to be abandoned?

-Noël Hume (1979:19)

ABSTRACT

Understanding the processes of European expansion remains one of the key interests of historical archaeology. The study of colonization invariably crosses the boundaries between historical, indigenous, and maritime archaeologies, and demands that we draw upon a broad palette of theoretical and methodological approaches from all three fields as well as from cognate disciplines. In this essay I explore some of the structures of colonization, using my current research on the failed 16th century Spanish colonizations of the Solomon Islands. In particular I consider the separated halves of the 1595 Mendaña expedition: one group having a short-lived colony with a surviving documentary record, while the other survives only as an archaeological site where the nature and duration of occupation and the eventual fate of the colonists remains unknown. In trying to understand the apparent differences in the archaeological records of the two sites, I consider the importance of context as well as the significance of understanding the processes and pattern of colonization as means of comparison.

Introduction

Despite the progressive broadening of research interests in the discipline of historical archaeology, Deetz's classic definition of it being "the archaeology of the spread of European culture throughout the world since the fifteenth century and its impacts on indigenous peoples" (Deetz 1977:5) still inspires us. During this critical period of expansion, the fleets of Spain and Portugal deliberately moved beyond their homelands and circled the globe from opposite directions exploring, establishing ports and settlements, and ultimately, creating a technological and cultural network of connections that formed the basis of the modern world (Orser 2004:14). Although much of the archaeological interest in the Iberian expansion has been on the more developed colonies and practices of colonialism (c.f. van Buren 2010), recent scholarship has encouraged us to look beyond the monolithic structures of empire and explore the diversity of colonizing experiences across time and space. These differences stem from each group's complex internal structures and external relationships with multiple influencing factors, including local environments and interactions with indigenous populations (Gasco 2005:70).

The epigraph above is taken from Ivor Noël Hume's *Martin's Hundred* (1979), the warts and all account of his archaeological investigations of a 17th century English colony in Virginia. The book remains a favorite of mine, both for its strong sense of the adventure of historical archaeology, but also for the way in which the recovery and interpretation of the material evidence of the colony drives the story of the research. However, in this essay I would like to focus on how we understand the structure of these early phases of exploration and colonization; the cognitive and material preparations for journeying to and establishing new settlements, and the reactions to encounters with new environments, cultures, and circumstances. People's decisions and responses were expressed in material ways, not least in the location and nature of sites (including their abandonment) and the selection, disposition and use of material culture.

For new colonies, sometimes extremely isolated from their home cultures and without any form of support or supply, the situations they found themselves in could be very different from those originally anticipated, or could change suddenly and unexpectedly, and in some instances, radically. What these colonists had been prepared for suddenly became irrelevant as they struggled to survive in unfamiliar environments and circumstances.

In order to explore diversity between colonizing events, we need to understand the archaeological signatures of colonization and conceive of frameworks that allow us to identify and compare different experiences and strategies. The ideal sites for exploring the archaeology of initial colonization are those in which the evidence has not been destroyed by later development; in essence, failed settlements. Because of its nature, the archaeological study of colonization invariably crosses the boundaries between historical, indigenous, and maritime archaeologies, and demands that we draw upon a broad palette of theoretical and methodological approaches from all three fields as well as from cognate disciplines. This sort of integration is exactly the sort of challenge put forward by the authors in *Historical Archaeology and the Importance of Material Things.*

To illustrate this approach, I provide a narrative of the development of my current research on the archaeology of colonization, investigating a series of unsuccessful attempts by Spain to settle the Solomon Islands in the SW Pacific, 700 kilometres east of New Guinea (Figure 1). The focus is a comparative study of the archaeology of the separated parts of Alvaro de Mendaña's 1595 expedition. The first site is his short-lived settlement on Santa Cruz Island, for which there is a surviving documentary record. The second is an archaeological site on Makira Island that may be evidence that the crew and passengers aboard a galleon that became separated from the rest of the expedition may have attempted to establish their own colony. This latter site was previously unknown and has no associated documents, leaving archaeology as the only means of exploring the nature of the occupation and the fate of the lost vessel and its people. One of the aspects which drew me to the project is that the different contexts experienced by the two halves of the expedition left what appear to be very different archaeological signatures. The obvious challenges of investigating and comparing these two sites demands the integration of approaches suggested above. I must stress that the research is ongoing, and that this paper is a consideration of approaches rather than an

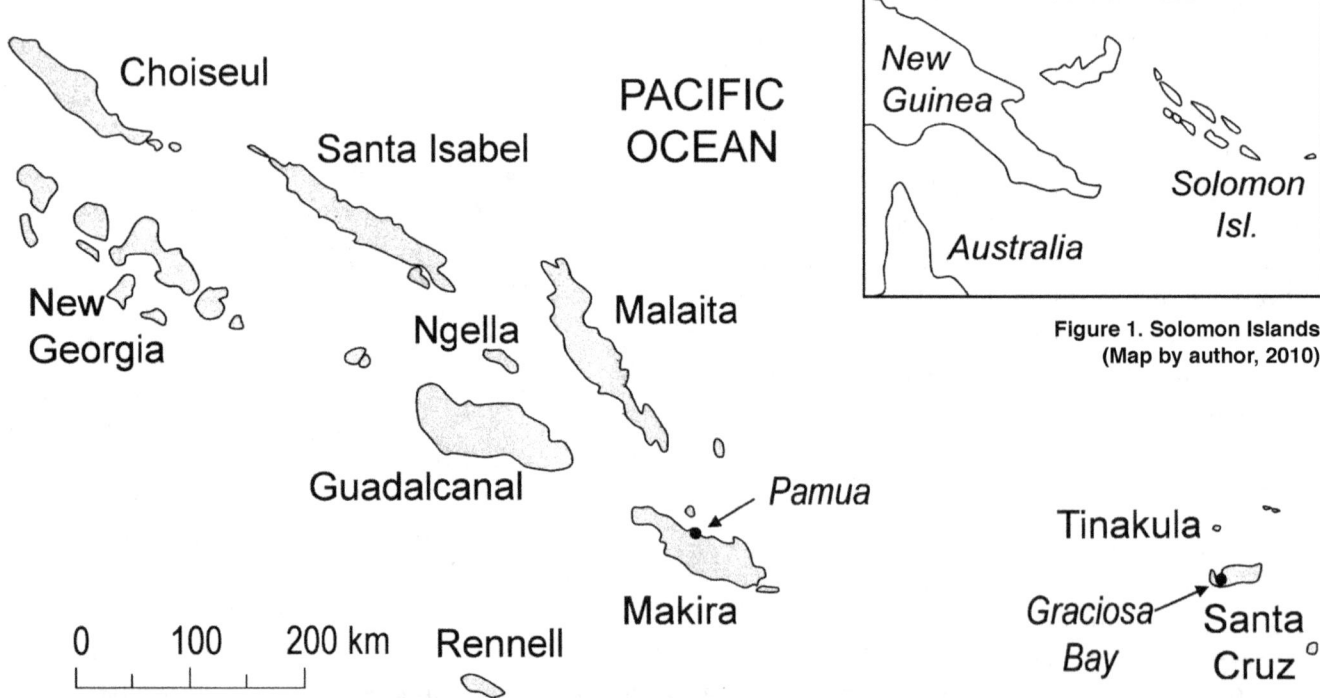

Figure 1. Solomon Islands.
(Map by author, 2010).

attempt resolve the archaeological problems being investigated. Instead, it will attempt to do three things. First, the essay will introduce a general comparative framework for understanding the stages and processes of colonization. Second, it will set out the general context for the Iberian expansion towards Asia and the Spanish search for the Solomon Islands, as well as the historical and archaeological evidence for Alvaro de Mendaña's 1595 expedition. Finally, it will consider the Mendaña expeditions in light of the framework in an attempt to define the ambiguities to be explored between the two sites.

The Archaeology of Colonization

There have been many approaches to the archaeology of colonization (Rockman and Steele 2003; Dietler 2005), so I make no claim that what I am proposing here is especially new or innovative. In general my understanding of colonization follows the framework outlined in Stein's (2005) review of the concept, although here I would like to address some of the process-oriented concerns about how it happens, emphasizing the cognitive and material nature of each stage. Perhaps most importantly, each of the stages discussed below and the shifts between them is potentially detectable within the archaeological record.

Pre-Voyage Phase

The colonization processes that are captured in the archaeological record begin to form long before the physical movement to the settlement site. Even the basic motivations for colonization would influence the location, nature, and organization of the intended enterprise. Rockman (2003:9) has described these as "push" factors (conditions encouraging movement to a new environment) versus "pull" factors (conditions making colonization attractive) leading to decisions to migrate and colonize, and later to stay or abandon settlements. Stein (2005:11) sets out the various *reasons* colonies were established, the most common being trade and/

or resource extraction, although other settlements were military or administrative outposts for conquered areas, points of resettlement for conquered populations, refuges, outposts for the spread of specific ideologies (such as Spanish missions), "settler colonies" for excess population, or capital investments in agriculture.

Initially, intending colonists actively collected information and developed expectations of the natural, social, and economic environments that they would experience or develop. More importantly they made decisions regarding appropriate supplies and materials and possibly sought experience or training to facilitate their plans (Cameron 1981; Gibbs 2002a; 2006). These efforts were influenced by factors such as the accuracy of the information they obtained, the conditions imposed by those in authority, or by the individual's social, educational and economic status, capabilities, and circumstances, including expectations of their likely roles and prospects (Blanton 2003). Organizers faced similar issues while also addressing broader conceptual, political, administrative, economic, and practical concerns. Formal permissions may have been required, along with patronage and funding, all of which carried various obligations including rules setting out the where and how of the settlements and their subsequent development. Organizers would also require frameworks for the proposed political, legal, and administrative structures and processes including reporting back to the homeland, developing relations with other polities, arranging trade and supply, making further explorations, negotiating the rights and obligations of colonists, and so on. Practical issues would include arranging transport, selecting colonists with appropriate skills and capabilities, assembling a military force if necessary, determining what supplies were required for the voyage and the establishment of the colony, and a host of other items. At this stage and subsequently, during preparation, decisions and responses would be influenced by the perception and evaluation of risk, the development of risk avoidance and mitigation strategies, or the decision to ignore risk and proceed regardless.

An obvious link between maritime and historical archaeology is if the colonizing group was water-borne. Vessels would have to be selected, modified, or constructed to undertake the task, with their size, nature, capabilities and operation providing various constraints to other aspects of the expedition. The choice of route, sailing time, and even the choice of an initial landing place would be dependent upon the ship. With space at a premium a balance would need to be struck between equipment for ship operation, supplies for the voyage, the corporate colonizing equipment and personal cargo, as well as supplies to sustain the infant settlement until food could be found. Living space would then have to be allocated for officers, crew, and the different status groups of passengers. A colonizing ship therefore embodied the initial expectations of how the settlement process might proceed (Scott-Ireton 1998).

Voyage Phase

The process of traveling to the proposed settlement site, which might include finding a site if none had been chosen previously, is often neglected in considering colonization. The journey held its own dangers from a multitude of human and natural causes. Voyages, especially those for an extended period of weeks or months, could see internal difficulties such as structural or mechanical problems with the ship, navigation errors, a shortage of supplies, or illness devastating crew and passengers. There could be tension between shipboard authority and the colonist's leaders as to decision-making, or conflict between other groups and individuals which might even result in mutiny and violence. External attacks, storms, becalmed conditions, or other mishaps may lead to shipwreck or stranding. Colonizing expeditions could be abandoned before the destination was even reached, or end up in different places and circumstances than those originally intended.

Colonization Phase

Once ashore the colonizers would potentially move through several stages. I have a predilection for an early explanatory framework developed by Australian historical archaeologists known as the *Swiss Family Robinson* model (Birmingham and Jeans 1983). As the title suggests, the authors used Wyss's 1812 novel as

a paradigmatic account of colonization, the analogy being particularly apt here as the Robinsons were part of a group intending to establish a settlement in the South Seas, before being shipwrecked and forced to survive by drawing upon the contents of the wreck as well as the resources of their new land (Birmingham and Jeans 1983). Although originally applied to the analysis of planned settlements, elements have also served my own work investigating how shipwreck survivors organized themselves on land (c.f. Gibbs 2003). In its original graphic form the *Swiss Family Robinson* model was in flow-chart form with feedback loops for decisions. Colonization is divided into the three main stages:

- **Exploratory:** where colonists entered the new environment with their existing socio-economic structures, technologies, skills, material culture, and expectations. In this period there was reliance upon imported stores of food and equipment while the colonists made a preliminary assessment of the natural and cultural environment, identified potential resources and selected a possible production system. Perception of environment, as filtered through the cultural lenses of the colonists, was a critical factor (Rockman and Steele 2003). Contact and relations with indigenous populations - ranging from amicable to hostile - would be established. In this period, presumably before further ships arrived, there was a finite set of human resources and material culture aboard the ship.
- **Learning:** where the initial production system was implemented. If unsuccessful, the technologies or processes were either rejected or revised based on further learning about environment and resources and tried again, or alternatives implemented. Colonies were often beset by remote decision making from government or company administrators back in the home country, forcing settlers to respond to inappropriate or even dangerous rules, protocols and practices (Bairstow 1984). If successful, the colonists passed into the Developmental stage.

- **Developmental:** where reinforcements and refinements were made, influenced by increasing knowledge of or changes in the cultural and biophysical environments, the arrival of new technology and skills, local innovations, changes in the commercial environment, or other factors.

Kirch (1980:125) describes the processes of adaptation when colonizing as "revolutionary," where selective pressures were at their highest and likely to induce the greatest range of variability in a cultural system. These stress situations could lead to rapid increases in experimentation and innovation, which might include testing and implementation of previously maladaptive or detrimental behaviors (Kirch 1980:116). Observation of and intelligence from indigenous inhabitants, as well as their participation, were obvious sources of knowledge and inspiration (Harrison and Williamson 2004; Silliman 2005). There was also a psychological factor to colonization and how people responded in these stressful situations, and especially when failure seemed likely or imminent, which also needs to be explored (c.f. Gibbs 2002a).

Abandonment

At any point a failure to adapt to the new environment and conditions, including internal and external political, social and economic pressures, could overweigh the push-pull factors which originally encouraged the settlement. Unanticipated changes in circumstances such as shipwreck, lack of group cohesion, attack from external forces, epidemic, or natural disasters (flood, storm, drought) could also force radical changes upon a group and as a result its responses. This could result in abandonment by all or part of the group, potentially including salvage of materials on the site, and relocation to a new site, to another existing settlement, or even return to the homeland. In the extreme cases a failure to adapt or accommodate changed circumstances could result in death (Blanton 2003).

Adopting a simple and robust framework allows us to order the various forms of data and provide sufficient commonality for comparative analysis, not just between different sites but also for identifying changes over time within the one group. There is also the potential for introducing further structures and categories for organizing investigations, such as authority and social structures, site location and organization, subsistence, material culture, shelters and structures, health, and mortality. Almost as importantly, these same categories can also apply to shipwreck survivors and the unintentional settlements they were forced to create (Gibbs 2003). In this way we can recognize similarities between groups and sites, but more importantly it allows us to distinguish and consider the causes of difference.

The Iberian Expansion

Kathleen Deagan (2003:3) has aptly described the processes of the 15th and 16th century Spanish colonial project as "simultaneously an invasion, a colonization effort, a social experiment, a religious crusade, and a highly structured economic enterprise." This is largely true of the Portuguese as well. For both groups the roots of their movement beyond Europe lay in the weakening of Moslem power on the Iberian Peninsula, although even before this occurred both were maritime nations. By the mid-15th century Portuguese fishermen and then explorers had already probed southwards along the West African coast and the Canary Islands. Part of this push beyond Europe was economic, especially the possibility of finding an alternative path to the Orient which would bypass or supplant the traditional overland trade routes. There was a degree of religious fervour, with the possibility of spreading the faith and confirming the rumours of distant Christian empires (such as of Prester John). Scientific interest and the desire to explore also played roles in what were usually joint royal-private ventures, even when initial economic returns were poor. However, by 1498 Vasco de Gama had reached the Cape of Good Hope and travelled along the East African coast to eventually reach India (Scammell 1981). By 1520 the Portuguese had established colonies and trade entrepots in the Spice Islands (Indonesia) and as far eastward as Timor, with connections through to China. The shift from exploration, to trade, to conquest was rapid.

The Spanish expansion started slightly later, with much of their energy directed towards the *Reconquista,* completed in 1492. Portugal was already in Africa and beyond, so Spain was receptive to Columbus' proposals to try to reach the Orient by a westward route. The discovery of Hispaniola and its mistaken identification as being close to the Indies was matched by a series of Papal Bulls attempting to resolve the spheres of exclusivity and influence. This culminated in the 1494 *Treaty of Tordesillas,* marked by a line of longitude determining which lands (and any potential new lands) would fall to the exclusive rights of Spain or Portugal. The original terms of the treaty were somewhat vague, so there was considerable dispute over its exact position. In general Spain had exclusive rights westwards including the New World excepting Brazil, whereas Portugal claimed Africa and eastwards through to Asia. However, given the navigational limitations of the time, there was great uncertainty where its antipodean extension would be (Hinton 1969:2).

By the first decades of the 16th century the Spanish were already exploring beyond Hispaniola and establishing colonies through the rest of Caribbean. This process continued on to the main continental land masses with several initial failed attempts to colonize in North America (La Florida) (Milanich and Milbrath 1989:3). Settlements were progressively established along the northern coast of South America and then, after Balboa crossed the Isthmus of Panama in 1513, north and south along the Pacific coast. The leaders of successful expeditions, usually referred to as *conquistadors*, were given lands, rights, titles and Honors, often becoming the Governors of their new territories (Kicza 1992:237). The conquered area of the Mesoamerican Aztec Empire (Mexico) eventually became the core of the Viceroyalty of New Spain, while the area of the conquered Inca Empire was incorporated into the Viceroyalty of Peru.

Although eventually successful, in many respects Spain's American project remained an interlude towards completing the connection towards Asia. Magellan's expedition to circumnavigate the globe reached Cebu in the Philippines in 1522, although it was not until 1564 that Urdaneta established a route that would allow ships to return eastward to Acapulco in New Spain, making regular trade viable. An expedition from New Spain to conquer and colonize the Philippines followed, with permanent settlements acting as trade entrepots with China and the Spice Islands established at Cebu in 1565, Manila in 1571, and Vigan in 1574 (Skowronek 1998:47). This heralded the start of the renowned "Manila Galleon" trade that exchanged the riches of the New World for the silks and spices of the Orient (Camino 2008).

For both Spain and Portugal these were programs of deliberate expansion, with fortunes to be made in distant lands through trade, war, and pillage. Together they blazed trails across the seas, developed new forms of navigation and technologies of watercraft, and replaced the former land routes and trade systems with seaborne empires linking Europe to Africa, Asia, and the Americas. South (1990:331) described the imperatives of the Spanish colonial system as "economic exploitation, fortification for protection of the settlement population, and control of the native people through the mechanism of evangelization into the Catholic faith." Each empire was supported by a network of forts, settlements, ports, trade stations and factories. As well as the economic impact of empire there was the intellectual experience of coming into contact with new lands, environments and cultures, as well as the evolution of systems for acquiring and controlling their new territories (Scammell 1981). Indigenous populations were integral to the operations of empire, with Spain especially employing subjugation and Christianization to co-opt or coerce their economies and labour into mining, agricultural and pastoral concerns (Scammell 1981:301). However, while the temptation is to see the Iberian nations as juggernauts, there were many instances where *entradas* or colonies were unsuccessful. Kicza's (1992:244) analysis of the structure of Spanish expeditions includes several examples of failure from a variety of causes, not the least the failure to find any resources of value to export, being unable to sustain themselves independently, and being unable to control indigenous peoples, as well as other difficulties ranging from epidemic to inadequate transport systems. All of these factors should be borne in mind when considering the case study of the failed settlements of the Solomon Islands.

The Spanish Search for the Isles of Solomon

Establishing the Tordesillas line was not only to determine rights of access to Asia, but also any potential claims to Tharshish and Ophir, the lands from where King Solomon derived his wealth of gold, should they be discovered (Jack-Hinton 1969:4). There had been lengthy conjecture that these biblical sites were synonymous with the as yet undiscovered southern continent had been predicted since Classical times (Kelsey 1986). The idea of a southern land regained currency when the warrior-scholar Pedro Sarmiento de Gamboa collected Quechua stories of Tupac Yupanqui's fleet which had allegedly found islands to the west of Peru containing black people and gold (Spate 1979:121; Camino 2005:33). In 1568 Sarmiento gained the support of the Viceroy of Peru to mount an expedition to find the 'Islands of Solomon', obtain their wealth and convert their people. The potential of an alternate route to the Spice Islands under the control of Peru may also have been attractive. The Viceroy placed the voyage of exploration and colonization under the control of his inexperienced 25 year old nephew Alvaro de Mendaña, who was named *Adelantado* and given the rights to conquer and claim territory. Mendaña's expedition of two ships and 150 men was fraught with tension, propagated in part by the supplanted Sarmiento.

After nearly three months sailing westward Mendaña's ships discovered a group of large islands in the SW Pacific, nearly 14,000 km from Peru. This led to six months of explorations and numerous encounters with indigenous groups, but no gold. With supplies and ammunition running low, the ships rotting and increasing internal dissent, a decision was made to abandon any plans of colonizing and instead depart for the Philippines (Camino 2005). To prepare for this homeward voyage, the Spanish took over an indigenous village in the northern part of Makira (San Cristoval), spending three weeks careening their ships, raiding local villages for supplies, and killing a number of Islanders in several conflicts (Amherst 1901:177, 206-7).

Still holding the title of "Adelantado of the Western Isles" (Hill 1913:656), for 26 years Mendaña made constant appeals for resources to return and finish the mission of colonization (Spate 1979). Finally, he was allowed four vessels that departed Peru on 16 June 1595 carrying approximately 400 people (Kelly 1965:161, 399). The expedition intended to establish a colony on Makira, using married soldiers, their wives, children, and servants as settlers. Due to an under estimation of the distance sailed in 1568 this outward voyage took significantly longer than anticipated, so by September the Solomon Islands still had not been reached and food and water were critically low. Admiral Lope de Vega commanding the Almiranta *Santa Isabel* begged Mendaña for a boat load of wood, saying that "for want of fuel, they had burnt boxes, and were using the upper works of the ship" (Markham 1904:35). While Mendaña (who was also his brother-in-law) granted this request, de Vega's appeals for water were refused, despite his claims that he had only nine jars remaining for the 180 men, women, and children aboard (Markham 1904:35).

On 7 September 1595 the convoy spotted a dense cloud of smoke, which we now know was from an eruption of the Tinakula volcano in the Santa Cruz group. The frigate was sent ahead to investigate whether this meant land was nearby and a system of lamp signals organized for them to warn the Capitana and Almiranta of any dangers. Although the Almiranta was seen at 9:00pm, when the frigate returned several hours later and sent signals reporting land nearby and advising the fleet to stop, no response signal was seen from her. When morning came the *Santa Isabel* had vanished. Several attempts to find her were unsuccessful and the Almiranta and its crew were never seen again, although Mendaña and the other colonists believed that they had probably continued on the fleet's last heading towards Makira.

Unsure of the location of the Solomon Islands, Mendaña decided to take the remaining 220 persons and establish a colony on a nearby island which he named Santa Cruz (Nendö). After a heated argument between Mendaña and the Camp Master (Field Commander), a site at the bottom (south) end of Graciosa Bay adjacent to a fresh water stream was selected for the settlement, and work begun to clear land

and construct a church and houses. At least one faction wanted to take over an existing settlement, although the area eventually chosen was noted as not having an indigenous village on it (Markham 1904:46). Contact with indigenous groups was however a daily event, with extraordinary efforts made by the Paramount Chief of the island to negotiate amicable relations. Despite this, the constant demands by the Spanish, especially for food, quickly created conflict. The colony suffered from internal political troubles, as well as discontent with the conditions and the lack of the lands, gold, and other rewards promised at the outset of the voyage. With tensions between the Spanish and islanders also increasing, some of the sailors mounted a deliberate campaign of antagonism and violence hoping it would force a return to Peru. These incidents were only partially quelled through intervention by Mendaña who oversaw the execution of the Camp Master, the leader of a dissenting faction, along with several followers.

Fatal illnesses also ravaged the group, so after the death of nearly 50 Spanish (including Mendaña) the decision was made to abandon the settlement. The ships departed 18 November 1595 after only two months (Green 1973). One final unsuccessful attempt to locate the Almiranta was made as they sailed for the Philippines, a voyage that took nearly three months and saw at least another 50 people die of illness and starvation (Camino 2005:56).

A final Spanish expedition to find the southern land departed Peru in 1616, commanded by Mendaña's former navigator Pedro de Quiros. This epic voyage - guided initially by Quiros' religious convictions and then confounded by his increasingly erratic behavior - also failed in its quest. It was nearly 200 years before Europeans again sailed through the region, by which time the Spanish expeditions to find the Isles of Solomon had become benchmarks in the history of European exploration into the Pacific.

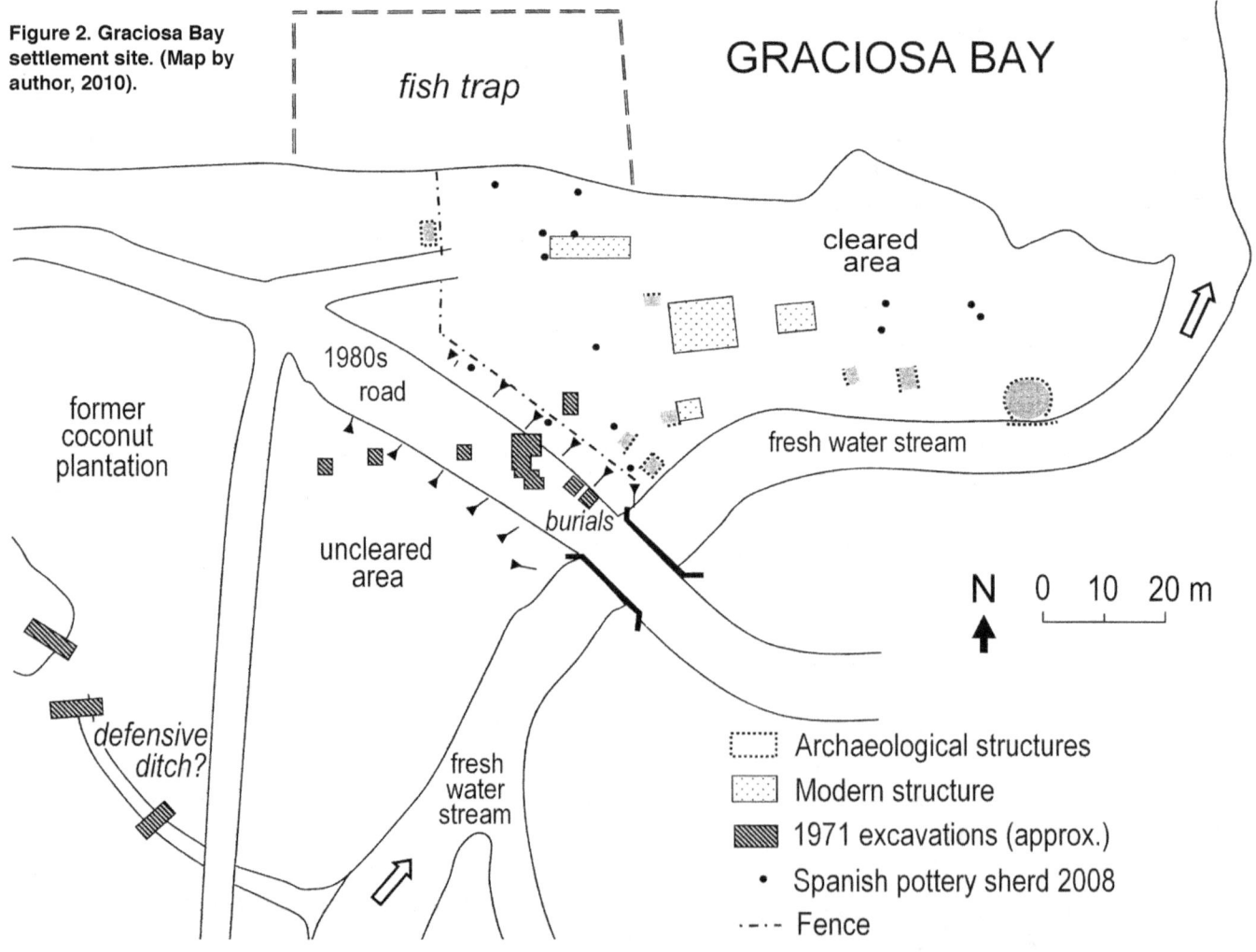

Figure 2. Graciosa Bay settlement site. (Map by author, 2010).

The Archaeology of the 1595 Expedition

Archaeological interest in the failed Spanish colonies began in 1970 when pre-historian Roger Green relocated the site of Mendaña's 1595 settlement in the southeast corner of Graciosa Bay on Santa Cruz (Figure 2). In addition to a surface scatter of Spanish pottery, test excavations uncovered a rectangular crushed coral pad which he interpreted as potentially associated with a Spanish structure on the basis that most traditional Santa Cruz houses were circular (Allen and Green 1972; Allen

1976). To the south and west of this area Green also found a ca. 2 m wide curving ditch, originally 1.25 m deep, with a bank of soil on the inner (north and east) side (Allen and Green 1972). With no clear natural or indigenous origin, Green suggested this may have been a defensive trench associated with the Spanish settlement. Unable to obtain funding, no further field investigations followed these initial explorations.

Soon after returning home to New Zealand in 1970 Green stumbled across a collection of sherds in the Otago Museum which were identical to those from Santa Cruz, but collected by missionaries from Pamua on the coast of Makira (San Cristobal) Island, 450km further west (Figure 3). After several visits to Pamua,

Figure 3. Pamua Archaeological sites. (Map by author, 2010).

Mwaoraha Isl.

0   500 m

● Pottery
◔ Elevated Areas
⬡ Reef
⋯ Modern buildings

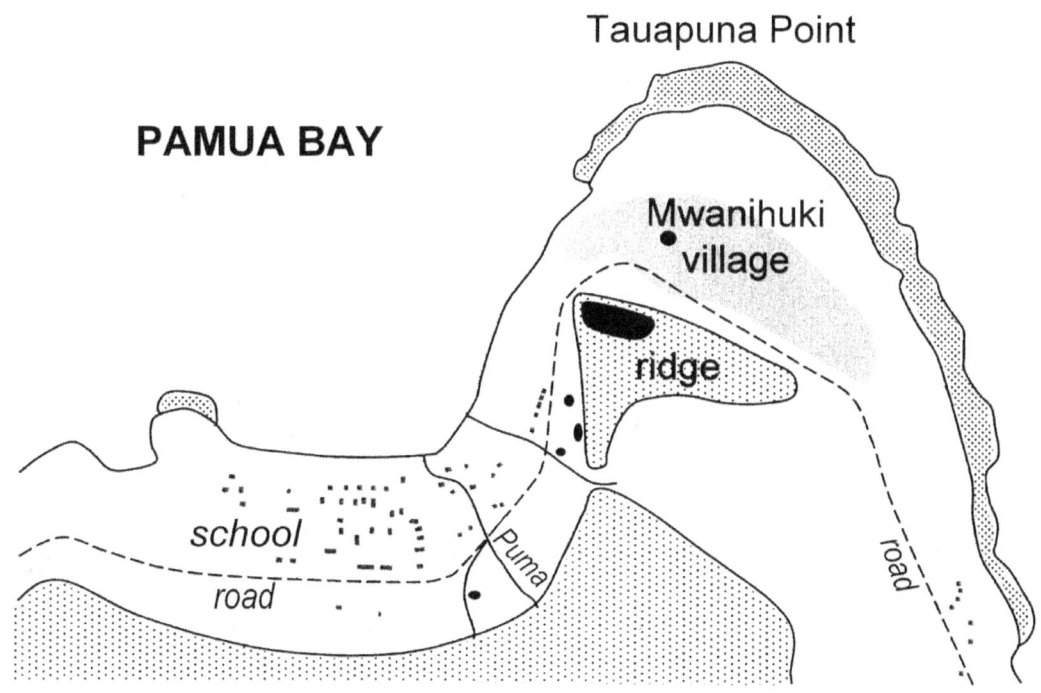

PAMUA BAY

Tauapuna Point

Mwanihuki village

ridge

school

road

Puma

road

Green located a scatter of Spanish sherds on a 30 m high ridge to the northeast of the current St. Stephens School. Green and his assistant Michael Kaschko plotted a surface scatter of over 200 sherds, mostly within a 100 x 30 m area (Figure 4). Several excavations yielded further ceramics and an identifiably Spanish iron spike (Green 1973). One test pit contained what they described as a coral-lined rectangular hearth with charcoal dating 360+/-90 B.P (I-6177), while an ash lens in another trench produced a date of 320+/-90 B.P. (I-6176). These dates and the ceramic vessel forms suggested a late 16th to early 17th century origin (Green 1973:26). Petrographic analysis, identifying the mineral composition of the fabric of the sherds,

confirmed that the Pamua red ware sherds were from the same source as the Graciosa specimens (Dickinson and Green 1973). Based on the historical and archaeological evidence Green hypothesized that Pamua was associated with the lost Almiranta *Santa Isabel*.

In 1975 Kaschko (1979) returned to investigate the indigenous cultural sequence of Pamua, excavating a village site known as Mwanihuki situated on the coastal flats less than 100 m north of the ridge top Spanish site. Mwanihuki is spread over at least several hundred meters, with a dense surface scatter of stone artifacts and faunal remains, many large midden mounds and a series of coral and stone features interpreted as burial structures. Kaschko also recorded a small collection of Spanish sherds concentrated around one large midden mound, which he felt implied that they had

**Figure 4. Pamua Ridge Site –
distribution of Spanish Pottery 1981,
2008, 2010. (Map by author, 2010).**

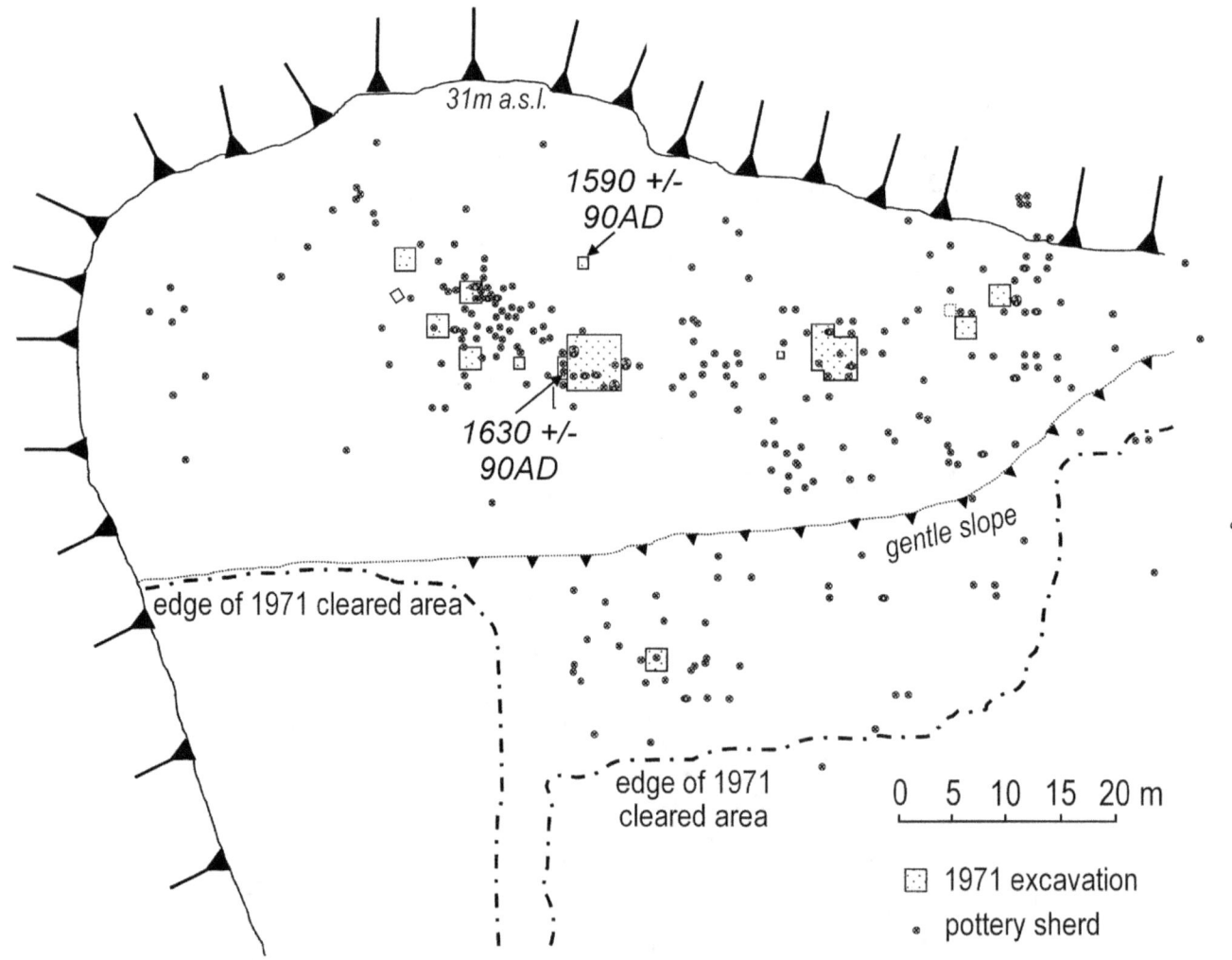

31m a.s.l.

1590 +/-
90AD

1630 +/-
90AD

gentle slope

edge of 1971 cleared area

edge of 1971
cleared area

0 5 10 15 20 m

▢ 1971 excavation
• pottery sherd

been discarded in the context of the active cultural system of the village. A basal date from the ca. 1.7 m deep deposit suggests the site was first occupied ca. AD 1350, with the Spanish sherds appearing on the surface and first few cms of deposit, which Kaschko interpreted as marking the terminal use (Kaschko 1979). One of the most exciting discoveries was from his excavation of a coral lined structure on the top of this mound, revealing an extended burial at a depth of approximately 40 cm. The body, tentatively identified as a 17-24 year old male (Carroll 1981), had a metal object in the area of its upper chest. Although initially thought to be a projectile point (Spriggs 1997:237), later re-analysis identified it as an *aiglet*, a metal sheath used in the 16th century to cap the ends of the laces used to fasten clothing (c.f. Deagan 2002:175).

In 2008, my colleagues and I relocated the Graciosa Bay and Pamua Spanish sites to determine their potential for further investigation. Graciosa Bay has now been partially cleared of dense tropical vegetation, revealing additional sherds and evidence of at least two rectangular coral pads similar to the ones excavated in 1971. However, the probable area of the 1971 excavation has been destroyed by a 1980s road, with villagers recalling four skeletons and pottery being uncovered during construction. The ditch was also relocated and remains ambiguous as to its origin or purpose. One surprising discovery was a series of coral and stone alignments from a previously unidentified prehistoric indigenous village. The pottery lay above these features, supporting Spanish claims that the area was not occupied at that time. Due to tensions over land ownership, only a brief survey and surface collection was possible. However, interviews with several knowledgeable older men provided interesting information on traditional practices such as protocols for treatment of visitors which may bear on indigenous responses to the Spanish, as well as their insights and interpretations of some of the historically documented events. They also related that the site is home to a powerful and malevolent spirit who is believed to have caused illness and/or influenced the deaths of the Spanish, especially that of Mendaña.

Resurvey of the Pamua ridge site in 2008 and 2010 located more Spanish sherds, bringing the count to over 400. A fluxgate gradiometer (Geoscan FM256) survey has indicated several high intensity anomalies, some of which may be caused by metals or hearths, although test excavations of several of these produced only further sherds and no structural remains. The Mwanihuki village suffered some disturbance from gardening and quarrying, although the 2010 excavations on several of the mounds will hopefully confirm the sequence of occupation and possible abandonment. While interviews with the traditional land owner yielded no stories directly relevant to the Spanish, she related more general information, including that Mwanihuki had been her clan's original village, until the "white people" came, after which they moved into the mountainous interior. When asked why they had never returned, she said that this was because some years later missionaries had occupied the area, which we know was in 1911 (Fox 1958:231). Given that the Spanish ceramics are at surface level, presumably marking the terminal use of the village, this begs the question of the identity of the "white people" described.

Investigating the 1595 Mendaña Expedition

Even though the investigation of the Spanish colonies in the Solomon Islands has only just begun, it is already possible to restructure the historical, archaeological, and oral evidence into the framework described above, identifying some of the differences and ambiguities worthy of further exploration.

Pre-Voyage Phase

Before discussing difference it is worth identifying commonalities, especially in expectation and preparation. As with most Spanish expeditions, in his planning for the Solomon Islands Mendaña perceived the potential for finding gold or other resources, converting a sizeable indigenous population to Christianity, and elevating the status of himself and his family (hence the placement of relatives such as his brother-in-law Admiral de Vega into positions of authority). Other individuals participated with expectations of reward, primarily through improved social and economic status, especially through ownership land and indigenous labor.

By the time of the 1595 expedition to the Solomon Islands the Spanish had considerable experience from their colonizing efforts in North and South America, including responding to a range of non-European environments and cultures. The records of Mendaña's 1568 expedition shows rapid deployment of exploration strategies including well-developed processes for engaging with and learning from indigenous groups (Amherst 1901; Markham 1904; Kelly 1966). Information from this journey also informed preparations for the 1595 expedition. The surviving documents suggest some of the preparations for the voyage, the expectations of the participants and some of the personalities, social hierarchies, and tensions involved. Although given Royal consent and assistance, this was not a crown expedition and the post-voyage account of the expedition's pilot, Pedro de Quiros, makes it clear that Mendaña was forced to cut corners:

Figure 5. Sample of earthenware and glazed sherds from Pamua-Graciosa. (Photograph by author, 2010).

The Adelantado met with some difficulties and obstacles in fitting out the expedition... The disorders which took place in this expedition were numerous; and in order that this history may be clear, it is necessary to say something of them, as it seems to me that they were the cause of the unfortunate ending of the enterprise (Markham 1904:4).

Although the documents state that Mendaña purchased two galleons, a frigate and a galliot, these labels provide only a notion of the types of vessel and little of their actual nature, whether they were constructed in Spain or the Americas, of what timber and design, or if they had been modified for the expedition or for Pacific Ocean conditions. The ships appear to have been in poor condition, to the extent that after failing to convince Mendaña to replace the Almiranta the crew then drilled holes in the hull to force him to swap her for a "new and strong" ship (Markham 1904:8). During the voyage there were still complaints that the replacement galleon was in a dismal state and badly ballasted (Markham 1904:35). Deterioration of the other vessels was also a factor in the eventual abandonment of the Graciosa Bay colony. Should the wreck of the Almiranta be found, at least some of these questions regarding structure and condition could be addressed, as might others regarding preparations and stowage. The near-contemporary colonizing vessels excavated at Pensacola would provide an excellent comparative archaeological data set (Scott-Ireton 1998; Smith et al. 1998, 1999).

Mendaña had difficulties finding the appropriate quality and quantity of supplies for the voyage and was forced to sail his vessels to various ports and harbors of Peru to scrounge materials, food, and water (Markham 1904:10-11). Further research on what was purchased, in what quantities and from where is necessary, but the archaeological evidence has already brought an interesting aspect to light. While the pottery from both Graciosa Bay and Pamua have recognizably Spanish vessel forms, the fabric of the majority of the sherds — mostly coarse red earthen wares and a few finer red wares — bears almost no similarity to pottery examined from contemporary sites in the eastern United States (Figure 5). Only a handful of the olive jar sherds are

of a pinkish-white fabric similar to those found on the latter sites (c.f. Deagan 1987; South et al. 1988; Marken 1994). There are a few sherds with light and dark green glazing and some whitish-cream pieces that might be a form of Panama plain, but no evidence of highly colored majolica. Given the origin of the Solomon Island expeditions from the west coast settlements in Peru, it seems likely that the Pamua - Graciosa assemblages must represent some of the earliest products of the Peruvian or Mesoamerican Spanish colonial pottery industry (c.f. Rice 1994). Several sherds have been tentatively identified as south Asian in origin (Green 1973:25), while at least one white porcelain sherd has been recovered suggesting these are products of the Manila galleon trade flowing back through the system (Skowronek 1998:48). Several sherds may also be of a much more exotic fabric and may be of indigenous South American production (c.f. Chatfield 2007). Sourcing analysis of the sherds using petrological identification and other analytical techniques such as Raman and XRF are being undertaken to compare the Solomon Island material to those found in other Spanish, colonial, and shipwreck sites to confirm these connections. Consequently, the deposits on the short duration Spanish settlements might be considered a snapshot of ceramic production and trade in the Viceroyalty of Peru in the late 16th century in exactly the same way as would be provided by a shipwreck assemblage.

Voyage Phase

The 1595 expedition suffered various internal tensions throughout the voyage, partly based on Mendaña's uncertainty about the location of the Solomon Islands and the likely sailing time, with the journey taking several months rather than the several weeks he had confidently expected and equipped for the voyage. However, this extended period left the fleet with little food or water and the ships in deteriorating condition, while demoralizing the participants and calling Mendaña's credibility and authority into question. Most importantly, it forced the decision to colonize Santa Cruz rather than push on an unknown distance to the Solomons and the intended site on Makira.

Exploratory Phase

The separation of the Almiranta from the rest of the fleet took place only days before the decision to establish a settlement on Santa Cruz. The documentary and archaeological record from Graciosa Bay provides some insights into the colonization strategies the group as a whole expected to pursue and their perceptions of and responses to indigenous contacts. These will be dealt with first, before considering the Pamua site.

Graciosa Bay

Many of the basic expectations for where and how Spanish colonies were to be established were set out in King Philip II's 1573 *Royal Ordinances for New Towns* (Nuttall 1921; Deagan 1995:424). For instance:

> 111. Having chosen the place where the town is to be made, which as above-said must be located in an elevated place, where are to be found health, strength, fertility, and abundance of land for farming and pasturage, fuel and wood for building, materials, fresh water, a native people, commodiousness, supplies, entrance and departure open to the north wind. If the site lies along the coast, let consideration be had to the port and that the sea be not situated to the south or to the west. If possible, let there be no lagoons or marshes nearby in which are found venomous animals and corruption of air and water (Nuttall 1921:750).

However, several writers have noted the degree of variability in how Spanish settlements were founded due to local decision making (Gasco 2005; Fowler 2009: 434; Van Buren 2010). As described, although Mendaña had decided on a site at the entry to Graciosa Bay, the Camp Master preferred a location at the bottom of the bay and simply started clearing the area (Markham 1904:46-47). It is arguable which site would have best fitted the Ordinances. They also instruct that settlements were to be in vacant areas to avoid harm to indigenous populations, which would explain Mendaña's refusal to allow an existing village to be occupied (Markham 1904:46). Subsequent sections of the Ordinances deal with the specifics of layout, with the initial phase of occupation as follows:

> 128. Having made the plan of the town and the assignment of building lots, each of the settlers shall set up his tent on his plot if he should have one. For this purpose the captains shall persuade them to carry tents. Those who do not possess tents shall build their huts of such materials that can be obtained easily, where they may have shelter. As soon as possible all settlers shall make some sort of a palisade or ditch (Nuttall 1921:752).

One of the roles of the Camp Master seems to have been to direct the establishment of the settlement, presumably to meet these requirements, and it was he who was ashore and guiding work while the ailing Mendaña mostly remained on his ship until such time as a house was erected for him (Markham 1904:46, 53). There are hints as to the nature of the camp, as well as arrangements being made for the further development of the settlement:

The next time the Adelantado went on shore was to arrange and mark out with the Camp Master a site for a stockade to be used as a fort. Touching this, and the ground for sowing, and other matters relating to the administration of the settlement, he had to give his attention and to hear much folly (Markham 1904:60).

Textual references indicate that the group had erected tents, constructed framed thatched houses, a church, and a guardhouse. It is uncertain how the different status groups were situated in the camp or how decisions were influenced by the tensions within the group. Defensive systems seem to have been established quickly, with references to the "gate" of the camp (Markham 1904:86) implying a fence, palisade, and/or ditch had been established, as well as a *corps de gardes* within the camp and another "at a distance," which may indicate a forward defensive post (Markham 1904:82). Given the stream and beach would define the eastern and northern boundaries, the archaeological evidence of the ditch and bank along the south and west sides seems consistent with enclosing the settlement area. Apart from scant documentary hints, the structure and organization of this initial settlement remains unknown. Consequently, the archaeological survival of what may be foundations or floor surfaces provides some hope of exploring this further.

Similarly, the realities of subsistence and survival in Graciosa Bay over the two months of occupation are vague in the documentary account. The extended sea voyage had left the Spanish with limited supplies, presumably forcing them to rely on local food sources immediately. There was an expectation that indigenous groups would trade or provide food, resources and labor as required, but while the expedition was equipped with trade goods such as bells, beads and caps, whether these were desired by the islanders in return for resources the Spanish wanted is questionable. Despite attempts by the Paramount Chief of Graciosa Bay to draw the Spanish into a structured relationship, their increasing demands, especially for food, created intense friction. Not only did Spanish needs exceed local subsistence production, but their harassment of the islanders for meat in the form of pigs was the source of serious tension and eventually violence. In Melanesian cultures pigs are not food but wealth, required for specific social and ritual transactions including consumption at ceremonial events. The fact that the Islanders conceded to their Paramount Chief's requests to hand over the animals to the Spanish is indicative of the degree to which they were attempting to achieve conciliation and accommodation. Archaeological deposits may provide insights into the balance between the imported foods, those foraged for by the Spanish, and those extracted from the indigenous groups.

Health and mortality as a category for investigation is also significant, as the Graciosa camp was gripped with various health problems including a spiraling death rate from what may have been malaria and typhus, although the pathology is uncertain. Others died from accidents, indigenous attacks, and violence between the different Spanish factions. A burial ground was established, although whether in the camp or beyond it, in what configuration, or using what internment practices is unknown. Upon the death of Mendaña he was placed in a coffin and buried, although it is unlikely that this honor was extended to others (Markham 1904:88). As described, the 1980s road construction through the site uncovered at least four skeletons. Although it is possible this identifies the Spanish burial ground, the fact of the earlier village in the area means these could be indigenous, as traditional Santa Cruz practice was to bury the dead beneath houses. The Spanish presence also meant increased mortality for the indigenous inhabitants of Graciosa Bay, most obviously through violence, although contact most likely saw transmission of diseases, infections and genetics.

In addition to the worsening relations with the Islanders, food shortages and ill health, one of the arguments raised in support of abandoning Graciosa Bay was the deteriorating condition of the ships:

> The ships have many defects, and we cannot careen them, we have no cables, and the rigging is rotten. As for provisions, we have nothing left but a little flour, and the jars for water are diminished in number, as many of them have been broken; while the barrels are out of order, there being no one who can repair them (Markham 1904:66).

There was a fear that waiting too long would mean that the vessels would simply sink and strand the colonists on Santa Cruz, or worse, not survive the homeward journey. Similar reasoning had been a major factor in the decisions to not attempt a settlement in the 1568 expedition. The departure of the Spanish from Graciosa Bay after only two months means that the group had remained very much in the exploratory phase of the colonization process, without really advancing into colonialism (c.f. Dietler 2005:52-54).

Pamua

If the location and organization of Graciosa Bay can be seen as a compromise with the Ordinances, then the archaeological evidence at Pamua brings with it many ambiguities suggesting that they pursued a very different strategy. At this point we have no idea of the circumstances or duration of the

158

Spanish presence, their relationships with the indigenous inhabitants, or the ultimate fate of the settlers and the ship. The choice of the Pamua locale for settlement seems rational, given it is on the same latitude that the fleet had been following and therefore would be where any subsequent vessels might search for the Almiranta (Figures 6 and 7). It is also the only semi-sheltered anchorage on the north Makira coast, with the bay and the small island providing some protection from winds and current as well as a protected sandy beach which would be easy to land on. There is a strip of flat and fertile land several hundred meters wide which then rises steeply into the mountains that characterize the interior of the island, as well as several small freshwater streams running into the corner of the bay.

As described, the archaeology consists of the pottery on the northwest corner of the ridge above the

Figure 6. Pamua – view from ridge site to Mwaoraha Island. Mwanihuki village in trees below. (Photograph by author, 2010).

east side of the bay, a group of sherds on a midden in the village, the burial with the aiglet on the same mound, and several sherds scattered to the west of the ridge. However, standing on the ridge site presents two immediate insights. First is that it has a spectacular view over the anchorage and eastward towards Santa Cruz, while the Mwanihuki village is immediately north of the site. Second is that the 30m steep sides cliff provides a formidable defensive aspect. Several major scenarios and variants might be proposed to account for aspects of the currently known archaeological record and allows us to generate testable predictions.

In a *short duration* scenario the ridge might represent a temporary lookout post established as the Almiranta waited for the other vessels to arrive. However, the spread of several hundred sherds over a wide area of the ridge is suggestive of more complex activity than a simple lookout of even several weeks duration.

An *immediate or near immediate shipwreck* scenario resulting from natural causes (e.g. storm),

Figure 7. Aerial view of Pamua. Ridge site and Mwanihuki village on the point on the left. (Photograph by author, 2010).

human error (navigation or handling), structural failure of the ship, or indigenous attack (c.f. Koorsgaard 2010) could have forced colonists into an urgent transfer to land, establishment of a camp, and implementation of short to long-term survival strategies (Gibbs 2002a). Loss of the ship might mean no further access to the material culture aboard, and no chance of departure. In these circumstances the immediate establishment of a defensible position might have been considered imperative.

An *attempted colonization* scenario could have several variants. The first is a short-term occupation of weeks or months followed by complete abandonment, such as at Graciosa Bay. Second is an attempted colonization with changing circumstances (e.g. epidemic, attack, internal dissent, loss of the ship). This latter variant introduces the possibility of (radical) alterations to the colonizing strategy after an initial

settlement had been established, changed priorities in the structure or location of the colony, departure (if possible), the death of some or all of the colonists, or even voluntary/involuntary incorporation (assimilation) into indigenous populations (Gibbs 2002a:136; Stein 2005:17).

If the ridge site was the primary settlement, it does not appear to correspond to either the Ordinances or the decisions seen at Graciosa Bay. The Almiranta group, separated from the rest of the expedition, may have held limited knowledge of the Ordinances, or the ridge may be a different interpretation of a settlement needing to be in an "elevated place". However, it is difficult to access and several hundred meters from the nearest place where a boat can easily land, stretching the connection to the ship at a critical time when it represented the major source of subsistence and protection. There is limited area for gardening and no fresh water, meaning a climb with heavy ceramic jars down to the streams at its base. Breakage from dropped jars may explain the several sherds found at the base of the track up the hill, as well as near the streams. However, if the colonists felt immediately under threat they may have decided there was an urgent need for a defensible site. As noted, shipwreck with the loss of any capacity to depart might produce such a response. Alternatively, the primary settlement may have been situated elsewhere and has not yet been discovered, (such as somewhere on the flat area near the current St Stephens School, or even within the Mwanihuki village) and the ridge may represent either a special function site such as a lookout, church, or sub-settlement for a particular group of colonists, or even a secondary and more defensible settlement established after circumstances changed.

Spanish colonizing strategy would suggest that close proximity to an indigenous community would have been seen as a positive factor, with the expectation that they would provide food, labor, and religious converts (c.f. South 1992; Ewen and Hann 1998; Beck et al. 2006; Deagan 2008). Although the Santa Cruz response was an attempt at accommodation, the records of other European expeditions through the region shows that Melanesian reactions to outsiders were fluid and complex, ranging from immediate economic and social rationalization to spiritual supplication, contests of symbols, and armed confrontation. For both sides, encounters were influenced by local political and social circumstances and ambitions, the physical environment in which encounters took place, and the composition and disposition of each group at the time (Torrence and Clarke 2000:9). Fatal conflict was an ever-present possibility, and changed circumstances (such as loss of the ship) could alter relations. It should be recalled that only 25 years earlier Mendaña's first expedition had murdered many Makirans and destroyed their villages and property less than 50km from Pamua. Even if relations with the Mwanihuki group had been amicable, there could have been immediate attempts at retribution from other groups.

The location of the Spanish material in only one area of the Mwanihuki site, atop the highest mound in the village site and co-located with the burial containing the aiglet, suggests various possibilities. It could indicate special relations with one specific component of the village population, various modes of trade or acquisition, or a special purpose for the site: for instance, on all three Solomon Islands expeditions

there are numerous instances of the Spanish erecting crosses on beaches and hills and using these places as the focus for religious conversion and activities, or to claim, or sanctify sites (e.g. Amherst 1901:38, 231, 303; Markham 1904:30, 185, 200, 249). The material might have purely indigenous agency, with post-Spanish collection or even salvage from a wreck. The same may conceivably be true for the pottery on the ridge above the village. Until an analysis is made of the skeleton (now in process), the question remains of whether this was a Spanish person buried in the indigenous site, or an Islander buried in Spanish clothing.

Another factor related to the possible fate of the Almiranta group is its diverse composition. There were 180 people aboard including men, women, and children of Spanish, African, indigenous South American and mixed-descent, from a range of social classes, with various family or other relationships (Markham 1904:35; Kelly 1965). This group carried a vast array of experiences, skills, capabilities, as well as basic perceptual differences of the environments and cultures they were encountering. These differences may have impacted the organization of the original settlements and then have influenced group cohesion and responses if the situation changed or deteriorated. A person's age, sex, physical characteristics, skills, etc., would have given them different "values" in relations with indigenous communities (Gibbs 2002b). Stein (2005:9) and Gasco (2005:98) also identify this sort of heterogeneity within colonizing groups and within the "host" cultures as a significant aspect when considering the nature of internal and external engagement.

Conclusion

In writing this essay about developing an approach towards the investigation of the Spanish colonization of the Solomon Islands, I have tried to emphasize that a concern with pattern, process, and comparison is still central to historical archaeology. Recognizing similarities and differences and identifying ambiguities drives the project.

First, there is the overarching context of Spanish/Iberian expansion and the broader structures of Spanish colonizing strategy and material culture. Although wider comparison has not been a central concern of this paper, there are numerous published studies of successful and failed Spanish settlements of different types, operating in the various environmental, social and political circumstances of the New World (Deagan 1995, 2002; South 1992; Funari 2006) and western Pacific (Headley 1995; Skowronek 1998, 2009). The early phases of St Augustine, Santa Elena, and Puerto Real have been the focus of extensive historical and archaeological study and are particularly relevant (South 1992; Deagan 1995, 2008). Investigations of the archaeology of exploratory expeditions (Ewen et al. 1998; Beck et al. 2006) and the wrecks of colonizing vessels (Scott-Ireton 1998; Smith et al. 1998) also offer valuable insights into the material culture, settlement structures, and processes of Spanish colonization. There are also several general models of Spanish New World colonization strategy which should be considered (South 1990; Crouch 1991; Hoover 1992). However, the Spanish focus should not exclude evaluation of the wider literature on failed colonies in the non-Spanish world and the "why" and "how" of their demise (Wright 2009).

A second point which I have tried to make is that there is a need to explore how different contexts can lead to different colonization outcomes. While the 16th century Spanish explorations of the Solomon Islands were part of a wider process of expansion of the Spanish Empire, we need to recognize the diversity of colonizing experiences and the internal and external factors which produce these. Interaction with indigenous populations is one of the most important factors in the Solomon Islands example, although the nature and role of indigenous encounters is a complex area which could only be addressed minimally here. There is a large body of archaeological studies of New World Spanish-Indigenous contact which offers insights into ways to approach the Solomon Islands data (Smith 1987; Rothschild 2003; Thomas 1989; Gasco 2005; Voss 2005). There is an equally extensive literature on the social, economic and symbolic aspects of cross-cultural contact in Oceania which explores the dynamic, context-driven, and multivalent nature of these engagements (Appadurai 1992; Sahlins 1996; Torrence and Clarke 2000; Dening 2004). There are also many anthropological studies of the materiality of cross-cultural exchanges in Melanesia (e.g. Thomas 1991; Gosden and Knowles 2001), as well as a growing body of archaeological studies tracing the longer-term trajectories of change in the region as a result of, or continuities despite, contact (Torrence 2000; Walters and Sheppard 2000).

While the documentary and archaeological records for Graciosa Bay show a general structure to the colonization which has continuities with other Spanish sites, the specific nature of the settlement, its short-lived operation and decline was a function of the personal expectations and capabilities of the colonists, and the context they found themselves in. Graciosa Bay clearly stayed within the *exploratory* stage remaining in the initial camp and dependent upon the supplies from the ship. Although they had not yet identified local resources, the crew was in the process of planning the formal settlement. Despite the existence of historical records, archaeology still offers the only means for resolving some of the questions surrounding architecture and construction, site layout, defense, subsistence, and trade and interaction with the Santa Cruz Islanders. More importantly, these additional details will provide further comparative material for the Pamua sites.

Based on the current evidence, the nature and duration of the Spanish occupation at Pamua remains unclear. Although the absence of identifiable structural features may indicate that they never advanced beyond the *exploratory* stage, further survey and excavation on the ridge site, the Mwanihuki village, and in the wider landscape may still present a longer and more complex story. Locating evidence that the *Santa Isabel* wrecked at Pamua would also significantly narrow the possibilities, as well as provide an opportunity to examine the material basis of the colonizing effort (Gibbs 2006). Understanding relationships with and impacts upon the indigenous communities in and around Pamua will clearly be a key element in the investigations. In this regard, the collection of oral histories and information on traditional practice and indigenous perspectives concerning "contact" with new cultures will also expand our comprehension of possible events surrounding the fate of the *Santa Isabel* and her people.

162

Acknowledgements

The *Beyond the New World* project is funded by the Australian Research Council grant DP1093168 and is undertaken in collaboration with the Solomon Islands National Museum. The discovery aspect of this project owes much to the original 1970s investigators: the late Prof. Roger Green (Auckland University), Prof. Jim Allen (Latrobe University) and Michael W. Kaschko (formerly University of Hawaii). Thanks to my colleagues Dr David Roe (Port Arthur Historic Site Management Authority) and Lawrence Kiko (Solomon Islands National Museum) and to my students and field assistants Natalie Blake, Sarah Kelloway, Richard Tuffin, Kevin Edwards, Stephen Manebosa and Ryan Hovingh. Bishop Karibongi of Hanuato'o (Makira) Diocese and Principal Samuel Aruhu of St Stephens School Pamua kindly gave their permissions stay at Pamua and work on those parts of the site on school grounds. Deputy Principal Fr. Paterson Tako and the rest of the staff and students of St Stephens School made us welcome during our visit. I am also grateful to Mrs. Noelene Haghamaoto and Chief Ramoni of Pamua and Frank Samui, Martin and Henry Note of Santa Cruz for their knowledge and assistance. Dr Brad Duncan kindly took the time to comment on a draft of this paper. I would like to thank Mark Leone, Joe Joseph and Julie Schablitsky for the opportunity to contribute to the volume, but especially to Julie who has the patience of a saint when it comes to shepherding wayward authors. Finally, this paper is dedicated to my wife Melissa and daughter Eliza, who was only three months old when her daddy ran off to the Solomon Islands on the first season of this fieldwork.

References

ALLEN, JIM

1976   New light on the Spanish settlement of the Southeast Solomons: an archaeological approach. In *Southeast Solomon Islands Cultural History: a preliminary survey*, Roger Green and Mary Cresswell (editors), pp. 19-29. Royal Society of New Zealand, Wellington.

ALLEN, JIM AND ROGER GREEN

1972   Mendaña 1595 and the fate of the lost Almiranta: an archaeological investigation. *Journal of Pacific History* 7:73-91.

AMHERST, LORD (EDITOR)

1901   *The Discovery of the Solomon Islands by Alvaro de Mendaña in 1568*. Hakluyt Society, London.

APPADURAI, ARJUN

1992   *The Apotheosis of Captain Cook: European mvth-makinq in the Pacific*. Princeton University Press, Princeton.

BAIRSTOW, DAMARIS

1984   The Swiss Family Robinson Model: a comment and appraisal. *Australian Journal of Historical Archaeology* 2:3-6.

BECK, ROBIN, DAVID MOORE AND CHRISTOPHER RODNING

2006   Identifying Fort San Juan: A Sixteenth-Century Spanish Occupation at the Berry Site, North Carolina. *Southeastern Archaeology* 25 (1): 65–77.

BIRMINGHAM, JUDY, AND DENNIS JEANS

1983   The Swiss Family Robinson and the archaeology of colonisations. *Australasian Journal of Historical Archaeology* 1:3-14.

BLANTON, DENNIS R.

2003   The weather is fine, wish you were here, because I'm the last one alive: "learning" the environment in the English New World colonies. In *Colonization of Unfamiliar Landscapes: The Archaeology of Adaptation*, Marcy Rockman and James Steele (editors), pp. 190-200. Routledge, London, England.

CAMERON, JAMES
1981   *Ambition's Fire: The Agricultural Colonization of Pre-Convict Western Australia.* University of Western Australia Press, Nedlands.

CAMINO, MERCEDES
2005   *Producing the Pacific: Maps and Narratives of Spanish Exploration.* Rodopi, New York, NY.
2008   *Exploring the Explorers: Spaniards in Oceania 1519-1794.* Manchester University Press, Manchester, England.

CHATFIELD, MELISSA
2007   From Inca to Spanish Colonial: Transitions in Ceramic Technology. Doctoral dissertation, Department of Anthropology, University of California. Santa Barbara.

CARROLL, SANDRA K.
1981   *An Osteological Analysis of Burials Recovered from Makira, S. E. Solomon Islands.* Unpublished student report (Anthropology 699), Department of Anthropology, University of Hawaii.

CROUCH, DORA
1991   Roman models for Spanish Colonization. In *Columbian Consequences: Volume 3. The Spanish Borderlands in Pan-American Perspective*, David Thomas (editor), pp. 21-36. Smithsonian Institution Press, Washington, D.C.

DEAGAN, KATHLEEN
1987   *Artifacts of the Spanish colonies of Florida and the Caribbean, I500-1800.* Smithsonian Institution Press, Washington, D.C.
1995   After Columbus: The sixteenth-century Spanish-Caribbean frontier. In *Puerto Real: The archaeology of a sixteenth-century Spanish town in Hispaniola*, Kathleen Deagan (editor), pp.419-455. University Press of Florida, Gainesville.
2002   *Artifacts of the Spanish colonies of Florida and the Caribbean.* Smithsonian Institution Press, Washington, D.C.
2003   Colonial Origins and Colonial Transformations in Spanish America. *Historical Archaeology* 37(4):3–13.
2008   Archaeology at the Fountain of Youth Park (8-SJ-31) 1934-2007. Final Report to the Florida Department of State, Tallahassee, FL.

DEETZ, JAMES
1977   *In Small Things Forgotten: The Archaeology of Early American Life*, Anchor Press/Doubleday, Garden City, NY.

DIETLER, MICHAEL
2005   The archaeology of colonization and the colonization of archaeology. In *The Archaeology of Colonial Encounters*, Gil Stein (editor), pp. 33-68. School of American Research Press, Santa Fe, NM.

DENING, GREG
2004   *Beach Crossings: Voyaging Across Times, Culture and Self.* Melbourne University Press, Melbourne, Australia.

DICKINSON, WILLIAM AND ROGER GREEN
1973   Temper sands in 1595 A.D. Spanish ware. *Journal of the Polynesian Society* 82:293-300.

EWEN, CHARLES AND JOHN HANN
1998   *Hernando de Soto among the Apalachee.* University Press of Florida, Gainesville.

FERGUSON, LELAND (EDITOR)
1977   *Historical Archaeology and the Importance of Material Things*, Leland Ferguson, editor, pp.5-8. The Society for Historical Archaeology, Special Publication Series No.2.

FOWLER, WILLIAM
2009   Historical Archaeology in Yucatan and central America. In *International Handbook of Historical Archaeology*, Teresita Majewski and David Gaimster (editors), pp. 429-44. Springer, New York,NY.

FOX, CHARLES
1958   *Lord of the Southern Isles: Being the story of the Anglican Mission in Melanesia, 1849-1949.* Mowbray, London, England.

GASCO, JANINE
2005   Spanish Colonialism and processes of social change. In *The Archaeology of Colonial Encounters*, Gil Stein (editor), pp. 69-108. School of American Research Press, Santa Fe, NM.

GIBBS, MARTIN

2002a   Behavioral models of crisis response as a tool for archaeological interpretation – A case study of the 1629 wreck of the V.O.C. Ship Batavia on the Houtman Abrolhos Islands, Western Australia. In *Natural Disasters, Catastrophism and Cultural Change*, John Grattan and Rob Torrence (editors), pp. 66-86. Routledge, New York, NY.

2002b   The Enigma of William Jackman 'The Australian Captive' - Fictional character or shipwreck survivor? *The Great Circle* 24(2):3-21.

2003   The Archaeology of Crisis: Shipwreck Survivor Camps in Australasia. *Historical Archaeology* 37(1):128-145.

2006   Cultural site formation processes in Maritime Archaeology: Disaster response, salvage and Muckelroy 30 years on. *International Journal of Nautical Archaeology* 35(1): 4-19.

GOSDEN, CHRISTOPHER AND CHANTAL KNOWLES

2001 *Collecting Colonialism: Material Culture and Colonial Change*. Berg, Oxford, England.

GREEN, ROGER

1973   The Conquest of the Conquistadors. *World Archaeology* 5:14-31.

HARRISON, RODNEY AND CHRISTINE WILLIAMSON (EDITORS)

2004   *After Captain Cook: The archaeology of the recent indigenous past in Australia*. AltaMira, Walnut Creek, CA.

HEADLEY, JOHN

1995   Spain's Asian Presence, 1565-1590. *The Hispanic American Historical Review* 75(4): 623-646.

HILL, ROSCOE

1913   The office of Adelantado. *Political Science Quarterly* 28(4):646-668.

HOOVER, ROBERT

1992   Some models for Spanish colonial archaeology in California. *Historical Archaeology* 26:37-44.

JACK-HINTON, COLIN

1969   *The Search for the Islands of Solomon 1567-1838*. Clarendon Press, Oxford, England.

KASCHKO, MICHAEL W.

1979   Field Report: 1975 Excavations on Site BB-2-15, Makira, S.E. Solomons'. Report for the Department of Anthropology, University of Hawaii, Honolulu.

KELLY, CELSUS

1965   *Calendar of Documents: Spanish voyages in the South Pacific*. Franciscan Studies, Madrid, Spain.

KELLY, CELSUS (EDITOR)

1966   *La Australia del Espiritu Santo*. Hakluyt Society, Cambridge.

KELSEY, HARRY

1986   Finding the Way Home: Spanish Exploration of the Round-Trip Route across the Pacific Ocean. *The Western Historical Quarterly* 17 (2): 145-164.

KICZA, JOHN

1992   Patterns in Early Spanish Overseas Expansion. *The William and Mary Quarterly* 49: 229-253.

KIRCH, PATRICK

1980   The Archaeological Study of Adaptation: Theoretical and Methodological Issues. *Advances in Archaeological Method and Theory 3:101*-156.

KOORSGAARD, ANNIKA

2010   Shipwrecks of the Solomon Islands. Bachelor of Arts thesis, Department of Archaeology, University of Sydney, Australia.

MARKEN, MITCHELL

1994   *Pottery from Spanish Shipwrecks, 1500-1800*. University Press of Florida, FL.

MARKHAM, CLEMENTS (EDITOR)

1904   *The Voyages of Pedro Fernandez Quiros*. Hakluyt Society, London, England.

MILANICH, JERALD, AND SUSAN MILBRATH

1989   *First Encounters: Spanish Explorations in the Caribbean and the United States, 1492-1570*. University of Florida Press, Gainesville.

NOËL HUME, IVOR

1979   *Martin's Hundred.* University Press of Virginia,
        Charlottesville.

NUTTALL, ZELIA

1921   Royal Ordinances Concerning the Laying out of New
        Towns. *Hispanic American Historical Review* 55(4): 743-
        753.

ORSER, CHARLES

2004   *Historical Archaeology.* HarperCollins, New York, NY.

RICE, PRUDENCE

1994   The Kilns of Moquegua, Peru: technology, excavations,
        and functions. *Journal of Field Archaeology* 21: 325–44.

ROCKMAN, MARCY

2003   Knowledge and Learning in the Archaeology of
        Colonization. In *The Colonization of Unfamiliar
        Landscapes: The archaeology of adaptation.* Marcy
        Rockman and James Steele (editors), pp. 3-24.
        Routledge, London, England.

ROCKMAN, MARCY AND JAMES STEELE (EDITORS)

2003   *The Colonization of Unfamiliar Landscapes: The
        archaeology of adaptation.* Routledge, London, England.

ROTHSCHILD, NAN

2003   *Colonial Encounters in a Native American Landscape.*
        Smithsonian Books, Washington, D.C..

SAHLINS, MARSHALL

1996   *How "Natives" Think: about Captain Cook for example.*
        University of Chicago Press, Chicago, IL.

SCAMMELL, GEOFFREY

1981   *The World Encompassed. The First European Maritime
        Empires, c.800-1650.* Methuen, London, England.

SCOTT-IRETON, DELLA

1998   An analysis of Spanish colonization fleets in the age of
        exploration based on the historical and archaeological
        investigation of the Emanuel Point shipwreck in Pensacola
        Bay, Florida. Master's thesis, Department of Anthropology,
        University of West Florida, Pensacola.

SILLIMAN, STEPHEN

2005   Culture contact or colonialism? *American Antiquity*
        70(1):55-74.

SKOWRONEK, RUSSELL

1998   The Spanish Philippines: Archaeological Perspectives.
        International Journal of Historical Archaeology 2(1):45-71.

2009   On the fringes of New Spain: The Northern Borderlands
        and the Pacific. In *International Handbook of Historical
        Archaeology.* Teresita Majewski and David Gaimster
        (editors), pp. 471-503. Springer, New York, NY.

SMITH, ROGER, JOHN BRATTEN, J. COZZI, AND KEITH PLASKETT

1998   The Emanuel Point Ship Archaeological Investigations
        1997-1998. Report No. 68, Archaeology Institute,
        University of West Florida, Pensacola.

SMITH, ROGER C., JAMES SPIREK, JOHN BRATTEN, AND DELLA SCOTT-IRETON

1999   The Emanuel Point Ship: Archaeological Investigations,
        1992-1995. Preliminary Report, Bureau of Archaeological
        Research, Tallahassee, FL.

SMITH, MARVIN

1987   *Archaeology of Aboriginal Culture Change in the Interior
        Southeast: Depopulation during the Early Historic Period.*
        Ripley P. Bullen Monographs in Anthropology and History
        No. 6, University Press of Florida, Gainesville.

SOUTH, STANLEY A.

1977   Foreword. In *Historical Archaeology and the Importance
        of Material Things.* Leland Ferguson (editor), pp.1-2. The
        Society for Historical Archaeology, Special Publications
        Series No. 2.

1988   Santa Elena: Threshold of Conquest. In *The Recovery of
        Meaning,* Mark Leone and Parker Potter (editors), pp. 27-
        71. Smithsonian Institution Press, Washington.

1990   From Thermodynamics to a status artifact model. In
        *Columbian Consequences: Volume 2. Archaeological
        and Historical Perspectives on the Spanish Borderlands
        East.* David Thomas (editor), pp. 329-341. Smithsonian
        Institution Press, Washington, D.C.

1992   *Archaeology at Santa Elena: Doorway to the Past.* South
        Carolina Institute of Archaeology and Anthropology,
        Columbia.

166

SOUTH, STANLEY A., RUSSELL SKOWRONEK, AND RICHARD JOHNSON
1988   *Spanish Artifacts from Santa Elena*. South Carolina Institute of Archaeology and Anthropology, Columbia.

SPATE, OSCAR
1979   *The Spanish Lake*. Croom Helm, London, England.

SPRIGGS, MATTHEW
1997   *The Island Melanesians*. Blackwell, Oxford, England.

STEIN, GIL
2005   Introduction: The comparative archaeology of colonial encounters. In *The Archaeology of Colonial Encounters*, Gil Stein (editor), pp. 3-32. School of American Research Press, Santa Fe, NM.

THOMAS, NICHOLAS
1991   *Entangled Objects*. Cambridge University Press, Cambridge, England.

TORRENCE, ROBIN
2000   Just another Trader? In *The Archaeology of Difference*, Robin Torrence and Annie Clarke (editors), pp. 101-141. Routledge: London, England.

TORRENCE, ROBIN AND ANNIE CLARKE
2000   Negotiating Difference. In *The Archaeology of Difference*, Robin Torrence and Annie Clarke (editors), pp. 1-31. Routledge, London, England.

VAN BUREN, MARY
2010   The Archaeological Study of Spanish Colonialism in the Americas. *Journal of Archaeological Research* 18:151–201.

VOSS, BARBARA
2005   From Casta to Californio: Social Identity and the Archaeology of Culture Contact. *American Anthropologist* 107(3):461-474.

WALTER, RICHARD AND PETER SHEPPARD
2001   Nusa Rovianna. *Journal of Field Archaeology* 27:295-318.

Martin Gibbs
Department of Archaeology
School of Philosophical & Historical Inquiry
University of Sydney
New South Wales, 2006
Australia

Matthew H. Johnson   English Culture in the Atlantic World

It is terribly important that the small things forgotten be remembered. For in the seemingly little and insignificant things that accumulate to create a lifetime, the essence of our existence is captured. We must remember these bits and pieces, and we must use them in new and imaginative ways so that a different appreciation for what life is today, and was in the past, can be achieved... Don't read what we have written; look at what we have done.

-Deetz (1996:259-260)

ABSTRACT

The essays by James Deetz and Henry Glassie in the 1977 *Historical Archaeology and the Importance of Material Things* volume set out their thoughts on the transition between 'pre-Georgian' and 'Georgian' (1714-1830) cultural and material forms in the American colonies. In the last 30 years, much has been written about the 18th century, but much less on the dawning of the early 17th century. This paper focuses on the first horizon that Deetz laid out. Using the model as a basis, I consider the antecedent conditions in 16th and early 17th century England that framed the everyday life and world-view of the colonists. Two general points emerge from this discussion. First, "culture" is less a blueprint or mental template as it is a set of material practices. Second, there was no simple translation of a core or essential English medieval culture to the New World, but there was a refraction of particular structural tensions and processes between the Old World and the New. I argue for a tracing of structural tensions and processes to complement existing work on regional origins and influences in the archaeological study of the migration from England.

Introduction

The subject of this paper is English culture, and its material and archaeological form, at the start of the 17th century. Broadly speaking, my focus is on the material dimensions of English culture at what is arguably a key horizon in historical archaeology: the first moment at which numbers of English men, women, and children were migrating in large numbers from the Old World to the New. My paper represents part of an initial phase of a long-term project: to articulate a few elements of a theoretical framework for understanding the archaeology of the Atlantic world, one that incorporates but moves beyond previous conceptions and models. Such previous models include simpler ideas of "progress" or European "superiority"; although most scholars would now overtly reject such models, they still surface implicitly and habitually from time to time. I also question simpler models and ideas of colonialism, and traditional narratives of the American frontier (Turner 1920).

In order for archaeologists to better interpret the subtle traces of the 17th century, they must first understand two points related to English culture at the time of the first migration. First, a description and critical understanding of the archaeology of English culture around ca.1600 is a necessary basis for sketching out a broader framework for understanding 17th century transformations and diasporas at a series of scales, ranging from the individual, small-scale and local to the Atlantic world as a whole.[1] Second, such a description and understanding should be incorporated into the analysis of material culture and theoretically in the idea of materiality, which I define in a very loose and preliminary fashion as an acknowledgement of the importance of the "stuff" we find in the ground.

In the spirit of this volume and its predecessor (Ferguson 1977), I want to emphasize material things as important. Stuff – houses, fence boundaries, fields, roads, gravestones, skillets, thimbles, clay pipes, chairs, maritime and terrestrial landscapes from the local to the global scale – was and is more than just a reflection or expression of some underlying subject of study. Despite its inanimate status, stuff plays an active role. It defines who people are as much as it reflects who people are; it is part of and mediates social processes as much as it is a reflection of social process. As Deetz insists in the prefatory epigraph, it accumulates to create people's lives and identities, and to imperfectly shape our interpretations of what those identities were in the past.

An emphasis on materiality in these terms raises a host of difficult theoretical issues: pots may define who people are, but people in turn make new pots. As a result, there is a very extensive and complex theoretical literature on materiality encompassing a range of different views on the notion, and the relation between people and objects (Demarrais et al. 2005; Miller 2005; Preucel 2006; Webmoor and Witmore 2008; Hodder 2011). "Materialisation" is an awkward and clumsy word to use; but perhaps, in this context, its slightly jarring note is appropriate. If material things are important, it follows that they are not just secondary to ideas. In other words, material things are not simply or only "expressions" of cultural values, imperfect manifestations of processes, norms or mental templates, manifestations of some zeitgeist or spirit of the age ("this house displays the spirit of Georgian society to perfection") or means of "display" of some prior status or reality.

All of these phrases – process, expression, norm, spirit, display – are deceptively smooth. If not deployed carefully and rigorously, they can imply that material things are secondary; what archaeologists and historians should be studying, in this view, are the ideas and processes that have no direct material existence, but which somehow go on behind those material things to define their meaning. Such reasoning is persuasive in part because it has very deep roots in the "taken-for-granteds" of Western culture. It goes back to the Platonic distinction between body and soul, surface and essence, and the prioritization of the latter.

If materiality is important, it disrupts some of the ways archaeologists have traditionally thought about the world, and a little disruption of the English language is therefore appropriate in this context.

Small Things, Big Issues

My starting point in this paper is a passage from James Deetz's *In Small Things Forgotten* (1977a; 1996). This little book is still, in my view, one of the two or three most important books in defining the study of historical archaeology, and a book that amplified and gave depth and shape to his preliminary observations in his contribution to *Historical Archaeology and The Importance of Material Things* (Deetz 1977b). *In Small Things Forgotten* fired my imagination as a student. I was struggling with the task of assimilating and understanding the archaeology of medieval and postmedieval England, and trying to fit typologies of clay pipes and pottery, observations of field systems, and the minutiae of carpentry techniques to the many theories and interpretive frameworks then used to understand the transition between those two worlds. Deetz gave me a distinctive archaeological framework to place these studies of pottery typologies and house-plans in a wider context. He showed me how one could understand houses, pots, everyday rubbish, and gravestones as more than just lots of stuff that generated lots of particular studies with no particular end result. He proposed a clear and simple model into which detailed observations of particular contexts and classes of material could be organized.

Most importantly, and especially pertinent to this volume, is the observation that Deetz placed material things at the center of his argument. Pots were not simply indices of economic progress or levels of wealth; their form, appearance and decoration was important as well; artifacts were profound statements of people's view of their world. Deetz shared Henry Glassie's passionate commitment to folk culture as important, as a profound statement about world-view, and to the place of material culture as a statement of world-view that was much more than what could be found in documents (Glassie 1975).[2]

In this way, Deetz moved beyond traditional post-1500 archaeology as practiced in Britain, which continues to use archaeological material to address questions defined by historians (cf. Johnson 2007). His model was fundamentally an archaeological one, with two cultural horizons – the early 17th century and the mid-18th century; the archaeological concept of "horizon" upon which his model depended was laid out with customary clarity in *Invitation to Archaeology* (Deetz 1967:59-61).

Deetz (1977:36) wrote about the opening of the 17th century migration as follows:

The tiny ship that dropped anchor in Plymouth Harbor in the December cold of 1620 carried a precious cargo. Its passengers, English emigrants who had come to the New World for a variety of reasons, brought with them a blueprint – in their minds – for re-creating the culture they had left behind. Like their counterparts who preceded them to Virginia and would follow them to other colonial outposts along the Eastern Seaboard, they were carriers of a tradition that owed much of its form to the English Middle Ages, recently drawn to a close. The Renaissance, which revolutionized our view of ourselves and our world, had not yet made its impact on the simple people of England, and it would be more than a century before its effects could be measured among their counterparts in North America.

In the second edition, this passage was altered, significantly and appropriately, to equally acknowledge the African contribution to early settlement in the New World, and also to move away from prioritizing New England over the Chesapeake:

The tiny ships that crossed the Atlantic in the early seventeenth century... all carried a precious cargo. Their passengers, English emigrants who had come to the New World for a variety of reasons, brought with them a blueprint – in their minds – for re-creating the culture they had left behind. Likewise, the unwilling passengers aboard the thousands of slave ships that made the same crossing brought with them, against enormous odds,

traditions from their West African homelands which would endure in a new and hostile environment. Both would come together in the New World, and combine in complex ways through both resistance and accommodation to form a new culture, one not seen before and one that would become a vital component of our modern society. For the English, theirs was a tradition that owed much of its form to the English Middle Ages, recently drawn to a close. The Renaissance, which revolutionized our view of ourselves and our world, had not yet made its impact on the simple people of England, and it would be more than a century before its effects could be measured among their counterparts in North America (Deetz 1996: 59).

Like so much of Deetz's writing, this is a tremendously rich passage, with a host of ideas embedded within it. Many of these ideas were not followed up in the text: in the later chapters of the book, and in the subsequent scholarship of others, much more attention was paid to the second cultural horizon, the transformation of the 18th century known as the "Georgian Order". The concept of the Georgian Order and of Georgianization in terms of common principles of order, symmetry and segregation observable across different classes of things such as ceramics, houses, gravestones and landscapes was developed by Mark Leone and his students in subsequent decades (Leone 1984, 2005; Courtney 1996).[3] The study of "Georgianization" has overshadowed the analysis of the earlier, 17th century horizon, perhaps in part due to the sheer quantity of archaeological material that can be related to the later transformation, and perhaps also to its status as an index of nascent capitalism and modern life.

The passage also needs to be set alongside Deetz's more detailed accounts of human beings and everyday life. Deetz has been criticized for propounding a kind of ahistorical structuralism, in which the patterns and structures that his model articulates somehow bypass or fail to engage with real human lives, and particularly with the inequalities and injustices of colonialism. Loren and Beaudry (2006:253) have noted that "the outcome of ahistorical structuralist analyses like Deetz's is that the colonial aspect of early colonial life gets overlooked." Such a criticism is pertinent to the structuralist model used, and arguably to the book in itself, but less so to Deetz's work as a whole. Criticizing Deetz for failing to engage with humans can only make sense if one fails to set alongside *In Small Things Forgotten* his much more detailed and humane explorations of the lives of early Americans in his other studies, most notably *Flowerdew Hundred* and *The Times of Their Lives* (Deetz 1993, 2000).

In what follows, I want to unpack some of the ideas embedded in Deetz's passage, and amplify, deepen and extend some of the concerns raised, with particular reference to material patterns.

The Tiny Ships

It is well known that the 17th century diaspora was dependent on changes in maritime technology and prior shifts in patterns of economic activity, most obviously fishing. The harvesting of shoals of herring was a particularly important component on medieval European economic activity, in part due to religious injunctions to avoid meat at particular times of the year. From 1450 onwards herring fleets moved across the North Atlantic in response to changing movements of herring shoals. This ecological shift, dependent on the climatic fluctuations of the Little Ice Age, ultimately led to new techniques of ship construction, which in turn enabled further, faster, and longer voyages and wider patterns of marine exploitation. "Doggers" set off from the British Isles to Iceland from the 15th century onwards, leading to political confrontation between England and Iceland over who had the right to fish in different waters in the North Atlantic around Iceland (Fagan 2000: 78-9). Further encounters with Greenland and Newfoundland in search of herring shoals led to European settlement (Tuck et al. 1999) and exploration and mapping of the New England coast from ca.1500 onwards.

I am influenced here by maritime colleagues; the development of maritime technologies seem to play relatively little part in much of what is written about historical archaeology, yet material conditions like the decreasing journey time between the Old World and the New are surely crucial, for example in the difficulty

of speedy communication between Europe and colony, and hence the relative autonomy and development of "rogue capitalism" in colonial contexts. Dawdy (2009), for example, paints a compelling picture of the "devil's empire" that was 18th century New Orleans; the complex and often chaotic picture of "rogue capitalism" that she delineated was a situation made possible, in part, by the insuperable difficulty of the long journey time between France and Louisiana, and the consequent impossibility of close imperial control of the town. Maritime archaeology is in a particularly strong position to further elucidate the crucial impacts of technology and its effect on the development of early European settlement. Jon Adams' work on changes in ship design in the 16th and 17th centuries has shown how the process was much more complex than simply improvements in construction. The production of faster, bigger ships was also the result of a new conceptual and social organization of shipbuilding and design (Adams 2011). If the production of ships needs further attention, so does the social experience of the passage and the social organization of life both on board ships and in the port cities and towns, and wider maritime landscapes, that served those ships. Documentary accounts, most obviously Governor Bradford's retrospective propaganda description of the passage in terms of divine Providence, suggest that the lived experience of the "passage" (Murphy 1981:66-71), and the way it was represented, played a central role in the lived experience of 17th century English migrants (Gibbs, this volume).

A Precious Cargo

A proper anthropological understanding of the English families traveling on the tiny ships has been inhibited by two contrasting, if often implicit, moral valuations. The first is that of traditional American history: that these English colonists were the ancestors and forebears of American values of freedom of conscience, liberty, and so forth. The second diametrically opposed view is that the migrants were essentially colonial oppressors. Neither of these views is wrong. Ideas of equality before the law, of individual liberty, and of constitutional limits to royal power, were powerful and at times, violently contested ideals in 17th century England. These principles were upheld by contemporaries, who cited a long legal genealogy stretching back to Magna Carta and beyond to the Anglo-Saxons. Radical ideas of liberty and equality were articulated in the English revolution; these ideas claimed legitimacy by looking back to Anglo-Saxon freedoms. Historians have traced these ideas forward, as a key component of American ideas of liberty expressed in the American Revolution and U.S. Constitution (Hill 1972).

At the same time, the colonial nature of the English migration is immediately evident. Englishmen may have asserted liberty and equality as ideals, but it cannot be over stated that the English migration can never be decoupled from the17th century diaspora of enslaved Africans. The slave trade was not, as some have implied, a moral imperfection or deviation from the otherwise onward march of progress and libertarian ideals. Rather, the institution and practice of slavery was a core structural element of European involvement with the Atlantic world. The English engaged in the slave trade from the very beginning of the early modern period, from the 1550s onwards (Williams 1944; Froude 2005).

However, a moral valuation is only part of the story. With apologies to Willey and Phillips (1958:2), archaeology is anthropology or it is nothing, and anthropology studies cultural and moral systems dispassionately and in comparative perspective. An understanding of the English emigrants has to start with their worldview (though it is necessary to add that it must never finish there). It is a paradox, but nevertheless true, to observe that 17th century English communities were, in part, motivated by fear. For many contemporary commentators, the rest of Catholic Europe seemed united in conspiracy against the kingdom of England; regular collections for English victims of Turkish and north African pirates were held in churches up and down the country (Colley 2003).

We easily forget that English emigrants could not be aware that their country was on the high road to imperial domination. The 17th century is too easily seen through the lens of 18th and 19th century colonial domination; even the word "colony" itself is problematic in this context. But the world in 1600 was a very different place. Bruce Lenman (2001:1-2) has pointed out that it was not until the last decades of the 18th century that the term "colony" acquired a definition resembling anything like its contemporary meaning; before this date, the word used by contemporaries was "plantation".

A Blueprint – in Their Minds – for Recreating the Culture They had Left Behind

Deetz deploys a particular view of culture that combines structuralism with a normative approach. A structural view of culture shows how the forms of various and diverse artifacts – a toothbrush, a gravestone, a slipware dish, a timber-framed house – are generated by a set of common structural principles. This set of principles has no material existence; it exists between the ears of members of a culture. Such an approach is now out of fashion, but I do not believe this makes it wrong. Nor does it necessarily contradict a stress on materiality. A structural approach of this kind does have the merit of starting with material things and looking for patterns, relationships, and common principles between them, rather than engaging in an immediate assimilation to historical questions and issues.

The English Middle Ages, Recently Drawn to a Close

What were the Middle Ages and in what sense had it drawn to a close? How was its closure related to the migration across the Atlantic? Was the ending of the Middle Ages a fundamental transition? What role can archaeology play in the long-standing and wide-ranging historical debate on the medieval-to-Renaissance transition (Gaimster and Stamper 1997)? Deetz does not have to answer any of these questions. His task is to present a satisfactory narrative of 17th and 18th century North America; in a sense, his protagonists arrive on the coast of North America pre-formed at the start of his narrative. For Deetz, then the question of medieval origins does not have to be addressed for his account to be intellectually complete. But for the archaeologist of late and postmedieval England, seeking to understand the origins of the Atlantic migration, these questions are fundamental; the difficulty is knowing where to start with a vast historical literature involving processes as various and as intensively studied as: the end of feudalism; the Black Death and the underlying causes and demographic consequences; 14th century economic collapse and structural transformation; religious reformation; the onset of the Little Ice Age; and the cultural impact of the post 1492 encounter with the New World.

The Renaissance... Had not yet Made its Impact on the Simple[r] People

Deetz is invoking a model here of cultural diffusion. In this view, "the Renaissance" started at the top of society and took its time to work down the social scale. Instead of a top-down idea of change in the 16th and early 17th century, in which a set of pre-formed "Renaissance values" were diffused geographically from Italy and socially from the elite downwards, I depict a society driven by transformation from within, in which cultural values and their materialization were constantly in a state of being reformed.

Deetz's first edition opens with "the tiny ship that dropped anchor in Plymouth Harbor," but this particular moment in American and world history was also much more than the chance volition of a group of individuals establishing a new settlement. It was a complex coming together of individual decisions, social and economic forces, changing technologies, and complex climatic variables (Rockman 2010).[4] People did indeed migrate for "a variety of reasons," but those reasons were proximal rather than ultimate causes, just one facet of a much larger kaleidoscope of intersections and transformations.

Some of those intersections and transformations can be considered within the context of England and her immediate neighbors such as the material life of the household and the market, along with England versus Britain, during the period 1550-1650. These two tensions operated at different and complementary scales ranging from the nation-state and beyond incorporating the material worlds of the region down to the village level and throughout the minutiae of a household. I suggest that these material dynamics prompted a series of structural transformations within English society. Among these transformations were the phenomenon of migration and the origins of empire.

Furthermore, the dynamics of change from household to national levels were all tied to particular kinds of material practices, and are, therefore, woven into the everyday stuff of archaeology. A key point I want to stress is that a search for these structural tensions is not a particularly complex and deep exercise in theory. As Deetz stresses, they can be found in the artifacts, site structure, and the physical form of the house and landscape – in what people have done. Many of the themes I want to highlight are best evidenced not through a difficult search for hidden complexities, but rather through basic observations of patterning in the archaeological record.

House and Household

I want to consider the archaeology of the house and households before moving on to the regional, national, and global levels. The archaeology of England in the 16th and early 17th centuries is the archaeology of houses. This is admittedly a rather sweeping statement; I mean several things by it.

First, the house and household was the central guiding political and cultural metaphor of the period, from the elite to the socially middling, to the humble (Johnson 2010).[5] The kingdom or commonwealth was a social pyramid, consisting of the King, the aristocracy, the gentry, yeoman and husbandman classes down to the laboring poor. Political commentators varied the precise terms used, but all took for granted that each level consisted of a number of households. They insisted that the male head of household governed in his own home in the same manner as the king governed the Commonwealth.

Second, most people lived in rural areas. This simple observation is too easily obscured by the biases of the practices of British postmedieval archaeology. Much archaeological research has been in urban areas, as a result of excavation in advance of redevelopment of town centers, and ensuing post excavation work. At the same time, these urban sites are very rich in ceramics and other artifacts when compared with their rural counterparts; in the countryside, refuse was often gathered in the manure heap and then broadcast across the fields rather than being concentrated in trash pits so beloved by the archaeologist. Consequently, the impressive artifact assemblages associated with densely occupied bourgeois households have disproportionately influenced our understanding of postmedieval life in general (Gaimster 1999). It is easy to forget in the face of this material that four out of five households were rural rather than urban. Furthermore, urban households were the exception rather than the norm in terms of contemporary social schema. The urban classes occupied ambiguous positions in social commentaries and did not fit easily into the hierarchies outlined by political commentators.

Whether urban or rural, the archaeology of the period is defined in terms of the domestic material remains of structures (property boundaries, gardens, buildings) both above and below ground and the artifacts associated with those remains. Excavated pottery assemblages are characteristically household assemblages, records of personal preference, class status, and consumption within the postmedieval household. The bread-and-butter analysis of these assemblages is also an exploration of the economy of these households in the broadest sense, that is, their production and consumption of goods (cf. Yentsch 1991). Foodways in England, and the ceramic and artifacts that materialized those foodways, were so much more than what Joan Thirsk calls "phases, fads and fashions" (Thirsk 2007); they constituted the house as a social unit.

The English countryside was dominated by houses, thousands of which survive today (Figure 1). Their form is well known: the overwhelming majority were rectangular in shape, consisting of two to four rooms on the ground floor, and constructed of local building materials. These households, headed by socially middling yeomen and husbandmen, contained numerous young servants who would eventually establish households of their own. The physical and social grammar of the house – that is, its layout around upper and lower ends, its relationship to surrounding farm and ancillary buildings, its position within the property boundaries of the toft and croft, its position within a village or wider community – is precisely the

Figure 1. Monks Eleigh, Suffolk, eastern England. In one sense, a "typical English village," with houses surviving from the 15th to 17th centuries clustered around a green with a medieval church at its head. In another sense, a display of the building blocks of early modern political authority – a series of households or little commonwealths within a village community. (Photograph by author, 1992).

subject of traditional studies of vernacular buildings (Johnson 2010).

At this time, larger houses, whether of the gentry or of the aristocracy, were exactly that – larger versions, occupied by larger households with many rather than few servants, but deploying a fundamentally similar social grammar. Montacute House, for example, built by the Speaker of the House of Commons Sir Edward Phelips in 1599, is in its form a very large version of an H-plan house, with a hall at its center, and a service and parlor on either side (Figures 2a and 2b). Phelips' social inferiors, themselves socially middling male heads of household, would have sat as guests in his hall, and recognized the physical and social layout of Montacute as a larger version of their own homes. What the common social grammar of large and small houses shows us is that the conceptual linkage between the house and cultural order – the idea that the male householder ruled in his home just as the lord ruled in his great house and the king ruled over his kingdom -- was an extremely powerful part of a common cultural and political vocabulary.

However, the common social grammar was inherently weak as well as strong; however powerful its elements, it was also simultaneously being pulled apart. In the first place, it rested on a set of gender relations

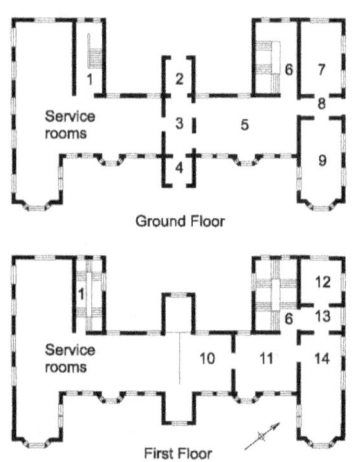

Figure 2. Montacute House, elevation and plan. A great house, nevertheless centered around a great hall with upper and lower ends. (Photograph by author, 2008).

Ground Floor

First Floor

Key
1 South stairs
2 Rear porch
3 Front porch
4 Screens passage
5 Great Hall
6 North stairs
7 Parlour chamber

8 Lobby
9 Parlour
10 Best chamber
11 Withdrawing room
12 Garden chamber
13 Lobby
14 Dining room
Not to scale

that were constantly open to subversion. Wendy Wall (2002) has looked at foodways and other household practices through the lens of cook books and other household manuals. She shows how solid sufficiency and order of the socially middling sort, and the cultural values that went with it, concealed an unstable underside. Women engaged in activities that contradicted the orthodoxy of male supremacy. Men were held by [male] legal theorists and political commentators to be in a position of authority over the household, but women were in charge of the practical activity around it – transforming nature into culture through cooking, controlling the production of beer, cheese and other dairy products. Behind political order, then, was always a contradiction, and anxiety was expressed though the many instances of contradictory advice given to housewives by the male writers of advice books around everyday activities such as cooking and cleaning. Wendy Wall (2002) discusses, for example, advice books urging the ever more curious and fanciful production of pastries and sweetmeats while at the same time exhorting the housewife to economy and frugality.

At the same time, new forces were acting on the house and household that struck at its role as the basic building block of society. In reality, the house had never been self-sufficient. Excavations of 14th and 15th century peasant dwellings have revealed a range of traded goods, including pottery, foodstuffs and metal artifacts that reveal the household as an active participant in market activity. Excavations of rural peasant households of the 15th century have revealed goods traded over long distances, for example metal dress accessories (Hinton 2005, 2010; Smith 2009), as well as the presence of fish on inland sites (Grant 1988:143).

If the household was the basic unit of political culture, then the household was maintained by husbandry. Husbandry was cultural and social as well as economic labor and its purpose was to maintain the commonwealth (Johnson 1996: 83-86). Work by the head of the farming households along with his field and house servants and laborers maintained and consolidated its economic position. Husbandry was an expression of the values of the house and of the community, but it was also the terrain of a set of norms that were undercut by cultural tension, such as the benefits of improvement and anxiety over enclosure (Tawney 1912; Burt and Archer 1994). Again, these tensions are materialized in the everyday interactions that are the bread and butter of archaeology, in this case landscape archaeology and history. The historical literature on the 15th and 16th centuries is full of little stories of peasants improving their land, consolidating holdings, and wrangling over ownership of property (Dyer 1997), for example:

In 1605 a dispute was brought before the Court of Exchequer by the inhabitants of Marsham against Thomas Thetford, owner of the manor, and regarding the imposition of a fold course... thirty years previously Clement Paston had gained 'by action at the common lawe' the several land and fold course from the tenants of Marsham... since then Thomas Wright grazed four hundred sheep within this fold course, and it was claimed that during that time, no inhabitants of Marsham pastured their sheep on the several doles... when [John Brown's servants] attempted to drive Thetford's sheep from his crops of corn the 'servants of Thetford 'did beat and miseuse' him (Whyte 2009:103).

Indeed, archaeology contributes to the complex historic landscape created by historians: numerous studies of regional communities have shown a consistent viewpoint of enclosure, improvement, and rural industry, sitting often uneasily alongside a strong sense of community and a powerful set of local practices affirming that community (Whyte 2009). One artifact of this emergent tension between classes was the genre of advice books. These were written by male members of the gentry classes who explicitly addressed socially inferior men and women, specifically socially middling households. These advice books, as one might expect, express a traditional view of social values. The house is placed at the center of their discourse, and conceived of as a productive unit; however, the structure and pattern of household life they advocate so stridently diverged from what the middling sort were actually building. Gervase Markham's famous house plan from *The English Husbandman* (1613) is often cited in normative terms, as an expression of the cultural values framed around the house (cf. Thompson 1995). But, its form varies in terms of scale from the compact rectangular boxes that socially middling farmers were actually building. The middling sort envisioned compact rectangular boxes for themselves, not a traditional H-plan manor house.

This disjuncture between what the gentry classes were prescribing for the middling sort, and what the middling sort actually built for themselves, can be seen by comparing Figures 3 and 4. This tension can also be seen, at a very basic and obvious level, in artifacts and artifact assemblages.

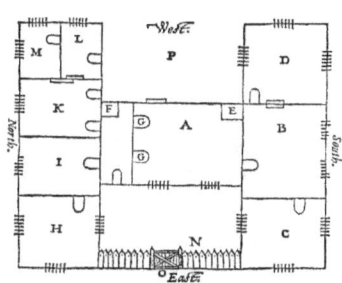

Figure 3. Gervase Markham's idealized plan of a socially middling husbandman's farmhouse. The letters indicate different rooms (A is the hall, K is the kitchen, and so on) (Markham 1613).

The later 16th and early 17th century is known as the period of the "Great Rebuilding," an era of material improvement of houses, including the steady rise in the number, level, and provision of goods within the house. These include the brightly colored ceramics, clay pipes and associated tobacco, vessel and window glass-- the typical fodder of postmedieval archaeology. All of this material culture added to the comfort and beauty of the home. It was fitted, literally, into the traditional concept of the domestic unit. The ceramic dishware on the kitchen shelves, the pewter spoon set on the dining table, and the cooking pots around the hearth, all constituted the domestic environment. But these

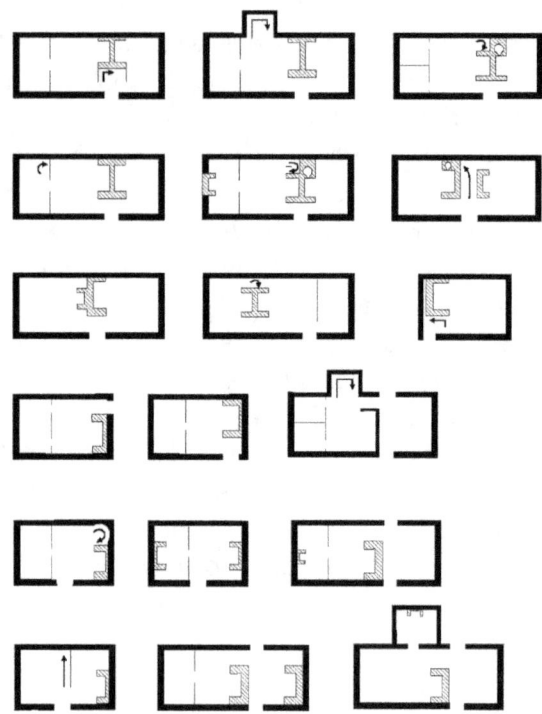

FIGURE 4. Plans of surviving farmhouses from the later 16th and 17th centuries from different regions of England. Compare with Figure 5. (Plan by Penny Copeland, 2010.)

goods also bound the house to a wider network of economic relationships, in particular the market – both a physical market in the form of the central area of the local small town, and the growing network of market relations represented by traveling tinkers, peddlers and the like (Spufford 1984). All of these goods and improvements materialized the tension between the ideal of solid sufficiency and the reality of a diverse set of practices including material aggrandizement. The period after 1450 has been termed the "postmedieval ceramic revolution," "characterized urban increasing multiplicity and dimensionality of body, form, surface treatment and ornament, which transformed pottery vessels from the strictly functional product of the mid-1400s into a medium with diverse utilitarian and social purposes by c.1650" (Gaimster 1999:214). In other words, as social commentators celebrated ever more stridently the ideal of the house as a self-sufficient social unit of production with values of self-sufficiency and frugality, so it was becoming more and more an arena of bright, colorful consumer goods emblematic of market relations.

Why is this material analysis of the English household relevant to the wider Atlantic world? Because it delineates a series of tensions – between household as self-sufficient unit and household as locus of market forces, between the ideals of patriarchy and the realities of a complex set of gender and other relations, between a solid sufficiency and the acquisition of more goods and rise in material comforts – that went on in turn, I argue, to structure relations at a wider scale, across the Atlantic world. For example, these tensions can be also seen in the concept of "plantation" and specifically in the early settlement of New England. The charter and funding for Plymouth Plantation was framed around the settlement's purpose in terms of exploitation and trade, specifically fishing (Cressy 1987; Deetz and Deetz 2000). However, the aims and intentions of the Puritan settlers were different, centering around the creation of a series of Godly households. The genesis and form of Plymouth Plantation was a material rendition of an emergent and long-term tension within and around the English house.

England and the British Isles

The household and the village community were, in the cultural and political orthodoxy of the time, the English kingdom writ small. But what exactly was the English kingdom? The basic archaeological patterns of the period show us a strong normative ideal of England as a kingdom, not least through the overt proclamations of royal propaganda in the form of heraldry, monumental architecture such as royal palace-building (Thurley 1993) and so on. However, archaeology also shows us a series of contradictions subverting this ideal of a geographically and ethnically homogenous country. Far from being an island kingdom, a "precious stone set in the silver sea" as extolled by Shakespeare in the famous speech of John of Gaunt (Richard II, Act II Scene I), England had difficult, complex and shifting land boundaries on its western and northern sides. Before ca.1600, there had been a tension between an idealized conception of the self-sufficient kingdom of England on the one hand, and structure of domination and attempted incorporation of the "margins" of the British Isles on the other. This tension was not eased after the accession of

King James VI of Scotland to the English throne in 1603; James' attempts to unify England and Scotland failed, and he and his successors reigned as monarchs of the two kingdoms with two separate parliaments and two sets of religious institutions, with political consequences that contributed to civil war in the 1640s (Morrill 1993).

This tension is materialized in the basic stuff of archaeology, particularly the distribution map and particularly the relationship of different artifact and monument distributions to the physical geography of the British Isles, as opposed to the kingdom of England. In the 1930s, Cyril Fox (1938) delineated a northern and western 'highland zone' and southern and eastern 'lowland zone' characterized by the geology of the British Isles. He showed how different patterns and distributions of settlement stretched far back into prehistory. Fox's observations have often been distilled into a vulgar determinism in which southern and eastern England have always been wealthier and more "progressive" than Scotland, Ireland, Wales and northern and western England. However, the enduring

value of Fox's work is his insight into the way a normative conception of the kingdom of England, dominated by London and consisting of nucleated villages surrounded by arable fields, was based around a very partial view of southern and eastern England. If as archaeologists we look at settlement beyond these areas from ca.1100 onwards, a very different picture emerges.

The Anglo-Normans had annexed large areas of Welsh-speaking territory in the 11th and 12th centuries, and areas of the island of Ireland from the 1160s. The landscapes of these areas were divided along feudal lines, with a structure of English counties being created and a network of castles and associated towns established. Edward I's famous new castles, such as Beaumaris, Caernarvon, Conway, Harlech, Rhuddlan, and Flint, were built at huge royal expense in the later 13th century as part of the annexation of north Wales and

Figure 5. Caernarvon: a "new town" planted in the later 13th century as part of the English King Edward I's conquest of north Wales, on the site of an earlier Welsh settlement whose origins date back to the Roman period (John Speed 1611).

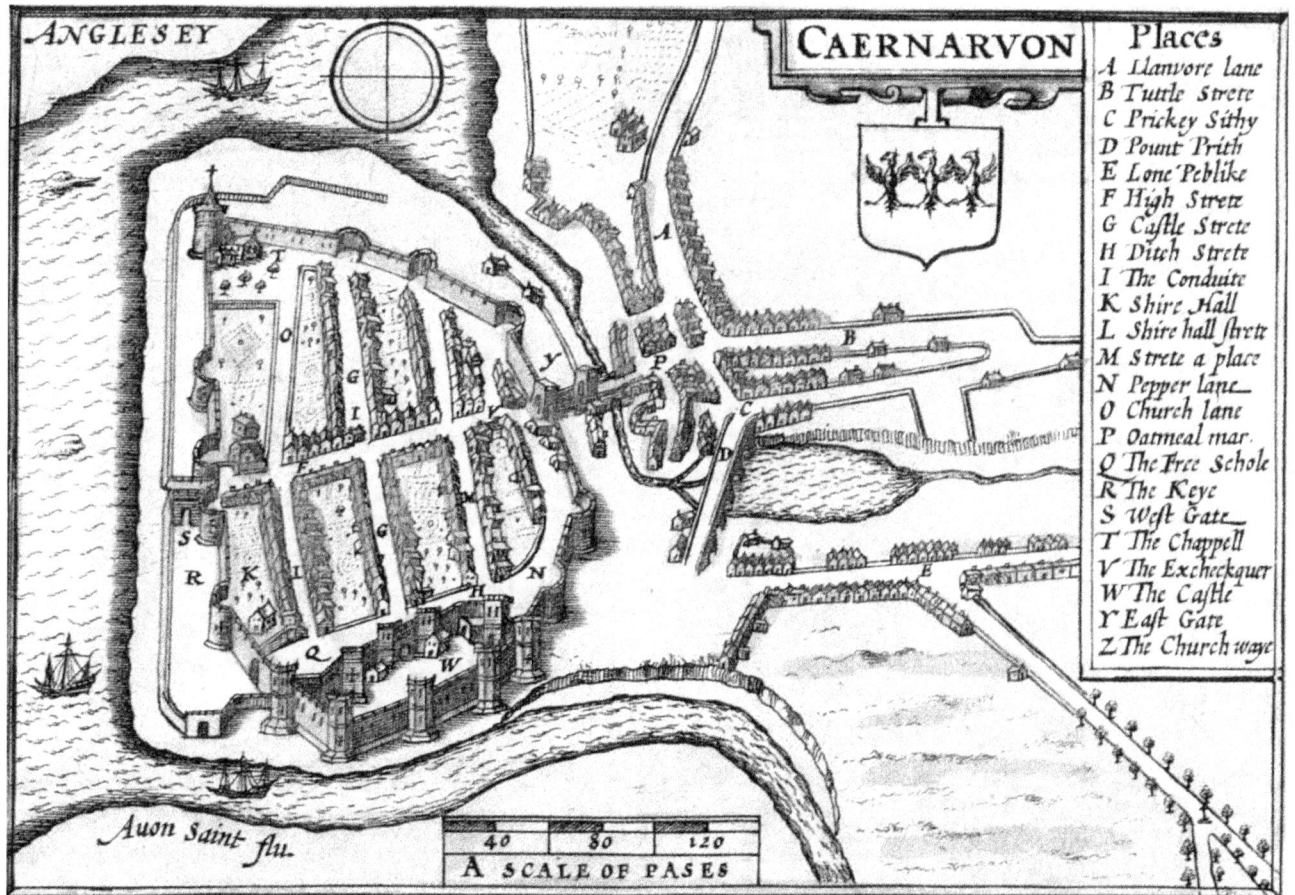

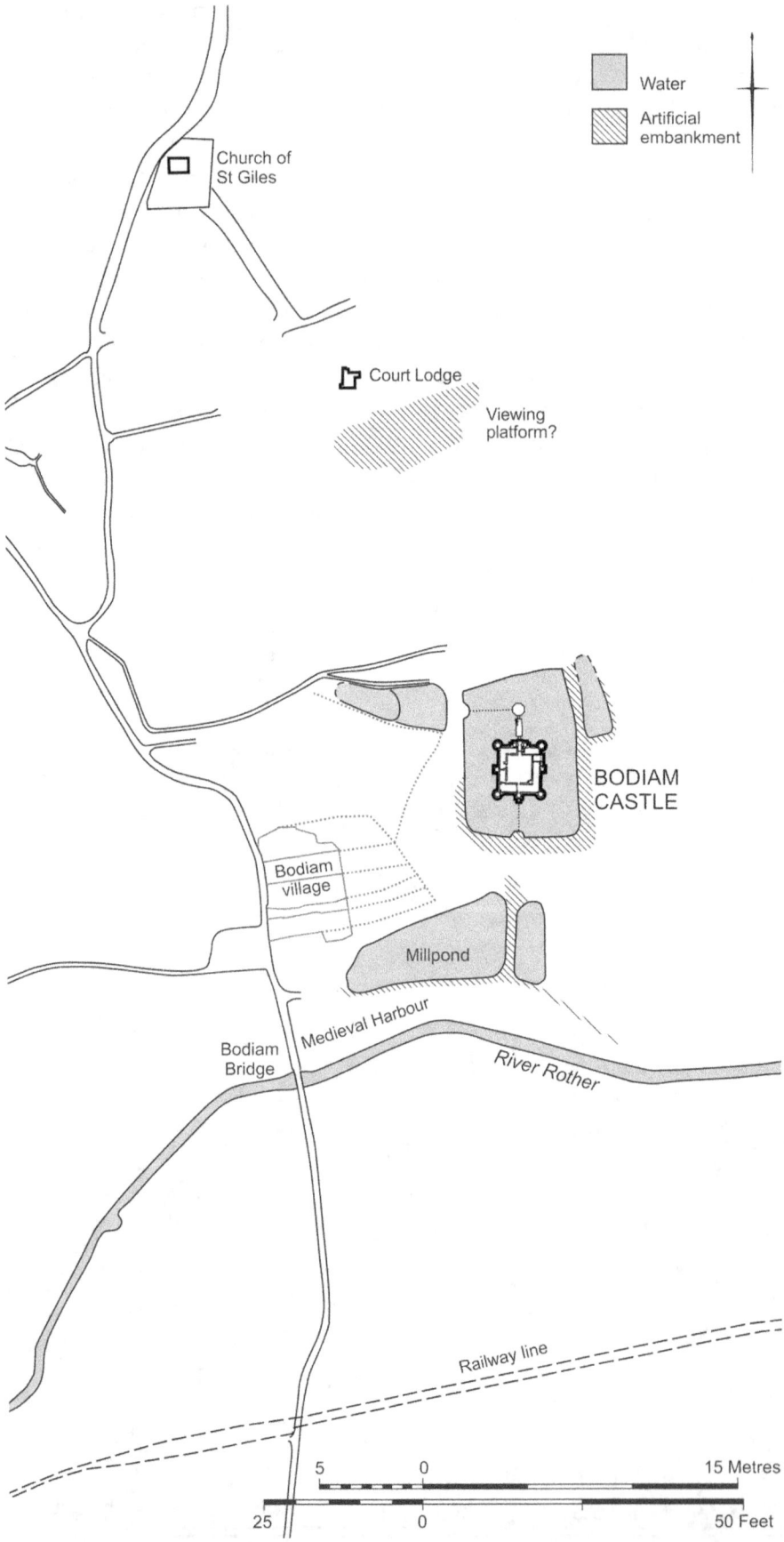

Figure 6. The landscape around Bodiam Castle, south-eastern England. The castle was built and an elaborate system of water features was created, including a bridge, harbour, mill and millpond, in the 1380s. The millpond is to the south; the site of the mill is uncertain, but may be immediately to the south of the castle. A row of houses to the west of the castle forms a small, ideal version of a medieval village. The castle and landscape could be viewed from an elevated location north of the castle adjacent to the earlier site of Court Lodge, possibly used in this period as a 'viewing platform.' (Plan by Penny Copeland, 2011.)

were paired with fortified new towns on regular plans (Figure 5). The Irish Pale around Dublin, the most fertile area of the island of Ireland, was initially the subject of feudal conquest and was again subject to a pattern of feudal settlement. It is arguable that the first creation of ordered colonial landscapes occurred within the interstices of a feudal system of government, not a nascent capitalist or colonial one in the modern sense. Great caution is therefore required in deploying terms like colonialism and capitalism in such early contexts, such as Eric Klingelhofer (2003:102, 117) when he describes Ireland as "England's first colony." In fairness, he goes on to note the "vexing" difficulties regarding the definitions of colonialism and imperialism (Horning 2006).[6]

In recent years, archaeologists have discerned numbers of "designed landscapes" created by medieval lords to reflect an idealized view of the landscape (Creighton 2009). For example, in the 1380s, after the crisis of feudalism of which the 1348-1349 Black Death was but one symptom, Edward Dallingrygge laid out an idealized feudal landscape around his new castle of Bodiam in southeast England. This landscape included the battlemented and symmetrical form of the castle itself, a carefully constructed setting including the artificial lake or moat around the castle, a system of bodies of water, a mill and millpond, and possibly a planned village. This landscape has recently been the subject of geophysical and topographical survey by the University of Southampton (Figure 6), a survey which has clarified and further defined elements of this landscape, as well as elucidating its relationship to the river Rother below the site. It was created a century after Edward's planned Welsh settlements, and a century before the earliest English settlement of the New World. Bodiam represents an attempt to create an ordered landscape that is an idealized physical and social representation of a landscape that might be termed "feudal," in the sense of materializing a feudal community: the private residence of a lord, surrounded by church, village, and mill. However, it was created at a moment in time when the structure of feudalism, however defined, was falling apart; it was laid out in the same decade as the Peasants' Revolt, the famous uprising against lordly oppression (Whittick 1993).

The 16th and 17th centuries have often been seen as a time of unprecedented state formation (Braddick 2000), using technologies such as the map. Helgerson (1992:105-146) has explored the role of the map in presenting an ideal of the nation-state, but also and at the same time discussed how the map created an idea of the nation that was conceptually independent of the monarch. It has also been seen in terms of a new sense of ethnic consciousness, most famously seen in Shakespeare's Henry V, in which Shakespeare creates an ideological portrayal of English, Scots, Welsh and Irish fighting together under the young King. Shakespeare's creation, of course, says very little about the events of Henry's campaign of 1415 and everything about the context of the play's first production in 1599, specifically the propaganda and underlying political anxiety surrounding the invasion of Ireland by Queen Elizabeth's favorite, the Earl of Essex (Shapiro 2005:98-104).

There is a tension between the ideal of an English kingdom, and the reality of a complex and fractured British Isles, the margins of which experienced different forms of settlement and domination from the 11th century onwards. However, this experience can only be called colonial in the very loosest sense, and its initial stages are certainly better understood within the framework of feudal conquest than of nascent capitalism.

Definitions of England, of Britain and the British Isles, and of all the nations of the Atlantic world were fashioned and refashioned constantly and dialectically from the medieval to the Victorian worlds. In other words, England was not some immutable core or essence, but was redefined as other nations and colonies redefined themselves. The so-called English Civil War was in fact, among other things, a war involving all the regions of the British Isles; further, it saw the creation and definition of new forms of national identity based on ethnic homogeneity: the New Model Army, created by the Puritans, was an explicitly ethnically homogenous creation, a conscious rejection of the use of non-English mercenaries and others (Stoyle 2005). This very new consciousness of State and ethnicity was materialized using the vocabulary of older, chivalric forms: for example, references to King Arthur in the architecture of the period (Johnson 2002:133); and propaganda depictions referencing Queen Elizabeth as the Virgin Mary (Hackett 1995).

The material forms of settlement across the Highland and Lowland Zones materialized this complex set of relationships. They also point to wider patterns and processes across the Atlantic world – for example, the use of tower-houses and "bawns" (fortified enclosures) in the Highland Zone of the British Isles was also a grammar of settlement that was played out from Ireland to Virginia (St George 1990), while the use of castles in conjunction with new towns, and the imposition of the language of townships and counties, were traditional materializations of feudal authority deployed in new World contexts from the Caribbean to New England.

Conclusion: England and the Atlantic World

Scholarly discussion of the material life and culture of what has become known as the "great migration"[7] has been quite incomplete in certain respects. This may sound like a strange statement to make. After all, 17th to 19th century European and African settlement in the Chesapeake, New England and elsewhere has been very extensively researched by historians and archaeologists. At the same time, every aspect of the culture of later 16th and early 17th century England has been studied in detail; the period 1540-1640 has been named "Tawney's Century" after the great socialist historian Richard Tawney, who saw in that century the origins of the modern world (Tawney 1912, 1926; Fisher 1961). The economic, social, intellectual and cultural origins of the English Civil War of the 1640s have been, it seems to the outside observer, almost studied to death (Hill 1972; Morrill 1993; Stoyle 2005).

What has been lacking is detailed consideration of the great migration from the point of view of English history and archaeology, as opposed to North American history and archaeology. The primary focus in New World scholarship is, quite appropriately, on "becoming American".[8] Cressy's (1987, vii) comment that "it is rare that one finds references to America, New England or Massachusetts in the indexes of modern texts and monographs about Stuart England" remains partly true over 30 years later.[9] Genuinely comparative studies that represent sustained empirical attempts to link England with New England and the other colonies are not common (for exceptions see Yentsch 1991; Horn 1994; Cheek 1997; Horning 2011).

Archaeologists have conspired with this English parochialism of historians for a variety of reasons. There is an enduring particularism in much English medieval and postmedieval archaeology. This is partly due to the continuing dominance of culture-historical approaches in much of the field, but there are other theoretical currents also at work also. The influence of local and landscape history on the English tradition has led to a stress on small-scale processes, as has the more recent postprocessual stress on the individual (Johnson 2005, 2007; Whyte 2009).[10]

I am arguing here for a broadly based and comparative archaeology not simply of the regional origins of the English, but of the structural conditions and tensions that framed English culture at the opening of the 17th century. I have identified tensions within English society at two different levels; I could have delineated a series of intermediate levels, for example of the village, the congregation of the church, and the county and regional community. I could also have delineated the level of the individual, and talked about the structural conditions and tensions that underlay the idea of liberty as it developed in 17th century England and America.[11] The 17th century, then, was not simply or only a matter of an English culture or mind set getting up and moving across the Atlantic. The processes that underlay the Great Migration were the same that articulated the New World in new and different ways. They underlay the creation of the Renaissance State, and of Britain as opposed to England.

At each level, these tensions had material form; they were the stuff of material life. The very basic patterns that can be seen in the archaeology of the period materialized these tensions. When the postmedieval archaeologist sorts through pottery assemblages, consults maps, traces the inventories of peasants, pores over distribution maps of the Highland and Lowland Zones, she or he is dealing with the material working-through of a set of ideas and values that were Janus-faced. On the one hand, they were powerful cultural norms, a mental template if you will, that was strongly subscribed to in the orthodoxy of the period. On the other hand, they were also and immediately open to subversion, in part due to a new set of forces – the pull of market relations, changes in understandings and practices of gender, new practices of the nation-state.

If we look not just at what 16th and 17th century Englishmen and women wrote, but also at what they did, we find that pottery, maps, houses, and landscape materialize a powerful set of norms, but they also materialize a process of becoming and of constant subversion. It is in this tension and duality that an important and overlooked perspective on the Great Migration is to be found.

Acknowledgments

My first acknowledgement should be to James Deetz. He took the time to talk to an anonymous young student visiting Flowerdew, and to encourage my early work, with an intellectual openness and generosity and refreshing lack of pretension. Conversations with Jon Adams informed the discussion of maritime technology. I thank Mark Leone and Julie Schablitsky for asking me to write this paper, for their thoughtful and detailed encouragement and feedback, and for their patience during its production.

References

ADAMS, JONATHAN
2011   *A Maritime Archaeology of Ships: Innovation and Social Change in Medieval and Early Modern Europe.* Oxbow, Oxford, England.

BRADDICK, MICHAEL J.
2000   *State Formation in Early Modern England c1550-1700.* Cambridge University Press, Cambridge, England.

BURT, RICHARD AND ARCHER, JOHN M. (EDITORS)
1994   *Enclosure Acts: Sexuality, Property and Culture in Early Modern England.* Cornell University Press, Ithaca, NY.

CARSON, CARY, HOFFMAN, RONALD AND ALBERT, PETER J (EDS)
1994   *Of Consuming Interests: The Style of Life in the 18th Century.* United States Capitol Historical Society, Charlottesville, NC.

CHEEK, CHARLES D.
1999   An Evaluation of Regional Differences in Colonial English Foodways. In *Old and New Worlds*, Geoff Egan and Ronald L.Michael, editors, 349-357, Oxbow, Oxford, England.

COLLEY, LINDA
2009   *Britons: Forging the Nation 1707-1837.* Second edition. Yale University Press, New Haven, CT.
2003   *Captives: Britain, Empire and the World.* Pimlico, London, England.

COURTNEY, PAUL
1996   In Small Things Forgotten: the Georgian World View, Material Culture and the Consumer Revolution. *Rural History* 7, 87-95.

CREIGHTON, OLIVER H.
2009   *Designs Upon the Land: Elite Landscapes of the Middle Ages.* Boydell, Woodbridge, England.

CRESSY, DAVID
1987   *Coming Over: Migration and Communication Between England and New England in the 17th Century.* Cambridge University Press, Cambridge, England.

DAWDY, SHANNON L.
2009   *Building the Devil's Empire: French Colonial New Orleans.* University of Chicago Press, Chicago, IL.

DEAGAN, KATHLEEN AND CRUXENT, JOSÉ MARIA
2002   *Archaeology at La Isabela: America's First European Town.* Yale University Press, New Haven, CT.

DEETZ, JAMES F.
1967   *Invitation to Archaeology.* Natural History Press, New York, NY.
1977a   *In Small Things Forgotten: The Archaeology of Early American Life.* Anchor, New York, NY.
1977b   Material Culture and Archaeology – What's the Difference? In *Historical Archaeology and the Importance of Material Things*, Leland Ferguson, editor, 9-12. SHA Special Publication Series 2. Society for Historical Archaeology.
1995   *Flowerdew Hundred: The Archaeology of a Virginia Plantation, 1619-1864.* University of Virginia, Charlottesville, VA.
1996   *In Small Things Forgotten: An Archaeology of Early American Life.* Second revised edition. Anchor, New York, NY.

DEETZ, JAMES F. AND DEETZ, PATRICIA S.
2000   The *Times of Their Lives: Life, Love and Death in Plymouth Colony.* Anchor, New York, NY.

DEMARRAIS, ELIZABETH, CHRIS GOSDEN, COLIN A. RENFREW (EDITORS)
2005   *Rethinking Materiality: Engagement of Mind with the Material World.* McDonald Institute, Cambridge, England.

DEMOS, JONATHAN
1970   *A Little Commonwealth: Family Life in Plymouth Colony.* Oxford University Press, Oxford, England.

DYER, CHRISTOPHER C.
1997   Peasants and Farmers: Rural Settlements in an Age of Transition. In *The Age of Transition: The Archaeology of English Culture AD1400-1600,* David Gaimster and Paul Stamper, editors, 61-76. Oxbow, Oxford, England.

EGAN, GEOFF AND RONALD L. MICHAEL (EDITORS)
1999   *Old and New Worlds.* Oxbow, Oxford, England.

FAGAN, BRIAN
2000   *The Little Ice Age: How Climate Made History.* Basic Books, New York, NY.

FISHER, FREDERICK J.
1961   Tawney's Century. In *Essays in the Economic and Social History of Tudor and Stuart England: in Honour of R. H. Tawney.* Frederick Fisher, editor, 1-14. Cambridge University Press, Cambridge, England.

FOX, CYRIL
1938   *The Personality of Britain: Its Influence on Inhabitant and Invader in Prehistoric and Historic Times.* National Museum of Wales, Cardiff, England.

FROUDE, J. ANTHONY
2005   Sir *John Hawkins and the African Slave Trade.* Kessinger, London, England.

GAIMSTER, DAVID
1999   The Postmedieval Ceramic Revolution in Southern Britain c.1450-1650. In *Old and New World*, Geoff Egan and Ronald Michael (editors), 214-225. Oxbow, Oxford, England.

GAIMSTER, DAVID AND PAUL STAMPER (EDITORS)
1997   *The Age of Transition: The Archaeology of English Culture AD1400-1600.* Oxbow, Oxford, England.

GLASSIE, HENRY
1975   *Folk Housing in Middle Virginia: A Structural Analysis of Historic Artifacts.* University of Tennessee Press, Knoxville.
2000   *Vernacular Architecture.* University of Indiana Press, Bloomington.

HACKETT, HELEN
1995   *Virgin Mother, Maiden Queen: Elizabeth I and the Cult of the Virgin Mary.* St. Martin's Press, New York, NY.

HAZELWOOD, NICK
2004   *The Queen's Slave Trader: John Hawkyns, Elizabeth I, and the Trafficking in Human Souls.* Harper Collins, New York, NY.

HELGERSON, RICHARD
1992   *Forms of Nationhood: The Elizabethan Writing of England*. University of Chicago Press, Chicago, IL.

HICKS, DAN AND AUDREY HORNING
2006   Historical Archaeology and Buildings. In *The Cambridge Companion to Historical Archaeology,* Dan Hicks and Mary C. Beaudry, editors, Cambridge University Press, Cambridge, England.

HILL, CHRISTOPHER
1972   The *World Turned Upside Down: Radical Ideas During the English Revolution*. Temple, London, England.

HINTON, DAVID A.
2005   *Gold and Gilt, Pots and Pins: Possessions and People in Medieval Britain*. Oxford University Press, England.
2010   Deserted Medieval Villages and the Objects From Them. In *Deserted Villages Revisited. Explorations in Local and Regional History 3*, C. Dyer and R. Jones, editors, 85-108. University of Hertfordshire Press, Hertford, England.

HODDER, IAN
2011   Human-thing Entanglement: Towards and Integrated Archaeological Perspective *Journal of the Royal Anthropological Institute* 17:1, 154-177.

HORN, JAMES
1994   *Adapting to a New World: English Society in the 17th Century Chesapeake*. University of North Carolina Press, Chapel Hill.

HORNING, AUDREY
2006   Archaeology, Conflict and Contemporary Identity in the North of Ireland: Implications for Theory and Practice in Comparative Archaeologies of Colonialism. *Archaeological Dialogues* 13(2):183-200.
2011   *Ireland in the Virginian Sea: Comparative Colonialism in the British Atlantic World*. University of North Carolina Press, Chapel Hill.

JOHNSON, MATTHEW H.
1996   *An Archaeology of Capitalism*. Blackwell, Oxford, England.
2005   On the particularism of English landscape archaeology. *International Journal of Historical Archaeology* 9(2):111-122.

2007   *Ideas of Landscape*. Blackwell, Oxford, England.
2010   *English Houses 1300-1800: Vernacular Architecture, Social Life*. Longman, London, England.

KNIFFEN, FRED B.
1965   Folk Housing: Key to Diffusion. *Annals of the Association of American Geographers* 55:4, 549-77. Reprinted in *Common Places: Readings in American Vernacular Architecture*, Dell Upton and J.Michael Vlach, editors, 1986, 3-26. University of Georgia Press, Athens.

KLINGELHOFER, ERIC
2003   The Architecture of Empire: Elizabethan Country Houses in Ireland. In *Archaeologies of the British: Explorations of Identity in Great Britain and its colonies 1600-1945*, Susan Lawrence, editor, 102-118. Routledge, London, England.

LENMAN, BRUCE
2001   *England's Colonial Wars 1550-1688: Colonial Empire and National Identity*. Pearson, London, England.

LEONE, MARK P.
1984   Interpreting Ideology in Historical Archaeology: Using the Rules of Perspective in the William Paca Garden in Annapolis, Maryland. In *Ideology, Power and Prehistory*, Daniel Miller and Chris Tilley, editors, 25-36, Cambridge University Press, Cambridge, England.

2005   *The Archaeology of Liberty in an American Capital: Excavations in Annapolis*. University of California Press, Berkeley.

LOREN, DIANA DIPAOLO, AND MARY C, BEAUDRY
2006   Becoming American: Small Things Remembered. In *Historical Archaeology*, Martin Hall and Stephen W. Silliman, editors, Blackwell, Oxford.

MARKHAM, GERVASE
1613 *The English Husbandman. The First Part: Contayning the Knowledge of the true Nature of Every Soyle within the Kindome*. T.S. for J. Browne, London, England.

MILLER, DANIEL (EDITOR)
2005   *Materiality*. Duke University Press, Durham, NC.

MORRILL, JOHN
1993   *The Nature of the English Revolution: Essays.* Longman, London, England.

MURPHY, FRANCIS (EDITOR)
1981.   *Of Plymouth Plantation 1620-1647.* Random House, New York, NY.

NEIMAN, FRASER
2008.   The Lost World of Monticello: An Evolutionary Perspective. *Journal of Anthropological Research* 64, 161-94.

O'KEEFFE, TADHG
1992   Medieval Frontiers and Their Tortification: the Pale and its Evolution. In *Dublin City and County: From Prehistory to Present - Studies in Honour of J.H. Andrews*, Aalen, F.H.A. and Whelan, Kevin , editors, 57-77, Geography Publications, Dublin, Ireland.

ORSER, CHARLES E.
1996   *An Historical Archaeology of the Modern World.* Plenum, New York, NY.

RICHARDSON, CATHERINE
2006   *Domestic Life and Domestic Tragedy in Early Modern England: The Material Life of the Household.* Manchester University Press, England.

PREUCEL, ROBERT W.
2006   *Archaeological Semiotics.* Blackwell, Oxford, England.

ROCKMAN, MARCY
2010   New World with a New Sky: Climatic Variability, Environmental Expectations, and the Historical Period Colonization of Eastern North America. *Historical Archaeology* 44(3):4-20.

ST GEORGE, ROBERT B.
1990   Bawns and Beliefs: Architecture, Commerce and Conversion in Early New England. *Winterthur Portfolio* 25(4):89-125.

SHAPIRO, JAMES
2005   *1599: A Year in the Life of William Shakespeare.* Farber, London, England.

SMITH, SALLY V.
2009   Materializing Resistant Identities Among the Medieval Peasantry: an Examination of Dress Accessories from English Rural Settlement Sites. *Journal of Material Culture* 14(3):309-332.

SPEED, JOHN
1611   *The Theatre of the Empire of Great Britaine.* Sudbury and Humble, London, England.

SPUFFORD, MARGARET
1984   *The Great Reclothing of Rural England: Petty Chapmen and Their Wares in the Seventeenth Century.* Hambledon, London, England.

STOYLE, MARK
2005   *Soldiers and Strangers: An Ethnic History of the English Civil War.* Yale University Press, New Haven, CT.

TAWNEY, RICHARD H.
1912   *The Agrarian Problem in the 16th Century.* Longman, London, England.
1926   *Religion and the Rise of Capitalism: A Historical Study.* Penguin Books, London, England.

THIRSK, JOAN
2007   *Food in Early Modern England: Phases, Fads and Fashions.* Hambledon, London, England.

THOMPSON, MICHAEL W.
1995   *The Medieval Hall: The Basis of Secular Domestic Life, 600-1600 AD.* Scolar Press, Aldershot, England.

THURLEY, SIMON
1993   *The Royal Palaces of Tudor England.* Yale University Press, New Haven, CT.

TUCK, JAMES A., BARRY GAULTON, AND MATTHEW CARTER
1999   A Glimpse of the Colony of Avalon. In *Old and New Worlds*, Geoff Egan and Ronald Michael, editors, 136-146. Oxbow, Oxford, England.

TURNER, FREDERICK J.
1920   *The Frontier in American History.* Holt, New York, NY.

WALL, WENDY

2002   *Staging Domesticity: Household Work and English Identity in Early Modern Drama.* Cambridge University Press, Cambridge, England.

WEBMOOR, TIM AND CHRIS L. WITMORE

2008   Things are us! A Commentary on Human/Things Relations Under the Banner of a 'Social' Archaeology. *Norwegian Archaeological Review* 41(1):53-70.

WHITTICK, CHRISTOPHER

1993   Dallingridge's Bay and Bodiam Castle Millpond–Elements of a Medieval Landscape. *Sussex Archaeological Collections* 131, 119-23.

WHYTE, NICOLA

2009   *Inhabiting the Landscape: Place, Custom and Memory 1500-1800.* Windgather, Macclesfield, England.

WILLEY, G.R. AND PHILLIPS, P.

1958   *Method and Theory in Archaeology.* University of Chicago Press, IL.

WILLIAMS, ERIC

1944   *Capitalism and Slavery.* University of North Carolina Press, Chapel Hill.

YENTSCH, ANNE

1991   Chesapeake Artefacts and Their Cultural Context: Pottery and the Food Domain. *Postmedieval Archaeology* 25, 25-73.

Endnotes

1   My work concentrates on the English, but similar points could be made in terms of the antedecents of Hispanic settlement in the New World, for example Deagan and Cruxent's (2002) discussion of La Isabela.

2   Glassie in turn is drawing on Kniffen (1965) and the intellectual and cultural values of the American folklife tradition in general; I am grateful to Chuck Orser for pointing this out to me.

3   For some. the Georgian Order is no longer a helpful concept, seen as either "indigestible" (Carson et al. 1994) or just "another normative model of change in material culture and the built environment" (Hicks and Horning 2006, 280). I believe this view is overstated, and would point to the absence of competing models in the attempt to explain change in the 18th century.

4   See also Neiman (2008) for a Darwinist perspective on migration.

5   See Demos (1970) for a New England perspective on the house as "a little commonwealth."

6   See also Horning (2006) and ensuing discussion from a variety of viewpoints.

7   This is a term used by Cressy (1987, vii) in relation to New England only.

8   For example the title of Loren and Beaudry (2006).

9   Stoyle (2005) on ethnic definitions and conflicts within the British Isles; Lenman (2001) on colonial wars; Horn (1994, 10-11) discusses the continuing lack of dialogue.

10   Whyte (2009) is a detailed and sensitive study that nevertheless refuses to move beyond the small-scale and the local.

11   A comparison of the conceptions of liberty articulated by Hill (1972), writing about England in the 1640s, and Leone (2005), writing about colonial Annapolis, would be instructive in this context.

Matthew H. Johnson
Department of Anthropology
Northwestern University
1810 Hinman Ave
Evanston, IL 60208